UNLOCKING THE LAW

UNL
ENVIRON
LAW

C000131042

Simon Sneddon

Routledge
Taylor & Francis Group

LONDON AND NEW YORK

Designed cover image: Galeanu Mihai/Getty Images ©

First published 2024
by Routledge
4 Park Square, Milton Park, Abingdon, Oxon OX14 4RN

and by Routledge
605 Third Avenue, New York, NY 10158

Routledge is an imprint of the Taylor & Francis Group, an informa business

British Library Cataloguing-in-Publication Data
A catalogue record for this book is available from the British Library

Library of Congress Cataloging-in-Publication Data
Names: Sneddon, Simon, author.
Title: Unlocking environmental law / Simon Sneddon.
Description: Abingdon, Oxon [UK] ; New York, NY : Routledge, 2023.
Series: Unlocking the law | Includes bibliographical references and index. |
     Summary: — Provided by publisher.
Identifiers: LCCN 2023023817 | ISBN 9780367683719 (hardback) |
     ISBN 9780367682873 (paperback) | ISBN 9781003137214 (ebook)
Subjects: LCSH: Environmental law. | Environmental law—Moral and ethical
     aspects. | Environmental law—Political aspects. | Environmental justice. |
     Climatic changes—Law and legislation.
Classification: LCC K3585 .S64 2023 | DDC 344.04/6—dc23/eng/20230608
LC record available at https://lccn.loc.gov/2023023817

ISBN: 978-0-367-68371-9 (hbk)
ISBN: 978-0-367-68287-3 (pbk)
ISBN: 978-1-003-13721-4 (ebk)

DOI: 10.4324/9781003137214

Typeset in Palatino
by Apex CoVantage, LLC

Contents

Detailed contents

Guide to the Book

Unlocking the Law books bring together all the essential elements for today's law students in a clearly defined and memorable way. Each book is enhanced with learning features to reinforce understanding of key topics and test your knowledge along the way. Follow this guide to make sure you get the most from reading this book.

AIMS AND OBJECTIVES

Defines what you will learn in each chapter.

Definitions

Find key legal terminology at a glance.

LEGISLATION

Provides extracts from global legislative provisions, such as global treaties, national and international acts, declarations, regulations and directives.

ARTICLE

Defines articles of major treaties and Conventions, such as the EC Treaty or of the European Convention on Human Rights.

CLAUSE

Shows a bill going through Parliament or a draft bill proposed by the Law Commission.

CASE

Illustrates the law in action.

JUDGMENT

Provides extracts from judgments on cases.

Note

Provides additional considerations or comments on the text.

QUOTATION

Encourages you to engage with primary sources.

ACTIVITY

Enables you to test yourself as you progress through the chapter.

KEY FACTS

Draws attention to essential points and information.

CRITIQUING THE LAW

Highlights academic debate within controversial areas of the law.

SAMPLE ESSAY QUESTIONS

Provides you with real-life sample essays and shows you the best way to plan your answer.

SUMMARY

Concludes each chapter to reinforce learning.

SAMPLE PROBLEM QUESTIONS

Provides you with real-life sample problem questions and suggests the best way to plan your answer.

Figures

Table of Cases

Table of Legislation

UK Secondary Legislation

Non-UK National Legislation

Table of EU Legislation

Table of International Legislation

Acknowledgements

I would like to thank everyone at Routledge for their support and patience, especially Russell George, who started the ball rolling, and Chloe James, Chloe Herbert, and Emily Kindleysides for keeping me on track.

I would also like to thank my environmental law and biosphere law students at the University of Northampton for their feedback on the usability of the drafts.

Most of all, I want to thank my wife, Katie, without whom I could not have done this.

1

Introduction to Environmental Law

In this chapter, you will explore the underpinnings of environmental law. Understanding what the environment is will be fundamental to unlocking environmental law, and it will be very difficult to consider the environmental issues without a legal context. Bell et al.[1] suggest that issues around the definition of environmental law are problematic and yet central to the study of the topic.

What Bell et al. are alluding to is the fact that as lawyers, we recognise that accurate definitions are crucial, but there are many contradictory and competing definitions of the "environment."

The vast majority of environmental law is fundamentally based on conceptual frameworks, and so in this chapter we will explore the primary frameworks and concepts on which it is founded.

The development of environmental law, from a set of inchoate, unrelated policies and laws into a recognised body of law, will be explored. Knowing how environmental law evolved to its current form, and why, will help your understanding of the area.

Some of these concepts are ones with which you are likely to be familiar at some level. Sustainability and sustainable development, for example, are one of the cornerstones of 21st-century life, whether it is the United Nations' Sustainable Development Goals (SDGs) (the specifics of which are covered in Chapter 5) or as part of the strategies of schools, colleges, universities, and businesses. Others, such as anthropocentrism and ecocentrism, may be newer to you.

AIMS AND OBJECTIVES

After reading this chapter, you should be able to:

- Identify the key similarities and differences between definitions of the environment.
- Explain the key points in the development of environmental law.
- Explain the application of the precautionary principle and polluter pays principle.

DOI: 10.4324/9781003137214-1

1.1 What Is the Environment

Environmental law as a discrete topic area is relatively recent, particularly when contrasted with areas of law such as tort and criminal law. However, the relative newness of the area should not lead you to think that the individual elements of environmental law are equally new. The links between environmental quality and the health of humans and livestock have been understood for centuries.

One of the fundamental questions for the environmental lawyer is to identify the scope of environmental law. The simple answer, of course, would be "laws which impact upon the environment" in some way. That is true, but unhelpful. For lawyers, definitions are of crucial importance – the rules of judicial interpretation will offer some comfort where a term is not adequately defined in statute, but where a term is not consistently defined outside statute, potential problems are manifest. Contrast these three different definitions of "the environment":

....

Definitions

"The environment is everything which is not me" (Albert Einstein, reputed comment).

"The environment is where we all live" (Gro Harlem Brundtland, in the introduction to WCED, 1987, Report of the World Commission on Environment and Development: Our Common Future, Vienna: United Nations Department of Economic and Social Affairs, UN General Assembly, A/42/427).

"The 'environment' consists of all, or any, of the following media, namely, the air, water and land; and the medium of air includes the air within buildings and the air within other natural or man-made structures above or below ground" (S1(2) Environmental Protection Act 1990).

"'[E]nvironment' means waters (including groundwaters, surface water, transitional waters, coastal waters and marine waters), sediment, soil, air, land, flora and fauna (indigenous or not), and any interrelationship between them, and any relationship with other living organisms" (Reg 2(1), the Plant Protection Products (Sustainable Use) Regulations 2012 SI 2012/1657).

These four definitions, two of which are statutory, have different impacts. Einstein's conceptualisation, based as it is on "everything," would seem to be the broadest. Taking that forward as an approach to environmental law would essentially mean it is the law relating to everything. All law is thus environmental law. The Environmental Protection Act definition is clearly much more specific, giving what appears to be an exhaustive and much narrower list of things which might be included under the auspices of environmental law. Interpreting this definition means we are set to exclude any living organism (including humans) from the environment. The third definition, by contrast, specifically *includes* flora and fauna, their interrelationships, and their relationships with other living organisms. Most statutory definitions will overcome any contradiction with other statute by specifying that the definition applies for the purposes of that specific act or regulation, so in practice, although there are differences, they do not have a particularly marked impact on enforcement. Other definitions include cultural, aesthetic, and other intangible characteristics.

In many ways, the precise meaning of "the environment" can be seen as a red herring. Although there are many pieces of legislation, both domestic and international, which include the phrase in their titles, almost none are quite that generic in their application. Instead, they focus on specific, relevant aspects of the environment. This could be specific pollutants, activities, or species, for example, which will be much more tightly defined.

....

Recent legislation has made valiant attempts to define environmental law, but as you can see in what follows, such attempts are not without their problems:

SECTIONS

44 Meaning of "natural environment"
In this Part the "natural environment" means –

(a) plants, wild animals and other living organisms,
(b) their habitats,
(c) land (except buildings or other structures), air and water, and the natural systems, cycles and processes through which they interact.

45 Meaning of "environmental protection"
In this Part "environmental protection" means –

(a) protection of the natural environment from the effects of human activity;
(b) protection of people from the effects of human activity on the natural environment;
(c) maintenance, restoration or enhancement of the natural environment;
(d) monitoring, assessing, considering, advising or reporting on anything in paragraphs (a) to (c).

46 Meaning of "environmental law"

(1) In this Part "environmental law" means any legislative provision to the extent that it –

(a) is mainly concerned with environmental protection, and
(b) is not concerned with an excluded matter.

(2) Excluded matters are –

(a) disclosure of or access to information;
(b) the armed forces or national security;
(c) taxation, spending or the allocation of resources within government.

SS 44–46, Environment Act 2021

So "environmental law," according to the most recent legislative provision, is mainly (but not exclusively) about protecting plants, animals, habitats, air, water, and land from people (and vice versa), as well as monitoring and enhancing, provided it does not concern spending money or accessing information.

As a working outline, however, thinking of environmental law as a linked series of laws which impact in some way on the environment is a solid starting point, despite its circular, self-referencing arguments.

The key aspect of how environmental laws work, whether local, national, regional, or international, is how they are designed to alter the behaviour of persons in some way – these can be physical or legal persons. No legislation can influence the manner in which a tree grows, or a salmon spawns, and so what is left is a series of measures setting out what we may do, what we must do, and what we must not do, depending on the specific circumstances.

1.2 Development of Environmental Law

Environmental law is often, and in my view, incorrectly, regarded as being both a relatively new and relatively narrow area of law focusing on issues such as climate change, species extinction, and plastic pollution.

The underlying concepts and ideas behind what is now regarded as environmental law have developed and evolved over decades from very loose ideas to much tighter ones which, as we have already seen, impact on every aspect of life. Hughes et al.[2] talk of the emergence of a "more coherent" system of environmental law which emerged from a series of diverse, ad hoc, and unrelated pieces of legislation at international, European, and domestic level.

There are perhaps as many ways of dividing environmental law into time periods as there are environmental lawyers, but here we will be looking at pre-19th century, the period from around 1830 to 1970, the late 20th century, and the 21st century. Some of the issues you will cover in the next pages will blend across those boundaries, however.

1.2.1 Pre-19th Century

Traditionally, humans have been viewed by many cultures as being separate from the environment, and the view that humans should be able to exert power over the rest of the world is found in many religious texts. Early in the Old Testament of the Bible, Genesis verse 26 sets out the relationship between humans and the environment very clearly, saying:

> [L]et us make man in our image, after our likeness: and let them have dominion over the fish of the sea, and over the fowl of the air, and over the cattle, and over all the earth, and over every creeping thing that creepeth upon the earth.
>
> (Genesis 1–26)

This level of dominion can also be seen in the fundamentals of the English language – natural habitats are the *wild*erness, fauna is *wild*life, and "to wilder" (as in bewilder) means to lead astray. Similarly, humans "settle" and "tame" new lands – the natural world is hostile and needs to be forcibly shaped into a kinder, tamer version of itself.

A slightly different approach is taken in the Jātakamāla (a text written by the Indian Buddhist poet Āryaśūra in the 3rd or 4th century BCE). The hierarchical relationship between humans and animals is established, albeit with the caveat that the power should be exercised responsibly.

QUOTATION

"Because animals are dull by nature we should have sympathy for them. When it comes to being happy and avoiding suffering, all beings are the same. Therefore if you find something unpleasant you should not inflict it on others."

Āryaśūra's Jātakamāla, in Dhammika, S., 2015, *Nature and Environment in Early Buddhism*, Kandy, Sri Lanka: Buddhist Publication Society, p. 11

However, this is not the case for all religions and cultures, as will be explored in more depth in Chapter 3. In Hinduism, for example, the goddess Bhumi (originally called Puhumi in Sanskrit) represents the earth itself. There are clear similarities with other cultures which embody a personification of the earth. The Greek goddess Gaia/Gaea was seen as the mother of all life and is one of the fundamental deities. In Rome, the goddess Tellus Mater/Terra Mater represents the earth itself and is one of the 20 principal deities. In New Zealand, the Māori word *kaitiakitanga* represents a way of managing the environment by acting as a guardian, or *kaitiaki*.

For most of English history, there was no overarching environmental law, although there were localised "pockets" of lawmaking which would today be included under the environmental umbrella. In the 7th century, for example, St Cuthbert, the bishop of Lindisfarne, passed laws to protect seabirds (especially the eider duck) on the remote Farne Islands off the North-East Coast. Given that the Farne Islands were mostly inhabited by occasional hermits, these laws did not have a huge reach. Several hundred years later, and soon after his invasion of England, William the Conqueror established the New Forest in Hampshire, which was to be maintained as a royal hunting reserve. To manage the forest, a system of verderers (judicial and administrative officers), agisters (livestock managers), and commoners (Land users) was established, which had the knock-on effect of protecting the flora and fauna from all development.

More broadly speaking, there was no system of unified law in any aspect. King Henry II expanded the Curia Regis (King's Law) in the 12th century by developing a system of itinerant justices who travelled the country, ensuring that the same law was enforced everywhere. This became known as the common law.

Even with the development of the common law, there was still no single system of *environmental* law, however. Interestingly, many of the same issues which affect human health and the wider environment today were beginning to become problematic even in the 12th and 13th centuries. Smoke from the burning of wood became so unbearable in the 12th century that Queen Eleanor of Aquitaine, the wife of King Henry II, has been forced to leave Tutbury Castle in Lancashire. A century later, when coal was used more widely, another Queen Eleanor, this time of Provence and wife of Henry III, fled the noxious air of Nottingham to seek solace *in* Tutbury Castle.[3]

King Edward I, son of Henry III and husband to yet another Queen Eleanor (of Castile), passed laws to ban the use of "soft coal" (low-grade coal, containing higher sulphur levels) in 1273, following concerns about the impact on human health in London. Three decades later, in 1306 or 1307, Edward passed new laws which forbade the use of sea coal in London (the term "sea coal" is used both for coal which washes up on the seashore and coal which is transported by ship from the North-East of England to London) and appointed a Royal Commission to ensure that the law was being followed, and to punish those who broke it. This is widely regarded as being the first air pollution commission anywhere in the world. The rules, however, were largely unenforceable, because with the felling of trees in the vicinity of London, there was no longer an alternate affordable fuel available for cooking and heating.

It was not just the air quality which was beginning to suffer as cities became larger. In 1357, King Edward III travelled though London and was so appalled by the pollution levels in the river that he caused a Royal Order to be addressed to the mayor and sheriffs.

LEGISLATION

"[F]or saving the body of the river, and preserving the quays . . . for lading and unlading, as also for avoiding the filthiness that is increasing in the river and upon the banks of the Thames, to the great abomination and damage of the people, there shall henceforth no rubbish or filth be thrown or put into the rivers of Thames and Flete [Fleet], or into the Fosses [moats or ditches] around the walls of the City, but must be taken out of the City by carts."

Royal Order 1357, cited in Simon, J., 1890, *English sanitary institutions: reviewed in their course of development, and in some of their political and social relations*, London: Cassell & Company Ltd., p. 40

The common theme of the regulatory regime in this long period of history is that the laws were fragmented, largely ineffective, and almost exclusively passed for the benefit of the nobility, rather than the wider populace, or indeed the environment.

1.2.2 Industrial and Agricultural Revolutions to 1970s

The second time period which we will look at is the period which starts with the Industrial and Agricultural Revolutions and ends in the 1970s. The period sees a transition in approaches to the environment from regarding it primarily of a resource (e.g. of timber or coal) to increasing awareness of the intrinsic importance of the environment.

The Industrial Revolution is widely regarded as starting in around 1760 and running to the mid-19th century, and the Agricultural Revolution started a little earlier and ran to about the same time. There is more debate about the specific time periods of the Agricultural Revolution, with some arguing that there was a series of four "revolutions" from the 15th to the 19th centuries.[4] During the century preceding the 1860s, production per agricultural worker more than doubled, and the population of England rose from around five million to over 16 million, with over two million living in London by 1850.

With increased population and increased urbanisation comes increased concentration of pollution and issues around sewerage and other waste. Just prior to stepping down from the House of Lords in 1741, Lord Tyrconnell, the MP for Grantham, simultaneously praised London for its wealth and commerce and criticised it for the "heaps of filth" he found in every street.

Against this backdrop of overflowing cesspits, slums, untreated sewerage flowing into drinking water, and rotting animal carcasses in the streets, it is little wonder that outbreaks of disease were routine. A series of four outbreaks of cholera in 1832, 1848–1849, 1853–1854, and 1865 claimed close to 110,000 lives in England and Wales[5] – equivalent to half a million deaths when calculated against current population levels.

These outbreaks led to changes in the law. Early on, the Cholera Morbus Prevention (England) Act 1932,[6] alongside its equivalent for Scotland, provided local boards of health with a limited range of powers to clean properties, but it had little impact, as the outbreak was too well-established by the time the powers were given. During and after the second outbreak, several acts were passed to try to contain the impact.

The Public Health Act 1848

The Act for Promoting Public Health[7] was passed on the back of a report by Edwin Chadwick which had demonstrated that there was a causal link between poor living conditions, susceptibility to disease, and a shorter life expectancy. The Act gave the newly created General Board of Health the power to appoint an inspector to visit towns with unusually high death rates to launch a public inquiry about the state of local sewerage and water supply (Section VIII).

LEGISLATION

> "[T]he General Board of Health may, if and when they shall think fit, direct a Superintending Inspector to visit such City, Town, Borough or Place, and to make public Inquiry, and to examine Witnesses as to the Sewerage, Drainage and Supply of Water . . ."
> Section VIII, Act for Promoting Public Health 1848

Crucially, this was expressed as a power rather than a duty, so there was no compulsion of the board to do anything. Equally problematic was Chadwick's adherence to the "miasma theory," which was prevalent at that time, the idea that diseases are spread through foul-smelling air rather than contaminated drinking water. Chadwick thought it was the smell of human waste that caused cholera, and his actions resulted in an increased flow of sewerage into the river Thames and actually *increased* the risk of cholera.

The Nuisances Acts 1848, 1849, and 1855

The Nuisances Removal and Diseases Prevention Act 1848[8] and the Nuisances Removal and Diseases Prevention (Amendment) Act 1849[9] gave powers to local authorities to appoint inspectors to bring those suspected of creating a nuisance injurious to health before the local Justice of the Peace (Section XII). What constituted a nuisance for the purposes of these acts was set out under Section VIII:

SECTION

The Word "Nuisances" under this Act shall include –
 Any Premises in such a State as to be a Nuisance or injurious to Health:
 Any Pool, Ditch, Gutter, Watercourse, Privy, Urinal, Cesspool, Drain, or Ashpit so foul as to be a Nuisance or injurious to Health:
 Any Animal so kept as to be a Nuisance or injurious to Health
 Any Accumulation or Deposit which is a Nuisance or injurious to Health:
                              Section VIII, Nuisances Removal and Diseases Prevention Act 1848

The Nuisances Removal Act for England 1855[10] was a part consolidation act and part amendment act which repealed the earlier acts and added new provisions, without fundamentally changing the approach.

Metropolis Local Management Act (Amendment) Act 1858

Following the 1848–1849 London outbreak, John Snow, a physician, wrote that cholera was spread through untreated water, rather than being airborne. The miasma theorists ignored Snow's work, but despite this, he was able to use epidemiological data to trace the Soho infections of the 1853 outbreak to a single contaminated water pump in Broad Street.

In the hot summer of 1858, the woeful sanitation situation in London led to the "Great Stink" – a period of two or three months when high temperatures and a lower water level served to concentrate the impact of pollutants in the river.

In June, even before the worst impacts of the stink were being felt, the Chancellor of the Exchequer, Benjamin Disraeli introduced what was to become the Metropolis Local Management (Amendment) Act 1858,[11] saying that the Thames had been reduced to a "stygian pool" and was "reeking with ineffable and intolerable horrors" that posed a risk to health. The Act allowed the Metropolitan Board of Works to borrow money to finance Joseph Bazalgette's new sewer system, which had been designed to remove the smell (and thus the miasma-related risk to health) from raw sewerage as rapidly as possible from the city to the sea.

By the time of the 1865 outbreak, Bazalgette's redevelopment of the main sewerage system in London had been completed. The epicentre of the outbreak was the one part of London not yet connected to the system, and the miasma theory was overturned once and for all.

Outside London

Although the majority of cholera deaths in England occurred in London, other cities were affected and took measures to tackle the outbreaks. In Liverpool, the Liverpool Sanitation Act 1846[12] made various provisions to improve the sewerage and drainage system of the city. Many of the provisions of this Act were in fact carried over to the Public Health Act 1848. The Liverpool Sanitation Act was amended by the Liverpool Sanitary Amendment Act 1854,[13] which allowed for the completion of the city's sewerage network – a feat which was achieved in 1969 and led to a doubling of human life expectancy in the city.

In Birmingham, the Birmingham Improvement Act 1861[14] stipulated, *inter alia*, that all new dwelling houses had to be connected to the new main water system rather than relying on wells, many of which were polluted.

What this episode demonstrates is fourfold:

Firstly, environmental lawyers need to work alongside other disciplines and professions in creating laws.

Secondly, it is vital that the consequences of any environmental measure are planned out to avoid to the greatest extent possible and unintended consequences.

Thirdly, reactive ad hoc laws have a tendency to be disjointed, and this lessens their effectiveness.

And finally, as we saw at the start of the chapter, environmental laws overlap and mingle with laws on nuisance, public health, and employment.

Richard Macrory suggests that Lord Ashby, the first president of the Royal Commission on Environmental Pollution, regards this reactive element of environmental lawmaking as being part and parcel of the process.

QUOTATION

"In his view, any serious advances in environmental law or policy required a detailed analysis of the problem and what was needed to deal with it, but then some 'ignition' event, such as a major pollution event, to drive the politics."

Macrory, R., 2020, *Irresolute Clay: Shaping the Foundations of Modern Environmental Law*, London: Bloomsbury, p. 130

Outside the preoccupation with sewerage, the period also saw the creation and use of a vast number of new industrial measures and processes. With these came new forms of *artificial* pollution which had not previously been a problem, and these new forms of pollution required yet more reactive legislation to be passed.

At the close of the 18th century, a French physician, Nicolas Leblanc, invented a scientific process for making alkali from sea salt. Soda ash, as the alkali was called, was a vital part of several other industries, from glassmaking to paper manufacturing to soap production. The process of producing soda ash is relatively complex but involves the emission of hydrogen chloride gas (which turns into hydrochloric acid as soon as it contacts any water). Hydrochloric acid, also known as *muriatic acid*, is harmful to human, animal, and plant life.

To control the ill-effects of the industrial emissions from this industry, the Alkali Act 1863[15] was passed, which created a new inspectorate to monitor the factories involved in the process.

In the parliamentary debate on the Alkali Bill, doubts were expressed as to why this particular industry was being singled out for regulation when other industries which were equally or more polluting were not. During the debate, the Rt Hon. Edward Pleydell-Bouverie, MP for Kilmarnock, questioned why "greater evils" produced by emissions from other industries were excluded from the bill.

Interestingly, unlike modern industrial pollution control legislation, there was nothing in the Alkali Act to monitor the process itself; it merely made it mandatory for Leblanc Alkali works to absorb 95 per cent of the muriatic acid in their emissions.

Almost 100 years after the Alkali Act, and 650 years after Edward I's attempts to clean coal smoke from the air, the Clean Air Act 1956[16] was passed. This Act was another piece of reactive legislation, which was brought in after the "Great Smog" of 1952 in London, when an estimated 10,000 people died as a result of poor air quality. The case was the increased use of low-grade coal (similar to that banned by Edward I), which was being used out of necessity – with higher-grade coal being sold off to repay debts incurred during the Second World War. Coal smoke, vehicle emissions, and fog combined with a temperature inversion, which prevented the fumes from escaping. The end result was four days of smog.

The Clean Air Act forbade the emission of "dark smoke" (see Chapter 9) and introduced smoke control areas where the use of certain fuels was prohibited. In those areas, householders could reclaim between 70 and 100 per cent of the cost of replacing a coal fire with a less-polluting gas fire (Section XII).

Throughout this period, there were laws passed which undoubtedly had a beneficial impact on the wider environment – flora, fauna, and habitat. Cleaner air, cleaner water, lower pollution levels all have a wide benefit. None of the measures, however, was specifically intended to do that, and any environmental benefit was incidental. The main focus was on human health, partly from a growing belief that it was the morally right thing to do, but tempered by a sense that it was of benefit to businesses to have a supply of healthy and happy workers. It is no coincidence that this period also saw the building of idealised communities, like Saltaire in Yorkshire, Port Sunlight in Merseyside, and Bourneville in Birmingham, by, respectively, the industrialists Titus Salt, the Cadbury Brothers, and the Lever Brothers.

Most case law of the period was dealt with under tort law, particularly the laws relating to nuisance. Tort is largely reactive in nature, and so from an environmental perspective, this is not an ideal approach – often, once the damage is done, it is irreparable, and although landowners can be recompensed, the environment will never recover.

This was not a period bereft of individuals and groups concerned about environmental issues, however.

The Cruel Treatment of Cattle Act 1822[17] (better known as "Martin's Act," after the MP who introduced it) was a flawed attempt to prevent the ill-treatment of some animals, but the ill-treatment needed to be reported within ten days in order for a prosecution to take place. Two years later, the Society for the Protection of Animals was founded, to bring those who were cruel to animals to justice. The Society received its royal charter in 1840 and, as the RSPCA, continues to bring prosecutions today.

It was not just land animals which were being afforded a level of protection by this time. In 1869, the Sea Birds Preservation Act[18] became the first piece of UK legislation to protect wild birds. It was far from universal protection and only covered listed species of birds (including the eider duck originally protected by St Cuthbert in the 7th century), and the protection only extended to the breeding season. The rationale for the Act was that seabird colonies across the UK were disappearing because of over-exploitation. The parliamentary debate made it clear that a strong trigger was the fact that seabirds are useful to humans. Flocks of gulls mark out shoals of fish, which can then be caught by fishermen, and they also serve as a warning of rocky shores, garnering the nickname of the "Flamborough Pilots."

The Society for the Protection of Birds was founded in 1889, to campaign on limiting the use of exotic feathers as decorations in hats. The Society was awarded its royal charter in 1904, and the RSPB pushed for both the Importation of Plumage (Prohibition) Act 1921,[19] which again concerned the use of feathers in hats, and the Protection of Birds Act 1954,[20] which offered more general protection to native wild birds.

CASE

Partridge v Crittenden (1968) 1 WLR 1204

In this case, Mr Partridge placed an advert in a magazine for "A B C R [aviary-bred, close-ringed] Bramblefinch cocks, Bramblefinch hens, 25s each." Bramblefinch is another name for brambling.

Mr Partridge was charged by the RSPCA for breaching Section 6(1) and Schedule 4 of the Protection of Birds Act 1954. Section 6(1)(a) prohibits the sale, offer for sale, or possession for sale of any bird listed in Schedule 4.

Mr Partridge was convicted, but the conviction was quashed on appeal, as the RSPCA had decided to prosecute for "offer for sale" rather than "sale," and the High Court held that Mr Partridge's advertisement was an invitation to treat, rather than an offer for sale.

Had Partridge been charged with selling a wild bird, then it is likely that the conviction would have stood.

Towards the end of this period, two influential reports were produced, which led to the creation of the National Parks and Access to the Countryside Act 1949:[21]

- Conservation of Nature in England and Wales 1945 (the Wildlife Conservation Special Committee – the Huxley Committee)
- Final Report on Nature Reserves in Scotland 1949 (the Scottish Wildlife Conservation Committee – the Ritchie Committee)

The Act recognised both the recreational and educational benefits of protecting areas of the country and created national parks (Section 5), nature reserves (Section 16), sites of special scientific interest (SSSIs) (Section 23), and provisions relating to rights of way and access to the countryside. Chapter 7 covers these aspects in more detail.

Over the course of this period, we can see a clear dichotomy. There are those laws which are designed to alleviate specific incidences relating to industrial or other pollution and for the protection of human health. There are those which concern the protection of animals and birds, although there is inconsistency as to whether this is just to preserve stocks for future exploitation or to preserve them for their own benefit. At the end of the period, the "environment" seems to be shifting from an entity which produces financial benefits to one which also produced educational and recreational benefits.

1.2.3 Late 20th Century

The past 50 years or so have seen a greater awareness among the public and law-makers about the knock-on effects of damage to animals, the ozone layer, and plant life, which could then affect the economy.

We have also seen the emergence of the impacts of the industrialisation and innovation of the late 19th and 20th centuries. Climate change and the climate crisis are the clearest sign of this, but consider also the impacts of urban spread and the extractive industries on biodiversity. Before considering specific legislation and case law, it is worth considering the overall context within which it occurred.

The period started with the United Nations Educational, Scientific and Cultural Organisation (UNESCO) setting up the Man and Biosphere (MAB) programme in 1971. The MAB programme focuses on improving the relationship between humans and their environments and has created a network of over 700 "biosphere reserves," areas where potential solutions to global environmental issues can be researched. There are seven biosphere reserves in the UK:

Wester Ross, Galloway and Southern Ayrshire (Scotland)

North Devon, Brighton and Lewes Downs, Isle of Wight (England)

Biosffer Dyfi (Wales)

Isle of Man

Between them, they cover over two million hectares and range from upland down to salt marshes to sand dunes. Most of these reserves gain no legal protection from their status, but many are protected as nature reserves (local or national) or sites of special scientific interest under the National Parks and Access to the Countryside Act 1949.

In 1972, the United Nations Conference on the Human Environment (UNCHE) took place in Stockholm, Sweden. It was the first time that a global governmental conference had been convened to specifically cover environmental issues. The conference ended with the "Stockholm Declaration," which made environmental and developmental issues inexorably linked and raised the importance of a need for global dialogue on the links between development, environment, pollution, and so on.

LEGISLATION

"Man is both creature and moulder of his environment, which gives him physical sustenance and affords him the opportunity for intellectual, moral, social and spiritual growth. In the long and tortuous evolution of the human race on this planet a stage has been reached when, through the rapid acceleration of science and technology, man has acquired the power to transform his environment in countless ways and on an unprecedented scale. Both aspects of man's environment, the natural and the man-made, are essential to his well-being and to the enjoyment of basic human rights the right to life itself."

Stockholm Declaration of the UN Conference on the Human Environment, 1972

In addition to the Declaration, the UNCHE was responsible for the creation of the UN Environment Programme (UNEP), which remains responsible nearly

50 years later for coordinating global environmental and sustainable development programmes, including the UN Sustainable Development Goals (SDGs).

A key outcome of UNCHE was Principle 21, which essentially allowed for states to do what they wanted, provided their activities did not damage the environment in other states. As a declaration, it is *soft law* and had, and has, no binding force, but it is an early recognition of the problems of transboundary pollution.

LEGISLATION

> "States have, in accordance with the Charter of the United Nations and the principles of international law, the sovereign right to exploit their own resources pursuant to their own environmental policies, and the responsibility to ensure that activities within their jurisdiction or control do not cause damage to the environment of other States or of areas beyond the limits of national jurisdiction."
>
> Principle 21, UNCHE, 1972

Whilst neither the MAB programme nor the UNCHE created any specific legislative measures to protect the environment, in 1973 the Convention on International Trade in Endangered Species of Flora and Fauna (CITES) was opened for signature. The purpose of CITES was to protect species which had already been designated as being endangered from further exploitation through international trade. Species were placed onto one of three appendices, and the international trade in those species was restricted or banned.

Bermuda Village, Nuneaton, the Deposit of Poisonous Waste Act 1972, and the Control of Pollution Act 1974

In February 1972, 36 drums filled with sodium cyanide ash were dumped overnight in the village of Bermuda, close to Nuneaton in the Midlands. Sodium cyanide ash is potentially highly toxic, as on exposure to moisture it releases hydrogen cyanide gas, which is deadly to humans, animals, birds, and plants. The site where the drums were dumped was a brownfield site which had previously been a brickworks and which was also a site where local children often played.

The public outcry over this event led to the very rapid enactment of the Deposit of Poisonous Waste Act 1972,[22] which received royal assent on 30 March, a mere five weeks after the sodium cyanide ash had been dumped. It was a very short act, running to only eight sections, and was intended to be a stopgap measure before more lengthy and considered legislation could be brought in.

The new legislation was the Control of Pollution Act 1974 (CoPA),[23] which was passed in July 1974. CoPA had a far wider coverage than the 1972 Act and covered air, water, and noise pollution as well as pollution by toxic substances.

The Flixborough Disaster and the Health and Safety at Work Etc. Act 1974

In June 1974, a leak at the Nypro chemical plant in Flixborough, in North Lincolnshire, caused what is to date the largest peacetime explosion in the UK: 28 people were killed, and 36 injured, and had the explosion not occurred on a Saturday, when the plant was not fully staffed, the impact would have been much larger. The chemical leak also caused the nearby river Tent to be closed to fishing. The accident is often cited as being the push which was needed for the enactment of the Health and Safety at Work Etc. Act 1974 (HASAWA),[24] which received royal assent a little over a month afterwards. The bill was introduced in June, but this was not the beginning of the process. In January 1973, Parliament had debated the Report of the Robens Committee into Safety and Health in Employment. HASAWA regulates workplace safety for employees and members of the public but does not consider longer-term risks to the environment.

Both of these incidents illustrate well the point made by Lord Ashby, cited earlier, that there is a difference between having the legal framework to create new legislation and the political urgency to push it through. They also illustrate that human health still took precedence over environmental concerns despite a growing recognition and acceptance of the inherent importance of the environment.

The end of the 1970s and the whole of the 1980s saw increasing recognition that some environmental issues are too large to be successfully dealt with by one state.

In 1979, the United Nations Economic Commission for Europe (UNECE) Long-Range Transboundary Air Pollution Convention (LRTAP) was introduced, which was the first piece of legislation to link together North America, Europe, and Russia in an attempt to better model, and thus better control, the impacts of airborne pollutants. The LRTAP was partly triggered by the recognition that pollution emitted by one state could cause damage in another state. This in itself was not new, but what LRTAP did was establish strict limits and targets on pollutant levels.

CASE

Trail Smelter Arbitration

A smelter in British Colombia, Canada, caused damage to forests and other crops both locally and across the border in Washington State. The company operating the smelter had been fined in 1924 following arbitration with local farmers, but no new regulations were introduced. The company lengthened the chimneys in an attempt to disperse the smoke. This was beneficial locally but polluted farms in Washington.

There was no law in place at the time of the arbitration, and transboundary air pollution had never been arbitrated previously. The case was also the first use of the polluter pays principle (see later text) in an international air pollution dispute.

United States v. Canada (1938 and 1941) 3 RIAA 1905

In 1986, a nuclear accident in reactor 4 of the Vladimir Lenin Nuclear Power Plant (more commonly the Chernobyl Nuclear Power Plant) in Ukraine caused radioactive material to be widely dispersed. High levels were recorded in Ukraine, Belarus, and Russia, but within a month, detectable levels of radiation were found across the Northern Hemisphere. Despite Russia, Belarus, and Ukraine all being member states of UNECE and all being signatories to LRTAP, no action has been taken for the pollution caused by the Chernobyl accident.

A year before the Chernobyl accident, in March 1985, the United Nations opened a new convention for signature. The Vienna Convention for the Protection of the Ozone Layer explicitly linked back to the UNCHE Principle 21 and is equally explicit in recognising the threat to human health *and* the environment. The Convention itself does not make any specific provisions in relation to pollutants; rather, it sets in place a framework for research (Article 3), cooperation (Article 4), and information sharing (Article 5). The details were left to the Montréal Protocol (Montréal Protocol on Substances That Deplete the Ozone Layer) and the several subsequent amendments made to it.

Legislative frameworks which govern how states work with each other in tackling global environmental issues are extremely important, but one of the other impactful changes in this period was the ability of ordinary people to access information on the state of the environment in their area. Registers for different activities had been around for a long time, but they were often not accessible in any meaningful way.

In 1990, Directive 90/313 on the Freedom of Access to Information on the Environment was passed. It did not grant universal access, as it only applied to information held by public authorities (Article 1), but it was a sea change from previous approaches. Member states were given until the end of 1992 to pass enabling legislation, and the UK duly passed the Environmental Information Regulations 1992[25] in December. Access to information is useful, and knowledge may be power, but without a viable conduit for exercising that power, it becomes a pyrrhic victory. This was to change in 1998, when the UNECE brought in the Convention on Access to Information, Public Participation in Decision-making and Access to Justice in Environmental Matters in Aarhus, Denmark (the Aarhus Convention). Not only did this Convention extend the access to environmental information; it also sought to widen the possibility for public engagement in environmental decisions and ensure greater environmental justice. The Convention entered into force in 2001 and again extends only as far as requiring public bodies to provide information.

Indisputably, one of the events with the most far-reaching consequences was the UN Conference on Environment and Development (UNCED), held in Rio de Janeiro, Brazil, in 1992. UNCED is the spiritual successor to the UNCHE two decades earlier and produced a wealth of legislative frameworks which continue to shape our relationship with the environment to this day.

UN Framework Convention on Climate Change (UNFCCC)

The UNFCCC will be covered in greater detail in Chapter 9, but in essence, it is the framework which allows the "developed country Parties" to report on their efforts to reduce carbon emissions and other pollutants. As of August 2022, there are 198 parties (197 states and the European Union).

ARTICLE

> "[W]ith the aim of returning individually or jointly to their 1990 levels these anthropogenic emissions of carbon dioxide and other greenhouse gases not controlled by the Montreal Protocol."
>
> Article 4 (2)(b) UN Framework Convention on Climate Change 1992 (extract)

Under the umbrella of the UN Framework Convention on Climate Change, we have seen the creation of the Kyoto Protocol (1997, 192 parties) and the Paris Agreement (2015, 193 parties), and it is these latter two instruments which contain more detailed targets and processes for emissions reduction.

The requirements of the UN Framework Convention on Climate Change are not therefore universal. Firstly, the convention does not require states to address emissions of pollutants which are covered by the Montréal Protocol to the Vienna Convention (cited earlier), even where there may be pollutants which both impact the ozone layer and are linked to climate change. In addition, there is a recognition that the bulk of the work needs to be carried out by those states which have already industrialised, as they are responsible for the majority of the historic damage to the climate.

UN Convention on Biological Diversity (CBD)

The CBD, which will be discussed in more detail in Chapter 8, recognises that biological diversity of species in enormously important for the health of humans and of the planet. It has been ratified by every UN member state, with the exception of the United States of America, which has variously expressed concerns over intellectual property rights, cost of implementation, and infringement of sovereignty.

ARTICLE

"The objectives of this Convention . . . are the conservation of biological diversity, the sustainable use of its components and the fair and equitable sharing of the benefits arising out of the utilization of genetic resources, including by appropriate access to genetic resources and by appropriate transfer of relevant technologies, taking into account all rights over those resources and to technologies, and by appropriate funding."

Article 1, UN Convention on Biological Diversity

The CBD reaffirms the sovereign right of states to exploit resources in their own territory and pairs that right with a responsibility not to damage the environment of other states, or the global commons (see Chapter 2).

There are two protocols to the Convention, the Cartagena Protocol on Biosafety (2003, 170 parties) and the Nagoya Protocol on Access to Genetic Resources and the Fair and Equitable Sharing of Benefits Arising from Their Utilization to the Convention on Biological Diversity (2010, 137 parties).

Agenda 21

Agenda 21 is fundamentally about sustainability, which will be covered in Section 1.3.1 later and in Part 3 of the book. Unlike the FCCC and CBD, Agenda 21 is not a binding piece of legislation; it is an advisory text. The *21* in the title refers to the initial hope that global sustainable development would have been achieved by the start of the 21st century, but this has not happened. It was Agenda 21 that was the trigger behind the Millennium Development Goals (MDGs), introduced in 2000, and the Sustainable Development Goals (SDGs), adopted in 2015.

CRITIQUING THE LAW

The FCCC, CBD, and Agenda 21 have failed to achieve their stated objectives on reducing emissions to 1990 levels, preserving biodiversity, and achieving global sustainable development by 2000.

Does this mean that they have all failed as international instruments?

This period marked a change in approach from the height of the Industrial Revolution and perhaps the beginning of the end of the dominant Western discourse about "man's dominion" over nature. Prior to 1973, there were no truly global environmental conventions, and by the end of the century, there were many, covering thus:

■ Wildlife trade (1973 CITES Convention)

■ Wetlands (1971 Ramsar Convention on Wetlands of International Importance Especially as Waterfowl Habitat)

■ Chemical use (1998 Rotterdam Convention on the Prior Informed Consent Procedure for Certain Hazardous Chemicals and Pesticides in International Trade)

■ Hazardous waste transportation (1989 Basel Convention on the Control of Transboundary Movements of Hazardous Wastes and Their Disposal)

■ Air quality (Convention for the Protection of the Ozone Layer [Vienna Convention] 1986, UN Framework Convention on Climate Change 1992)

As we moved from the 20th to the 21st century, this shift in policy direction gathered pace.

1.2.4 21st Century

This final section of the chronology will look at current issues in environmental law. The conclusion to the book will revisit this aspect and try to predict where environmental law is likely to go in the near future.

In the last two decades, we have seen a growth in public awareness of environmental issues, triggered by mainstream television programmes (e.g. the BBC *Blue Planet* series from 2001 and, more dramatically, the follow-up *Blue Planet II* from 2017), online-streamed media (e.g. Netflix's 2021 *Seaspiracy*), and social media (e.g. the remarkable efforts of Greta Thunberg).

Much of the policy and legislative framework of earlier eras was driven largely by the views of experts, whether scientific, legal, or industrial. The boom in *citizen science* and the impact this has had on legislative processes are discussed in Chapter 4.

There has also been an increase in extra-legislative measures adopted voluntarily by businesses and sectors. The ban by nearly 50 airlines on carrying hunting trophies, for example, was not mandated by any policy or legislative requirement but was a reaction to public opinion. Equally, the rise in "green" stock markets (e.g. the Luxembourg Green Exchange, the London Stock Market's Sustainable Bond Market and UNEP's Sustainable Stock Exchanges Initiative) demonstrates that there is a market for companies to go beyond any threshold which they may have been required to meet – going beyond US Supreme Court Justice Oliver Wendell Holmes Jr's conceptualisation of the "bad man," and perhaps even towards to "good man."

QUOTATION

"If you want to know the law and nothing else, you must look at it as a bad man, who cares only for the material consequences which such knowledge enables him to predict, not as a good one, who finds his reason for conduct, whether inside the law or outside of it, within the vaguer sanctions of his conscience."

Holmes, O. W., 1897, "The Path of the Law," 10 *Harvard Law Review* 457

From a legislative perspective, recent years have seen a raft of legislative provisions that have been triggered by the Brexit process. Between 2018 and 2022, there have been over 1,000 UK Statutory Instruments linked to "EU exit," although only a fraction of that number to date related to environmental provisions. In addition to these more procedural amendments, there have been regulations focused on specific environment-related issues, such as:

■ The Water Supply (Water Quality) Regulations 2016,[26] which gave effect to EU laws about the quality of water for drinking and cooking

- The Environmental Protection (Microbeads) (England) Regulations 2017,[27] which banned the use of microbeads in "rinse-off personal case" products
- The Environmental Protection (Plastic Straws, Cotton Buds and Stirrers) (England) Regulations 2020,[28] which banned, with certain exception, the supply of single-use plastic straws, stemmed cotton buds, and drink stirrers
- The Single Use Carrier Bags Charges (England) (Amendment) Order 2021,[29] which amended the similarly named 2015 Regulations, putting up the price of single-use carrier bags from 5p to 10p

ACTIVITY

Identify what you consider to be the most dramatic changes caused by environmental law since the 19th century.

These changes may have had positive impacts for society or the environment, or they may have had negative impacts.

The Environment Act 2021[30] is interesting to note here, as it is the latest attempt to pull together many of the different strands of environmental law into one place. It is a relatively large piece of legislation, running to 149 sections and 21 schedules, and at the time of writing, not all the Act is yet in force. Broadly, the Act covers aspects of waste and resource efficiency (Part III), air quality and the recall of products which do not meet environmental standards (Part IV), water (Part V), nature and biodiversity (Part VI), and conservation (Part VII).

The Act introduced the idea of "environment improvement plans" (SS 8–15), which must be set by the Secretary of State and which must last longer than 15 years. This recognition that environmental issues might not be solvable in a short time period is a contrast to older statute which set much more short-term goals. The Act retrospectively designates the 2018 government publication "A green future: our 25 year plan to improve the environment" as an environmental improvement plan.

In addition, the Act created a new body, the Office for Environmental Protection, which will have the power to prosecute, and its role will largely replace the role previously undertaken by the European Commission.

ACTIVITY

Imagine you are drafting a new legislative provision which is designed to regulate total emissions from the UK manufacturing sector.

The goal of the legislation will be to reduce total emissions by 50 per cent by a given future date.

Consider the issues are you going to have to factor in if the target date is ten years in the future.

Would these be different if the target date were 25 years in the future?

Over the course of the chapter so far, we have seen that the area which would now be called environmental law has evolved from a series of unconnected, retrospective, poorly enforced ideas into a much more coherent, anticipatory, aspirational, and broad framework. This evolution has seen standards get tightened as scientific understanding has improved, whether that understanding relates to the transmissibility of cholera, to the potential extinction of entire species, or to the impact of industrial pollution by one state on the environment of another.

Despite this dramatic shift over the centuries, it is possible to identify a number of concepts and principles which have underpinned the laws to a greater or lesser extent. Many of these now form part of the enforceable legislative framework, but many are "borrowed" from older or other cultural frames of reference and were adapted to their current use.

1.3 Concepts of Environmental Law

In this section we will consider five of the key concepts which underpin environmental law. Some of them you will have encountered at some level previously; others may be new to you. The more common ones will have been explicitly included in legislation, and there will be case law that has added interpretation to the legal skeleton, but others exist much more in the background.

1.3.1 Sustainability and Sustainable Development

At its core, an activity is sustainable when it can be carried on for an indeterminate period of time with little or no impact on its ability to be carried out. The sun, for example, is sustainable in that the nuclear chain reaction which takes place at the heart of the sun will continue unabated for around five billion years. It will eventually break down, the core will contract, and the sun will become a red giant, destroying Mercury, Venus, and the Earth.

Neither the sun nor the moon represents suitable environments for life, however. In practical terms, *sustainability* has come to mean a way of avoiding the over-exploitation of natural resources in such a manner that they are given time to naturally replenish and will not be exhausted. The term itself has been in use for around 300 years, since being coined (in German) in 1713 by Hans Carl von Carlowitz,[31] who was concerned that the mining industry in the German state of Saxony was using lumber faster than it could be reproduced. What von Carlowitz called "nachhaltende Nutzung" is usually translated as "sustained use" or "sustainable use."

The concept of sustainability, though, especially in the context of construction, is far older, and there are examples of it in Ancient Greece and Rome as well as Indonesia, India, Cambodia, and Morocco. If we think back to the use of coal in domestic fires in 13th-century London, part of the rationale for doing this was that the trees in the surrounding counties had been felled at a rate much faster than they could reproduce. It was not just building materials which were being consumed too quickly. In the early 20th century, the director of the Bronx Zoo in New York, William Hornaday, argued passionately that wildlife was being hunted at an unsustainable rate, or "very much more rapidly than it is breeding."[32]

Sustainable development has strong formal roots in two economics texts from the early 1970s: *The Limits to Growth* from 1972, and *Small Is Beautiful* from 1973. In *The Limits to Growth*, Donella Meadows, Dennis Meadows, Jørgen Randers, and William Behrens III modelled what would happen if human population and economic growth continued in a world with finite resources. The book concluded that humanity has everything it needs to create a society in equilibrium which would last for generations, and that failure to create this equilibrium would lead to exponential growth and the collapse of the Earth.

The Limits to Growth also used the analogy of the "chessboard story" to illustrate the effects of exponential growth. In the story (which has many different versions), the protagonist asks for payment of one grain of rice (or wheat) on the first square of a chessboard, two on the second, and doubling on every square after that. By the time the story reaches the 64th and final square, it would require 18 quadrillion grains (264), and there are not enough grains in the kingdom (of Persia, India, or China, depending on the version of the story).

In the 1973 text *Small Is Beautiful*, E. F. Schumacher continues the argument that humans are consuming resources at a rate far greater than they are being regenerated, by drawing a contrast with a business owner whose company is using up its capital faster than it regenerates. Neither pattern of behaviour, he argues, can be continued indefinitely.

It is this link between sustainability, construction, and economic growth which led most clearly to sustainable *development* becoming an almost-separate concept from sustainability. Most famously defined by the Brundtland Commission in the late 20th century (see following text), *sustainable development* has become one of the underpinning elements of modern life.

Definition

Sustainable development is development that meets the needs of the present without compromising the ability of future generations to meet their own needs. It contains within it two key concepts:

■ the concept of 'needs', in particular the essential needs of the world's poor, to which overriding priority should be given; and

■ the idea of limitations imposed by the state of technology and social organization on the environment's ability to meet present and future needs.

WCED, 1987, Report of the World Commission on Environment and Development: Our Common Future, Vienna: United Nations Department of Economic and Social Affairs, UN General Assembly, A/42/427, p41

The Brundtland definition goes beyond environmental sustainability and looks also at social and economic sustainability, and these have become known as the "three pillars" of sustainability. There is an assumption in all legislation concerning sustainability that it is possible to ascertain at the start of a process whether it is, or is not, truly sustainable.

In legal terms, "sustainable," whether in terms of sustainable development or sustainability, is not defined in UK law; none of the five acts which have the term as part of their title gives a definition of "sustainable."

■ The Sustainable Energy Act 2003[33]

This Act amended the Utilities Act 2000 and made a provision about the development and promotion of a sustainable energy policy. The Act required the Secretary of State to publish an annual "Sustainable Energy Report" covering efforts made to cut carbon emissions and reduce fuel poverty, both of which would fall within the broad remit of sustainability, but also on energy security. The Act does not define what is meant by sustainable energy.

■ The Sustainable and Secure Buildings Act 2004[34]

This Act primarily amended the Buildings Act 1984[35] and added new requirements for building regulation to include fuel and water efficiency, environmental protection, sustainable development, and crime reduction. There is also a requirement on the Secretary of State to produce a bi-annual report on progress in relation to these matters. The Act does not set out what it means by *sustainable* or *sustainable development*.

■ The Climate Change and Sustainable Energy Act 2006[36]

This Act builds on several of the provisions of the Sustainable Energy Act 2003, in terms of alleviation of fuel poverty, reduction of GHG emissions, and promotion of microgeneration and renewable energy. The Act required the Secretary of State to report annually on the UK GHG emissions (S2), and this was repealed and replaced by a similar duty in Section 16 of the Climate Change Act 2008.[37] A second requirement on the Secretary of State to set targets for microgeneration (S4) and a third to produce reports on heat generated from renewable resources (S21) were scrapped by Section 57 of the Deregulation Act 2015.[38] The Act does not set out what it means by *sustainable energy*.

■ The Sustainable Communities Act 2007[39] (and the 2010 Amendment Act[40])

The purpose of the Act is to promote "the sustainability of local communities" and gives a duty to the Secretary of State to "assist local authorities in promoting the sustainability of local communities" (S1(4)). The schedule to the Act lists a range of matters which local authorities must bear in mind when proposing projects to promote sustainability, and a further range of definitions, but nothing to set out what is meant by *sustainability*.

If none of the acts define the terms which are key to their provisions, then courts must look to the ordinary usage of the terms when it comes to enforcement. Unfortunately, we have no judicial guidance in this regard, as there have only been a handful of reported cases brought under these acts, and those which have been brought did not hinge upon the interpretation of *sustainability* or *sustainable development*.

We can see that sustainability and sustainable development therefore offer certain advantages as approaches, even allowing for some flex in the definitions. They consider environmental protection, but not to the exclusion of social and economic development, which makes them rather pragmatic. When effectively implemented, the concepts also take into account the differing needs of developed and developing nations, the current and future generations (of humans, of course), and balances this against the potential benefits and threats of technological advances.

Table 1.1 Cases on Sustainability Brought under Four Selected Acts

Sustainable Energy Act 2003	*Scottish Power v National Grid Electricity Transmission PLC, E.ON UK PLC* (2005) EWHC 2324 (Admin)
Sustainable and Secure Buildings Act 2004	No reported cases
Climate Change and Sustainable Energy Act 2006	*R. (ex. p Friends of the Earth) v Secretary of State for Energy and Climate Change* (2009) EWCA Civ 810
Sustainable Communities Act 2007	*Forest of Dean DC v Wright* (2017) EWCA Civ 2102 *Samuel Smith Old Brewery (Tadcaster) v Selby DC* (2015) EWCA Civ 1107 *Brent LBC v Risk Management Partners Ltd* (2009) EWCA Civ 490

1.3.2 The Precautionary Principle

The precautionary principle applies to a far wider range of activities than just environmental law. It emerged into European environmental policy in the latter half of the 20th century but has its roots in the earlier German *Vorsorgeprincip*, or "anticipation through foresight," and potentially the old English proverb "better to be safe than sorry."

In terms of operation, the principle requires a predictive, proactive, or anticipatory approach to policymaking, which contrasts sharply with the largely reactive approach which has been the touchstone of earlier legislation. In this, it is thematically linked to sustainability, as a more accurate understanding of the impacts of a project will allow for a more accurate determination of its sustainability.

Definition

In order to protect the environment, the precautionary approach shall be widely applied by States according to their capabilities. Where there are threats of serious or irreversible damage, lack of full scientific certainty shall not be used as a reason for postponing cost-effective measures to prevent environmental degradation.

UN General Assembly, 1992, A/CONF.151/26 (Vol. I) Report of
the United Nations Conference on Environment and Development,
Annex I: Rio Declaration on Environment and Development, Principle 15

In practice, the precautionary principle involves looking at a proposed project, and if there is a risk of "serious or irreversible" damage, then the fact that there is no scientific certainty as to the size of the risk should not be used as a reason to allow the project to continue without any remediation or risk reduction measures in place.

Definition

When an activity raises threats of harm to human health or the environment, precautionary measures should be taken even if some cause and effect relationships are not fully established scientifically. In this context the proponent of an activity, rather than the public, should bear the burden of proof.

Wingspread Statement on the Precautionary Principle, 1998

There are different ways of interpreting the precautionary principle as an approach to decision-making, and these will have very different impacts:

- The project *should not* be allowed to proceed unless it has been demonstrated that it *will not* lead to harmful environmental consequences.

- The project *should* be allowed to proceed unless it has been demonstrated that it *will* lead to harmful environmental consequences.

The first of these approaches is far more restrictive in terms of development, and the second is very permissive. From an environmental protection perspective, it is the restrictive interpretation which offers the most protection, although Cass Sunstein[41] argues that the restrictive interpretation effectively prevents all development and paralyses the system.

It was the restrictive approach which was used by the Northern Ireland Court of Appeal in the 2017 case Re Friends of the Earth Ltd Application for Judicial Review. Friends of the Earth were seeking a review of a decision by the Department of the Environment not to issue a stop notice in relation to unauthorised dredging of sand from Lough Neagh, which was a special protection area, a Ramsar site, and an area of special scientific interest (see Chapter 7).

JUDGMENT

Re Friends of the Earth Ltd Application for Judicial Review [2017] NICA 41, [2018] Env. L.R. 7

"[T]hese operations are considered likely to have significant impact, that the nature and extent of that impact has not been established, that prior to the grant of permission is the requirement to establish that there will be no significant impact and that it is imperative that the precautionary principle be applied."

(Per Weatherup LJ @163)

In terms of legislative provision, there is only one mention of the precautionary principle in any UK act. The Environment Act 2021[42] includes it as one of the five "environmental principles" which are identified in Section 17 as being the basis of a "policy statement on environmental principles" which the Secretary of State must produce. The remaining principles overall follow:

SECTION

Policy statement on environmental principles

(1) The Secretary of State must prepare a policy statement on environmental principles in accordance with this section and section 18.

(2) A "policy statement on environmental principles" is a statement explaining how the environmental principles should be interpreted and proportionately applied by Ministers of the Crown when making policy.

(3) It may also explain how Ministers of the Crown, when interpreting and applying the environmental principles, should take into account other considerations relevant to their policy.

(4) The Secretary of State must be satisfied that the statement will, when it comes into effect, contribute to –
    (a) the improvement of environmental protection, and
    (b) sustainable development.

(5) In this Part "environmental principles" means the following principles –
    (a) the principle that environmental protection should be integrated into the making of policies,
    (b) the principle of preventative action to avert environmental damage,
    (c) the precautionary principle, so far as relating to the environment,
    (d) the principle that environmental damage should as a priority be rectified at source, and
    (e) the polluter pays principle.

S17, Environment Act 2021

Whilst it is still too early to identify any groundbreaking cases brought under the Environment Act 2021, the wider case law on the precautionary principle is extensive. Several of the cases relate to the interpretation of whether or not the proposed development would cause "significant environmental harm,"

CASE

***R (on the application of Trevone Objectors Group) v Cornwall Council* (2013) EWHC 4091 (Admin)**

A local authority had decided to depart from the planning policy and grant permission for the development of 15 affordable homes in the North Cornish village of Trevone. The planning officer had found that there would be a high probability of permanent environmental damage, but the local authority concluded that significant environmental effects were unlikely, and therefore there was no needs for an environmental impact assessment.

The High Court found that this was legal, and the objector's judicial review failed.

Whilst there appears largely to be clarity on the nature of the precautionary principle, there is still a large subjective element at work in its operation. The European Union identifies that terms such as "irreversible harm," "lack of scientific certainty," and "serious threat" have been described as ambiguous and ill-defined. More troubling for some, this could lead to legislative uncertainty, as courts and tribunals may apply the rules inconsistently.

CRITIQUING THE LAW

Should an independent environmental impact assessment be a requirement of all development proposals over a certain threshold?

To avoid the type of paralysis that concerned Sunstein, von Schomberg[43] has identified four scenarios where she feels the precautionary principle should and should not be used. The principle should not be used in situations where the risk is purely hypothetical, or where standard risk management approaches are appropriate. It should be used where there is a threat of harm but there is insufficient scientific consensus about the effects, or where the harm is understood but the causal relationship is unclear.

1.3.3 The Polluter Pays Principle

The third of the concepts to be covered is the polluter pays principle.

Definition

"The principle to be used for allocating costs of pollution prevention and control measures to encourage rational use of scarce environmental resources and to avoid distortions in international trade and investment is the so-called 'Polluter-Pays Principle.' This principle means that the polluter should bear the expenses of carrying out the above-mentioned measures decided by public authorities to ensure that the environment is in an acceptable state. In other words, the cost of these measures should be reflected in the cost of goods and services which cause pollution in production and/or consumption. Such measures should not be accompanied by subsidies that would create significant distortions in international trade and investment."

Organization for Economic Cooperation and Development, 1972, Recommendation of the Council on Guiding Principles concerning International Economic Aspects of Environmental Policies, recommendation Aa)4

Shortly after the OECD adopted the polluter pays principle as an underpinning principle, the European Commission adopted the 1st Environmental Action Programme, which included a commitment to using the principle.

LEGISLATION

"The Member States and the Commission have advocated the adoption of the 'polluter pays' principle. This should be taken as the guiding principle for applying economic instruments to carry out the environmental programme without hampering the progressive elimination of regional imbalances in the Community."

Declaration of the Council of the European Communities and of the representatives of the Governments of the Member States meeting in the Council of 22 November 1973 on the programme of action of the European Communities on the environment, OJ C 112, Chapter 9(A)

The early Environmental Action Plans did not have any statutory authority, and the principle was not formally embedded into EU law until 2004, with Directive 2004/35/CE of the European Parliament and of the council of 21 April 2004 on environmental liability with regard to the prevention and remedying of environmental damage.

CASE

Raffinerie Mediterranee (ERG) SpA v Ministero dello Sviluppo Economico (C-378/08)

This was a European Court of Justice case in which the court concluded that the polluter pays principle as set out in Directive 2004/35 meant that the only thing that needed to be proven was a causal link between the activities and the pollution. There was no need to prove any fault, negligence, or intent.

The court regarded the polluter pays principle as establishing strict liability.

Within the broad umbrella of the polluter pays principle, it is possible to include development such as "*shared responsibility*," which was introduced into EU law by the 5th Environmental Action Programme as a replacement for the "command-and-control" approach to regulation. It involves government, industry, and the public to share the responsibility for engaging in policies and actions to prevent environmental degradation. This recognises that there is a cyclical relationship between governments as rule-makers, the public as consumers, and the industrial sector as the creators/manufacturers. We all share in the creation of the pollution; thus, we should all share in the burden of paying for it.

One of the most straightforward examples of the polluter pays principle in action in the UK is the Environmental Permitting Regime. This will be covered in much more detail in Chapter 12, which focuses on regulation of corporations. In essence, the Environmental Permitting Regime grew out of the EU integrated pollution control and, later, integrated pollution prevention and control systems. The UK system was introduced in 2007 and pulled different licensing regimes within one framework. The intention was to reduce the administrative burden on both industry and regulators without compromising on the environmental and human health standards which had previously been delivered by the separate regimes. The Environmental Permitting (England and Wales) Regulations 2010[44] and subsequent amendments brought yet more regimes into the permitting system and streamlined the "administrative burden" further.

The Environmental Permitting Regime is a good example of the polluter pays principle. It requires anyone who wishes to carry out a potentially polluting activity to apply for a licence before they carry out the activity. The cost of the licensing pays for the monitoring and enforcement regime, and so if you wish to pollute, you must pay. It is also a good example of the precautionary principle, since the use of the best available techniques (BAT) approach to require license holders to identify the most effective techniques to prevent environmental harm.

The polluter pays principle is not without its flaws, however. For large corporations and large pollution incidents, the assessment of damage caused and the payment of fine and remediation costs can take many years.

The supertanker *Exxon Valdez*, travelling between Alaska and California, ran aground in Prince William Sound in March 1989, spilling 37,000 tonnes of crude oil, contaminating 1,300 miles of Alaskan coastline, and causing immense damage to wildlife in the region. Exxon has paid in the region of US$3bn in fines and clean-up costs, but the International Tanker Owners Pollution Federation (ITOPF), which assists with ship-based oil and chemical spills, estimates the clean-up cost amounts to around US$7bn.

ACTIVITY

The Portuguese-owned company *Empresa de óleo sujo* (Edos) has been convicted of causing 10,000 litres of oily residue to leak into the river Purple, close to their factory in Midshires, UK. The court wishes to use the polluter pays principle to calculate the level at which the fine imposed on Edos. Consider which of the following four options would be the most effective way of calculating this.

Applying the polluter pays principle, how should the costs of pollution incidents be assessed?
Actual/potential damage to property?
Actual/potential damage to amenity?
Actual/potential damage to natural resources?
Actual/potential damage to flora and fauna more widely?

SUMMARY

■ Environmental law is multidisciplinary – law needs science, and science needs laws.

■ Many issues (for example, climate change) are too large to be dealt with by one country.

■ Some countries may need financial and technical assistance to achieve globally beneficial goals.

- Law operates in societal context, and society changes – more global focus.
- Move from reactive and ad hoc (waiting for damage and then legislating the specifics) to proactive and comprehensive (attempting to predict outcomes).
- More use of concepts and principles – sustainability, precautionary principle, polluter pays principle.
- Effects of environmental damage can be cumulative (the rise in microplastics in the water system); some are irreversible (e.g. species extinction), and some may be both (e.g. the effects of deforestation and the reduction in carbon sinks on climate change).
- Legal solutions need to take account of political and economic constraints.
- Collaboration between states to meet common goals is essential.

SAMPLE ESSAY QUESTION

Using examples, assess the extent to which it is important to have a unified definition of "the environment" for enforcement of environmental law.

1. State definition of "the environment" in EPA 1990 and in other selected legislation (both domestic and international).
2. Discuss what aspects of the environment are subject to statutory protection – is it ever "the environment" as a whole, or is it more specific elements, for example, water quality, air quality, or biodiversity?
3. Assess how this links with approaches such as the precautionary principle and polluter pays principle. Do either rely on a tight definition of the *environment*?
4. Conclude. Ensure that your conclusion follows the internal logic of the rest of your answer – do not, for example, provide examples suggesting a unified definition is not important and then conclude that it is important.

Further Reading

Bell, S., McGillivray, D., Pederson, O., Lees, E., & Stokes, E., 2017, *Environmental Law*, 9th ed., Oxford, OUP

Du Pusani, J.A., 2006, Sustainable Development – Historical Roots of the Concept, *Environmental Sciences*, 3(2), 83–96, http://doi.org/10.1080/15693430600688831

Hughes, D., Jewell, T., Lowther, J., Parpworth, N., & de Prez, P., 2002, *Environmental Law*, 4th ed., Oxford: OUP

Meadows, D.H., Meadows, D.L., Randers, J., & Behrens, W., 1972, *The Limits to Growth: A Report for the Club of Rome's Project on the Predicament of Mankind*, Falls Church, VA: Potomac Associates

O'Riordan, T., & Cameron, J., 1994, *Interpreting the Precautionary Principle*, London: Routledge

Schumacher, E.F., 1973, *Small is Beautiful: A Study of Economics as if People Mattered*, London: Blond & Briggs

WCED, 1987, *Report of the World Commission on Environment and Development: Our Common Future*, Vienna: United Nations Department of Economic and Social Affairs, UN General Assembly, A/42/427

Notes

1 Bell, S., McGillivray, D., Pederson, O., Lees, E., & Stokes, E., 2017, *Environmental Law*, 9th ed., Oxford: OUP, p. 7

2 Hughes, D., Jewell, T., Lowther, J., Parpworth, N., & de Prez, P., 2002, *Environmental Law*, 4th ed., Oxford: OUP, p. 3

3 Allaby, M., 2003, *Dangerous Weather: Fog, Smog and Poisoned Rain*, New York: Facts on File Inc., pp. 64–65

4 Mingay, G.E., ed., 1977, *The Agricultural Revolution: Changes in Agriculture 1650–1880*, London: Adam & Charles Black, p. 3

5 Underwood, E.A., 1947, The History of Cholera in Great Britain, *Proceedings of the Royal Society of Medicine*, XLI, 165–173

6 (2 and 3 Will. 4 c. 10)

7 (11 and 12 Vict. c. 63)

8 (11 and 12 Vict. c. 123)

9 (12 and 13 Vict. c. 111)

10 (18 and 19 Vict. c. 121)

11 (21 and 22 Vict. c. 104)

12 (9 and 10 Vict. c. 127)

13 (17 Vict. c. 15)

14 (24 and 25 Vict. c. ccvi)

15 (26 and 27 Vict. c. 124)

16 (4 and 5 Eliz. 2 c. 52)

17 (3 Geo. 4 c. 71)

18 (32 and 33 Vict. c. 17)

19 (11 and 12 Geo. 5. c. 16)

20 (2 and 3 Eliz. 2 c.30)

21 (12, 13, and 14 Geo. 6. c. 97)

22 c. 21

23 c. 40

24 c. 37

25 SI 1992/3240

26 SI 2016/614

27 SI 2017/1312

28 SI 2020/971

29 SI 2021/598

30 c. 30

31 von Carlowitz, H.C., 1713, *Die Sylvicultura Oeconomica, oder haußwirthliche Nachricht und Naturmäßige Anweisung zur wilden Baum-Zucht* (On Economic Forestry, or Domestic Message and Natural Instruction for Wild Tree-Cultivation), Leipzig: Verlegts Johann Friedrich Braun, pp. 105–106

32 Hornaday, W.T., 1913, *Our Vanishing Wild Life: Its Extermination and Preservation*, New York: Charles Scribner's Sons, p. ix

33 c. 30

34 c. 22

35 c. 55

36 c. 19

37 c. 27

38 c. 20

39 c. 23

40 Sustainable Communities Act 2007 (Amendment) Act 2010 c. 21

41 Sunstein, C.R., 2005, *Laws of Fear: Beyond the Precautionary Principle*, Cambridge: CUP, p. 15

42 c. 30

43 von Schomberg, R., 2012, The Precautionary Principle: Its Use Within Hard and Soft Law, *European Journal of Risk Regulation*, 3(2), 147–156

44 SI 2010/675

2

Philosophy and Ethics

Law students, and others, may be forgiven for thinking that environmental law as a coherent system is a relative newcomer to the legal canon – old stalwarts like equity, criminal law, and contract certainly have a longer tradition. As we saw in Chapter 1, environmental law did not, however, emerge fully formed alongside current discussions on plastic pollution and climate change.

What we will see in this chapter is that whilst it is true that a body of law loosely categorised as "environmental law" has not been around for very long, the concepts and ideas upon which it is based have developed over decades, centuries, even millennia. Loose, seemingly unconnected ideas and approaches have evolved into much tighter ideas, which have a significant impact on every aspect of life on Earth.

Coyle and Morrow[1] suggest that it might seem strange to question the "philosophical foundation" of environmental law, and while this is true, the fact remains that behind every environmental law passed, whether it is the UK or elsewhere, there will be a set of philosophical or ethical values. These values may be explicit or implicit and will reflect the dominant worldview of those who supported the bill on its journey through Parliament.

It is also fair to say that the dominant philosophical and ethical views have changed over time, such that the views which were expressed by 18th-century lawmakers are not necessarily those which are dominant today. This is not to say that "old" philosophical perspectives are somehow automatically "wrong" – some are widely viewed today as being inappropriate or abhorrent, but others remain dominant. It is crucial, of course, to identify that while in the UK the Western philosophical tradition (stemming from the Ancient Greeks) remains dominant, other regions of the world follow differing traditions – Eastern, African, Islamic, and so on.

Ethics, on the other hand, while linked inexorably to philosophy, are considerably more varied. Ethics can be thought of as either a way of doing things or a way of being (or both, perhaps), and it is not uncommon to find inherent contradictions or cognitive dissonance in the stance taken by individuals. Sometimes this will draw a distinction based on species ("bees are good, but wasps are bad"), and sometimes it will be more complex – recognising the right of nations to develop, but with concern over the climate impacts of allowing this development.

DOI: 10.4324/9781003137214-2

In this chapter, we will explore some of the varied views that have been dominant over the years, considering both their importance at the time and their shadows which can be discerned in current environmental laws and policies. Some of these approaches were covered in Chapter 1, and so they will be revisited in this chapter to explore their links to philosophies and ethics. Other concepts, for example, ecocentrism and anthropocentrism, may be less well-known to you. The chapter will also cover Garrett Hardin's "tragedy of the commons" (or "tragedy of the unmanaged commons," as Hardin later renamed it) and explore the application of the allegory in relation to extending legal protection beyond national boundaries, for example, the high seas.

At the end of the chapter, I recommend some texts which will be of use to you if you want to explore this topic further, for it is of such a scale that one chapter can only touch the surface.

AIMS AND OBJECTIVES

After reading this chapter, you should be able to:

■ Identify the links between ethics, philosophies, and environmental lawmaking.

■ Explain the key differences between anthropocentrism and ecocentrism.

■ Understand the connections between the "tragedy of the commons" and the philosophical and ethical basis of environmental law.

2.1 Environmental Philosophies and Ethics

As we saw in Chapter 1, in the UK there are elements of common law which would today be considered environmental in nature. Laws on nuisance, for example, although they require the claimant to have an interest in land, do protect against smells, noise, heat, and so on. The protection given is very limited, however, and the focus is entirely on protecting the affected landowner rather than the wider population or the environment as a whole.

The basis of this lack of protection for non-human life is twofold. Traditionally, in Western philosophy, humans were regarded as being separate from the environment. More recently, the interconnectedness of all life on the planet has become a more dominant discourse, and this has been driven partly by increased scientific understanding.

In terms of an environmental philosophy, there are many different belief systems which have a role in modern society, and there are many people who may feel that elements of different philosophies or belief systems appeal to them. There is no particular system which is "right" or "wrong," and you will be able to see many elements which overlap, both with your own views and with the policies and laws which are in existence.

2.1.1 Gaia Hypothesis

Whilst the Gaia hypothesis has its roots in much earlier cultural belief systems, the hypothesis of the planet as a self-regulating, complex system was proposed by James Lovelock in the late 1960s, although the term was not popularised until the late 1970s and 1980s.

QUOTATION

The argument is based on the idea that the planet is a self-regulating system which incorporates all organic and inorganic elements. The network is acknowledged to be extraordinarily complex, and the logical progression of that argument is that it is impossible to know which, if any, elements of that network are superfluous. This uncertainty works because it repositions the actions of humans to "save the planet" from being altruistic to essentially egoistic – by saving the planet, we are saving ourselves.

There are those, particularly evolutionary biologists and theorists, who criticise the Gaia approach. Stephen Jay Gould dismissed the hypothesis as "a metaphor not a mechanism."[2] Richard Dawkins, for example, felt that it ignores the Darwinian theory of evolution and natural selection and is therefore illogical.[3] Others, too, were happy to criticise Gaia – Dobson argued that the adoption of Gaia by political ecologists "betrays either a woolly thinking or latent anthropocentrism."[4] Nonetheless, the idea has gained traction and, indeed, has become more or less mainstream.

ACTIVITY

Discuss the application of the Gaia hypothesis in the following situations:

1. A highly contagious fungal infection is discovered in humans. The effect of the fungus is initially to render its host temporarily catatonic, and it is calculated to be fatal in one in ten hosts. A vaccine which would kill the fungus is available.
2. Scientists have developed a new form of limitless, pollutant-free energy which will reduce anthropogenic greenhouse gas emissions to almost zero. It will allow for expansion of every urban area on Earth with no additional air pollution.

In both these scenarios, to protect one type of life will necessitate damage to other organisms. If Gaia is a mechanism by which "living organisms have always, and actively, kept their planet fit for life," should we kill the fungus or allow human population to be reduced by 10 per cent? Should we reduce airborne pollutants and allow more urban expansion or protect the terrestrial environment at the cost of increased air pollution?

2.1.2 Eco-Socialism

For centuries, indigenous communities regarded the environment as an entity which needed to be respected rather than exploited. As we saw in Chapter 1, the Māori people of New Zealand use the word *kaitiakitanga* to represent their traditional way of managing the environment by acting as a kaitiaki. The Earth itself was deified as a goddess, for example, to Hindus (Bhumi), Māori (Papatūānuku),

Ancient Greeks (Gaia), Ancient Romans (Terra), the civilisations of the Andes (Pachamama), many Native Americans (Spider Grandmother), and Old Norse (Jörð or Fjörgyn) and across many other cultures. The concept of ownership of the environment, or any element of it, was unthinkable to many of these cultures. Chief Seattle (sometimes spelled *seathl*) was a 19th-century chief of the Suquamish and Duwamish people in North-Western United States. The city of Seattle in Washington State is named after him. In what is now regarded as most likely being an inaccurate transcription of a speech he possibly gave in 1864, Seattle is quoted as saying, "All things are connected. Whatever befalls the earth befalls the sons of the earth."[5] Whatever the truth of what Seattle said, the sentiment is likely to be genuine and represents the broad view of many pre-industrialised societies.

From these ancient roots, the modern eco-socialist movement emerged in the late 19th century and was popularised by writers such as Karl Marx and William Morris. It is based on the belief that the capitalist system, with its corresponding drive for greater production and more profit, is at the root cause of the environmental issues which face the world. Corporate bodies are indeed the largest polluters, but it is important to bear in mind that corporations do not necessarily pollute purely out of malice. They are largely satisfying demand from consumers (whether those are individuals or other companies), and it is this unsustainable drive for commodities which leads to the levels of pollution and emissions we currently live with.

Eco-socialists are often considered to be more extreme than other environmental movements and are placed within the wider "deep green" or "fundamentalist greens," which are discussed later. However, as with any movement, there are internal divisions, and *green anarchism* is often regarded as being an even more extreme part of the wider eco-socialist approach. While eco-socialists may push for a post-capitalist and post-state world, green anarchists take the approach that all hierarchies should be abolished – including those which exist between humans and non-human animals.

Eco-socialists are generally critical of other approaches to environmentalism, which are seen as being too "cosy" with the capitalist system. Organisations such as Greenpeace International, which in 2020 employed directly about 500 people (and over 3,000 people across the Greenpeace Network) and had current assets of €44m, are an example of the type of organisation which eco-socialists would consider to be too embedded into the system.

The counterargument is that unless an organisation acts within a system, it has less ability to influence the direction of travel of that system. As we saw in Chapter 1, *The Limits to Growth*, published in 1972, predicted that the current patterns of consumption and development would lead to catastrophe. That text, along with Ehrlich's *The Population Bomb*, saw over-population as being the main cause of this potential disaster, but the eco-socialist movement saw capitalism itself as the root cause of the problem.

From a formal, politico-legal perspective, eco-socialism is a long way from being mainstream, but as we will see in Chapter 5, when we look at the creation of environmental laws, politicians are swayed by their own belief systems, and those of their constituents.

The anarchist and social ecologist Murray Bookchin, writing in the early 1980s, saw clear parallels between the recognition of humans as part of a web (rather than at the top of a pyramid) and the dissolution of hierarchies between humans.

QUOTATION

Using this web as the basis for a new (and almost utopian) society would, he argues, lead to a series of small, networked communities which would recycle their own waste and produce their own power, and where food would be raised and hunted locally. Bookchin suggested that material possessions such as cars and clothes would be made of a higher quality, enabling them to be passed down through the generations.[6] The appeal of this type of "off-grid" living rose to the fore during the COVID pandemic, when record numbers of people were looking to move from cities and other high-population centres into villages and more rural locations. With the end of the pandemic came a realisation for many that they were too reliant on the services afforded to them by urban living, and they re-embedded themselves into city life.

The Brundtland Commission definition of *sustainable development* can be argued to have quite close thematic links to eco-socialism, as it focuses on the "needs" of current and future generations rather than the "wants," as well as equality between developed and underdeveloped nations. Eco-socialists, however, tend to favour sustainability without the development, which they feel is the most appropriate way for societies to progress. Eco-socialism effectively requires a dismantling of existing governmental and power structures, which perhaps makes it less feasible as a dominant approach.

2.1.3 Ecofeminism

In the same way that eco-socialism places the responsibility for the planet's environmental issues at the door of capitalism, ecofeminism regards the (largely Western) patriarchal societal structure as being at fault. Françoise d'Eaubonne, the French environmentalist and feminist, coined the term *ecofeminism* in her 1974 book *La Féminisme ou la Mort* (Feminism or Death), which built on the wider feminism movement of the 1960s. She called for the eradication of social injustice more widely, as well as arguing that the domination and oppression (by men) of women and other marginalised groups was linked to the domination and oppression of nature by the patriarchy.

QUOTATION

As with eco-socialism, the end goal for ecofeminism is to either replace the existing global system with one which is equitable or cause the existing system to evolve rapidly into a truly equitable state.

In some ways, this mirrors wider concerns – the full name of the UN Sustainable Development Goal 5 (gender equality) is "Achieve gender equality and empower all women and girls." It recognises that without gender equality, sustainable development will be difficult, if not impossible, to achieve. The UN Environment Programme, too, recognises the importance of gender equality.

Definition

"Gender inequality is one of the most pervasive threats to sustainable development. It has negative impacts on access to, use of and control over a wide range of resources, and on the ability to meet human rights obligations with respect to enjoyment – by women and men – of a clean, safe, healthy, and sustainable environment."

UN Environment Programme, 2016, Global Gender and
Environment Outlook, Vienna: UNEP, pii

There is a divergence within ecofeminism, however. On the one hand, there are those who believe that the traditionally gendered role of nurturing and caregiving ascribed to women makes them best placed to solve current and future environmental issues. On the other hand, there are those who argue that it is the domination and oppression by the patriarchal capitalist system of both women and nature that puts them in this role. Those in the second group criticise those in the first group for "essentialising" women, that is to say, attributing fixed immovable qualities to a gender, rather than recognising the social construction of gendered differences.

2.1.4 Green Conservatism and Eco-Capitalism

If eco-socialism and ecofeminism are both on the left-wing side of the political spectrum, green conservatism and eco-capitalism are much more right-wing approaches to environmental protection. Taken together, they are sometimes called "blue greens."

At its heart, both apply the same approach to environment as they do to every other aspect of life. Simply put, the solution to environmental issues is not increased government action and more legislative provisions; it is to leave it to the market to come up with innovative solutions. The difference between the two is that green conservatives would prefer to leave everything to the market and to reduce state input and regulation. Eco-capitalists, on the other hand, recognise the idea of "natural capital" and that future wealth requires that the market should be allowed to exploit this capital.

Proponents argue that free market, or guided market, is much more pragmatic than setting up large-scale, complex international targets (such as those put in place under the Kyoto Protocol to the UN Framework Convention on Climate Change). They will point to the fact (as will be covered in more detail in Chapter 9 on air pollution) that none of the targets ever set at any of the Conferences of the Parties (COPs), from COP 1 in Berlin to COP 27 in Sharm El-Sheikh, have ever been met. Under the Kyoto Protocol (COP 3), for example, states agreed to reduce GHG emissions to 18 per cent below 1990 levels. In 1990, the 38 member states of the Organisation for Economic Cooperation and Development (OECD) produced 15.3 gigatonnes (GT) of CO_2. Instead of the target drop of 18 per cent, OECD emissions actually rose by around 7 per cent and had still not hit the target in 2019 (15.4 GT). Within these overall figures, there are some successes – the UK dropped from 794m tonnes in 1990 to 453m tonnes in 2019, but green conservatives would argue that individual state accomplishments are rendered meaningless by global failures.

Edmund Burke, regarded as the father of modern conservatism, recognised in the late 18th century that leaving a "ruin instead of a habitation"[7] was the inevitable outcome of a revolutionary approach to policy, and that a more conservative, evolutionary approach was required. His approach was to suggest that every member of society should consider what they "received from their ancestors" and equally that they should not feel empowered to waste this inheritance. If such an approach were to be repeated by several generations, then the fabric of society would be destroyed.

One of the best-known eco-capitalism mechanisms is the emissions trading system (ETS), whereby a limited market is created for carbon emissions, in the form of "carbon credits." The total available stock is reduced over time, and the theory is that this increasing scarcity will drive up the price, and so players in the market who are more efficient (and operating below their individual limit) will be able to trade their "spare" capacity to players who are operating above their limit. Thus, if the system works effectively, players who reduce their emissions are rewarded, and vice versa, and the total emissions levels falls. Critics of ETS identify issues of total availability being too high, and that there are too many emitters who are not in the system.

Eco-socialists, ecofeminists, green conservatives, and eco-capitalists all recognise that the majority of the world's environmental problems stem from the patterns and practices which began in the Industrial Revolution period of the mid-19th century. Where they disagree is both on the specifics of why this happened and also on the ways to solve the issues.

Whilst not overtly adhering to a consistent philosophical viewpoint, most current Western legislative frameworks fall within the capitalist, conservative side of the debate. They recognise the root cause of issues such as climate change as being industrial pollution emissions, but are wedded to the embedded capitalist ideology, using taxes and market-based mechanisms to shape environmental behaviour.

ACTIVITY

Different philosophical perspectives all recognise the same cause of pollution levels. Given this similarity, how important is it to agree on whether the pollution levels were caused by lack of scientific understanding at that time, the inherent unfairness of the capitalist system, or the domination by the patriarchy?

Would we be better to tackle the issue of pollution first and deal with the philosophical foundations second, or is an understanding and acknowledgement of systemic and institutional failures essential to solve the pollution problem?

Draw up a list of the advantages and disadvantages of the approaches that have just been outlined.

2.1.5 Environmental Ethics

Ethics can be thought of as either a "code of conduct" or a way to behave, or as a "state of being" central to all an individual's beliefs. As with philosophical approaches, it is possible for an individual to hold different ethical standpoints for different environmental issues. For example, there will be people who are committed to animal protection and conservation on the one hand and are simultaneously happy to include meat in their diet on the other.

QUOTATION

In this section, we will cover a range of ethical standpoints, but it is important to recognise that this by no means is an exhaustive list.

Definition

Ethics are "the idea of an ecological consciousness connecting the individual to the larger world."

Bunyard, P., and Morgan-Grenville, F., 1987, *The Green Alternative Guide to Good Living*, London: Methuen, p. 282

The ethics of ecology grew out of the wider field of evolutionary biology and recommends human restraint in relation to the environment so can be considered a code of conduct. Within the field exists a range of different standpoints, which have been described both as ethics and philosophies.

Anthropocentrism, Biocentrism, and Ecocentrism

Anthropocentrism literally means "human being centred," and as an ethical/philosophical approach, it means that the values and experiences of humans are regarded as taking precedence over the values and experiences of nature. There is an inherent circularity in this approach insofar as the quality of the environment has a significant impact on the quality of life of humans, but this is generally downplayed.

There has been an element of pragmatism and self-preservation for governments to veer towards an anthropocentric approach in the past, since governments need to be in power in order to create laws and are thus more likely to create laws which benefit whoever puts them into power. As we saw in Chapter 1, there is a strong biblical basis for an anthropocentric approach (Genesis 1:26), although some argue that this part of the Bible should be interpreted as meaning God is supreme and humans are just one part of a wider creation – so effectively making Genesis 1:26 "theocentric" rather than anthropocentric.

Nonetheless, the anthropocentric approach to lawmaking has been the dominant one for many centuries, and it appears that it is likely to remain so for the foreseeable future.

Biocentrism gives value to all living things on Earth and, by omission, does not give value to non-living entities, such as water and air. Taylor[8] identifies four rules that need to be met in order to have a truly biocentric approach:

1. The rule of nonmaleficence
2. The rule of noninterference
3. The rule of fidelity
4. The rule of restitutive justice

He goes on to expand these rules and to argue that nonmaleficence (do no wrong) would only apply to deliberate actions or inactions by moral beings which would cause harm to other living beings. It would not, therefore, cover damage to the inert natural environment. Noninterference comes with a further requirement not to be speciesist and to leave natural events to unfold rather than act to protect one species over another. Preventing the "cute" zebra calf from being killed and eaten by the "mean" spotted hyena, for example, raises many value judgments and would not be deemed appropriate by a biocentrist. The rule of fidelity would apply only to humans and would require a cessation in "tricking" other species, for example, by the use of hunting lures. Finally, restitutive justice would require the setting aside of land, for example, in proportion to the level of harm historically inflicted. This last provision has echoes of the discussions at COP 27 in 2022 concerning payments by richer countries for historic climate and environmental damage. However, the significant difference is that the COP 27 agreement involves humans making reparations to other humans, and the biocentric approach would involve restitution being given by humans to nature.

Ecocentrism, on the other hand, ascribes value to the non-living natural world. The original idea was put forward by the American philosopher Aldo Leopold in his *Sand County Almanac and Sketches Here and There*, which was published posthumously in 1949. Leopold viewed ethics as an iterative approach, starting with relations between individuals and evolving into relations between individuals and society. The problem, he argued, is that the next level of ethics, which would cover humanity's relations with the natural world, has not yet evolved beyond the idea that the natural world is there for the economic benefit of humans, with no obligations on our part to repay nature.[9]

Ecocentrism has developed since Leopold's beginning and now envisions an equality and recognition of intrinsic value for all of human and non-human nature, which is a form of biospherical egalitarianism as promoted by Arne Næss's deep ecology, or ecosophy approach.

Arne Næss's Shallow and Deep Ecology, and Ecosophy

Arne Næss was a 20th-century Norwegian philosopher who argued that all who subscribed to an ethics of ecology, whether shallow or deep, shared the desire to fight against resource depletion and pollution. These, he felt, were the minimum requirements for anyone taking this worldview. They are also, as you will see in other sections of the book, the most mainstream elements of environmental law and policy and the areas which have received the most legislative and judicial attention.

QUOTATION

"The emergence of ecologists from their former relative obscurity marks a turning-point in our scientific communities. But their message is twisted and misused. A shallow, but presently rather powerful movement, and a deep, but less influential movement, compete for our attention."

Næss, A., 1973, *The Shallow and the Deep: Long-Range Ecology Movements: A Summary*, Inquiry, 16, 95–100

Shallow ecology, or "everyday" ecology, Næss suggests, has as its central objective the health and affluence of people in developed countries, and this would make it incompatible with ideas of environmental and climate justice (see Chapter 3).

Næss's view on what he called deep ecology, on the other hand, was much more strongly aligned with ecocentrism, the idea that humans were part of the environment, and what he called "biospherical egalitarianism," which, as was discussed earlier, is a form of ecocentrism.

In common with many of the red/green approaches to environmental thinking, and with the principles of environmental and climate justice (see Chapter 3), deep ecology recognises that there is an inherent class element in the debate, and that an anti-class posture would lead to better environmental quality. Warwick Fox[10] agrees that this approach is beneficial from an environmental perspective, as it shifts the basis for justification of decisions. Currently, he argues, those who want to protect the non-human world are required to justify themselves, and the new approach would be that those who wish to damage the non-human world would need to do so instead. This has echoes in the discussion of the precautionary principle in Chapter 2.

Næss also argues that *ecology* is an etymologically incorrect term, as it takes its roots from "eco" and "logy," which in turn derive from the Greek *oîkos* (house) and *logía* ([scientific] study of). He argues that *ecosophy* would be more appropriate, representing the approach as more philosophical than scientific.

ACTIVITY

Would you consider that you are a shallow or a deep ecologist?
Do you fit more into the ecocentric or anthropocentric model?
Is your answer the same for all environmental issues?
Is pragmatism the most useful approach to environmental law in practice?

Whether these approaches are more accurately included within philosophies or ethical approaches is a matter for discussion. What is important is to recognise the wide range of belief systems which operate in relation to environmental issues. Decisions made by individuals, corporations, governments, legislatures, and non-governmental organisations are all value-driven to some extent, and understanding where those values originated will help you contextualise those decisions.

ACTIVITY

The Gaia hypothesis as constructed by Lovelock is a relatively modern construction.
Find examples from non-Western philosophies and First Nation approaches which overlap with the Gaia hypothesis. How much credit should be given to these "proto-Gaia" hypotheses?

KEY FACTS

Anthropocentrism	Effect on humans is the key driver of decision-making. A decision which would involve the destruction of habitat but create favourable living conditions is acceptable.
Biocentrism	All living things have value (not necessarily equal value). No interference with natural processes, even to save endangered species.

Ecocentrism	*Shallow ecology*. Recognition of the idea of equal value for all life, but limitations in the practical application focus on health and well-being of humans, largely in the developed world.
	Deep ecology. Incorporates a strong anti-class aspect and focuses on equality for humans and species in a global context.
	Ecosophy. Not a rejection of science but a strong recognition of the philosophical importance of ecocentrism.

2.2 The Tragedy of the (Unmanaged) Commons

The idea of the tragedy of the commons, as with the other concepts discussed in the chapter, is far older than the name. The Greek philosopher Aristotle talked about what is common to the greatest number getting the least attention, but the concept may be even older than that. The name was coined by the American ecologist Garret Hardin in 1968, although 20 years later, he revised the name to the "tragedy of the *unmanaged* commons." The concept is based on a pasture which is open for grazing to any herdsman who wishes to use it. It is unmanaged (hence the revised title), and there are no rules on how many cattle each herdsman keeps.

QUOTATION

It is to be expected that each herdsman will try to keep as many cattle as possible on the commons. Such an arrangement may work reasonably satisfactorily for centuries because tribal wars, poaching, and disease keep the numbers of both man and beast well below the carrying capacity of the land. Finally, however, comes the day of reckoning, that is, the day when the long-desired goal of social stability becomes a reality. At this point, the inherent logic of the commons remorselessly generates tragedy.

As a rational being, each herdsman seeks to maximize his gain. Explicitly or implicitly, more or less consciously, he asks, "What is the utility to me of adding one more animal to my herd?" This utility has one negative and one positive component.

1. The positive component is a function of the increment of one animal. Since the herdsman receives all the proceeds from the sale of the additional animal, the positive utility is nearly +1.
2. The negative component is a function of the additional overgrazing created by one more animal. Since, however, the effects of overgrazing are shared by all the herdsmen, the negative utility for any particular decision-making herdsman is only a fraction of − 1.

Adding together the component partial utilities, the rational herdsman concludes that the only sensible course for him to pursue is to add another animal to his herd. And another; and another. . . . But this is the conclusion reached by each and every rational herdsman sharing a commons. Therein is the tragedy. Each man is locked into a system that compels him to increase his herd without limit – in a world that is limited. Ruin is the destination toward which all men rush, each pursuing his own best interest in a society that believes in the freedom of the commons. Freedom in a commons brings ruin to all.

Hardin, G., "The Tragedy of the Commons," *Science*, Vol 162
Issue 3859, pp. 1,243–1,248

There are examples of equivalents to this model in real life. Consider, for example, the naturally occurring *gyres* (large system of circulating ocean currents) in the North and South Pacific, North and South Atlantic, and Indian Ocean. Over time, plastic and other floating rubbish have been borne by ocean currents to these gyres and accumulated as huge floating masses of rubbish.

The main piece of international legislation which covers the oceans is the UN Convention on the Law of the Sea (UNCLOS), which was signed in 1982. The details of legislation covering marine pollution are covered in Chapter 10.

National jurisdiction extends for a distance away from the shoreline of a coastal country. There are four different categories of sea-based territory, and for all of them, the mean (average) low-water mark acts as the baseline for measurements:

- Territorial Sea (Arts 2 *et seq.*)
  - This extends for 12 nautical miles (14 miles) from the baseline. Provided they comply with UNCLOS and other international laws, states are empowered by Article 21 to pass legislation to conserve living resources, protect the environment, and prevent, reduce, and control pollution.
  - Ships from other states may pass through territorial waters, and any pollution incidents will be dealt with by the laws of the coastal state itself.
  - Within territorial waters, the state's control extends to the seabed (and anything under it), the water (and anything in it), the water's surface (and anything on it), and the air and space above it.
- Contiguous Zone (Arts 33 *et seq.*)
  - This extends a further 12 nautical miles from the extent of territorial waters. Within this zone, the state's authority only extends as far as the sea, and seabed, not to the air and space above it. The primary purpose of the contiguous zone is to allow states to deter and catch criminals.
- Exclusive Economic Zone (Arts 55 *et seq.*)
  - This extends for 200 nautical miles from the baseline. In this area, the state has exclusive rights to exploration, exploitation, conservation, and management of any resources – this would include generating power from wave energy, for example, by floating "sea-snake" type of generators (see Chapter 7).
- Article 56
  - This gives the state jurisdiction over the protection and preservation of the marine environment within the EEZ.
- Extended Continental Shelf
  - This is covered by UNCLOS Article 76 and is the part of the continental shelf which extends beyond the EEZ. The rights over this zone are not automatically generated and must be considered by the UN Commission on the Limits of the Continental Shelf.

For both the territorial waters and EEZ (and by dint of the fact it falls within the EEZ, the contiguous zone), Article 211 gives the state the right (but, interestingly, not the *duty*) to take whatever measures it sees fit to prevent, reduce, and control marine pollution from foreign ships, which would usually be regarded as the sovereign territory of another state.

In all these cases, there will inevitably be situations where the full extent of one state's area will encroach into another state's area. Since they cannot both have control over the same area, the default position is that the boundary is midway between the baselines of the relevant states.

ARTICLE

....

Measures to prevent, reduce and control pollution of the marine environment

. . .

2. States shall take all measures necessary to ensure that activities under their jurisdiction or control are so conducted as not to cause damage by pollution to other States and their environment, and that pollution arising from incidents or activities under their jurisdiction or control does not spread beyond the areas where they exercise sovereign rights in accordance with this Convention.

Article 194, UNCLOS 1982

Article 194 thus gives states the duty to control pollution incidents from any activity which occurs in their territory. Beyond the extent of any claimed extended continental shelf, the sea, seabed, and any resources are not controlled by any state, and any claim to sovereignty is denied by UNCLOS. They are the "high seas" and are covered by Part VII of UNCLOS.

The high seas are not completely lawless and unmanaged, however, so while they are the closest area to a true "global commons," they are not precisely equivalent. Article 65, which covers the right of states to preserve marine mammals, is deemed by Article 119 to apply to the high seas, for example. States also have the right to fish in the high seas, subject to provisions in Articles 63–67 about overfishing.

Almost by definition, a global unmanaged commons does not have legislative provision to shape the behaviour of individuals and corporate bodies within that space. What exists in its place tends to be regulatory frameworks covering specific industries. Pollution from ships has been covered extensively, for example. The International Maritime Organization's 1969 International Convention Relating to Intervention on the High Seas in Cases of Oil Pollution Casualties (which was amended subsequently to cover substances other than oil) applies to all ships and "seagoing vessels except warships or other vessels owned or operated by a State and used on Government non-commercial service." Later conventions included the IMO International Convention for the Prevention of Pollution from Ships 1973 (the MARPOL Convention).

Other than the high seas, the closest approximation to a global commons occurs off planet. Outer space is deemed to start at the Kármán line (named after the Hungarian American physicist and aerodynamic theoretician Theodore von Kármán), which is around 100 kilometres above sea level. It is covered by the United Nations Outer Space Treaty of 1967, which effectively designated space as a commons, and the 1974 United Nations Convention on Registration of Objects Launched into Outer Space, which requires any state from which an object is launched into outer space to register it.

ARTICLE

....

I The exploration and use of outer space, including the moon and other celestial bodies, shall be carried out for the benefit and in the interests of all countries, irrespective of their degree of economic or scientific development, and shall be the province of all mankind.

Outer space, including the moon and other celestial bodies, shall be free for exploration and use by all States without discrimination of any kind, on a basis of equality and in accordance with international law, and there shall be free access to all areas of celestial bodies.

> There shall be freedom of scientific investigation in outer space, including the moon and other celestial bodies, and States shall facilitate and encourage international co-operation in such investigation.
>
> II Outer space, including the moon and other celestial bodies, is not subject to national appropriation by claim of sovereignty, by means of use or occupation, or by any other means.
>
> Articles I and II, UN Treaty on Principles Governing the Activities of States in the Exploration and Use of Outer Space, Including the Moon and Other Celestial Bodies

In practice, it is currently far harder to exploit outer space and the moon, and to date, people from only 44 nations have been into space. The rockets used for peopled flights were predominantly from state operators – the USSR/Russian Federation (26), the United States of America (12), and the People's Republic of China (1) – although three flights were made in 2021 and 2022 by the commercial company New Shepard.

In addition to flights carrying humans, the UN Office for Outer Space Affairs lists 13,450 objects which have been launched into outer space. Recently, the American SpaceX company has launched almost 3,000 Starlink satellites, which makes it the single largest commercial operator in outer space.

The outer space, as well as being populated by commercial and military satellites, is also filled with orbital debris, or space junk. This is any manmade item in orbit which no longer serves a purpose, and the US Space Surveillance Network run by NASA is currently tracking over 23,000 pieces of orbital debris that are larger than 10 centimetres in diameter, more than 500,000 lager than 1 centimetre in diameter, and 100 million of around 1 millimetre in diameter. These pieces of debris travel at more than 20 times the speed of sound and can potentially cause catastrophic damage to any satellite or spacecraft they hit. In addition, every such contact creates more space debris and exacerbates the problem.

ACTIVITY

The moon, although not yet inhabited, contains several objects of terrestrial origin. Some of these were left behind by moon landing missions, such as the Apollo 11 (1969). Others are deliberate, such as the crashing of the NASA LRCROSS mission in 2009, or accidental, such as the crashing of the booster rocket from the Chinese Chang'e 5-T1 mission in 2022.

Who should bear the responsibility of removing this debris?

Unmanaged global commons poses problems for lawmakers and policymakers, and a balance needs to be struck between allowing sovereignty to extend to these areas and protecting the resources for all.

2.3 Personhood and Non-Human Entities

With some exceptions, most adult humans currently have legal rights, duties, and powers ascribed to them by the legal system of the state in which they are currently present. This was not always the case, and at different points in history and in different states, women, slaves, and non-landowners had all been excluded from those who had legally enforceable rights. In some states, those rights, duties, and powers date back for thousands of years. The first legal code was in Sumer, the civilisation which existed around 4500–1900 BCE in what is now central Iraq. The first written legal system was the Code of Hammurabi, created in 1760 BCE by King

Hammurabi of Babylonia (now parts of Iraq and Syria), and copies of this were erected on stone tablets across the kingdom.

Over time, legal systems became more plentiful, more complex, and more wide-ranging, but it was Roman law which began to recognise the possibility that things other than humans could possibly be given some sort of enhanced legal status. In Roman law, there were five types of contract recognised:

- Emptio-venditio (buying/selling)
- Locatio conductio (letting/hiring)
- Emphyteuticary (close to leasehold)
- Mandate (gratuitous agency)
- Societas (association for trading purposes)

Societas evolved into what we would recognise today as an early form of partnership. Towards the end of the Roman Empire, Emperor Constantine formally recognised Christianity as a religion, and the Church began to "own" buildings. In England, with the diminution of feudalism in around the 14th century, a more formalised system emerged whereby the Church could own property *in abstractio* (in its own right), and the relevant Church officials could therefore conduct business and carry out transactions on behalf of the Church.

This idea of a non-human entity being empowered to own things spread to corporations (in the sense of the Corporation of London, rather than modern companies, which were still in their infancy and almost entirely unregulated).

QUOTATION

"Corporations have neither bodies to be punished, nor souls to be condemned; they therefore do as they like."

Poynder, J., 1844, *Literary Extracts from English and Other Works; Collected During Half a Century: Together with Some Original Matter*, London: John Hatchard & Son, p. 268

"Did you ever expect a corporation to have a conscience, when it has no soul to be damned, and no body to be kicked?"

Coffee, J., "No soul to damn. No body to kick: An Unscandalized Inquiry into the Problem of Corporate Punishment" (1981) 79 Mich L. R. 386

Both quotes were ascribed to Edward, Baron Thurlow, Lord Chancellor, between 1778 and 1792.

The mid-19th century, and the massive changes to the country which were being wrought by the Industrial Revolution, also led to new and previously unconsidered scenarios involving corporate bodies. These scenarios necessitated change in the legal duties on companies.

CASE

R v Birmingham and Gloucester Railway Co (1842) 3 QB 223

This case concerned a statutory duty which was imposed upon the railway company to reconnect via a bridge two pieces of land which were severed by the construction of the railway line.

The company failed to do so, and the case marks the first time a company was found to be liable for the breach of an absolute statutory duty.

CASE

R v Great North of England Railway Co. (1846) 9 QB 315 (per Denman CJ)

In this case, the railway company blocked the highway by carrying out works which had not been authorised. It built on the Birmingham and Gloucester Railway case, as the court held that there was no longer a distinction in corporate liability between non-feasance (not doing a thing you are required to do) and mis-feasance (doing a thing you are not permitted to do).

The two railway cases had, in the space of just a few years, opened up corporations to potential liability for breaching their statutory powers. A decade or so later, Erle J extended the liability from criminal to civil matters.

JUDGMENT

Green v the London General Omnibus Company (1859) 141 ER 828

In this case, the bus company had wrongfully prevented Green (also a bus operator) from carrying out his lawful business.

"The whole course of the authorities . . . shews that an action for a wrong will lie against a corporation, where the thing that is complained of is a thing done within the scope of their incorporation, and is one which would constitute an actionable wrong if committed by an individual."

(Per Erle J @833)

The drive to give companies greater levels of rights and responsibilities was not universally applauded. Company owners were naturally opposed to such moves, and they were supported in this opposition by the philosopher, libertarian, and MP John Stuart Mill. Mill argued[11] that the best people to control a business were those who had a vested interest in that business, because when the business did well, the individual did well. Today, such an overt approach would raise questions about conflicts of interest, but there is still a very strong political divide between those parties who favour reduced corporate regulation and those who advocate higher levels of regulation.

JUDGMENT

Membery v Great Western Railway (1889) LR 14 App. Ca. 179

"The master says, here is the work, do it or let it alone. If you do it, I pay you; if not, I do not. . . .

The servant does the work and earns his wages, and is paid, but is hurt. On what principle of reason or justice should the master be liable to him in respect of the hurt?"

(Dissenting judgment per Bramwell LJ @188)

Despite the objection of Mill and others, the expansion of the range of duties and responsibilities of a corporation continued to grow, until by the middle of the 20th century it was possible to hold corporations liable for crimes which required a mens rea element, such as intention to deceive (*DPP v Kent and Sussex Contractors* [1944] KB 146) and intention to defraud (*R v ICR Road Haulage Ltd* [1944] KB 551).

By the mid-20th century, therefore, it was well-established that legal rights and duties could be ascribed to "legal persons" in the form of corporate bodies. Once this was normalised, and as Fitzgerald put it, "as many kinds of juristic persons have been created by law as society requires,"[12] the inevitable question followed – if the legal system can give rights and responsibilities to this type of non-human entity, can it do the same for other types of non-human entities?

The development of a rights-based approach to animals will be discussed in greater detail in Chapter 9, and the rest of this section will focus on the granting of rights to non-animal entities.

2.3.1 Te Urewera

Te Urewera is an area in the eastern side of North Island, New Zealand. In 1954, it was designated as a national park under the National Parks Act 1952, as it was designated as an area containing "scenery of such distinctive quality or natural features so beautiful or unique that their preservation is in the national interest" (S3(1)).

The Tūhoe people (Ngāi Tūhoe) are the traditional inhabitants of the area which became the national park, and from the late 1990s, there was a growing push to have the area returned to them. The Tūhoe Claims Settlement Act 2014 gave the Tūhoe financial, commercial, and cultural redress for historic harms. The Te Urewera Act 2014 abolished the national park and replaced it with a legal, rights-bearing entity called Te Urewera. The rights of the entity were governed on its behalf by a legal body, also called Te Urewera, which is co-governed by the Crown and the Tūhoe.

SECTION
....

3 Background to this Act

(1) Te Urewera is ancient and enduring, a fortress of nature, alive with history; its scenery is abundant with mystery, adventure, and remote beauty.

(2) Te Urewera is a place of spiritual value, with its own mana and mauri.

(3) Te Urewera has an identity in and of itself, inspiring people to commit to its care.

(4) For Tūhoe, Te Urewera is Te Manawa o te Ika a Māui; it is the heart of the great fish of Maui, its name being derived from Murakareke, the son of the ancestor Tūhoe.

(5) For Tūhoe, Te Urewera is their ewe whenua, their place of origin and return, their homeland.

(6) Te Urewera expresses and gives meaning to Tūhoe culture, language, customs, and identity. There Tūhoe hold mana by ahikāroa; they are tangata whenua and kaitiaki of Te Urewera.

(7) Te Urewera is prized by other iwi and hapū who have acknowledged special associations with, and customary interests in, parts of Te Urewera.

(8) Te Urewera is also prized by all New Zealanders as a place of outstanding national value and intrinsic worth; it is treasured by all for the distinctive natural values of its vast and rugged primeval forest, and for the integrity of those values; for its indigenous ecological systems and biodiversity, its historical and cultural heritage, its scientific importance, and as a place for outdoor recreation and spiritual reflection.

(9) Tūhoe and the Crown share the view that Te Urewera should have legal recognition in its own right, with the responsibilities for its care and conservation set out in the law of New Zealand. To this end, Tūhoe and the Crown have together taken a unique approach, as set out in this Act, to protecting Te Urewera in a way that reflects New Zealand's culture and values.

(10) The Crown and Tūhoe intend this Act to contribute to resolving the grief of Tūhoe and to strengthening and maintaining the connection between Tūhoe and Te Urewera.

4 Purpose of this Act

The purpose of this Act is to establish and preserve in perpetuity a legal identity and protected status for Te Urewera for its intrinsic worth, its distinctive natural and cultural values, the integrity of those values, and for its national importance, and in particular to –

(a) strengthen and maintain the connection between Tūhoe and Te Urewera; and

(b) preserve as far as possible the natural features and beauty of Te Urewera, the integrity of its indigenous ecological systems and biodiversity, and its historical and cultural heritage; and

(c) provide for Te Urewera as a place for public use and enjoyment, for recreation, learning, and spiritual reflection, and as an inspiration for all.

SS3–4, Te Urewera Act 2014

Te Urwera has the distinction of being the first natural resource anywhere in the world to have the same legal rights as a person.

2.3.2 Whanganui River

The Whanganui River runs from the centre to the east coast of North Island, New Zealand. Much like Te Urewera, it has highly significant cultural and historical importance to the Māori people of the region, who call it Te Awa Tupua. The decision to grant the river legal personhood was made in 2012, which made it the first time such a decision was made. The enabling act was the Te Awa Tupua (Whanganui River Claims Settlement) Act 2017, and so the river became the second natural resource in the world to be granted legal identity. Finlayson calls this a "novel legal theory"[13] which aligned 21st century legislative provisions with the ancient beliefs of the people who lived beside the river.

SECTION

Te Awa Tupua is a legal person and has all the rights, powers, duties, and liabilities of a legal person.

The rights, powers, and duties of Te Awa Tupua must be exercised or performed, and responsibility for its liabilities must be taken, by Te Pou Tupua on behalf of, and in the name of, Te Awa Tupua, in the manner provided for in this Part and in Ruruku Whakatupua – Te Mana o Te Awa Tupua.

S14, Te Awa Tupua (Whanganui River Claims Settlement) Act 2017

As with Te Urwera, the rights, etc., of Whanganui/Te Awa Tupua will be administered jointly by the Crown and the Māori, operating as Te Pou Tupua, or the legal face of the river.

2.3.3 India

The Ganges (or Ganga) officially starts at the town of Devprayag in Uttarakhand, although it has headwaters that extend far beyond that and also draws water from Himalayan glaciers. The Yamuna River starts in Yamunotri, also in Uttarakhand, and similarly draws water from Himalayan glaciers. The Yamuna flows into the Ganges in Allahabad/Prayagraj in the state of Uttar Pradesh, and the Ganges then flows into the Ganges Delta in the Bay of Bengal.

The state of Uttarakhand, in northern India, borders Nepal and Tibet and sits in the southern foothills of the Himalayas. In 2017, the Uttarakhand High Court declared that the river Ganges and all its tributaries would henceforth have legal personality. The court gave regard to Articles 48A and 51A(g) of the Constitution of India.

ARTICLE

Article 48A

The State shall endeavour to protect and improve the environment and to safeguard the forests and wild life of the country.

Article 51A(g)

It shall be the duty of every citizen of India –

. . .

(g) to protect and improve the natural environment including forests, lakes, rivers and wild life, and to have compassion for living creatures;

Excerpts from the Constitution of India, 1950 (as amended)

CASE

Mohd. Salim v State of Uttarakhand and Others (2017)

"Accordingly, while exercising the parens patrie [sic] jurisdiction, the Rivers Ganga and Yamuna, all their tributaries, streams, every natural water flowing with flow continuously or intermittently of these rivers, are declared as juristic/legal persons/living entities having the status of a legal person with all corresponding rights, duties and liabilities of a living person in order to preserve and conserve river Ganga and Yamuna" (Para 19).

Parens patriae is an old English common law mechanism which allows the attorney general to represent those who are unable to represent themselves. The High Court recognised that all Hindis have strong आस्था (Astha/belief or faith) in the rivers and that they are "central to the existence of half of Indian population and their health and well being" (para 17), and this was also the view of the first prime minister of India.

QUOTATION

As with the New Zealand examples, a group of people was empowered to act on behalf of the rivers, in this case being the state's chief secretary and advocate general and the director of the National Mission for Clean Ganga.

The decision of the High Court was made less secure by the fundamental issue of jurisdiction. The rivers are only flowing through Uttarakhand for a small portion of their total journey to the sea and, indeed, also flow through Bangladesh. As a result of what they called its impracticability, the Indian Supreme Court overturned the High Court's ruling within two months.

Nonetheless, the High Court ruling is significant, as it represents an attempt by one jurisdiction to grant legal personality to an entity which exists across jurisdictions.

2.3.4 Ecuador

As we have already seen, in New Zealand and India, rights were granted to specific non-human entities by specific court cases to give succour to the belief systems of specific groups of people. In Ecuador, by contrast, the 2008 Constitution included a new section which gave effect to the concept of *sumac kawsay*, sometimes translated as *buen vivir*, or good living, although it is more accurately "the plentiful life." Sumac kawsay is a relatively new term, but the concept has its origins in the ancestral belief systems of the Quechua people from the region of the Andes which now encompasses parts of Peru, Chile, Bolivia, Colombia, and Ecuador.

ARTICLES

Article 10

Persons, communities, peoples, nations and communities are bearers of rights and shall enjoy the rights guaranteed to them in the Constitution and in international instruments.

Nature shall be the subject of those rights that the Constitution recognizes for it.

Article 71

Nature, or Pacha Mama, where life is reproduced and occurs, has the right to integral respect for its existence and for the maintenance and regeneration of its life cycles, structure, functions and evolutionary processes.

All persons, communities, peoples and nations can call upon public authorities to enforce the rights of nature. To enforce and interpret these rights, the principles set forth in the Constitution shall be observed, as appropriate.

The State shall give incentives to natural persons and legal entities and to communities to protect nature and to promote respect for all the elements comprising an ecosystem.

Constitution of the Republic of Ecuador 2008

In a further divergence from the situations elsewhere, there is a small but growing body of case law relating to this constitutional right, beginning with the 2011 case of *Wheeler*.

CASE

Richard Frederick Wheeler y Eleanor Geer Huddle c/Gobierno Provincial de Loja, juicio 11121–2011–0010 (30 March 2011)

This case, which was held before the Provincial Court of Justice in Loja, in the south of Ecuador, concerned a local government road building project which dumped waste into the adjacent river. Rather than relying on property rights, local residents Wheeler and Huddle relied on the constitutional rights of nature.

The court held that if there were to be a conflict, the rights of nature would prevail over other constitutional rights.

The case has not been overturned by higher courts in Ecuador, and so the court's decision remains valid. It is important to understand that the more standard proprietary rights are not removed by the rights of nature; rather, they are enhanced by them.

Critics of this approach point to the fact that humans and companies, the two main physical entities given rights by laws, have corresponding responsibilities or duties, and despite the aspirational wording used, these are impossible to apply to rivers and natural areas without human intervention. The overturning of the High Court of Uttarakhand's decision by the Indian Supreme Court adds weight to the argument.

In UK law, there is no recognition of legal personhood for natural resources, and non-human legal personality is limited to companies and trusts.

SUMMARY

- Myriad of philosophical and ethical standpoints that relate to environmental law.
- They are all personal – your own views may fit within one or more of these categories, and there may also be situations where your views diverge from them.
- Global unmanaged commons shows risk of leaving decision-making to the logic of individuals.
- Emerging legal issue of personhood for non-humans, in the context of non-animals, brings together philosophical, religious, and societal world views that pre-existed much of the current legislative structure.
- Recognising the rights of nature is truly an emerging trend or is a return to an older state of understanding.

SAMPLE PROBLEM QUESTION

In 2023, the UK government announced plans to give the river Thames legal personality, to align it with the approaches taken in New Zealand for the Te Urwera and Whanganui/Te Awa Tupua Rivers. The Thames has historically been associated with the goddess Isis and has been personified as "Old Father Thames."

They have tasked you with drawing up the criteria for shortlisting groups who might be considered to have sufficiently relevant claims to be appointed as the "legal face" of the river.

What legal issues will be included in your shortlisting criteria?

1. Identify the similar provisions from New Zealand.
2. Assess the criteria which empowered the groups in New Zealand to be appointed as guardians – historic connection, spiritual beliefs.
3. Assess the difficulties that may arise from this approach – competing interests, different types of river (the New Zealand ones are rural).
4. Apply these rules to the UK – would this include those with longstanding commercial interests?
5. What problems with enforcement can you foresee?
6. What environmental benefits can you foresee?
7. Conclude.

Further Reading

Bookchin, M., 1982, *The Ecology of Freedom: The Emergence and Dissolution of Hierarchy*, Palo Alto, CA: Cheshire Books

Coyle, S., & Morrow, K., 2004, *The Philosophical Foundations of Environmental Law: Property, Rights and Nature*, Portland, OR: Hart Publishing

Dawkins, R., 1999, *The Extended Phenotype: The Long Reach of the Gene*, Oxford: OUP

Dobson, A., 1995, *Green Political Thought*, London: Taylor & Francis

Ehrlich, P.R., 1968, *The Population Bomb: Population Control or the Race to Oblivion*, New York: Ballantine Books

Grayling, A.C., 2019, *The History of Philosophy*, London: Penguin

Hardin, G., 1968, The Tragedy of the Commons, *Science*, 162(3859), 1243–1248

Katz, S.N., ed., 2009, *The Oxford International Encyclopaedia of Legal History Vols 1–6*, Oxford: OUP

La Follette, C., & Maser, C., eds., 2019, *Sustainability and the Rights of Nature in Practise*, Boca Raton, FL: CRC Press

Leopold, A., 1949, *A Sand County Almanac and Sketches Here and There*, Oxford: OUP

Lovelock, J.E., 1979, *Gaia: A New Look at Life on Earth*, Oxford: OUP

Mies, L., & Shiva, V., 1993, *Ecofeminism*, London: Bloomsbury

Ruse, M., 2013, *The Gaia Hypothesis: Science on a Pagan Planet*, Chicago, IL: University of Chicago Press

Taylor, P.W., 2011, *Respect for Nature: A Theory of Environmental Ethics*, 25th anniversary ed., Princeton, NJ: Princeton University Press

Notes

1 Coyle, S., & Morrow, K., 2004, *The Philosophical Foundations of Environmental Law: Property, Rights and Nature*, Portland, OR: Hart Publishing
2 Gould, S.J., quoted in Ruse, M., 2013, *The Gaia Hypothesis: Science on a Pagan Planet*, Chicago, IL: University of Chicago Press
3 Dawkins, R., 1999, *The Extended Phenotype: The Long Reach of the Gene*, Oxford: OUP, pp. 235–236
4 Dobson, A., 1995, *Green Political Thought*, London: Taylor & Francis
5 Smith, H.A., 1887, Early Reminiscences: Number Ten: Scraps from a Diary – Chief Seattle–A Gentleman by Instinct–His Native Eloquence, Etc., *Seattle Sunday Star*, 28 October
6 Bookchin, M., 1982, *The Ecology of Freedom: The Emergence and Dissolution of Hierarchy*, Palo Alto, CA: Cheshire Books, p. 344
7 Burke, E., 1790 (1909), *Reflections on the Revolution in France*, Vol XXIV, Part 3, Harvard Classics, New York: P.F. Collier & Son, p. 243
8 Taylor, P.W., 2011, *Respect for Nature: A Theory of Environmental Ethics*, 25th Anniversary ed., Princeton, NJ: Princeton University Press, p. 172
9 Leopold, A., 1949, *A Sand County Almanac and Sketches Here and There*, Oxford: OUP, p. 190
10 Fox, W., 1986, *Approaching Deep Ecology: A Response to Richard Sylvan's Critique of Deep Ecology*, Occasional paper (University of Tasmania. Board of Environmental Studies), 20, p. 84
11 Mill, J.S., 1869, *On Liberty*, London: J.W. Parker & Sons, Chapter V: Application, para 18
12 Fitzgerald, P.J., 1966, *Salmond on Jurisprudence*, 12th ed., London: Sweet & Maxwell, pp. 305–306
13 Finlayson, C., 2019, A River is Born: New Zealand Confers Legal Personhood on the Whanganui River to Protect it and its Native People, in La Follette, C., & Maser, C., eds, *Sustainability and the Rights of Nature in Practise*, Boca Raton, FL: CRC Press

3

Environmental Justice and Climate Justice

In recent years, the issue of the differential impacts of environmental problems has come to dominate discussions in a number of areas. The most obvious is the impact of climate change, where consequences such as a rise in sea level will have a serious impact on low-lying island nations than on EU member states, for example. Further to this, there is a recognition that the bulk of the emissions which are causing climate change was emitted by richer, more industrialised nations, and the impacts are going to be felt disproportionately by poorer, less industrialised nations.

This is widely referred to as either environmental injustice or climate injustice, and the corollary is the drive to achieve environmental justice and climate justice. In this chapter we will cover the essentials of both.

By looking at the different definitions, you will be able to frame the debate more accurately. We then look at some practical examples, both of climate and environmental injustice, and some occasions where this has been effectively remedied. The middle part of the chapter explores whether there is a human right to a clean and healthy environment, what this means, and how it can be developed as an approach to achieve climate and environmental justice. Neither concept is formally incorporated into legal systems, so we will look at principles which have been embedded, such as sustainable development and the polluter pays principle, to ascertain whether there are mechanisms within these which could be leveraged to achieve an end to injustice. As Sir David Attenborough put it in his introductory speech at COP 21 in Glasgow in 2021, "those who have done the least to cause this problem are being the hardest hit."

AIMS AND OBJECTIVES

After reading this chapter, you should be able to:

- Understand the key elements of environmental and climate injustice.
- Explain the links between these two concepts and human rights.
- Understand the application of these principles in relation to real-world examples.

DOI: 10.4324/9781003137214-3

3.1 Origins and Nature of Environmental and Climate Justice

The idea of a nation state is mostly felt to have developed in Europe in the 19th century, a time which, coincidentally or not, also saw the high point of the Industrial Revolution. Modern Italy and Germany, for example, were unified in 1861 and 1871, respectively. Before the nation state, Europe, Asia, and the Middle East tended to be broken up by empires, sultanates, caliphates, and similar types of structure, where a single ruler, or ruling house, governed across a number of what we would now consider to be different nations and, indeed, different continents.

Richer, more powerful nations have always taken advantage of poorer, less powerful nations. Initially, the power was militaristic in nature and led to the rise and fall of different imperial interests. Over time, this has evolved to include economic power. The British Empire was a hybrid of the two, as militaristic power was used to provide the foundations for economic power and access to resources. The current approach of the People's Republic of China in purchasing controlling stakes in mineral extraction companies across the world is a good example of this.

Within states, too, the domination of poorer areas by wealthier areas has been common practice for centuries. In England, for example, coal was the power behind the Industrial Revolution. The majority of the coal in England is found in the north of the country, so it would be logical to assume that the wealth generated by the most important power source of the Industrial Revolution would mostly be found in the north. However, to this day, life expectancy, income, educational achievements, and house prices are higher in the south, and unemployment and reliance on the benefit system are higher in the north. This is not uniquely an English phenomenon, however. Similar areas of deprivation can also be found in all the other G7 economies (Canada, France, Germany, Italy, Japan, and the United States), and these often overlap with current or one-time industrial areas. Detroit in the United States is a good example of this. Once the hub of the American motor industry, with half a million people directly employed by General Motors, Chrysler, and other companies, the city of Detroit itself filed for bankruptcy in 2013.

One consequence of this historic and contemporary approach (and there are many other socio-economic consequences) is that the areas which benefit most from the wealth generated by extractive industries and high-emission lifestyles are rarely the areas which suffer the most consequences. This disparity can occur within a city, or within a state, or a country, or internationally.

3.1.1 Environmental Justice

The formalisation of ideas around environmental justice dates to around the late 1970s and early 1980s, when scholars such as Robert Bullard started writing about the disproportionate impacts of pollution on poor Black communities in the United States.

QUOTATION

"[T]he principle that all people and communities have a right to equal protection and equal enforcement of environmental laws and regulations."

"Race and class still matter and map closely with pollution, unequal protection, and vulnerability. Today, zip code is still the most potent predictor of an individual's health and well-being."

Bullard, R., 2019, "About Environmental Justice," https://drrobertbullard.com/

Definition

It becomes clear that there are elements of race embedded within environmental injustice, and there is distinction between those who regard the two terms as interchangeable and those who regard environmental racism as an aspect of environmental injustice. Today, Banzhaf et al. argue that there is only one sensible and robust way to think about environmental injustice, which is to look for the link between "pollution, poverty and people of color."[1]

In the United States in 1994, President Clinton issued an executive order (which has the power of legislation) to require federal agencies to identify whether their actions are likely to cause environmental injustice, and to work to reduce this.

LEGISLATION

"To the greatest extent practicable and permitted by law, and consistent with the principles set forth in the report on the National Performance Review, each Federal agency shall make achieving environmental justice part of its mission by identifying and addressing, as appropriate, disproportionately high and adverse human health or environmental effects of its programs, policies, and activities on minority populations and low-income populations in the United States."

Executive Order 12898 of February 11, 1994

The executive order does not explicitly define *environmental justice*, but we can infer from the text that "disproportionately high and adverse human health or environmental effects" on "minority populations and low-income populations" are what is meant.

What all these concepts have in common is their inherent anthropocentric approach (see Chapter 1). They all concerned with disproportionate impacts of groups of humans, rather than on the environment as a whole. This has been criticised as a weakness in the approach, but to date, no viable ecocentric or biocentric version (see Chapter 3) alternative to environmental justice has become mainstream.

The most comprehensive attempt to create a series of underlying truths for environmental justice took place over 30 years ago in Washington., DC. The First National People of Color Environmental Leadership Summit gathered over 1,000 delegates from across the United States to discuss environmental injustices. The meeting ended with 17 principles, which, broadly speaking, still provide a framework to try to achieve environmental justice.

Definition

Principles of Environmental Justice

1. Environmental justice affirms the sacredness of Mother Earth, ecological unity and the interdependence of all species, and the right to be free from ecological destruction.

2. Environmental justice demands that public policy be based on mutual respect and justice for all peoples, free from any form of discrimination or bias.

3. Environmental justice mandates the right to ethical, balanced and responsible uses of land and renewable resources in the interest of a sustainable planet for humans and other living things.

4. Environmental justice calls for universal protection from nuclear testing, extraction, production and disposal of toxic/hazardous wastes and poisons and nuclear testing that threaten the fundamental right to clean air, land, water, and food.

5. Environmental justice affirms the fundamental right to political, economic, cultural and environmental self-determination of all peoples.

6. Environmental justice demands the cessation of the production of all toxins, hazardous wastes, and radioactive materials, and that all past and current producers be held strictly accountable to the people for detoxification and the containment at the point of production.

7. Environmental justice demands the right to participate as equal partners at every level of decision-making including needs assessment, planning, implementation, enforcement and evaluation.

8. Environmental justice affirms the right of all workers to a safe and healthy work environment, without being forced to choose between an unsafe livelihood and unemployment. It also affirms the right of those who work at home to be free from environmental hazards.

9. Environmental justice protects the right of victims of environmental injustice to receive full compensation and reparations for damages as well as quality health care.

10. Environmental justice considers governmental acts of environmental injustice a violation of international law, the Universal Declaration On Human Rights, and the United Nations Convention on Genocide.

11. Environmental justice must recognize a special legal and natural relationship of Native Peoples to the U.S. government through treaties, agreements, compacts, and covenants affirming sovereignty and self-determination.

12. Environmental justice affirms the need for urban and rural ecological policies to clean up and rebuild our cities and rural areas in balance with nature, honoring the cultural integrity of all our communities, and providing fair access for all to the full range of resources.

13. Environmental justice calls for the strict enforcement of principles of informed consent, and a halt to the testing of experimental reproductive and medical procedures and vaccinations on people of color.

14. Environmental justice opposes the destructive operations of multi-national corporations.

15. Environmental justice opposes military occupation, repression and exploitation of lands, peoples and cultures, and other life forms.

16. Environmental justice calls for the education of present and future generations which emphasizes social and environmental issues, based on our experience and an appreciation of our diverse cultural perspectives.

17. Environmental justice requires that we, as individuals, make personal and consumer choices to consume as little of Mother Earth's resources and to produce as little waste as possible; and make the conscious decision to challenge and reprioritize our lifestyles to insure the health of the natural world for present and future generations.

17 principles of environmental justice adopted by the First National People of Color Environmental Leadership Summit in Washington, DC, 1991

The following four examples, all of which have been suggested to be environmental injustice in operation, will help you identify the difficulty with the concept.

North Dakota

The US state of North Dakota borders Manitoba and Saskatchewan in Canada, and Minnesota, South Dakota, and Montana in the United States. It is the 19th largest state in the United States (c. 185,000 square kilometres) but the fourth most sparsely populated (four people per square kilometres). It produces large amounts of oil, shale gas, and lignite (brown) coal, which is uses to generate electricity. Almost 85 per cent of the electricity produced in North Dakota is exported to other US states, and the state has relatively high per capita income and low unemployment rates. However, the pollution caused by decades of coal mining, oil drilling, and more recently, shale gas extraction has started to take their toll, and White[2] suggests that every part of the 11,000-mile network of rivers and lakes is contaminated with mercury from the coal mining process. Data from the US Clean Air Task Force suggest that:

- More than 11,000 people live within 1 kilometre of an active oil or gas operation.
- More than 80,000 live in counties of North Dakota where the cancer risk is about the US Environmental Protection Agency's "level of concern" limit.

It is unarguable that the state of North Dakota benefits financially from the exportation of electricity, oil, and gas, which contribute US$4.7bn to the state coffers annually. Similarly, the highest income per capita is in the main oil-, coal-, and gas-producing areas of the state. Nonetheless, the health implications for the state are significant, and this propels many to argue that this is an example of environmental injustice. It does not fit the standard model, however, as the benefits and the costs disproportionately affect the same groups of people.

Colorado River

The 1,400-mile-long Colorado River starts in the Rocky Mountains in Colorado State. It flows from Colorado through Utah, Arizona, Nevada, and California before crossing the Mexican border and theoretically entering the sea in the Gulf of California, although water almost never reaches the sea now.

Over time, the river and its tributaries have seen 45 dams built, the oldest being the Laguna Diversion Dam in Arizona in 1905, and the most recent to date being the Ridges Basin Dam in Colorado in 2007. Some of these are used to divert water into canals (e.g. the Paolo Verde Diversion Dam on the Arizona–California border), others to create reservoirs for supplying municipal areas (e.g. the Jones Valley Dam in Utah), and others are used to generate hydroelectric power (e.g. the Hoover Dam on the Nevada–Arizona border). This brings benefits to the residents primarily of the US states through which the river flows. Estimates of the flow rate at the US–Mexican border suggest the flow rate has dropped from 1,200 cubic meter per second in 1900 to only 0.3 cubic meter per second in 2019. This dramatic fall has meant that several species of fish in the lower part of the river which used to be common are now listed as endangered. It has also had a dramatic impact on residents of north-western Mexico who were not allocated any water when the US–Mexican Morelos Dam Treaty was signed in 1944. Water *was* allocated to Mexico, but it was all allocated for farming irrigation rather than municipal supply.

Climate change has exacerbated the issue of the Colorado River's flow, or lack of it. Lake Mead in Nevada, for example, is the reservoir created by the construction of the Hoover Dam in 1936. The drought in the Western United States has seen the level of Lake Mead drop by 11 meters in the last five years. This is sufficiently dramatic that the bodies of alleged mafia victims which have been dumped into the lake over the years are now reappearing. The drop may not seem very large, but it puts the lake more than 55 meters below full level and only 40 meters above "dead pool" level, when water will no longer flow over the Hoover Dam into the Colorado River.

It is argued that the damming and diverting of the river by the United States is an act of environmental injustice to Mexico, in that the United States is reaping all the benefits from the river, and its actions are denying those benefits to Mexico. This is complicated slightly by the fact that the hydroelectric energy reduced is reducing reliance on fossil fuels and thus having an impact, albeit small, on the total US carbon emissions.

In 2012, however, the International Boundary and Water Commission, United States and Mexico, which controls the Morelos Dam, agreed on "Minute 319," which allowed for a "pulse flow" of water to be released into Mexico for 56 days in 2014 to help restore the habitat. This was a small victory and demonstrates that it is possible to rectify complex environmental injustices at least partly or temporarily.

LEGISLATION

"The United States and Mexico will implement a binational cooperative polit programme for the duration of this Minute. The binational project will generate environmental flows to benefit the riparian ecosystem and as a part of that effort a pulse flow will be implemented to the Colorado River Delta of approximately 105,832 acre-feet (130mcm) tentatively during 2014 but no later than 2016."

International Boundary and Water Commission,
United States and Mexico, 2012, Minute 319, p. 14

England

In the UK, the best meta-study focuses on England and was produced by Natural England in 2019. The study pulled together information form a range of publications and found that in the "most deprived areas" of England, people were over 80 per cent likely to experience at least one "least favourable" environmental condition. By contrast, those in the "least deprived areas" were only around 30 per cent likely to experience the same.

Specific examples in the UK are linked to airborne pollutants and deprived urban communities. This concept – that some areas are inherently meant to put up with conditions that other areas would consider a nuisance – is not a new one.

JUDGMENT

Sturges v Bridgman (1879) LR 11 Ch D 852

The case, which is a key case in the tort of nuisance, involved a consultant doctor (Sturges) who was unable to carry out his consulting because of the noise caused by machinery operated by a neighbouring confectioner (Bridgman). Sturges sued in nuisance. Bridgman tried unsuccessfully to rely on the fact that he had been carrying out his business for over 20 years and Sturges had only recently started his.

It is primarily remembered for the words "[W]hat would be a nuisance in Belgrave Square would not necessarily be so in Bermondsey."

(Per Thesiger LJ, @865)

Within the context of the tort of nuisance, the words of Thesiger J have been used to clarify that tortious nuisance is very much location-based rather than strictly activity-based. What they also suggest is that if an area is poor, industrial, and busy, then it is acceptable to carry out certain activities that would not be acceptable in affluent, residential, and quiet areas.

However, the Environmental Protection Act 1990 (as amended) sets out a list of statutory nuisances, which are not dependent upon location.

LEGISLATION

79 (1) Subject to subsections (1A) to (6A) [which follow], the following matters constitute "statutory nuisances" for the purposes of this Part, that is to say –

(a) any premises in such a state as to be prejudicial to health or a nuisance;
(b) smoke emitted from premises so as to be prejudicial to health or a nuisance;
(c) fumes or gases emitted from premises so as to be prejudicial to health or a nuisance;
(d) any dust, steam, smell or other effluvia arising on industrial, trade or business premises and being prejudicial to health or a nuisance;

. . .

[A]nd it shall be the duty of every local authority to cause its area to be inspected from time to time to detect any statutory nuisances which ought to be dealt with under section 80 below and, where a complaint of a statutory nuisance is made to it by a person living within its area, to take such steps as are reasonably practicable to investigate the complaint.

S79, Environmental Protection Act 1990 (excerpts)

This is not a comprehensive list, and it is later stated that "dark smoke" (see Chapter 9) is excepted from these provisions, as it is covered by other statute.

CASE

In November 2019, the Inner South London Coroner ruled that 9-year-old Ella Adoo Kissi-Debrah had died from acute respiratory failure, severe asthma, and air pollution exposure.

The coroner concluded that "[a]ir pollution was a significant contributory factor to both the induction and exacerbations of her asthma. During the course of her illness between 2010 and 2013 she was exposed to levels of Nitrogen Dioxide and Particulate Matter in excess of World Health Organization guidelines. The principal source of her exposure was traffic emissions. During this period there was a recognized failure to reduce the level of NO2 to within the limits set by the EU and domestic law which possibly contributed to her death."

Record of Inquest, www.innersouthlondoncoroner.org.uk/assets/attach/86/mnizari_16-12-2020_10-28-00.pdf

There has been widespread recognition for decades that air pollution levels are higher in areas with higher social deprivation, although there are micro-level differences, but this was the first inquest in the UK to officially link air pollution as a cause of death.

ACTIVITY

Consider whether there has been an environmental injustice in the following short scenarios.

Peter lives in a low-quality housing development in the centre of town. The local council has rerouted traffic away from a more high-quality area of town, and the resulting emissions have negatively impacted Peter's health.

Edith commutes from a village into the city to work as an investment banker. The air quality on the walk from the station to her office is poor, and this exacerbates an existing medical condition.

Geoff likes wild swimming. The river where he prefers to swim is now contaminated by raw sewage. He chooses to swim anyway and now suffers from recurring bouts of gastroenteritis.

Jane and her friends own and drive sports cars with large petrol engines. At the weekend, they like to race illegally along the street in the poorer end of town, as they are less likely to be arrested. The noise and emissions from their racing make it harder for local residents to sleep.

While the UK, unlike the United States, does not have any specific statutory provisions to prevent or remedy environmental injustice, it is identified in the 25-Year Environmental Plan published in 2018.

QUOTATION

"A healthier environment also helps deliver social justice and a country that works for everyone. For example, pollution affects us all, but it is the most disadvantaged in society who suffer more. The poorer you are, the more likely it is that your house, and your children's school and playground are close to highly polluted roads, and the less likely you are to enjoy ready access to green spaces.

Through this Plan we want to ensure an equal distribution of environmental benefits, resources, and opportunities. At present, children from minority ethnic backgrounds and lower income homes are the least likely to visit our countryside. This should change, so that everyone has the chance to benefit from getting close to nature and appreciating all it has to offer. In turn, they will want to protect and enhance the world around them."
Defra, 2018, "A Green Future: Our 25 Year Plan to Improve the Environment,"
Department of the Environment, Food and Rural Affairs, London, p. 16

Democratic Republic of the Congo

The Democratic Republic of the Congo (DRC) is the source of nearly two-thirds of the world's cobalt, which usually arises as a result of copper and nickel mining. Cobalt is an extremely useful mineral for the production of lithium-ion batteries, of the type used in mobile phones, laptops, and electric vehicles.

Around one-fifth of the cobalt mined in the DRC is mined in artisan or small-scale mines. From an environmental justice perspective, this could be a good thing, as it is likely to mean that the profits from mining are more likely to go to those who are involved in the process, so a fair distribution of benefit and cost. Unfortunately, the International Labour Organization has identified a significant issue, which is that children as young as 7 are routinely found to be working in the mines.[3]

Clearly, involving children of that age in work of this nature is unacceptable and violates at the least the UN Convention of the Rights of the Child. The situation is exacerbated by what the United Nations Security Council has called highly problematic levels of corruption in the country.

QUOTATION

"[L]ooting that was previously conducted by the armies themselves has been replaced with organized systems of embezzlement, tax fraud, extortion, the use of stock options as kickbacks and diversion of State funds conducted by groups that closely resemble criminal organizations."

UNSC, 2002, Final Report of the Panel of Experts on the Illegal
Exploitation of Natural Resources and Other Forms of Wealth of
the Democratic Republic of the Congo S/2002/1146,
Geneva: UN Security Council, p. 28

The impact of the injustice which is being meted out on the Congolese people is heightened by the fact that much of the cobalt is being used for recyclable Li-ion batteries, which are being used to reduce carbon emissions by electrical equipment and vehicles.

ACTIVITY

Which, if any, of the four examples (North Dakota, Colorado River, England, DRC) would you consider to be environmental injustice?
If an injustice has been perpetrated, identify:

- The perpetrators
- The victims
- The solution

The ideas behind environmental justice have been included in US legislative measures and in UK policy documents, and both of these are significant moves in the right direction.

3.1.2 Climate Justice

Climate justice is widely reckoned to be a subset of environmental justice, in the same way that environmental justice is likely a subset of social justice. Rather than focusing on the disproportionate environmental impact of all policies and practices, climate justice focuses on the impacts of climate change and the policies behind that. In 2002, a range of international NGOs created the 27 Bali Principles of Climate Justice, which were modelled on the 17 principles of environmental justice outlined earlier. The preamble to the principles leaves no room for doubt as to where the creators felt the blame for climate change should lie.

QUOTATION

"Whereas fossil fuel production and consumption helps drive corporate-led globalization;
Whereas climate change is being caused primarily by industrialized nations and transnational corporations;

Whereas the multilateral development banks, transnational corporations and Northern governments, particularly the United States, have compromised the democratic nature of the United Nations as it attempts to address the problem;

Whereas the perpetration of climate change violates the Universal Declaration On Human Rights, and the United Nations Convention on Genocide;

Whereas the impacts of climate change are disproportionately felt by small island states, women, youth, coastal peoples, local communities, indigenous peoples, fisherfolk, poor people and the elderly."

Preamble to the Bali Principles of Climate Justice

It is not solely the NGOs responsible for the 27 principles who see the exacerbated impacts of climate change on poorer nations.

QUOTATION

"The changes to the climate predicted by the IPCC and the impacts these will have 'will compound existing poverty. Its adverse impacts will be most striking in the developing nations because of their geographical and climatic conditions, their high dependence on natural resources, and their limited capacity to adapt to a changing climate.'"

ADB et al., 2022

Although it has been an issue for many years, climate justice has risen sharply up the agenda in the last few years, thanks largely to transnational organisations, like Extinction Rebellion and School Strike for Climate, and national groups, like Code Rood (Code Red) in the Netherlands, Centre for 21st Century Issues in Nigeria, Engajamundo (Engage the World) in Brazil, and the Philippine Movement for Climate Justice in the Philippines. The importance of protest will be covered in more detail in Chapter 4.

That climate change is a pressing issue for the world today is no longer an issue of debate. The Intergovernmental Panel on Climate Change, the foremost panel of climate change experts, has calculated that global average temperatures have risen by 1.1°C since the late 19th Century and forecasts that it will continue to rise of the foreseeable future. The mechanics of climate change and legal mechanisms to try to prevent it will be discussed further in Chapter 9, so here we will focus on the major effects and their impacts on those who are least resilient.

The ice cap in Greenland, for example, is melting nine times faster in 2019 than it was in 1992, and combined with the meltwater from other glaciers and ice sheets, it has contributed to a rise in global sea level of 23 centimetre since 1880 and the rate of rise is increasing, with another 30-centimetre rise predicted by 2050. This may not seem like a dramatic rise, but the impact of Small Island Developing States (SIDS) is likely to be catastrophic. Buildings will become uninhabitable, and as the freshwater table is affected, crops will no longer grow. Some islands will no longer be tenable for human life, and others will disappear. This was demonstrated to great effect in 2021 when the World Bank reported that the Marshall Islands will cease to exist as a nation and when the foreign minister of Tuvalu in the Pacific Ocean gave a speech to COP 26 in Glasgow while standing knee-deep in seawater.

Mainland, low-lying states will not escape this fate. In Bangladesh, for example, it is forecast that in the next three decades, around one-fifth of the country will be underwater, causing the displacement of 20 million people, which will exacerbate the stress placed on the remaining dry land.

Since it is developed countries which are responsible for the highest level of the carbon emissions which are causing sea-level rise, should they also be responsible for housing those peoples who are displaced as a result?

What legal mechanisms could be used (or created) to achieve this?

3.2 The Human Right to a Safe and Healthy Environment?

As we have already seen – and will continue to see throughout this book – there is an undeniable link between environmental quality and human physical and mental health. The argument that certain aspects of the environment are so strongly connected with human rights that to damage the environment is to be in breach of a human right has gained some traction in recent years.

Rephrasing environmental issues as human rights issues allows access to a swathe of human rights instruments which operate nationally, regionally, and globally.

The counterargument, and one which links back to the very core principles and concepts of environmentalism, is that categorising environmental issues as human rights issues is supremely selfish and anthropocentric. Such an approach, it is argued, risks prioritising what is good for "me" (human) over what is intrinsically good for "everything which is not me" (the environment).

This section will allow you to examine relevant human rights instruments to see whether, where, how, and if they link to environmental quality.

3.2.1 United Nations Provisions

The Bali Principles of Climate Justice (discussed earlier) specifically reference the 1948 Universal Declaration on Human Rights (UDHR) and the 1948 UN Convention on the Prevention and Punishment of the Crime of Genocide (Genocide Convention) as being "violated" by the "perpetration of climate change." In addition, this section will cover the 1966 International Covenant on Civil and Political Rights (ICCPR) and the 1966 International Covenant on Economic, Social, and Cultural Rights (ICESCR).

UDHR

The wording of the UDHR includes no mention of the words "environment," "pollution," "nature," "air," "water," or "climate." The closest to a provision which could be used to trigger environmental or climate injustice issues is Article 25.

ARTICLE

"Everyone has the right to a standard of living adequate for the health and well-being of himself and of his family, including food, clothing, housing and medical care and necessary social services, and the right to security in the event of unemployment, sickness, disability, widowhood, old age or other lack of livelihood in circumstances beyond his control."

Article 25(1), Universal Declaration on Human Rights, 1948

Even this provision is only obliquely linked to environmental issues. Some much-needed clarification was issued in 2008 by the United Nations High Commissioner for Human Rights as part of the 60th anniversary celebrations of the UDHR.

QUOTATION

"[T]he environment is never specifically mentioned in the UDHR but if you deliberately dump toxic waste in someone's community or disproportionately exploit their natural resources without adequate consultation and compensation, clearly you are abusing their rights.

As our recognition of environmental degradation has grown so has our understanding that changes in the environment can significantly impact on our human rights.

In no other area is it so clear that the actions of nations, communities, businesses and individuals can so dramatically affect the rights of others – damaging the environment can damage the rights of people, near and far, to a secure and healthy life."

Office of the UN High Commissioner on Human Rights

Genocide

Similarly, the Genocide Convention does not mention any of the terms previously listed. There are potentially elements of Article 2 which could be applied to environmental and climate injustice, for example, if the action is intended to degrade the environment to such an extent that a particular group is wholly or partly destroyed.

ARTICLE

In the present Convention, genocide means any of the following acts committed with intent to destroy, in whole or in part, a national, ethnical, racial or religious group, as such:

(a) Killing members of the group;
(b) Causing serious bodily or mental harm to members of the group;
(c) Deliberately inflicting on the group conditions of life calculated to bring about its physical destruction in whole or in part;
(d) Imposing measures intended to prevent births within the group;
(e) Forcibly transferring children of the group to another group.

Article 2, UN Convention on the Prevention and Punishment of the Crime of Genocide, 1951

There are several examples of activities and measures which have had the effect of causing significant damage to specific populations, but the issue of intent has never been satisfied. Cases on genocide and other crimes against humanity are brought before the International Criminal Court in The Hague. To date, there have been no cases brought at the ICC which relate to environmental or climate issues.

ICCPR and ICESCR

As with the previous two provisions, there is nothing specifically or overtly linked to environmental quality, climate quality, or the impacts of these in the ICCPR or ICESCR. One aspect which could be relied on more for *environmental* justice than *climate* justice is Article 1(2), a provision which is common to both covenants.

ARTICLE

> All peoples may, for their own ends, freely dispose of their natural wealth and resources without prejudice to any obligations arising out of international economic co-operation, based upon the principle of mutual benefit, and international law. In no case may a people be deprived of its own means of subsistence.
>
> Article 1(2), International Covenant on Civil and Political Rights, 1966
> Article 1(2), International Covenant on Economic, Social and Cultural Rights, 1966

The control of natural resources by a corporate or government body which is involved in asset-stripping without compensating the people on whose land the resources are found could potentially be breaching this provision.

The ICESCR does have an additional provision which could provide some support. In Article 12, the right to the highest standards of physical and mental health is recognised, and one of the contributory factors is recognised to be "environmental hygiene," which opens the way for discussion of the environmental quality.

ARTICLE

> 1. The States Parties to the present Covenant recognize the right of everyone to the enjoyment of the highest attainable standard of physical and mental health.
> 2. The steps to be taken by the States Parties to the present Covenant to achieve the full realization of this right shall include those necessary for:
>   (a) The provision for the reduction of the stillbirth-rate and of infant mortality and for the healthy development of the child;
>   (b) The improvement of all aspects of environmental and industrial hygiene;
>   (c) The prevention, treatment and control of epidemic, endemic, occupational and other diseases;
>   (d) The creation of conditions which would assure to all medical service and medical attention in the event of sickness.
>
> Article 12, International Covenant on Economic, Social and Cultural Rights, 1966

United Nations measures, while having the distinct advantage of a much wider reach than anything developed on a regional basis, do not appear to offer a significantly developed framework for using human rights as a route for environmental protection.

There is potential for the future, however. In October 2021, the United Nations Human Rights Council passed a non-binding resolution recognising the universal right to a clean, healthy, and sustainable environment. The terms "clean" and "healthy" are not defined in the resolution, but it remains a very interesting step.

ARTICLE

> 1. Recognizes the right to a clean, healthy and sustainable environment as a human right that is important for the enjoyment of human rights;
> 2. Notes that the right to a clean, healthy and sustainable environment is related to other rights and existing international law;
> 3. Affirms that the promotion of the human right to a clean, healthy and sustainable environment requires the full implementation of the multilateral environmental agreements under the principles of international environmental law;. . .
>
> Article 1–3, Resolution 48/13, the human right to a clean, healthy, and sustainable environment, resolution adopted by the Human Rights Council on 8 October 2021

3.2.2 Africa

The first of the regional provisions which will be covered is the African Charter on Human and Peoples' Rights, often referred to as the Banjul Charter, which came into force in 1986. The Charter was created under the auspices of the Organisation for African Union and has been ratified by all African nations other than Burundi and Morocco.

There are three main provisions within the Charter which could be triggered by environmental or climate injustices. These relate to physical and mental health, natural resources, and environmental rights.

ARTICLE

Article 16: Every individual shall have the right to enjoy the best attainable state of physical and mental health . . .

Article 21: All peoples shall freely dispose of their wealth and natural resources. This right shall be exercised in the exclusive interest of the people. In no case shall a people be deprived of it . . .

Article 24: All peoples shall have the right to a general satisfactory environment favourable to their development.

Selected articles, African Charter on Human and Peoples' Rights, 1986

Interestingly, unlike the recently identified "right to a clean, healthy and sustainable" environment like the UN, the Banjul Charter only extends to a "general satisfactory" environment. It was the first human rights instrument to include such a provision.

The Banjul Charter is overseen by the African Commission on Human and Peoples' Rights, which has the power to interpret the wording of the charter is asked to by any of the parties. To date, no party has asked for interpretation of any of the provisions.

Case law is equally scant, and in 36 years, only one case has been decided in relation to Article 24. It was brought against Nigeria, in 2001.

CASE

155/96 Social and Economic Rights Action Center (SERAC) and Center for Economic and Social Rights (CESR)/Nigeria

This case concerned the operations of the Nigerian National Petroleum Company (a joint venture between the Nigerian Government and Shell).

The allegation, which was upheld by the Commission, was that:

"[T]he oil consortium has exploited oil reserves in Ogoniland with no regard for the health or environment of the local communities, disposing toxic wastes into the environment and local waterways in violation of applicable international environmental standards. The consortium also neglected and/or failed to maintain its facilities causing numerous avoidable spills in the proximity of villages. The resulting contamination of water, soil and air has had serious short and long-term health impacts, including skin infections, gastrointestinal and respiratory ailments, and increased risk of cancers, and neurological and reproductive problems."

The Commission urged the Nigerian government "to ensure protection of the environment, health and livelihood of the people of Ogoniland."

3.2.3 Americas

In the Americas, the regional instrument is the American Convention on Human Rights 1969, often called the Pact of San José. The Convention was created by the Organization of American States, which also created an enforcement body (the Inter-American Commission on Human Rights) and a forum for cases to be heard (the Inter-American Court of Human Rights). There are two protocols to the Convention, the Protocol of San Salvador, which focuses on economic, social, and cultural rights, and the Asunción Protocol, which relates to death penalty.

In common with most of the other regional provisions, neither the Pact of San José nor the two protocols mention "environment," "pollution," "nature," "air," "climate," or "water." The closest potential link to environmental protection is Article 21, but even those provisions are not absolute, and there is a significant caveat of "public utility or social interest."

ARTICLE

Article 21: Right to Property

(1) Everyone has the right to the use and enjoyment of his property. The law may subordinate such use and enjoyment to the interest of society.

(2) No one shall be deprived of his property except upon payment of just compensation, for reasons of public utility or social interest, and in the cases and according to the forms established by law.

Article 21(1) and (2), American Convention on Human Rights, 1969

3.2.4 Asia

The Association of South-East Asian Nations (ASEAN) does not have an equivalent convention to Banjul or San José and instead has the ASEAN Human Rights Declaration 2012 (AHRD). There are two paragraphs in the Declaration, which is not legally binding, which have a link to environmental and climate justice.

LEGISLATION

Paragraph 28

Every person has the right to an adequate standard of living for himself or herself and for his or her family including:

a) The right to adequate and affordable food, freedom from hunger and access to safe and nutritious food
b) The right to clothing
c) The right to adequate and affordable housing
d) The right to medical care and necessary social services
e) The right to clean drinking water and sanitation
f) The right to a clean safe and sustainable environment

Paragraphs 35 and 36 (Extracts)

"The right to development should be fulfilled so as to meet equitably the developmental and environmental needs of present and future generations . . .

ASEAN member states should adopt meaningful people-oriented and gender responsive development programmes aimed at poverty alleviation the creation of conditions including the protection and sustainability of the environment."

ASEAN Human Rights Declaration

Since the AHRD is a "soft-law" declaration as opposed to a "hard-law" convention, there is no associated case law. There are clear links to sustainable development in paragraph 35, and the wording in paragraph 28 is broadly similar to that used by the UN Human Rights Council.

3.2.5 Europe

At a European level, the regional convention is the Convention for the Protection of Human Rights and Fundamental Freedoms, more commonly referred to as the European Convention on Human Rights (ECHR), which came into force in 1953. Created by the Council of Europe, the ECHR is enforced by the European Court of Human Rights (ECtHR), which sits in Strasbourg.

As with the UN provisions, neither the ECHR nor any of its seven amending protocols mentions "environment," "pollution," "nature," "air," "climate," or "water."

Because of lack of specific coverage in the Convention text, the ECtHR has become inventive about how it applies the Convention for maximum impact. None of the cases brought before the ECtHR specifically mention "environmental justice" or "climate justice," though there are clear links which can be drawn.

CASE

Öneryıldız v. Turkey (2004) ECHR 657

In this case, people were allowed to build their houses close to a domestic refuse site. Following a build-up of methane gas on the site, there was an explosion, which killed several people.

The ECtHR found that this was a violation of Articles 2 (right to life) and 13 (right to a domestic remedy) of the ECHR and Article 1 of Protocol No. 1 (right to peaceful enjoyment of possessions), as the state had failed in its duty to take adequate steps to protect its citizens.

The state was aware of the illegal site and had done nothing to close it. The benefit of the landfill site was felt by the state, and the people who were living on the site (and were among the poorest people in Turkey – now Türkiye) clearly bore the brunt of the conditions.

CASE

Brincat v Malta (2014) ECHR 900

In this case, the applicants were made seriously unwell and, in one case, died as a result of exposure to asbestos in their workplace. The ECtHR held that there had been a breach of Articles 2 (right to life) and 8 (respect to private and family life) as the state had failed to put in place the required measures to protect them from mesothelioma (a lung condition linked to working with asbestos).

In this case, too, the government allowed activities to take place which created the benefits of saving money on cheaper asbestos treatment. The cost was felt more heavily by those living and working nearby, and the benefit was enjoyed more fully by those who were at a distance.

This case, which is as yet undecided, involves the higher cancer risk in the "Tierra del Fuochi" ("Land of Fire") area of Campagna in the southern part of Italy. The risk is linked to the illegal dumping of hazardous and toxic waste in the region by organised crime groups, with the alleged complicity of government officials in northern Italy.

Once again, the benefits of this alleged conspiracy are felt in one area (northern Italy) and one group (corrupt officials and organised criminals), and the cost elsewhere (Campagna).

As with the UN, changes seem to be starting to happen within the Council of Europe. The Social Affairs Committee of the Parliamentary Assembly of the Council of Europe (PACE) proposed in September 2021 an additional protocol to the ECHR which would use the same wording as the UN Proposal, focusing on a right to a clean, healthy, and sustainable environment.

We can see therefore that across the universal and regional human rights provisions, there is a move towards including some kind of explicit right to a clean, safe, healthy, and sustainable environment. Case laws which have the ability to add some nuance to the interpretation, observation, and implementation of any future provisions take longer to develop, although you should keep in mind the different roles played by precedent in different jurisdictions.

The next section will focus on the links and overlaps between ideas of environmental and climate justice and some of the existing concepts and principles covered in Chapter 1.

3.3 Sustainable Development, the Polluter Pays Principle, and Environment and Climate Justice

Whilst looking at the underpinning theories and statutory and other provisions around environmental and climate justice, you will hopefully have been struck by the overlap with other areas of law. One of the largest areas of overlap is probably the idea of sustainable development (see Chapters 1 and 5) as a result of the horizontal and vertical effects of large-scale programmes. The other is likely to be the polluter pays principle, on the basis that when applied thoroughly, that principle requires a full internalisation of the environmental and social costs generated by the process.

3.3.1 UN SDGs

The UN Sustainable Development Goals are covered in considerably more depth in Chapter 5, but in essence, they were developed as a follow-on to the UN Millennium Development Goals that ran from 2000 to 2015. There are 17 SDGs, with the final one being more of an overarching one than a specific set of goals.

SDG 1   No Poverty
SDG 2   No Hunger
SDG 3   Good Health and Well-Being
SDG 4   Quality Education
SDG 5   Gender Equality
SDG 6   Clean Water and Sanitation
SDG 7   Affordable and Clean Energy
SDG 8   Decent Work and Economic Growth
SDG 9   Industry, Innovation, and Infrastructure
SDG 10   Reduced Inequalities
SDG 11   Sustainable Cities and Communities
SDG 12   Responsible Consumption and Production
SDG 13   Climate Action
SDG 14   Life below Water
SDG 15   Life on Land
SDG 16   Pease, Justice, and Strong Institutions
SDG 17   Partnerships for the Goals

All 17 of the SDGs strongly emphasise the importance of inclusiveness and pro-gress for all, and the very basis of sustainable development includes two major provisions which align to principles of environmental and climate justice:

■ Development which meets the needs of the present
■ No compromise on the ability of future generations to meet their own needs

The first of the two points is taken to be "horizontal" in impact, that is to say, it should apply equally across all peoples who are living currently. The second is "vertical," meaning, that meeting the horizontal criteria should not compromise the future generations.

What this means in practice is that sustainable development is, at its heart, a compromise. Figure 3.1 shows that in order to focus on the long-term, it is almost impossible to simultaneously focus on short-term impacts. Similarly, a focus on global impacts is not possible at the same time as a focus on local impacts. All four sectors of the grid are important, however, and this is where the compromise arises.

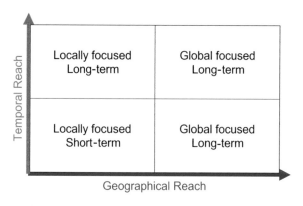

Figure 3.1 Horizontal and vertical impact of sustainable development.

Environmental justice is equally a compromise. The richer consumer suburb/city/region/state must accept that its consumption patterns need to change, and that the status quo cannot continue without causing huge damage to the poorer producer areas. Likewise, the producer areas which have historically suffered the worst environmental impacts may have to accept that the consequences of higher wages and better working conditions may be fewer employment opportunities, for example.

The compromise cannot go too far, however, lest it not achieve any of the desired outcomes of sustainable development.

LEGISLATION

"Human beings are at the centre of concerns for sustainable development. They are entitled to a healthy and productive life in harmony with nature."
Rio Declaration, Principle 1

Whilst all the SDGs can be tangentially linked to environmental and/or climate injustice, the five which arguably have the closest fit are SDG 1, SDG 3, SDG 5, SDG 10, SDG 12, SDG 13, and SDG 16.

SDG 1: No Poverty. Within this goal, there are subgoals which emphasise the importance of gender equality in terms of rights to economic resources, access to basic services, and ownership/control of land. Goal 1.5 calls for states to improve resilience of poorer communities to climate-related extreme events, as well as other economic and social issues. These are inherently important within environmental and climate justice approaches.

SDG 3: Good Health and Well-Being. This goal calls for a substantial reduction in deaths which happen as a result of air, water, and soil contamination – effects which are at the heart of environmental injustice.

SDG 5: Gender Equality. This goal includes subgoals which focus on reforming systems to give women better access to land ownership and control, economic resources, and more control over natural resources.

SDG 10: Reduced Inequalities. Inequality within and between countries is clearly identified as being concerning. This is one of the underpinning issues of environmental and climate injustice – that the negative impacts are focused on poorer areas/countries while the benefits are focused on the richer areas/countries.

SDG 12: Responsible Consumption and Production. The environmental and climate justice links to this are clear, in that one of the drivers for both types of injustice is the unsustainable consumption practices adopted in the Western world. The goal includes provision to encourage multinationals to be more sustainable and more open in their reporting, and to promote more sustainable public procurement.

SDG 13: Climate Action. Subgoal 13.3 focuses on the need for education, which almost exactly matches the call in principle 16 of the environmental justice principles (discussed earlier). Reducing the impact of climate change and promoting resilience are closely linked to climate justice.

SDG 16: Peace, Justice, and Strong Institutions. This goal includes measures to promote public access to information and creating and enforcing non-discriminatory laws for sustainable development.

There are natural overlaps and repetitions between the Sustainable Development Goals – it is impossible to end poverty without also assuring gender equality, for example.

ACTIVITY

In an attempt to meet the targets set by SDG 1 (no poverty), the government of the landlocked state of Erewhon decides to massively increase its steel production industry, as this will generate much-needed hard currency. The country relies on coal to power its steel mills, and as opposition politicians are opposed to the expansion, the government declares a state of emergency and bans all political parties and public protest.

These actions conflict with (at least) SDG 12, SDG 13, and SDG 16.

What would your advice be to the government as a way of balancing the competing and potentially contradictory targets in the different SDGs?

3.3.2 Polluter Pays Principle

We have seen in Chapter 1 that the OECD and the European Commission have adopted the polluter pays principle as the underpinning mechanism for deciding liability for population incidents. We have also seen that the ideas behind the principle are nothing new.

It is at its heart an economic instrument, and so it would be useful to focus briefly on the idea of internalising external environmental costs, which is an economics approach. Once all costs are internalised, the hope is that the least environmentally damaging option also becomes the least expensive.

Every good, or service, has a series of costs. Those costs which are internalised are reflected in the price paid for the good/service. External costs, on the other hand, are incurred in the production process but are not reflected in the price paid.

For illustrative purposes, we will look at the costs of a cotton T-shirt sold in the UK and identify the costs which are incurred from field to shelf.

Growing cotton requires a great deal of water – around 15,000 litres per kilo of raw (unprocessed) cotton. One T-shirt takes around 250 grams of raw cotton, so around 3,750 litres of water in the growing process.

Whilst it is possible to grow cotton indoors in the UK, the vast majority of the cotton sold is grown overseas. China, the United States, India, and Brazil are the four largest exporters of raw (unprocessed) cotton.

Let us say the raw cotton is shipped from China to Bangladesh, since that is one of the more popular cotton trading routes. This may be by ship, road, or air, all of which will contribute to CO_2 emissions. In Bangladesh, is it turned from raw cotton to processed cotton in a three-stage process (desizing, scouring, and bleaching). All these stages require substantial energy and water use, as well as other chemicals.

Once turned into processed cotton, the material will need to be turned into a recognisable T-shirt. Only 3 per cent of electricity in Bangladesh is generated from renewable sources, so the likelihood is that the factory will be powered by electricity from fossil fuels.

The T-shirts will then need to be shipped from Bangladesh to Europe, most likely Rotterdam, as Europe's largest deep-water container port. Shipping is recognised as being responsible for almost 3 per cent of anthropogenic carbon emissions.

From Rotterdam to the UK is also likely to be by ship, and then by road from Felixstowe or Southampton to the shop's distribution hub, and then into store.

Table 3.1 Phases of Production and Costs Incurred

Phase	Cost Incurred
Growing Phase	Employment
	Land use
	Fertiliser
	Water
Harvesting Phase	Employment
	Energy use
Processing Phase	Employment
	Export tax/import tax
	Transport to factory
	Energy use
	Water and chemical use
Manufacturing Phase	Employment
	Export tax/import tax
	Factory
	Transport
	Energy use
Shipping Phase	Employment
	Transport
	Energy use
Transport to UK	Employment
	Export tax/import tax
	Transport
	Energy
Retail	Employment
	Premises
	Energy
	VAT (unless children's clothes)

Naturally, this process is not triggered for a single T-shirt, and the costs incurred will be split between the thousands of garments in each shipment. However, in order to know how much the polluter should pay, they all need to be accounted for. This is crucial for achieving environmental and climate justice, as both require the costs and benefits to be shared equitably.

A further difficulty arises is attributing costs to environmental damage. Some things, particularly those which have value to humans and for which there is an existing market, are straightforward. A tonne of coal, a litre of water, ten kilos of cod all have a recognisable value. Harder to value are those things which have no market – should it cost more as a polluter if your pollution has killed 10,000 Hilsa fish in Bangladesh or five hectares of rain forest in Indonesia or caused an indigenous people to have to leave their homeland?

SUMMARY

- Environmental and climate justice are significant issues and are present at many levels – the town, city, state, region, and world.
- Underpinning problem is a sense that it is unjust and unfair for the benefits of something to be kept by one group whilst another group pays the cost.
- There may be an emerging trend in human rights provisions to formally include the right to a safe, healthy, and sustainable environment, but this is still some way away from implementation.
- There are overlaps between environmental and climate justice, sustainable development, and the polluter pays principle, highlighting the difficulties with quantifying costs.
- Easy (and satisfying), to lay the blame for environmental and climate injustices squarely and entirely at the door of multinational corporations. However, that would be to overlook and underplay the role that needs to be played by consumers, including ourselves.
- The solution to environmental and climate injustice is conceptually rather easy, but it is politically and economically much harder to implement.

The next chapter will cover the political process of lawmaking and link to the potential that citizens have to influence that process, whether from inside the system or outside.

SAMPLE ESSAY QUESTION

Using examples, assess whether the UK is giving sufficient weight to the issue of national or international environmental justice.

1. Define the different aspects of environmental justice and draw out the parallels between them.
2. Select an aspect of UK law and policy, for example, air pollution (see Chapter 9), water pollution (see Chapter 10), or biodiversity protection (see Chapter 7).
3. Assess the impacts of this policy on (a) different areas of the UK and (b) different types of state. For example, does the policy advocate building more waste treatment plants in particular types of demographic area? Does the policy contribute to higher levels of deforestation in less-developed countries?
4. Outline what more the UK could do to either remedy the environmental injustices you have identified or avoid them in the first place.
5. Conclude.

Further Reading

ADB et al., 2022, *Poverty and Climate Change: Reducing the Vulnerability of the Poor through Adaptation* (Joint publication of African Development Bank; Asian Development Bank; UK Department for International Development; EU Directorate-General for Development; German Federal Ministry for Economic Cooperation and Development; Netherlands Ministry of Foreign Affairs Development Cooperation; Organization for Economic Cooperation and Development; United Nations Development Programme; United Nations Environment Programme and The World Bank), www.oecd.org/env/cc/2502872.pdf

Banzhaf, S., Ma, L., & Timmins, C., 2019, Environmental Justice: The Economics of Race, Place, and Pollution, *Journal of Economic Perspectives*, 33(1), 185–208, 190, https://doi.org/10.1257/jep.33.1.185

Labonte, M., & Mills, K., eds., 2018, *Human Rights and Justice: Philosophical, Economic, and Social Perspectives*, London: Routledge

Natural England, 2019, *The Messy Challenge of Environmental Justice in the UK: Evolution, Status and Prospects*, Natural England Commissioned Report NECR273, www.gov.uk/natural-england

Robinson, M., 2019, *Climate Justice: A Man-Made Problem with a Feminist Solution*, London: Bloomsbury Publishing

Pali, B., Forsyth, M., & Tepper, F., 2022, *The Palgrave Handbook of Environmental Restorative Justice*, London: Palgrave

Skillington, T., 2016, *Climate Justice and Human Rights*, London: Palgrave MacMillan

White, K., 2018, Connection to Mother Earth Compels Indigenous Women to Protect It, *Truthout*, 8 October 2018, https://truthout.org/articles/connection-to-mother-earth-compels-indigenous-women-to-protect-it/

White, R., 2008, *Crimes Against Nature: Environmental Criminology and Ecological Justice*, London: Routledge

Notes

1 Banzhaf, S., Ma, L., & Timmins, C., 2019, Environmental Justice: The Economics of Race, Place, and Pollution, *Journal of Economic Perspectives*, 33(1), 185–208, 190

2 White, K., 2018, Connection to Mother Earth Compels Indigenous Women to Protect It, *Truthout*, 8 October 2018, https://truthout.org/articles/connection-to-mother-earth-compels-indigenous-women-to-protect-it/

3 ILO, 2019, *Child Labour in Mining and Global Supply Chains*, Geneva: International Labour Organisation, p. 2

4

Environmental Politics and Policymaking

Whatever the relevant legal system in place, legislative and policy provisions do not drop into place fully formed. There is a process involved which takes them from rough concept to legislation, and that is what we will focus on in this chapter. Initially, we will take a brief look at the legal systems in operation in the UK and the different approaches they have to environmental legislation. The bulk of the chapter focuses on the process of making law, and each stage is explained with examples. We then turn to public engagement in the decision-making process, and the opportunities which exist for this to happen.

AIMS AND OBJECTIVES

After reading this chapter, you should be able to:

- Identify the key stages in the policymaking cycle.
- Explain the role and importance of public engagement in this process.
- Understand the role played by protest and civil disobedience in driving change.

4.1 Brief Overview of the Legal Systems in the UK

The difference between Britain, England, and the United Kingdom is one which catches many law students out. This brief section will allow you to understand how the United Kingdom came into existence and hopefully help you avoid future mistakes.

As we saw in Chapter 1, the common law system in England dates back to the 12th century and evolved in the aftermath of the Norman Conquest in 1066. Over time, the territory ruled by different English monarchs waxed and waned. King Henry VI, for example, was King of England and Lord of Ireland from 1422 to 1461 and King of France from 1422 to 1435, although his claim to the

DOI: 10.4324/9781003137214-4

French throne was only recognised by the English and their allies. Sometimes territories were ruled in a monarch's personal capacity rather than being part of the country itself.

In terms of significant milestones, there are four which really stand out.

1542 Wales formally became part of England following two Acts of Parliament. The first Act, "An Acte for Laws & Justice to be ministred in Wales in like fourme as it is in this Realme"[1] (known as the Laws *of* Wales Act 1535), made Wales a part of England forever. The second Act, "An Acte for certaine Ordinaunces in the Kinges Majesties Domynion and Principalitie of Wales"[2] (known as the Laws *in* Wales Act 1542), was much more an administrative act and put into place councils and courts.

LEGISLATION

> "That his said Country or Dominion of Wales shall be and continue for ever from henceforth incorporated united and annexed to and with this his realm of England."
>
> Laws of Wales Act 1535, S1

1707 The entity known as Great Britain was created by the Acts of Union. It is *acts* rather than *act* as there were two acts. The first, "An Act for a Union of the Two Kingdoms of England and Scotland,"[3] was passed by the English Parliament in 1706, and the second, "An Act Ratifying and Approving the Treaty of Union of the Two Kingdoms of Scotland and England,"[4] was passed by the Scottish Parliament in 1707. Great Britain comprises only England (and thus Wales), Scotland, and the islands which belong to those countries. Various islands (including the Isles of Scilly and the Isle of Wight, but not the Isle of Man or the Channel Islands).

LEGISLATION

> That the two Kingdoms of England and Scotland shall upon the First day of May which shall be in the year One thousand seven hundred and seven and for ever after be united into one Kingdom by the name of Great Britain And that the Ensigns Armorial of the said United Kingdom be such as Her Majesty shall appoint and the Crosses of St. George and St. Andrew be conjoyned in such manner as Her Majesty shall think fit and used in all Flags Banners Standards and Ensigns both at Sea and Land.
>
> Act of Union 1706, Article I
>
> The text of the Scottish Act is almost identical, replacing the words "which shall be in the year one thousand seven hundred and seven" with "next ensuing the date hereof."

1801 As with Scotland, there were two acts which united Great Britain and Ireland. The first, "An Act for the Union of Great Britain and Ireland,"[5] was passed by the British Parliament in 1800, and the second, also called "An Act for the Union of Great Britain and Ireland," was passed by the Irish Parliament in 1801.[6] This created the United Kingdom of Great Britain and Ireland. The Irish Parliament was disbanded, and Ireland was given 100 seats in the new United Kingdom Parliament.

LEGISLATION

The wording in the 1801 Act is identical.

1921   The Government of Ireland Act 1920 ("An Act to Provide for the Better Government of Ireland")[7] separated Ireland into the 6 counties of Northern Ireland and the 26 counties of Southern Ireland. Both were to have their own House of Commons (S1), and a Council of Ireland was created to deal with issues that might affect the whole island (S2).

What was not anticipated was that Southern Ireland largely rejected the idea, and a civil war ensued. At the end of the civil war, the Anglo-Irish Treaty was signed, Article 12 of which allowed Northern Ireland the option of leaving the Irish Free State (which had dominion status) and re-joining the United Kingdom. The Irish Free State Constitution Act 1922[8] officially ratified the Treaty, and Northern Ireland did remain part of what became the United Kingdom of Great Britain and Northern Ireland.

ARTICLE

There are also several British Crown Dependencies in the geographical area known as the British Isles. They are not part of the United Kingdom and have their own lawmaking powers.

The Isle of Man. Whilst the Isle of Man has a separate Parliament (Tynwald) and separate laws, the government of the United Kingdom still has the responsibility for the defence of the island and for representing it in international fora, such as the United Nations. The Tynewald passes its own legislation, but in addition, UK Parliamentary Acts can apply to the island. Technically, UK Acts overrule Tynewald Acts, but this is being challenged recently.

The Bailiwick of Jersey. Jersey was part of William the Conqueror's lands in the 11th century but remained allied to (but not part of) England when Normandy was taken by the French in the 13th century. The island has its own Parliament (the States Assembly), laws, and court system (the Royal Court and the Jersey Court of Appeal).

The Bailiwick of Guernsey. Guernsey has its own assembly, the States of Deliberation, which also includes representatives from the neighbouring island of Alderney. Laws passed by the States of Guernsey need to be approved by the monarch. The Bailiwick of Guernsey also includes the island of Sark, which, unlike Alderney, has its own Parliament (the Chief Pleas).

CRITIQUING THE LAW

 Is it important for a group of territories in the same geographical space to have a harmonised series of laws relating to the environment?

4.1.1 Parliaments

The Westminster Parliament, in London, is the Parliament of the United Kingdom. For non-devolved matters, acts of the UK Parliament are binding on all of UK, although there may be separate sections that apply to Northern Ireland, Scotland, Wales, or the Crown Dependencies. Matters pertaining to the environment, water and flood defence, agriculture, fisheries, forestry, rural development, housing, and planning are devolved to the national assemblies, so when examining legislation in this area, you must be aware of the jurisdictional extent. The parliament is bi-cameral (two chambers) and has an elected lower house (the House of Commons), which draws members from all four home nations, and an unelected upper house (the House of Lords).

Senedd Cymru is the Welsh Parliament and sits in Cardiff. It became a Parliament in 2020, having previously been known as the National Assembly for Wales. The decisions of this unicameral parliament only have effect in Wales. A person cannot simultaneously be an MS (Member of Senedd) and an MP (Member of Parliament).

The *Pàrlamaid na h-Alba* is the Scottish Parliament and sits in Edinburgh. It is sometimes referred to as Holyrood, after the name of the building in which it sits. As with the other devolved nations, the Scottish Parliament is unicameral and fully elected. A person cannot sit as a Member of the Scottish Parliament (MSP) and a Member of Parliament at the same time.

Unlike the rest of the home nations, which are free to ignore EU law if it sees fit to do so, the Scottish Parliament passed the Withdrawal from the European Union (Continuity) (Scotland) Act 2020, which means that Scots law must continue to match EU law as it develops.

The Northern Ireland Assembly sits in the Stormont Estate in Belfast. The NI Executive sits in Stormont Castle. It is unusual in that there are two people leading the Assembly, the first minister and the deputy first minister. Despite the nomenclature, this is a shared leadership, and one is not the deputy of the other, despite the name. The first minister is nominated by the largest party of the largest denomination (in 2022, that was Sinn Féin as the largest Republican Party), the deputy first minister by the largest party of the second largest denomination (in 2022, that was the Democratic Unionist Party as the largest Unionist Party).

The Northern Ireland Assembly did not sit from 14 October 2002 to 8 May 2007 (1,667 days) or between 9 January 2017 and 11 January 2020 (1,097 days) and, at the time of writing, has not sat since 5 May 2022.

4.2 The Policymaking Cycle

Whether passed in Westminster, Cardiff, Edinburgh, or Belfast, laws come into existence via a political process. Generally, the political party with the largest representation will form the government, and the government will progress the vast majority of legislation. To put this into perspective, between 1983 and 2019, 1,603 Acts of Parliament were passed in Westminster, and 85 per cent of those started as government bills. More of the private member's bills (77 per cent) were introduced in the House of Commons.

The policymaking cycle in Figure 4.1 identifies the different stages which will occur between an issue first being identified and relevant legislation being passed. The timescales involved will vary widely, and some issues will not complete the cycle. The public has opportunities to get involved and influence the process at various stages, and these opportunities will be explored in Section 4.3 of this chapter.

4.2.1 Issue

The first stage in the process is when a particular issue begins to be noticed for the first time. In environmental law, this could be the increased death rates from cholera, or the identification of microplastics in the oceans, or the growing damage to the ozone layer, or the accelerating rate of biodiversity loss. The issues could be of local, regional, national, or global significance.

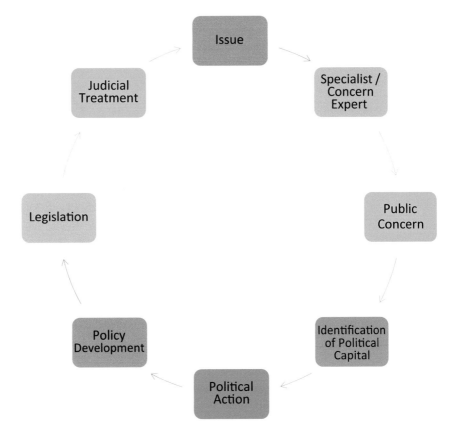

Figure 4.1 The policymaking cycle.

Once the issue has been identified as potentially problematic (or potentially beneficial), then there will potentially be more research conducted, either by academics or journalists or both, to determine whether what has been noticed was a one-off or whether it is a genuine issue that needed to be addressed.

The results of this research may be published, either in specialist academic press or in newspapers. There may or may not be a reaction from the relevant industrial body, government, regulator, or other researchers. Many issues do not get beyond this stage. For some, there may be a very long delay, and for yet others, there may be no delay at all.

QUOTATION

The fact that plastics can biodegrade into "numerous nondegradable fragments" in the oceans and on land has been known since at least 1990. In 2004, Thompson et al. suggested that "there is considerable potential for large-scale accumulation of microscopic plastic debris."

Their research identified microplastics in plankton samples dating back to the 1960s, but with a "significant increase in abundance over time."

Thompson, R. C.; Olsen, Y.; Mitchell, R. P.; Davis, A.; Rowland, S. J.; John, A. W. G.; McGonigle, D.; and Russell, A., 2004, "Lost at Sea: Where is all the plastic?" *Science* Vol 304, Issue 5672, p. 838

4.2.2 Specialist and Expert Concern

Once the issue has undergone preliminary investigation, expert and specialists in related fields may start to become concerned and voice those concerns. At this stage, it is possible that there will be a rise in research funding, and thus in research, to look more thoroughly at the issues.

Professor Nowotny[9] made the strong case over 40 years ago that the assumption that scientists agree on issues is a false one, and so there is likely to be a divergence of opinions.

It was not until 2009, four years after Thompson et al. found microplastics on beaches in South-West England and in plankton samples dating back to the 1960s, that the US National Oceanographic and Atmospheric Administration (NOAA) officially identified microplastics as being a problem and held the first International Research Workshop on the Occurrence, Effects, and Fate of Microplastic Marine Debris.

Specialists and experts were not concerned about microplastics, but there was no political or legislative measure being considered, and acquiring funding to undertake large-scale research would still have been relatively difficult.

4.2.3 Public Concern

Once an issue is of concern to experts, it may spark the imagination of the wider public. Not all issues need to go through this stage, as some of the expert concerns are in regard to issues which are so complex and esoteric that the public never get on board. Those issues may progress directly to the next stage.

If the public does become concerned, however, it can act as a snowball and raise the profile of the issue to a great degree. Environmental issues that involve cruelty to animals, particularly mammals and megafauna, fare very well in this regard, but 2022 also saw a big rise in interest in the discharge of untreated sewerage into the country's rivers, for example.

Eight years after the NOAA meeting, in December 2017, the *Blue Planet II* TV series aired on the BBC. Episode 7 of the series focused on microplastics, and the coverage provoked a dramatic rise in the number of newspaper articles and media coverage, and the market for non-plastic items (toothbrushes, cotton buds, shopping bags, etc.) exploded.

The petition.parliament.uk website saw over 200 new petitions being launched relating to plastic pollution. Even though fewer than 100 of these ever attracted any signatures, it is clear to see that the public interest was pricked, and that microplastic pollution had entered the public consciousness.

Public awareness and public action are, of course, two very different issues, and Dunn pointed out that despite the rise in awareness, there was no "observed change" in consumer's preference for actually buying plastic.[10]

4.2.4 Identification of Political Capital

The role of politicians is generally to represent the concerns of their constituents in the relevant Parliament. Once it becomes apparent that a particular issue is of concern to the public, it is likely that one or more politicians will start to identify that there is "political capital" in getting on board with the same cause. Often, this process will be simple, as politicians also form part of the general public and are as likely to be influenced by media coverage of a specific issue. Some politicians also come from specialist backgrounds, so it is possible that they will have become engaged at stage 2 of the cycle.

QUOTATION

> "He [the politician] gets his stock of influence by 'buying' a bit here and a bit there from the many small 'owners' who were endowed with it by the constitution-makers."
> Banfield, E. C., 1961, *Political Influence: A new theory of urban politics*, New York, NY: The Free Press of Glencoe/Crowell-Collier Publishing Co, p. 241–242

What Banfield (and later Bourdieu[11]) is alluding to is that, like financial capital, political capital is built up over time, and reckless use of it can leave a politician with no influence at all.

In the aftermath of the public's concerns, Hansard shows that in the Westminster Parliament, "plastic" was mentioned 146 times in the 12 months prior to the *Blue Planet II* TV series, and 447 times in the year following the broadcast. Furthermore, the pre-series mentions of plastic were mostly not in the context of plastic pollution, and the post-series mentions were almost exclusively on the context of pollution.

A cynical view of Parliament would conclude that MPs had identified that voters were concerned about plastic and wanted to make political capital and curry favour with the voters by discussing the issue. A less-cynical view is, the MPs became genuinely concerned about an issue they had been previously unaware of.

4.2.5 Political Action

Once it has become firmly established that an issue brings with it genuine political capital rather than being a short-lived public obsession, politicians are more likely to take action rather than just calling for others to take action. This resonates to some extent with the findings of Dunn (discussed earlier) in relation to the distinction between awareness and action on the part of the public.

In 2018, the year after the *Blue Planet II* series and the spike in public and political awareness, three private member's bills were introduced: the Plastic Pollution Bill, the Plastic Pollution (No. 2) Bill, and the Plastics Bill. The first two bills were both introduced by the Liberal Democrat MP for Orkney and Shetland, Alistair Carmichael, and both proposed setting targets for the reduction of plastic waste, with an associated strategy and annual reporting system. The third bill was introduced by Geraint Davies, Labour MP for Swansea West, and proposed much the same, with an additional requirement to align UK policy with EU policy. None of these three bills was successful – as we saw earlier in the chapter, only 15 per cent of legislation started as a private member's bill), but it is a marked shift in action. Prior to this, the most recent bill to specifically mention *plastic* in the title was the Plastic Glasses and Bottles (Mandatory Use) Bill introduced in 2012, which concerned the use of plastic polycarbonate bottles in pubs and bars.

4.2.6 Policy Development

Political action and public interest triggered the government to take action and look at developing policy. The government produced two large policy documents at either end of 2018.

The first, "A Green Future: Our 25 Year Plan to Improve the Environment," was launched in January 2018. It repeatedly included a pledge to "work towards eliminating all avoidable plastic waste by 2042"[12] and also a commitment to reducing marine plastic. In her speech launching the plan, Prime Minister Theresa May acknowledged the role played by the *Blue Planet II* TV series in highlighting the issue.

The second, launched in December 2018, was "Our Waste, Our Resources: A Strategy for England."[13] The ministerial foreword to the Strategy document by Secretary of State for the Environment, Food, and Rural Affairs Michael Gove namechecked the *Blue Planet II* series, thus cementing the role of this type of media in informing policy. The strategy was followed by consultations in 2019, and again in May 2021, where the government sought input from the public and organisations on their initial plans.

4.2.7 Specific Legislative Development

If a policy document is seen to be successful, then it is likely that the government of the day will introduce legislation to give effect to the policy. The specific mechanisms through which a bill proceeds through Parliament and becomes an act will not be covered here (see *Unlocking Constitutional and Administrative Law*[14]). This process may occur very quickly – the Coronavirus Act 2020 took only six days from first reading to royal assent, for example.

In the case of the Environment Bill, the process was considerably longer. The bill's first reading was in the House of Commons on 20 January 2020, and the bill finally received royal assent on 9 November 2021, a total of 660 days.

The Environment Act 2021[15] does contain provisions which obliquely build on the 2019 and 2021 consultations of the 2018 Waste Strategy. Section 1 of the Act gives the Secretary of State the power (note: not *duty*) to set long-term environmental targets, and Section 8 includes a further requirement to produce an "environment improvement plan" of at least 15 years' duration, though this was backdated to allow the 25-year plan from three years earlier to count.

> (1) The Secretary of State may by regulations set long-term targets in respect of any matter which relates to –
>   (a) the natural environment, or
>   (b) people's enjoyment of the natural environment.
>
> S1, Environment Act 2021

The Act mentions "plastic" only four times and does not mention "microplastic" at all. The implementation of specific legislation to reduce plastic waste is left to the Environmental Protection (Plastic Straws, Cotton Buds and Stirrers) (England) Regulations 2020,[16] which introduced three new offences, of applying single-use plastic straws, cotton buds, and drink stirrers to end users (though with a seemingly eternal exemption if the products were purchased before the regulations came into force).

4.2.8 Judicial Interpretation of Statute

Once regulations are approved or a bill becomes an act, there will be a period of stasis. Partly, this is because the date when the act enters into force will be later, to allow those impacted by the new legislation to take any necessary steps to comply.

The second reason is that it will take time for cases to be brought under the new legislation. In the summer of 2022, the National Audit Office said that average wait time for a criminal prosecution to come to court was 708 days, or close to two years. For civil cases, the delay is around 51 weeks for small claims cases and 78 weeks for larger cases. These are only the delays before the cases are heard and do not take into account any appeals to higher courts, which is where the bulk of judicial interpretation will occur. That could add years to the process.

CASE

Cambridge Water Co. Respondents v Eastern Counties Leather Plc. (1994) 2 AC 264

This is a case usually cited to demonstrate the issue of foreseeability, but it is also useful to consider the timescales involved.

"Before 1976," perchloroethylene (PCE) was spilled in the course of Eastern Counties Leather's business operations. The borehole of Cambridge Water was found to be contaminated with PCE in October 1983, and the source was traced to Eastern Counties Leather. The first action brought by Cambridge Water was dismissed in July 1991.

Cambridge Water appealed later in 1991, and the House of Lords found in their favour in December 1993.

It thus took a decade from the factual recognition of the cause of the contamination to be backed up with judicial recognition.

There are various rules, but essentially, where the language of the statute (act) is unclear or ambiguous, judges have the power to say what they believe it means. Under the rules of precedent, all lower courts must follow the interpretation given by the higher courts.

The Cabinet Office, which is essentially the corporate headquarters for government, outlines the process by which the government department "responsible" for an act will usually review the act between three and five years after it was passed. The "responsible" department will be the one whose remit most closely matches that of the act – it may not be an exact match, as some government departments (particularly those relating to the environment) are reorganised quite frequently.

Note

The current Department for Energy Security and Net Zero (DESNZ), for example, was created in February 2023 and took over the energy area from the Department of Business, Energy, and Industrial Strategy (DBEIS).

DBEIS was created in 2016 by merging the Department of Energy and Climate Change (DECC) and the Department of Business, Innovation, and Skills (BIS).

DECC had taken over the climate area of the Department for the Environment, Food, and Rural Affairs (DEFRA) in 2008.

DEFRA itself was created by merging the Ministry of Agriculture, Fisheries, and Food with parts of the Department of the Environment, Transport, and the Regions in 2001.

Once the review has been carried out, the department submits an assessment to the linked Commons committee, who then decides whether a more in-depth enquiry into the effectiveness of the act is warranted.

Part of this review process will be to consider the judicial treatment of the act and whether there is any restating of the law that has become necessary. There is also the possibility for judicial review actions to be brought by individuals or groups challenging the legitimacy of a particular action, or even the statute itself.

This cyclical process from issue to legislation, which is broadly the same in the devolved nations, demonstrates four issues:

1. In order for an issue to receive attention from policymakers, it is vital that it move from being a "niche" concern of specialists into a more mainstream issues and be brought into the public conscience.
2. The sheer length of time that the process can take – by the summer of 2022, it has been almost 70 years since microplastics started entering the ocean, over 30 years since it was identified, and nearly 20 since Thompson et al. identified it as being an issue of concern.
3. The creation of environmental laws (and other laws) is not linear but is truly circular and cyclical.
4. There are potentially many opportunities for "the public" in its widest sense to get involved with, and influence, policy- and lawmaking.

4.3 Public Engagement

Public engagement can come in many forms, involving many different levels of effort. It can also be direct engagement and indirect engagement, and all these nuances make for a wide range of effectiveness. Figure 4.2 illustrates different ways in which you can get involved in the decision-making process.

Figure 4.2 How to get involved.

It is entirely possible to influence the political system by voting in elections. Most elections do not have a full turnout, and often, the margin between victory and loss is smaller than the percentage of people who did not vote.

It is also possible to become part of the system and influence it from within by standing for election. Broadly speaking, anyone who meets the criteria for candidacy (these vary depending on location and type of election) can stand in an election.

4.3.1 Direct Involvement

All the devolved nations offer specific opportunities for the public and experts/specialists to become involved.

In the Westminster Parliament, a government department which is considering a policy development may publish a "Green Paper" in the early stages of the process. This is a consultation document open to any individual or group to give feedback. The department may or may not act out of any specific feedback and may choose to use it if there is to be a White Paper produced. A White Paper is published by the government, setting out proposals for future legislation. They are more detailed than Green Papers and will have taken into account the responses to the earlier consultation. Some White Papers, but not all, will serve as draft bills; some are more general. They offer a further opportunity for interested groups to be consulted with. Once a bill is introduced in Parliament, the opportunities for direct public involvement cease, although indirect influence may be brought through individual MPs.

In the Senedd, proposals for new legislation will be published, so there is an opportunity for feedback. Similarly, in the Scottish Parliament, bills will generally have undergone consultation before they are introduced. This is compulsory for committee bills, but not for members' bills. In Northern Ireland, there will be opportunities for consultation before a bill is presented to the Speaker of the Assembly, who will then decide whether the bill is within the competence of the assembly.

In all the different assemblies, influence may be brought to bear on individual members, who will be entitled to engage in debate on the bill, and to vote on whether or not to approve. This opportunity brings a focus from lobby groups, that is to say, paid or unpaid advocates for particular causes and issues.

Lobby groups (sometimes called political advocacy groups) can adhere to any political, philosophical, ethical, or other cause, and the lobbying process is governed by rules. A Member of Parliament is bound by the code of conduct not to accept money or other financial gain in order to vote in a particular way and must also register within four weeks anything which could reasonably be considered as likely to influence their actions.

12. No Member shall act as a paid advocate in any proceeding of the House.
13. The acceptance by a Member of a bribe to influence his or her conduct as a Member, including any fee, compensation, or reward in connection with the promotion of, or opposition to, any Bill, Motion, or other matter submitted, or intended to be submitted to the House, or to any Committee of the House, is contrary to the law of Parliament

Regulations 12 and 13 of the Code of Conduct for Members of Parliament

The activities of lobbyists are covered by the Transparency of Lobbying, Non-Party Campaigning, and Trade Union Administration Act 2014.[17] This is not a comprehensive register, however, and the UK Lobbying Register covers those not covered by the Act.

4.3.2 The Tyranny of the Majority

The idea that letting the majority of those involved decide the fate of the whole is at the heart of modern democracy. The most illustrative recent example of this is, of course, the 2016 referendum on the UK's membership of the European Union – 33 million votes were cast, from the 46 million eligible voters, and the Leave vote was 51.89 per cent of those votes (17,410,742), with the Remain vote receiving 48.11 per cent (16, 141,241). The referendum was not legally binding, but the government had promised to follow whichever path was voted for by the majority. This resulted in 17 million people deciding that the entire UK population of 67 million should leave the EU, including those in Northern Ireland and Scotland, who had voted overwhelmingly to remain in the EU.

This idea of majority rule has not been universally welcomed, however. John Adams, the second president of the United States, thought that without the checks and balances put in place by the US Constitution, the opportunities for tyrannical majority rule were rife.[18] His argument was that if the majority have power, then they will be supported by that majority, and there is little or nothing the minority can do to stop them, even if they were to behave unconscionably or despotically.

For Adams – and, a little later, for John Stuart Mill, the English philosopher, economist, and MP – simply letting the majority decide what was in the best interests of the state was an untenable prospect.

QUOTATION

"The will of the people, moreover, practically means the will of the most numerous or the most active part of the people; the majority, or those who succeed in making themselves accepted as the majority; the people, consequently may desire to oppress a part of their number. . . .

In political speculations, 'the tyranny of the majority' is now generally included among the evils against which society requires to be on its guard."

Mill, J. S., 1869, On Liberty, London: J. W. Parker & Sons, pp. 7–8

Adams, Mill, and others agree that left unchecked, oppression of a minority became a very real threat. Public consultation has been suggested as a way of limiting this. Rather than limiting involvement to a pre-determined group and instead giving everyone the chance to get involved means that it is not just the "usual suspects" who are heard, the argument goes. Judicial review (see Section 5.2.8) is also thought to be a way of ensuring decisions are rational and reasonable.

ACTIVITY

In 2016, the National Environment Research Council (NERC) launched a campaign to name their latest research vessel (www.nameourship.nerc.ac.uk). Following an Internet campaign, more than a third of the votes cast were for "RRS *Boaty McBoatface*," although NERC eventually opted to name the ship RRS *Sir David Attenborough* (which was the fourth most popular choice).

You have been given the task of carrying out a public consultation to ensure that a policy idea has sufficient support before it is introduced into Parliament.

How do you ensure that the public participation avoids both the "tyranny of the majority" and the "*Boaty McBoatface* effect"?

For those with an interest in the environment, the tension arises because despite a growth in environmental concerns across both the public and political agendas, they are rarely at the pinnacle of importance for most people. Until very recently, larger-scale environmental matters have often been framed as being longer-term, and thus, short-term issues become more immediate and important. For example, the global economic slowdown, the war in Ukraine, Brexit, and of course, the COVID-19 coronavirus pandemic have all involved urgent action by politicians and have had immediate deleterious impacts on populations. Climate change, on the other hand, despite requiring urgent action by policymakers, has impacts which will not be felt fully for several decades.

The "majority," therefore, are not currently prepared to do all that is necessary to protect the environment, and the system is led by the majority. Some jurisdictions (for example, Australia) make voting in elections compulsory, and this has led to a turnout of 89.8 per cent in the most recent (2022) federal elections (contrasting with 67 per cent in the 2019 UK General Election). Compulsory voting, leading to higher (but not complete) turnout, is argued to avoid Adams's point about it being "the most active part of the people" who make the decisions for everyone.

4.3.3 Access to Environmental Information

Giving people the right and ability to engage in the decision-making process is only part of the journey, however. "Knowledge itself is power,"[19] wrote Sir Francis Bacon in the late 16th century, and Ayeb-Karlsson expanded this in 2020 saying that "[t]here can be no power without the correlative constitution of knowledge, nor knowledge that does not produce or structure power."[20]

It is certainly an attractive proposition (particularly among academics) than the more informed a person is about a topic, the more they are empowered to make accurate decisions. It is not an absolute, however, and ill-informed people can make good choices just as frequently as well-informed people can make bad ones.

What these writers are alluding to is that just giving the public the power to influence policy without any training, education, or knowledge is half the battle at best. After all, without understanding the implications and consequences of two courses of action, it is harder to select the "preferable" one.

There have been different approaches taken by different states to try to provide understanding and knowledge about environmental issues to their publics. In the

United States, environmental information is covered by the Freedom of Information Act, passed initially in the 1960s[21] and then amended in every succeeding decade. In the EU, approaches were considerably more delayed. Initially, Directive 90/313/EC[22] gave EU citizens some rights to access information pertaining to the environment.

ARTICLE

Article 1:

The object of this Directive is to ensure freedom of access to, and dissemination of, information on the environment held by public authorities and to set out the basic terms and conditions on which such information should be made available.

Article 1, Directive 90/313/EC

Globally, though with no force, Principle 10 of the Rio Declaration also included provisions on access to environmental information and recognised the importance of citizen participation and the importance of environmental justice (see Chapter 4). The three "pillars" of Principle 10 are access to information, participation, and justice.

LEGISLATION

"Environmental issues are best handled with participation of all concerned citizens, at the relevant level. At the national level, each individual shall have appropriate access to information concerning the environment that is held by public authorities, including information on hazardous materials and activities in their communities, and the opportunity to participate in decision-making processes. States shall facilitate and encourage public awareness and participation by making information widely available. Effective access to judicial and administrative proceedings, including redress and remedy, shall be provided."

Principle 10, Rio Declaration

So we can see that globally, regionally, and in some cases, nationally, provisions are in place to try to ensure that information relating to environmental issues is available to the public.

In 1998, the United Nations Economic Commission for Europe (UNECE) passed the Convention on Access to Information, Public Participation in Decision-Making, and Access to Justice in Environmental Matters. This is usually referred to as the Aarhus or Århus Convention, after the town in Norway in which the signing ceremony took place. This builds on the three "pillars" of Rio Principle 10 and combines them with the intergenerational aspects of sustainable development.

ARTICLE

Article 1 OBJECTIVE

In order to contribute to the protection of the right of every person of present and future generations to live in an environment adequate to his or her health and well-being, each Party shall guarantee the rights of access to information, public participation in decision-making, and access to justice in environmental matters in accordance with the provisions of this Convention.

Article 2 DEFINITIONS

(3) "Environmental information" means any information in written, visual, aural, electronic or any other material form on:

(a) The state of elements of the environment, such as air and atmosphere, water, soil, land, landscape and natural sites, biological diversity and its components, including genetically modified organisms, and the interaction among these elements;

(b) Factors, such as substances, energy, noise and radiation, and activities or measures, including administrative measures, environmental agreements, policies, legislation, plans and programmes, affecting or likely to affect the elements of the environment within the scope of subparagraph (a) above, and cost-benefit and other economic analyses and assumptions used in environmental decision-making;

(c) The state of human health and safety, conditions of human life, cultural sites and built structures, inasmuch as they are or may be affected by the state of the elements of the environment or, through these elements, by the factors, activities or measures referred to in subparagraph (b) above;

Articles 1 and 2, UNECE Aarhus Convention

This allows for considerable transparency in looking at decisions which have been made and potentially opens the way for challenges to be brought against those decisions.

QUOTATION

"Progressive governments increasingly recognize and understand that environmental decisions will only be sustainable if reached through a transparent, participatory and accountable process. The Arhus Convention provides governments with standards to ensure this happens."

UNECE, 2014, Protecting your environment: The power is in your hands: A quick guide to the Aarhus Convention, United Nations Economic Commission for Europe, Geneva, p. 7

Whether it is the US FOIA, the EU Directive, UK Laws, or the Aarhus Convention, the one element that these all have in place is that they put in place a structure and a process. The application of the process is occasionally flawed, and the release of information which could potentially prove awkward for governments is resisted.

Some organisations, such as WikiLeaks, have taken it upon themselves to release a huge amount of detail which governments had deemed to be sensitive. Much of this concerns issues of national security and related issues, but there have been some environmental data released through WikiLeaks. The draft of the Trans-Pacific Partnership (TPP) agreement's environmental section, for example, was leaked back in 2015 and was highly criticised for its focus on trade rather than the environment. The TPP never came to fruition, but due to US President Trump's withdrawal in 2017 rather than as a result of the leak.

ACTIVITY

The right of the public to challenge decisions which have already been made, or to influence decisions which are currently being made, or to apply for relief against the impacts of a decision which has been made, is therefore reasonably well entrenched in legal frameworks. There are other processes which can be used. However, these are less about trying to change decisions in the system and more often about the desire to change the system itself.

4.4 Protest and Civil Disobedience

Protest and civil disobedience have a very lengthy history and a very wide range of approaches. They also have a wide range of consequences from nothing much really happening as a result to being the precursor of a full-blown revolution. There is no agreement on the "first" protest – where, when, why, what about, and who was involved are all open to discussion.

Some cite the "Revolt of the Barons" or the "First Barons' War" (1215–1217) as the first "proper" protest. It fits the stereotypical image of a protest, which is where people protest against authority in order to win concessions. It is unusual, for the protest was against the Crown ("the authority") but led by the landed gentry (and thus also "the authority"). It was led by Robert Fitzwalter (sometimes Robert FitzWalter de Clare), who was the marshal of the Army of God and the Holy Church. King John had signed the Magna Carta in 1215, and the protest centred on his refusal to abide by the terms. Ironically, the barons also largely ignored the terms of the agreement. The protest escalated into a full-blown civil war, with the help of Prince Louis of France. The revolt ended with the death of King John and the shift in the barons' loyalties to his son Henry III, who issued a revised Magna Carta in 1217.

For a protest which involved participants from outside the landed gentry, the Peasants Revolt of 1381 is usually seen as a starting point. Wat Tyler and John Ball led a group of protestors from London to Kent to protest about the introduction of a poll tax. Both Tyler and Ball were executed, but the revolt was seen as a success because no further poll tax was levied until the 20th century.

The first recorded protest about environmental issues was likely to be the protest which ended in the Khejarli massacre in 1730. Despite the name, the protest started out as peaceful, when Amrita Devi Bishnoi hugged a Khejri tree to prevent its being felled by the troops of Maharaja Abhai Singh Rathore, the local ruler. Devi was joined by her family, and other villagers, who protested that the trees were sacred to the Bishnoi community. She was killed by the troops, which meant other Bishnoi travelled to the site to hug trees. In total, nearly 400 were killed, and the maharaja, who had not authorised the massacre, travelled to the village to apologise. This protest is partly responsible for the "tree hugger" name given insultingly to environmentalists.

In terms of civil disobedience, although the practice predates him by many years, the American environmentalist Henry David Thoreau is widely credited with coining the term in 1849. Thoreau is also the writer of *Walden: or Life in the Woods*, widely regarded as one of the most fundamental environment texts.

QUOTATION

"Unjust laws exist: shall we be content to obey them, or shall we endeavor to amend them, and obey them until we have succeeded, or shall we transgress them at once?"

"It costs me less in every sense to incur the penalty of disobedience to the State than it would to obey. I should feel as if I were worth less in that case."

Thoreau, H. D., 1849, *On the Duty of Civil Disobedience*, Boston, MA: Ticknor & Fields

Mohandas K. (Mahatma) Gandhi's celebrated use of passive resistance, or *satyagraha*, predated his reading of Thoreau's book while in prison in South Africa. However, Gandhi adopted the phrase "civil disobedience" as a result, to better explain *satyagraha* to English readers.

Definition

"[C]ivil disobedience . . . [is] a public, nonviolent, conscientious yet political act contrary to law usually done with the aim of bringing about a change in the law or policies of the government."

Rawls, J., 1999, *A Theory of Justice*, revised edition, Cambridge, MA: Belnap Press/Harvard University Press, p. 320

Gandhi's preferred phrase, *satyagraha*, is a Sanskrit compound word meaning "holding firmly to truth." The "Champaran Satyagraha" in 1917 was a mass protest by indigo growers in the Champaran district of Bihar in the north-east of India. His protest led to a change in the laws.

Older, more mainstream, conservation-focused groups can trace their roots back to the 19th century. The Sierra Club in the United States (1892), the National Trust in the UK (1895), and the Field Naturalists Club of Victoria in Australia (1880) are examples of this type of organisation. Although at the time of their origins many of these groups were regarded as rather radical, they are today widely regarded as being part of the establishment.

The simplified diagram in Figure 4.3 represents the different levels of engagement with an issue that are most likely to occur. There are nuances that cannot be represented diagrammatically (such as "read a book"), and as with philosophical and ethical stances (see Chapter 2), we will all have different levels of engagement for different issues. In this section, we will look at some of the different approaches to protest, from the withdrawal of participation in mandatory events (e.g. School Strike for Climate) to mass occupation (e.g. Extinction Rebellion, Just Stop Oil), to sabotage of equipment and bombing campaigns (e.g. the Earth Liberation Front and Animal Liberation Front).

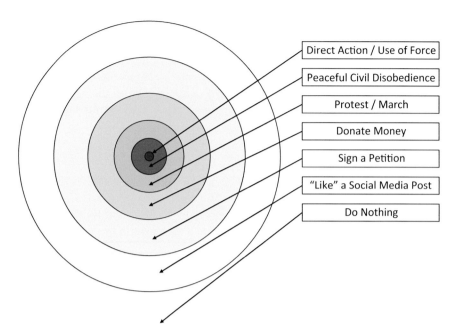

Figure 4.3 Layers of public engagement.

Note
If you are considering becoming involved in a protest, make sure you research the legal limits of what you can do in the place and at the time you are planning to do it.

The growth in interest and concern about the environment by the UK public is not limited to responses to opinion polls. Although the popularity of the School Strike for Climate movement expanded dramatically after the actions of Greta Thunberg in 2018, the first School Strike for Climate was in the UK in 2010, with a series of school walkouts linked to the various climate camps which ran from 2006 to 2011. In the February 2019 walkouts, an estimated 15,000 people took part.

A second wave of groups developed in the late 1960s and 1970s, with Friends of the Earth being founded by ex–Sierra Club member David Ross Brower in 1969, and Greenpeace starting as the "Don't Make a Wave Committee" in 1971. Both now operate as international networks of groups and campaigns of a range of issues, from promoting human rights, biodiversity, and peace to resisting nuclear power and hyper-consumption. Former Greenpeace president Patrick Moore departed Greenpeace in the 1980s as he felt the organisation had lost its way and become too confrontational.

QUOTATION

"By the mid-1980s, the environmental movement had abandoned science and logic in favor of emotion and sensationalism. I became aware of the emerging concept of sustainable development: balancing environmental, social and economic priorities. Converted to the idea that win-win solutions could be found by bringing all interests together, I made the move from confrontation to consensus."

Moore, P., 2005, "The Environmental Movement: Greens Have Lost Their Way," *Miami Herald*, 28 January 2005

In the 1980s and 1990s, a new wave of environmental groups started to emerge, which espoused more radical views than their predecessors. Manes called this "a new kind of environmental activism: iconoclastic, uncompromising, discontented with traditional conservation policy,"[23] and went on to say that the new generation of groups were less concerned with breaking the criminal law to get their point heard.

EarthFirst!, which, in stark contrast to Moore, regarded Greenpeace as being too "lethargic, compromising, and increasingly corporate," came into existence at the start of the 1980s. The organisation was inspired by a combination Arne Næss's "deep ecology" philosophical standpoint (see Chapter 2), Rachel Carson's 1962 *Silent Spring*, and the fictitious exploits of Edward Abbey's 1975 *The Monkey Wrench Gang* (which was also the source of "monkeywrenching" as a term to describe sabotage). By the mid-1980s, the group had a more radical, "direct action" approach to protest but moved to a more mainstream position in the 1990s.

Many of the more radical groups, whilst not directly advocating the use of violence, were prepared to accept it as a part of their mission. The Sea Shepherd Conservation Society, founded in 1981 by ex-Greenpeace member Paul Watson, has said that they will take action where necessary to prevent illegal activities (particularly whaling). Sea Shepherd is currently banned by a 2012 US Court of Appeal injunction from getting within 500 yards of any Japanese whaling ships, which demonstrates the impact the group was having on what they argued was illegal whaling.

CASE

Institute of Cetacean Research and Kyodo Senpaku Kaisha Ltd v Sea Shepherd Conservation Society and Paul Watson, No. 12–35266 DC No. 2:11-cv-02043-RAJ

"Defendants Sea Shepherd Conservation Society and Paul Watson, and any party acting in concert with them (collectively 'defendants'), are enjoined from physically attacking any vessel engaged by Plaintiffs the Institute of Cetacean Research, Kyodo Senpaku Kaisha, Ltd., Tomoyuki Ogawa or Toshiyuki Miura in the Southern Ocean or any person on any such vessel (collectively 'plaintiffs'), or from navigating in a manner that is likely to endanger the safe navigation of any such vessel. In no event shall defendants approach plaintiffs any closer than 500 yards when defendants are navigating on the open sea."

The Institute of Cetacean Research (ICR) is a Japanese research centre which, until 2020, killed whales for research purposes and sold "whale research by products" to Kyodo Senpaku Kaisha Ltd, which then sold them. The International Court of Justice ruled in 2014 (Whaling in the Antarctic (*Australia v. Japan: New Zealand intervening*) Judgment, ICJ Reports 2014, p. 226) that the ICR's programme was not scientific and thus amounted to illegal whaling. The ICR was ordered to cease killing whales.

The ultimate expression of willingness to use force to achieve environmental ends is likely to the be the Earth Liberation Front (ELF). Founded in 1992 in Brighton as a spiritual descendent of the Animal Liberation Front but an actual splinter of EarthFirst!, the ELF has no members or leadership, and actions are just claimed "on behalf of the ELF" by those who carry them out. Many of the activities carried out by the ELF are illegal, and in the United States, the group has been designated as being a domestic terrorism threat. Many arson attacks have been attributed the ELF over the years, as well as the destruction of several vehicles and apparatus used in the construction and logging industries.

Peaceful direct action for environmental issues is championed by the Extinction Rebellion (XR) movement. XR was launched by Roger Hallam and his colleagues from the Rising Up! NGO in October 2018, with around 1,500 people engaging in civil disobedience in Parliament Square, London. The group was designed from the outset to be a *holacracy*, or a network of self-organising teams, along the lines of the ELF. In its first three years, XR has grown to 1,178 local groups in 84 countries, although the current membership of XR is unknown, even to organisers.

The decentralised nature of both the ELF and XR means that both organisations run an inherent risk that events and attacks which they would not support can be attributed to them.

As Thoreau alluded to in the mid-19th century, civil disobedience and protest bring with them an increased risk to the participants. Martin Luther King made the point that "riot is the language of the unheard"[24] – in other words, people who are content with their inclusion and representation tend not to engage in violent protests or riots.

There can be a natural progression from ideas, concepts, and groups being considered "radical" or "extreme" to being more mainstream – no political parties at all had an environmental policy stream in the 19th century, but all do today, for example. One downside with this increasing ability for the radical side of environmental movements to garner screen time was set out by the Indian historian and environmentalist Ramachandra Guha. Guha makes the point that marginal voices within environmentalists are often ignored in favour of more headline-grabbing radicals, and that this can be detrimental as "only radicals are heard."[25]

Governments, too, have brought in measures to curb what they consider to be the more radical side of the environmental movement.

In the UK, the Police, Crime, Sentencing, and Courts Act 2022[26] (PCSCA) is a wide-ranging piece of legislation, running to 209 sections and 21 schedules. There are several provisions which will have an impact on the ability of protest groups to carry out what were previously legal activities.

For example, under the Public Order Act 1986,[27] conditions could be placed on a protest march if the senior police officer reasonably believed "it may result in serious public disorder, serious damage to property or serious disruption to the life of the community" (S12(1)(a)). The revisions to Section 12 introduced by the PSCSA expand this remit dramatically.

LEGISLATION

(aa) In the case of a procession in England and Wales, the noise generated by persons taking part in the procession may result in serious disruption to the activities of an organisation which are carried on in the vicinity of the procession,

(ab) In the case of a procession in England and Wales –

(i) the noise generated by persons taking part in the procession may have a relevant impact on persons in the vicinity of the procession, and

(ii) that impact may be significant

Section 12(1), Public Order Act 1986, as amended by PCSCA

If the noise from a protest may seriously disrupt the activities of a nearby organisation (say, for example, the organisation at which the protest is directed), it can be subjected to additional conditions, including being quiet. The question of "impact" is expanded later in the Act, and it is clearly designed to be able to stop the type of mass-sit-in event practised by XR. The Act also includes a new provision to apply the same standards to one-person protests.

It is possible that in the coming months, there will be a judicial review launched against these provisions, as some have argued they come very close to breaching the terms of the Human Rights Act 1988. The government has also announced that it intends to revise or replace the Human Rights Act and make it harder for judicial review cases to be brought.

CRITIQUING THE LAW

Should the right to protest about environmental issues be curtailed to avoid disrupting other people, or is a protest which causes no disruption not a protest?

SUMMARY

- We have traced the process of lawmaking and the opportunities which exist, or can be taken, to influence that policy.
- Taken note of the different jurisdictions in operation in the British Isles that mean that care needs to be taken when applying legal provisions.
- Followed the process whereby an initially minor issue of environmental concern may develop into a full-blown policy and legislative provision.
- Seen the influencers on policy – from voting, or standing in election, to protest, each has different rules and likelihood of success, whether they are in the short-, medium-, or long-term.
- Seen the possible pitfalls of the "tyranny of the majority" when the majority is given the power to act without consequences.

Part 3 of the book, which follows, focuses on sustainability, covering the UN SDGs in Chapter 5 and applying the rules of sustainability to the UK's energy policy in Chapter 6.

SAMPLE PROBLEM QUESTION

Kate is a teacher who wishes to protest about the decision by the academy she works with to cut down a number of mature trees around the playing field so that the land can be sold off to a developer.

She decides to chain herself to one of the trees and advertises this on social media, calling for others to join her in the protest.

Around 50 more people turn up. Some are carrying drums, some are carrying banners, and some build and occupy platforms in the trees. Many of the protestors walk up and down the street next to the trees, playing music and shouting slogans.

Which of these activities is likely to contravene Sections 11–14 of the Public Order Act 1986 as amended by PCSCA?

1. Outline the key provisions on the relevant sections of the Act (Sections 11–13 concern public processions, and Section 14 concerns public assemblies).
2. Identify the different actions from the question that you will need to focus on – Kate's actions and the actions of the different types of protestors – using the IRAC method (issue, rule, application, conclusion).
3. Conclude.

Further Reading

Adams, C.F., 1851, *The Works of John Adams*, Vol. V, Boston, MA: Charles C Little & James Brown

Ayeb-Karlsson, S., 2020, No Power without Knowledge: A Discursive Subjectivities Approach to Investigate Climate-Induced (Im)mobility and Wellbeing, *Social Sciences*, 9(6), 103,

Banfield, E.C., 1961, *Political Influence: A New Theory of Urban Politics*, New York: The Free Press of Glencoe/Crowell-Collier Publishing Co

Barritt, E., 2020, *The Foundations of the Aarhus Convention: Environmental Democracy, Rights and Stewardship*, London: Hart Publishing

Bourdieu, P., 1991, *Language & Symbolic Power*, Cambridge, MA: Harvard University Press

DiZoglio, D.A., 2022, *The Value of Political Capital*, 2nd ed., Lowell, MA: Loom Press

Graff-Zivin, J., & Krumholz, S., 2018, *Environmental Policy-Making; Theory & Practice*, Oxford: Rockefeller Foundation Economic Council on Planetary Health

Manes, C., 1990, *Green Rage: Radical Environmentalism and the Unmaking of Civilization*, Boston, MA: Little, Brown and Co

Nowotny, H., 1980, The Role of The Experts in Developing Public Policy: The Australian Debate on Nuclear Power, *Science, Technology & Human Values*, 5(2), 14

Thoreau, H.D., 1854, *Walden: Or Life in the Woods*, Boston, MA: Ticknor & Fields

Notes

1 27 Henry VII c. 26
2 34 and 35 Henry VIII c. 26
3 6 Ann c. 11
4 1707 c. 7
5 39 and 40 Geo. 3 c. 67
6 40 Geo. 3 c. 38
7 10 and 11 Geo. 5 c. 67
8 13 Geo. 5 c. 1
9 Nowotny, H., 1980, The Role of the Experts in Developing Public Policy: The Australian Debate on Nuclear Power, *Science, Technology & Human Values*, 5(2), 14
10 Dunn, M., 2020, Evaluating the Impact of the Documentary Blue Planet II on Viewers' Plastic Consumption Behaviors, *Conservation Science and Practice*, 2(10)
11 Bourdieu, P., 1991, *Language & Symbolic Power*, Cambridge, MA: Harvard University Press
12 The phrase appears variously as "Working to a target of eliminating avoidable plastic waste by end of 2042" (p29); "Work towards eliminating all avoidable waste by 2050 and waste by end of 2042" (p83); and "Achieving zero avoidable plastic waste by end of 2042" (p86)
13 PB 14552
14 Turner, C., & Foster, S., 2019, *Unlocking Constitutional and Administrative Law*, 4th ed., London: Routledge
15 c. 30
16 SI 2020/971
17 2014 c. 4
18 Adams, C.F., 1851, *The Works of John Adams*, Vol. V, Boston, MA: Charles C Little & James Brown, p. 490
19 Bacon, F., 1597/1996, *Meditationes Sacrae and Human Philosophy*, Whitefish, MT: Kessinger Publishing Company
20 Ayeb-Karlsson, S., 2020, No Power without Knowledge: A Discursive Subjectivities Approach to Investigate Climate-Induced (Im)mobility and Wellbeing, *Social Sciences*, 9(6), 103, p. 104
21 Freedom of Information Act 1966 5 USC §552

22 Directive 90/313/EEC of 7th June 1990 on the Freedom of Access to Information on the Environment
23 Manes, C., 1990, *Green Rage: Radical Environmentalism and the Unmaking of Civilization*, Boston, MA: Little, Brown and Co
24 King, M.L., 1968, The Other America, Speech Given at Grosse Pointe High School, *Grosse Point*, Michigan, 14 March 1968
25 Ramachandra Guha, in Gadjil, G., 2008, *Ramachandra Guha: The Trouble with Radical Environmentalists*, Pune: Infochange India
26 c. 32
27 c. 64

5

United Nations Sustainable Development Goals

This section of the book focuses on sustainable development. Half a century ago, the UN Conference on the Human Environment (UNCHE) in Sweden formally recognised that there was a link between economic development and environmental protection and declared that "[t]he protection and improvement of the human environment is a major issue which affects the well-being of peoples and economic development throughout the world"[1]

However, despite this watershed acknowledgement, the immediate impact was fairly non-existent. Many of the subsequent economic documents (e.g. the 1984 UN Resolution on the Charter of Economic Rights and Duties of States (A/RES/39/163)) took little account of the potential environmental impact of development. Similarly, many of the 1980s strategies for environmental protection did not take account of development.

It was not until the publication of the World Commission on Environment and Development Report (also referred to as "Our Common Future" or "The Brundtland Report") in 1987 that the two elements were effectively fused together. The WCED Report pointed to the need to ensure "sustainable development" to provide mechanisms to increase international cooperation.

Definition

Sustainable Development is:

> "Development that meets the needs of the present without compromising the ability of future generations to meet their own needs."
>
> Report of the World Commission on Environment and Development:
> Our Common Future, Part IV, Conclusion

The definition contains within it two key concepts:

- The concept of "needs," in particular, the essential needs of the world's poor, to which overriding priority should be given.
- The idea of limitations imposed by the state of technology and social organization on the environment's ability to meet present and future needs.

DOI: 10.4324/9781003137214-5

It is crucial to recognise that sustainable development is not simply an environmental approach – the environmental aspect is only one of the three pillars of sustainable development, the others being social and economic. In order for development to be truly sustainable, therefore, it must find a way to include all three pillars.

This chapter will allow you to take an in-depth look at the 17 UN SDGs, which we touched on in Chapter 3, and consider the links they have with other areas of environmental law.

The SDGs do not mark the first attempt of the United Nations to put in place goals for the improvement of environmental, social, and other standards. That accolade goes to the Millennium Development Goals, which were introduced in 2000 and ran to 2015.

AIMS AND OBJECTIVES

After reading this chapter, you should be able to:

- Identify the general parameters of the Sustainable Development Goals.
- Describe the practical application of the Sustainable Development Goals.
- Contrast the positive and negative aspects of the Sustainable Development Goals.

5.1 Millennium Development Goals

The Millennium Development Goals were focused on three areas: healthcare and education (categorised as "human capital"); "infrastructure," which covered access to water, environment, and sustainable farming; and "human rights," which covered a range of basic rights. There was a considerable overlap between the individual goals, which is to be expected. Improving maternal health (MDG 5), for example, has clear links with reducing child mortality (MDG 4).

- MDG 1 – Eradicate Extreme Poverty and Hunger
- MDG 2 – Achieve Universal Primary Education
- MDG 3 – Promote Gender Equality and Empower Women
- MDG 4 – Reduce Child Mortality
- MDG 5 – Improve Maternal Health
- MDG 6 – Combat HIV/ADIS and Other Diseases
- MDG 7 – Ensure Environmental Sustainability
- MDG 8 – Global Partnership for Development

MDG 7 is the most pertinent from an environmental perspective, and it contained within it four targets.

Millennium Goal 7 Targets

Target 7.1: Integrate the principles of sustainable development into country policies and programmes and reverse the loss of environmental resources.

Target 7.2: Reduce biodiversity loss, achieving, by 2010, a significant reduction in the rate of loss.

Target 7.3: Halve, by 2015, the proportion of the population without sustainable access to safe drinking water and basic sanitation.

Target 7.4: Achieve, by 2020, a significant improvement in the lives of at least 100 million slum dwellers.

The targets were largely not specific or precise, but they are a noteworthy attempt to improve the lives of those predominantly in the developing world, or in poorer areas of the developed world, allowing clear links to be drawn to the ideas of environmental and climate justice discussed in Chapter 2. The general nature of the goals was a deliberate move on the part of the UN. Rather than having a rigid standard which would be equally applicable in all countries, the generalist approach allowed for flexibility and for the most suitable application, taking into consideration the resources of a particular state.

The strength of the MDGs also proved to be something of a weakness, however, as the lack of many hard targets meant that states were able to pay lip service to the goals. There were also criticisms that poorer countries were not sufficiently involved in the drafting of the MDGs, which focused more on what the richer countries were doing, rather than on the extent to which the situation in poorer states was improving.

The 17 Sustainable Development Goals build on the 8 Millennium Development Goals, the targets for which were mostly unmet. The UN published an annual SDG report, and the 2022 report points out that whilst the world is over two-thirds of the way through the goal period for most of the SDGs (2000–2030), there are still enormous gaps in the level of reporting. This, of course, means that judging the relative successes of the goals individually or together is not easy.

5.2 SDG 1: No Poverty

It is widely understood that poverty can be both a cause and effect of environmental issues. As we saw in Chapter 2, the impact of global issues (e.g. climate change) will have greater impact on poorer communities than it does on richer countries. This may be because of fragile infrastructure or simple geography. Living in poverty also raises difficult scenarios for individuals and communities.

Whilst all agree that poverty is an issue which needs to be tackled, there will, of course, be different levels of income which lead to poverty, depending upon where you live. SDG 1 tackles this disparity by aligning to the World Bank's level of "extreme poverty," which is defined as living on less than US$1.90 per person per day.

CRITIQUING THE LAW

Is it morally acceptable for a person to kill a protected or endangered species of animal in order to get money to alleviate their family's poverty?

Should we take an ecocentric or anthropocentric (see Chapter 2) approach in this situation?

Should it be legally acceptable?

There is a double-edged sword here, however. The UN Environment Programme, among many others, has identified that the poorer a community or state is, the less it is able to spend to withstand the impacts of climate change, such as extreme weather or rising sea levels. Similarly, the poorer a community, the less it is able to spend on the cleaner technologies which would alleviate some of those impacts. Reducing the numbers of people in poverty will allow for a faster adoption of lower-polluting technologies.

Target 1.5   By 2030, build the resilience of the poor and those in vulnerable situations and reduce their exposure and vulnerability to climate-related extreme events and other economic, social, and environmental shocks and disasters.

The wealthier nations and the institutions which they support have a role to play here, of course. The International Monetary Fund (IMF) and World Bank launched the Heavily Indebted Poor Countries (HIPC) initiative in 1996. The purpose of HIPC was to try to make sure that the debts which these states owed to wealthier states were kept at manageable levels. Other debt-relief programmes have existed for some while, but HIPC was linked to the SDGs in 2005 and supplemented by the Multilateral Debt Relief Initiative (MDRI). MDRI allows for total reduction of eligible debts, but it does require that seven stringent criteria are met.

QUOTATION

"To be considered for HIPC Initiative assistance, a country must fulfill the following four conditions:

1) Be eligible to borrow from the World Bank's International Development Agency, which provides interest-free loans and grants to the world's poorest countries, and from the IMF's Poverty Reduction and Growth Trust, which provides loans to low-income countries at subsidized rates;

2) Face an unsustainable debt burden that cannot be addressed through traditional debt relief mechanisms;

3) Have established a track record of reform and sound policies through IMF- and World Bank – supported programs; and

4) Have developed a Poverty Reduction Strategy Paper (PRSP) through a broad-based participatory process in the country.

. . .

In order to receive full and irrevocable reduction in debt available under the HIPC Initiative, a country must

1) Establish a further track record of good performance under programs supported by loans from the IMF and the World Bank;

2) Implement satisfactorily key reforms agreed at the decision point; and

3) Adopt and implement its PRSP for at least one year.

Once a country has met these criteria, it can reach its completion point, which allows it to receive the full debt relief committed at the decision point.

IMF, 2021, Debt Relief Under the Heavily Indebted Poor Countries (HIPC) Initiative, International Monetary Fund, www.imf.org

Thirty-seven countries have so far been declared eligible for HIPC relief. Thirty-one are in Africa, five in Central and South America, and one in the Middle East.

The 2022 Sustainable Development Goals Report, published by the UN, notes the fragility of measures intended to meet SDG 1. The combined impact of the COVID-19 pandemic globally from 2020 to 2022 as well as regional and global impact of the Russian invasion of Ukraine in 2022 have led to a revised prediction of the number of people living in extreme poverty from 581 million to around 660 million.

5.3 SDG 2: No Hunger

Many of the SDGs overlap, and SDG 2 is no exception, as there is a clear link between poverty and hunger – richer people tend to go less hungry than poorer people.

There are many issues that contribute to hunger and the unequal distribution of food – climate, infrastructure, disease, war, and so on. The period 2019–2021 has seen both the COVID pandemic and the war in Ukraine. It also saw a rise in the number of people classed by the UN Food and Agriculture Organization (FAO) as facing hunger by 146 million. The FAO's prediction (in a world where 650 million people are classified as obese) is that 670 million people will be undernourished by 2030.

Unsurprisingly, the regions with the highest and lowest proportions of hunger (Africa is highest at around 20 per cent, and the United States is lowest at about 2 per cent) are reversed when looking at obesity rates (Africa is lowest at about 12 per cent, and the United States is highest at around 40 per cent). In addition to having the highest obesity rate in the world, the US Food and Drug Administration estimates that 30–40 per cent of all food in the United States is wasted. Obesity is linked to SDG 3 (good health and well-being), most closely Target 3.4.1, which aims to reduce death from non-communicable diseases, such as cardiovascular disease and other diseases linked to obesity. The food waste issues link to SDG 12 (responsible consumption and production), which aims to reduce food waste by half (Target 12.3).

QUOTATION

"A vast majority of the world's population lives in countries sourcing nearly all their staple crop imports from partners who deplete groundwater to produce these crops, highlighting risks for global food and water security."

Dalin, C., et al., "Groundwater depletion embedded in international food trade," *Nature*, 2017; 543(7647): 700–704

There is also a distinction in how food is grown globally. The FAO estimates that over 80 per cent of farms globally are small farms (those under 2 hectares) and produce around one-third of the world's food. By extension, therefore, 20 per cent of larger farms produce two-thirds of the world's food. Both of these approaches bring associated risks.

Small farmers are more likely to be financially unstable, more susceptible to global fluctuations in food prices, and at increased risk from any local climate issues. For example, in China, small farms contribute up to 80 per cent of the country's domestically produced food, but their size would make them more vulnerable to events such as the 2022 heatwave and associated drought.

Larger farms are more likely to be able to give over larger areas to monoculture – the wheat fields of Ukraine, Canada, and the United States are good examples of this. Perversely, their size makes them more vulnerable to crop-specific diseases and infestations of pests, thus requiring greater use of herbicides and pesticides.

People in richer countries buying out-of-season food imported from poorer countries generate additional income for poorer countries, but also additional road, rail, and air miles, thus contributing to climate change.

Buying only locally produced, seasonal products reduces consumer choice, reduces emissions, and reduces income for poorer countries.

Consider how a balance can be struck between these two competing positions.

5.4 SDG 3: Good Health and Well-Being

This SDG has clear links to other environmental policies, as it is difficult to achieve health and well-being among a population living in areas with high levels of air, soil, and water pollution.

There are much wider health-related aspects that are covered by the SDG, from improving maternal and child mortality rates (Targets 3.1 and 3.2) to reducing deaths from communicable and non-communicable diseases (Targets 3.3 and 3.4), reducing substance abuse and road traffic accidents (Targets 3.5 and 3.6), improving access to sexual healthcare and universal healthcare coverage (Targets 3.7 and 3.8), and more policy-related issues, such as reducing tobacco use, improving vaccine research, increasing health financing and recruitment, and strengthening capacity to deal with global health crises (Targets 3.a, 3.b, 3.c, and 3.d).

For the purpose of this section, we will focus on Target 3.9, which is the area most closely linked to environmental quality.

Target 3.9   By 2030, substantially reduce the number of deaths and illnesses from hazardous chemicals and air, water and soil pollution and contamination.

Indicators

3.9.1:   Mortality rate attributed to household and ambient air pollution.
3.9.2:   Mortality rate attributed to unsafe water, unsafe sanitation, and lack of hygiene (exposure to unsafe Water, Sanitation and Hygiene for All services).
3.9.3:   Mortality rate attributed to unintentional poisoning.

Household and ambient air pollution is a significant cause of death in many parts of the world and is estimated to kill around 7 million people prematurely each year. The causes of each are slightly different but linked. In Chapter 9 we will focus in much more detail on issues linked to air pollution, but in short, most problematic indoor air pollution is caused by the use of inefficient stoves and pollution fuel sources, such as dried animal dung and other biomass, or coal. The use of animal dung is a particular problem in areas like rural sub-Saharan Africa, which has suffered considerable deforestation, meaning, that wood is no longer a viable fuel source. By burning animal dung, people are not only forced to live with sub-optimal indoor air quality but are also losing a useful source of fertiliser for crop production.

The solutions to this are conceptually straightforward – replace the cooking methods for the 2.4 billion people who currently use open fires with non-pollution, or at least less-polluting, alternatives. Solar power, for example, would be a useful alternative in off-grid rural communities in areas like sub-Saharan Africa which benefit from relatively low cloud cover and high levels of sunshine.

Outdoor air pollution is largely caused by the burning of fossil fuels by industrial processes or in vehicles or other furnaces. This, as has been widely discussed, is a significant cause of climate change which, in turn, contributes to deforestation, and thus the increased need to use unsuitable fuels in indoor situations.

5.5 SDG 4: Quality Education

Education is seen as being an essential tool for communicating the message of sustainable development. The UN General Assembly confirmed the importance of education for sustainable development (ESD) as the "enabler" of all the other SDGs in 2017.[2]

The SDG does not focus solely on ESD, however. The other targets are all strongly liked to SDG 5 (gender equality) and emphasise the importance of education in the road to all.

Target 4.1: By 2030, ensure that all girls and boys complete free, equitable and quality primary and secondary education leading to relevant and effective learning outcomes.

Target 4.2: By 2030, ensure that all girls and boys have access to quality early childhood development, care and pre-primary education so that they are ready for primary education.

Target 4.3: By 2030, ensure equal access for all women and men to affordable and quality technical, vocational, and tertiary education, including university.

Target 4.4: By 2030, substantially increase the number of youth and adults who have relevant skills, including technical and vocational skills, for employment, decent jobs, and entrepreneurship.

Target 4.5: By 2030, eliminate gender disparities in education and ensure equal access to all levels of education and vocational training for the vulnerable, including persons with disabilities, indigenous peoples and children in vulnerable situations.

Target 4.6: By 2030, ensure that all youth and a substantial proportion of adults, both men and women, achieve literacy and numeracy.

Target 4.a: Build and upgrade education facilities that are child, disability, and gender sensitive and provide safe, non-violent, inclusive, and effective learning environments for all.

Target 4.b: By 2020, substantially expand globally the number of scholarships available to developing countries, in particular least developed countries, small island developing States and African countries, for enrolment in higher education, including vocational training and information and communications technology, technical, engineering, and scientific programmes, in developed countries and other developing countries.

Target 4.c: By 2030, substantially increase the supply of qualified teachers, including through international cooperation for teacher training in developing countries, especially least developed countries and small island developing States.

Whilst some of these targets create only fairly broad targets (e.g. "substantially increase . . ."), several of them are absolute in nature and require states to work towards completeness in terms of access to education and training at all levels. Currently, estimates vary for the numbers of children without access to education and the numbers of illiterate adults, but around 70 million primary school–age children are not attending school, and 700 million adults are illiterate.

The UN created three frameworks specifically to advance the ESD message, starting with the United Nations Decade of Education for Sustainable Development (2005–2014), followed by the Global Action Programme (GAP) on ESD (2015–2019), and now the UNESCO "ESD for 2030" roadmap.

Target 4.7   By 2030, ensure that all learners acquire the knowledge and skills needed to promote sustainable development, including, among others, through education for sustainable development and sustainable lifestyles, human rights, gender equality, promotion of a culture of peace and non-violence, global citizenship and appreciation of cultural diversity and of culture's contribution to sustainable development.

Target 4.7 speaks of "all learners," and of course, even if the other targets are achieved and all have access to education, not all will choose to access it at all levels. ESD has four strands:

Pedagogy and Learning Environment. It is intended that ESD become an integral part of the way that learning is designed, from the buildings to the levels of interactivity.

Societal Transformation. There is little point in learning about sustainable development purely as an abstract, theoretical notion. The learning needs to be linked to opportunities to make real changes to societies.

Learning Outcomes. The elements of learning which are assessed should be assessed on the basis of whether they allow for learners to achieve societal changes.

Learning Content. ESD should not be the unique purview of environment-related sources but needs to be embedded into all areas of teaching and learning.

There are obvious links to poverty here, as the poorer a country is, then the greater the pressure will be on children to work rather than study. Often, there is a significant gender disparity here as well.

5.6 SDG 5: Gender Equality

This SDG, like SDG 4, is one of the key goals which underpin all the others. The UN's summary of progress on this SDG to date does not make encouraging reading, however, as it says that the world is "not on track" to achieve gender equality by 2030. Worse still, the report says that the COVID pandemic has pushed things "further off track."[3]

From an environmental perspective, it is vital to understand the links that exist between gender inequality and environmental degradation. It is a two-way relationship, in that environmental degradation can be both a cause and a result of high levels of inequality.

Something as simple as water collection, for example, can have massive impacts. The UNEP estimated that three-quarters of the water which has to be collected off-premises (e.g. from a communal well) is collected by women, and in sub-Saharan Africa alone, 40 trillion working hours a year are lost to the women collecting the water. Improving the water infrastructure, therefore, would increase the amount of time which women had to become economically active and more financially equal.

Many countries have a patriarchal inheritance system, whereby land is passed from father to eldest son, rather than eldest child. This system denies women the opportunity to own land, particularly agricultural land, and the UN Development Programme (UNDP) says that women are more likely than men to share their knowledge and understanding of community well-being and are also more willing to adapt their practices to take account of environmental changes. Considerable research over the past decade or so has shown that women are more likely to be concerned about climate change and make more environmentally aware choices about energy use.

Women, despite being the majority of the world's population, are severely under-represented in national assemblies and parliaments, making up just over a quarter of representatives. This means that parliaments are less likely to follow a pro-environmental and pro-sustainability agenda.

QUOTATION

"Our results clearly show that nation-states with a greater proportion of women in national Parliament, controlling for other factors, typically are more prone to environmental treaty ratification than other nations.

[The reasons include] the fact that women have more pro-environmental values, are more risk averse, are more likely to participate in social movements, typically suffer disproportionately form environmental degradation, and sexism and environmental degradation can be mutually reinforcing processes."

Norgaard, K., and York, R., 2005, "Gender Equality and State Environmentalism," *Gender & Society*, (19)4, Aug 2005, 506–522, p519

Whilst the vast majority of the targets in SDG 5 are not directly linked to environmental issues, it is clear that any action taken to reduce gender inequality will allow for better decisions to be taken to benefit the environment.

5.7 SDG 6: Clean Water and Sanitation

Almost three-quarters of the planetary surface is covered by water, and SDG 6 combines with SDG 14 (life below water) to provide a set of targets designed to protect our water.

Within SDG 6 there are eight targets, and unlike some of the other SDGs, these all clearly link to environmental standards. The specifics of water pollution will be covered in depth in Chapter 10.

Target 6.1: By 2030, achieve universal and equitable access to safe and affordable drinking water for all. Currently, almost 2 billion people lack access to clean drinking water. This is down by almost half since 2000.

Target 6.2: By 2030, achieve access to adequate and equitable sanitation and hygiene for all and end open defecation, paying special attention to the needs of women and girls and those in vulnerable situations. The US centre for Disease Control say that over 3.5 billion people currently lack this.

Target 6.3: By 2030, improve water quality by reducing pollution, eliminating dumping, and minimizing release of hazardous chemicals and materials, halving the proportion of untreated wastewater, and substantially increasing recycling and safe reuse globally. Around 80% of wastewater is currently discharged untreated into the sea. [Recent events in the UK have revealed loopholes in legislation which allow water companies to release untreated sewerage into rivers and the sea; this will be discussed in more depth in Chapter 9.]

Target 6.4: By 2030, substantially increase water-use efficiency across all sectors and ensure sustainable withdrawals and supply of fresh water to address water scarcity and substantially reduce the number of people suffering from water scarcity.

Target 6.5: By 2030, implement integrated water resources management at all levels, including through transboundary cooperation as appropriate.

Target 6.6: By 2020, protect and restore water-related ecosystems, including mountains, forests, wetlands, rivers, aquifers, and lakes.

Target 6.a: By 2030, expand international cooperation and capacity-building support to developing countries in water- and sanitation-related activities and programmes, including water harvesting, desalination, water efficiency, wastewater treatment, recycling, and reuse technologies.

Target 6.b: Support and strengthen the participation of local communities in improving water and sanitation management.

All bar one of the targets has a 2030 deadline, but the deadline for Target 6.6 has already passed. As with many of the other targets, under-reporting has meant that a proper assessment is impossible, but even within the 97 states which have reported, only 60 per cent of the assessed water was in a "good condition."

Water has links to SDG 3 (good health and well-being), as contaminated drinking water is a cause of many communicable diseases, such as cholera (discussed in Chapter 1), typhoid, and dysentery, which between them kill around a million people a year. As with several of the other SDGs, the UN warns that despite good progress having been made early on, unless progress quadruples, the target will be missed, and "billions of people will lack access to these basic services."[4]

ACTIVITY

There is an inherent inequality present in the use of water, illustrated by the fact that in the UK the infrastructure is designed so that water used for washing and sanitation is of the same quality as drinking water, whereas 2 billion people lack access to clean drinking water.

What mechanisms could be used to improve achievement of SDG 6.1?

5.8 SDG 7: Affordable and Clean Energy

The links between energy policy and sustainable development in the UK are covered in more depth in Chapter 6.

SDG 7 focuses both on the generation and use of energy, as energy efficiency and increased use of renewable sources are both vital to avoid the worst effects of climate change. In addition, energy needs to be affordable and reliable; otherwise, the impact of its use will be greatly reduced.

With the exception of Target 7.1, none of the targets in SDG 7 are precise and quantifiable. Even so, the UN raises both the COVID pandemic and the war in Ukraine as factors impacting on the likelihood of achieving the goals.

Target 7.1: By 2030, ensure universal access to affordable, reliable, and modern energy services. Over 700 million people have no access to electric light and, as we saw earlier, 2.4 billion are using potentially lethal open fires for cooking. The UN recognises that progress has been good, but still falls short of the 2030 deadline without a doubling of the rate of increase in the next few years.

Target 7.2: By 2030, increase substantially the share of renewable energy in the global energy mix. Globally, renewable energy accounted for 17.7% of total global energy production in 2019 (but 26% of electricity generation).

Target 7.3: By 2030, double the global rate of improvement in energy efficiency.

Target 7.a: By 2030, enhance international cooperation to facilitate access to clean energy research and technology, including renewable energy, energy efficiency, and advanced and cleaner fossil-fuel technology, and promote investment in energy infrastructure and clean energy technology.

One good example of this was the announcement in 2020 of the "Viking Link" – a 760-kilometre high-voltage cable to be laid between Revsing in Denmark and Lincolnshire to provide zero-emissions electricity to the UK. The electricity provided via the Viking Link will equate to around 1.3 per cent of the UK's current electricity usage.

Target 7.b: By 2030, expand infrastructure and upgrade technology for supplying modern and sustainable energy services for all in developing countries, in particular least developed countries, small island developing States, and land-locked developing countries, in accordance with their respective programmes of support.

CRITIQUING THE LAW

Assess whether it is better from a global climate perspective to focus on turning the existing energy sector in the developed world into a zero-carbon system as opposed to focusing on creating a zero-carbon infrastructure in the developing world.

5.9 SDG 8: Decent Work and Economic Growth

This is one of the hardest SDGs to link *directly* to environmental benefit, but it is a combination of economic growth, social growth, and environmental protection which forms the basis of sustainable development, so indirect links are relatively straightforward.

The majority of the targets focus on growth, improved rights, and access to employment, and so it is left to Targets 8.4 and 8.9 to take the lead with the green agenda.

Target 8.4: Improve progressively, through 2030, global resource efficiency in consumption and production and endeavour to decouple economic growth from environmental degradation, in accordance with the 10-Year Framework of Programmes on Sustainable Consumption and Production, with developed countries taking the lead.

Target 8.9:   By 2030, devise and implement policies to promote sustainable tourism that creates jobs and promotes local culture and products.

The argument goes that the damage caused by natural disasters is very expensive to rectify, and so the better and more efficient our resource use, the more resilient we will become. As with the other SDGs, there is an overlap here – perhaps more so than with any other SDG, as the more people are in employment, the higher the individual and state revenues will become, and the more easily affordable the other goals will be.

Sustainable tourism is predicted to become a growth industry over the next few decades, although it is unlikely that it will replace "traditional" tourism in the short- or medium-term. Along with other forms of economic growth, however, the impact of the COVID-19 pandemic has been significant and mollified many of the more bullish predictions for growth.

Definition

Sustainable tourism should:

1. Make optimal use of environmental resources that constitute a key element in tourism development, maintaining essential ecological processes and helping to conserve natural resources and biodiversity.
2. Respect the socio-cultural authenticity of host communities, conserve their built and living cultural heritage and traditional values, and contribute to inter-cultural under-standing and tolerance.
3. Ensure viable, long-term economic operations, providing socio-economic benefits to all stakeholders that are fairly distributed, including stable employment and income-earning opportunities and social services to host communities, and contributing to poverty alleviation.

UNEP/WTO, 2005, "Making Tourism More Sustainable,"
United Nations Environmental Programme/World Tourism
Organisation, https://wedocs.unep.org/20.500.11822/8741, p11

Interestingly, the 2022 SDG Report published by the UN makes no mention at all of *sustainable tourism*, which underlines the likely impact of the pandemic on tourism as a whole.

Increasing poverty levels as a result of the pandemic are predicted to lead to an increase of 10 per cent by the end of 2022 in the numbers of children engaged in child labour compared to 2016. This clearly demonstrates the overlap between the SDGs, as in addition to being covered by SDG 8, this issue relates to elements of SDG 1 (no poverty), SDG 3 (good health and well-being), SDG 4 (quality education), SDG 9 (industry, innovation, and infrastructure), and SDG 11 sustainable cities and communities).

5.10 SDG 9: Industry, Innovation, and Infrastructure

This SDG has a much clearer link to sustainability than SDG 8, and it seeks to promote sustainable industrialisation and infrastructure, whether that involves the development of new industries or the retrofitting of existing ones.

Although almost all industrial sectors took a financial hit during the pandemic, the higher-technology industries rebounded more quickly, and this is touted as illustrating the importance of technological innovation for promoting sustainable development. This has also exacerbated regional differences, as only about one-fifth of manufacturing industries in Africa fall into the "medium- or high-technology" category, whereas nearly half of them do in Europe and North America.

One of the indicators aims to reduce this inequality, although the associated indicator does not give any specific goals to be achieved.

Target 9.a: Facilitate sustainable and resilient infrastructure development in developing countries through enhanced financial, technological and technical support to African countries, least developed countries, landlocked developing countries and small island developing States.

In addition to focusing on new and established industry and infrastructure, there is also a clear focus here on research and development. The idea is that the more, and more widely, research is carried out, the quicker new low- or zero-carbon techniques for manufacturing will become viable, and the more equally spread the financial benefits will be become.

The energy sector, which we will focus on in Chapter 6, has strong links here, as all industries, regardless of the sector in which they operate, require energy, most of which is produced off-site by specialist energy providers. Energy efficiency (also a focus of SDG 8 and SDG 12) is part of the drive, for using less energy will generally reduce costs and emissions and increase profitability, but more efficient energy production will lead to much greater emissions reductions.

Governments take different approaches to the SDGs, and it is this flexibility which has drawn both praise and criticism to the scheme. In the UK, for example, the government's implementation of SDG 8 includes a promise to "build more, better quality, safer, greener and more affordable homes." Linked to this strategy is an announcement that £450m has been put aside to pay for a £5,000 grant for households to upgrade to a new heat pump, combined with a ban on new gas-fired domestic boilers by 2035. This sounds promising and means that the UK government can legitimately claim to be working towards meeting SDG 8. In reality, however, there are two significant problems:

- The total grant fund is only sufficient to cover 90,000 houses, out of the UK's total housing stock of around 25,000,000 – 0.3 per cent.
- The grant value is far below the actual cost of a heat pump (currently around £14k).

SDG 9 places a relatively high reliance on the development of future technologies which do not currently exist in a commercial context, and some of these are discussed briefly in Chapter 11. There has been criticism of the SDG by those who favour focusing on reducing demand for energy rather than hoping that future technologies will remedy the issues caused primarily by past technologies. They point to the fact that in 1955, nuclear power was promoted as a means of generating electricity which would be "too cheap to meter"[5] and did not predict the significant problems caused by accidents and waste disposal.

5.11 SDG 10: Reduced Inequalities

There are strong links here to SDG 1 (no poverty) as it is the poorest communities who are most impacted by climate change and the resulting natural disasters, like fires and floods.

SDG 10 is one of the goals which focus squarely on economic and social sustainability, the argument being that the better off and more inclusive individuals, communities, and states become, the higher up the political agenda environmental issues will rise. Whilst there is considerable research that suggests concern about environmental issues is not necessarily income-dependent, the ability or willingness to do something about the underpinning issues is linked to income. Summers and Van Heuvelen[6] suggested in 2017 that there is a significant degree of separation between wealthier countries and the direct negative consequences of climate change, and this has resulted in a tendency towards complacency. With record temperatures and droughts occurring in Europe and the United States in the last two or three years, it is likely that this level of complacency is dropping.

Target 10.1 urges states to narrow the income gap between the poorest and wealthiest in their nation, as this will create a fairer and more equal community.

Target 10.1 By 2030, progressively achieve and sustain income growth of the bottom 40 per cent of the population at a rate higher than the national average.

At the macro-level, climate-related weather hazards are a significant cause of emigration from poorer states, and this has a double impact. Firstly, there are fewer people left in the state of origin to generate income and contribute to the economy, and secondly, there are more, often economically inactive people in the destination state, adding an additional cost. In February 2021, US President Biden issued Executive Order 14013[7] to the National Security Advisor to prepare a report on climate change and migration.

QUOTATION

"Although most people displaced or migrating as a result of climate impacts are staying within their countries of origin, the accelerating trend of global displacement related to climate impacts is increasing cross-border movements, too, particularly where climate change interacts with conflict and violence."

Executive Order 14013, "Rebuilding and Enhancing Programs to Resettle Refugees and Planning for the Impact of Climate Change on Migration"

The virtuous cycle which underpins SDG 10 is that if natural resources are managed more effectively and fairly (including through sound management of natural resources and critical ecosystems, as well as supporting institutional arrangements regarding the use and access to natural resources), then inequalities will be reduced, and if inequalities are reduced, then natural resources will be managed more effectively and fairly.

5.12 SDG 11: Sustainable Cities and Communities

KEY FACTS

- The world's cities occupy just 3 per cent of the Earth's land, but account for 60–80 per cent of energy consumption and 75 per cent of carbon emissions.
- Cities account for between 60 and 80 per cent of energy consumption and generate as much as 70 per cent of human-induced greenhouse gas emissions.
- 90 per cent of urban growth is forecasted to happen in Asia and Africa in the next 30 years.
- By 2050 70 per cent of the world population is predicted to live in urban settlements.

UN, 2022a, Goal 11: Make cities inclusive, safe, resilient, and sustainable, United Nations, www.un.org/sustainabledevelopment/cities/

The global trend towards urbanisation, which has been occurring for several centuries, has brought with it the inevitable concentration of pollution levels. As more and more people live in the same space, even if each individual produces no more pollution, there is more overall to cope with. We saw the impact of this on public health in Chapter 1, when looking at the 19th-century cholera outbreaks in England. Similarly, the more space that is given over to housing and industry to support a growing population, the greater will be the demand for food, and perversely, the less space will be available for food production.

The targets within the goal can be grouped into those which are focused on human health and those which have a broader focus. The human health–focused targets are for the removal of slums (Target 11.1), better access to transport (Target 11.2), reduction of deaths from waterborne illnesses and diseases and other disasters (Target 11.5), and better access to green spaces in urban areas (Target 11.7). Target 1.3 covers improved spatial and social planning in urban development, Target 1.4 covers improved protection of cultural and natural heritage, and Target 11.6 covers improving air quality (especially the emissions of PM_{10} and $PM_{2.5}$, which will be discussed in more detail in Chapter 9) and municipal waste control in urban areas.

As we have seen, Target 11.5 is concerned with reduction of deaths from natural disasters, and this links very directly with SDG 1 Target 1.5, which is about improving resilience and vulnerability to climate-related extreme events and disasters of those in poorer and more vulnerable areas. Rising sea levels, which are an ongoing result of the warming climate, are predicted to cause significant problems to cities across the world. From the following list, it is clear to see that with the exception of the three cities in the United States, all the cities most vulnerable to sea level rise are in the developing world.

Table 5.1 lists the ten cities with the highest predicted losses by 2050 caused by predicted sea level rise of 20 centimetres, their 2022 populations, and their predicted 2050 population.[8]

This predicted growth of almost 30 per cent in population across these ten cities underlines the importance of proper spatial planning, as highlighted by Target 1.3. As we saw earlier, the United Nations predicts that close to 75 per cent of the

Table 5.1 Populations of the Ten Cities Predicted to Suffer the Greatest Impact of Sea Level Rise

City	2022 Population	Forecast 2050 Population
Guangzhou (China)	14 million	13 million
Mumbai (India)	23 million	42 million
Kolkata (India)	15 million	33 million
Guayaquil (Ecuador)	3 million	4 million
Shenzhen (China)	13 million	11 million
Miami (United States)	0.4 million	7.5 million
Tianjin (China)	14 million	11 million
New York – Newark (United States)	9 million	24 million
Ho Chi Minh City (Vietnam)	9 million	12 million
New Orleans (United States)	0.4 million	0.5 million
Total	123.4 million	158 million

world's population will live in "urban centres" by 2050, so there is an imperative for these urban centres to develop in a way which does not compromise their inhabitants' access to green spaces and better housing.

5.13 SDG 12: Responsible Consumption and Production

This goal underpins a lot of the others, as irresponsible (and unsustainable) production and consumption are the root causes of many of the issues that are currently faced across the world. Targets 12.1 and 12.2 focus on national and individual use of resources and call for them to be much more sustainable.

We have seen earlier in the chapter in the discussions around SDG 2 (no hunger) that there is an enormous disparity in the distribution of food and nutrition across the world. Target 12.3 calls for a 50 per cent reduction in food waste (by consumers) and food losses (in the production and supply chain). Neither rate has changed significantly since the introduction of the SDG, remaining at around 27 per cent and 13 per cent, respectively.

Waste is covered by Targets 12.4 (chemicals and waste) and 12.5 (all waste), and the goal calls for increased recycling and overall better management of the waste stream. One of the issues identified by the UN is the ongoing subsidisation of the fossil fuel industry by different governments. This amounted to US$526bn in 2019 and US$375bn in 2020, though the UN suggests this drop was a temporary one and reflected low oil prices and reduced demand during the pandemic rather than structural reforms. To put these numbers into context, the Global Facility for Disaster Reduction and Recovery (GFDRR), which is a part of the World Bank, calculates that natural disasters, exacerbated by climate change, are costing the world US$520bn a year.

Softer targets are contained in Targets 12.6 and 12.7, which call for large and transnational companies to be encouraged to be more sustainable and for public procurement processes and practices to be more sustainable. The associated indicators both call for publication of information, and this links well with Target 12.7, which is to provide better access to information. We discussed the importance of access to information in Chapter 4, and it remains crucial to enhancing the ability of the public to engage in decision-making.

ACTIVITY

The rearing of cattle for beef production produces around 100 kilogrammes of carbon dioxide and consumes 2,700 litres of water per kilogramme of food. By contrast, the equivalent figures for rice are 4.5 kilogrammes and 2,400 litres, and for potatoes 0.5 kilogrammes and 59 litres.

Design a strategy for promoting the cessation of beef production as a means of protecting the environment and mitigating climate change.

You will have to consider the likely negative economic and social impact on countries and individuals involved in beef farming, transport, and processing and balance these with the likely positive global impacts and progress towards SDG 13.

5.14 SDG 13: Climate Action

Although it is not possible to ascribe specific climatic events to the effects of climate change, all the data suggest that the changing climate is increasing the frequency and intensity of extreme weather events. The increasing ferocity of cyclones and hurricanes, record heat levels, floods, droughts, and fires have a significant impact on global spending. As we saw in Section 5.13, the GFDDR calculates the direct cost of natural disasters as US$520bn a year. This is not the whole cost, however, and there are knock-on impacts on the cost of food, the cost of healthcare, and so on.

We will focus more closely on the issues around climate change in Chapter 9, but there are three broad targets set within SDG 13. None of them set specific emissions targets, but rather, they link to existing targets set by other international instruments and frameworks.

The "targets" for SDG 13 are more broadly expressed in terms of reducing the potential damage from climate-related disasters, embedding climate change into national policies, and improving public knowledge and education about climate-related issues. The focus on resilience is telling, as it indicates at least a tacit admission that stopping the impacts of climate change is no longer the only focus – dealing with the impacts that are already unstoppable has also entered the discussion.

Target 13.1 Strengthen resilience and adaptive capacity to climate-related hazards and natural disasters in all countries.

Target 13.2 Integrate climate change measures into national policies, strategies and planning.

Target 13.3 Improve education, awareness-raising and human and institutional capacity on climate change mitigation, adaptation, impact reduction and early warning.

It is, of course, impossible to link any single weather-related event conclusively to climate change. The IPCC and others, however, are united in their assertion that as the planet warms, the occurrence of such "extreme" events will be more frequent. The UN predicts that medium- to large-scale disasters will increase by 40 per cent by 2030. As we have seen elsewhere in this chapter, the impact of such events will be more keenly felt by poorer nations, who have, by and large, contributed much less to the causes of climate change. The importance of early-warning systems is emphasised by the World Meteorological Organisation.

QUOTATION

"A disaster related to a weather, climate or water hazard occurred every day on average over the past 50 years – killing 115 people and causing US$ 202 million in losses daily, according to a comprehensive new report from the World Meteorological Organization (WMO).

The number of disasters has increased by a factor of five over the 50-year period, driven by climate change, more extreme weather and improved reporting. But, thanks to improved early warnings and disaster management, the number of deaths decreased almost three-fold."

WMO, 2021, "Weather-related disasters increase over past 50 years, causing more damage but fewer deaths," World Meteorological Organization, https://public.wmo.int/en

Looking at the figures from various sources, we can see that one of the only benefits of the COVID pandemic was that global carbon emissions fell significantly during 2020 – by more than 5 per cent. This bucks the trend of previous decades, however, when, despite widely agreed and ratified targets being set in various international agreements since the 1990s, global emissions have risen annually every year except 2008. Since 2020, emissions have risen again, and energy-related emissions are now the highest they have even been. One of the major stumbling blocks of COP 27, which took place in Sharm el-Sheikh in Egypt in November 2022, was the level of financial responsibility which developed countries (which have contributed the largest share of historic global emissions) should bear for the cost of strengthening "resilience and adaptive capacity to climate-related hazards and natural disasters" (Target 13.1).

5.15 SDG 14: Life below Water

The ability of the sea to support life is being compromised by a combination of inefficient/unsustainable resource use (e.g. overfishing), pollution (microplastics, petrochemicals, sewerage), and ocean warming (causing widespread coral bleaching events). This significantly impacts the lives of the roughly 3 billion people who depend upon the sea for their livelihoods. This area is already partly covered by the UN Convention on the Law of the Sea (UNCLOS), which we covered in Chapter 2 and to which we will return in Chapter 10, but this is not very well adhered to, or very well enforced.

The targets can again be grouped thematically. There are those which are concerned with reducing pollution levels (Target 14.1, land-based water pollution, and Target 14.3, ocean acidification). There are also those which focus on reducing over-exploitation of marine resources (Target 14.4, end overfishing and illegal fishing, and Target 14.6, end fishing subsidies). There are also targets which focus on environmental protection (Target 14.2, strengthening marine and coastal ecosystems, and Target 14.5, conservation of coastal and marine areas). The only target which does not neatly fit into a single category is Target 14.7, which focuses on strengthening the financial capacities of Small Island Developing States and fits partly within all the categories.

The ocean is overall slightly alkaline in nature and has a pH level of around 8.1, where 7 is neural, 0–6.9 is acidic, and 7.1–14 is alkaline. The pH scale only applies to liquids, so although carbon dioxide is acidic in nature, it does not have a pH level. The alkaline nature of the ocean means it is well placed to absorb a significant quantity of the acidic carbon dioxide in the environment. One of the issues which this goal seeks to address is that of the increasing acidification of the ocean, which is reducing the carbon absorption potential. This, in turn, will speed up the level at which carbon is entering the atmosphere and increase the rate of climate change. Addressing ocean acidification, therefore, is seen as being fundamentally important to slowing this process.

More marine protected areas would allow species time to regenerate but also redistribute some of the profits from corporations to artisan fishers. Unlike many of the other SDG targets and indicators, this is an area for cautious celebration. The UN calculates that the average global score for the level of adoption of regulatory frameworks supporting small-scale fisheries and promoting participatory decision-making has risen from 3.5 in 2018 to 5.5 in 2022.

Plastic pollution is a significant problem for the oceans, and for human and other lives which depend upon the ocean. As we saw in Chapter 4, microplastics caused by the environmental degradation of larger plastic have been present in oceans for decades, but the rate at which plastic enters the oceans has increased dramatically. Whilst there is considerable momentum towards creating an international convention to control plastic pollution in the oceans, such a measure does not yet exist, meaning, reliance on imaginative interpretation of existing measures such as UNCLOS and the Basel Convention must continue.

5.16 SDG 15: Life on Land

Forests provide a number of useful functions to the planet. They are home to more than 80 per cent of terrestrial species of animals, plants, and insects, and so degradation of forest habitat compromises biodiversity. More than 1.5 billion people rely upon forests for their livelihood. Millions of hectares of forest are destroyed every year, and although the rate of destruction is slowing, Target 15.1 seeks to conserve and protect all ecosystems, especially forests, and Target 15.2 urges states to move towards sustainable forestry programmes. Interestingly, the deadline for both targets passed in 2020, and its scope only extended to ensure that states complied with their existing obligations under international instruments.

A similar approach was adopted by Targets 15.5 and 15.6. Target 15.5 focused on biodiversity loss. Rather than imposing new targets, it calls upon states to halt biodiversity loss by 2020, something many were already obliged to do under the Aichi Strategic Plan for Biodiversity agreed to by parties to the Convention on Biological Diversity. Target 2 of Aichi Strategic Goal A calls for the integration of biodiversity into planning, development, and poverty reduction strategies by 2020 *at the latest*. The UN reported in 2022[9] that slightly over one-third of countries were on track to meet their targets – two years after the deadline.

Target 15.6 focuses on the illegal trafficking of endangered species, a topic which is already comprehensively addressed by the 1973 convention on the International Trade in Endangered Species of Flora and Fauna (CITES). It is worth noting that neither the targets under 15.1, 15.2, or 15.5 were met by 2020.

The reporting on these issues is patchy, as it is with most of the other goals. One potential reason for this could be the number of "custodian agencies" involved with collecting and recording data. For the different facets of Goal 15, states will need to report to the following:

- Convention for International Trade in Endangered Species Secretariat
- Convention on Biological Diversity Secretariat
- Food and Agriculture Organization
- International Union for Conservation of Nature
- Organization for Economic Cooperation and Development
- UN Convention to Combat Desertification
- UN Environmental Programme
- UN Environmental Programme – World Conservation Monitoring Centre
- UN Office on Drugs and Crime
- World Bank

The complex nature of the SDG reporting requirements is one of the criticisms which has been levelled at the programme since its inception.

5.17 SDG 16: Peace, Justice, and Strong Institutions

Whilst there is nothing specific in Goal 16 which directly addresses environmental issues, there are many underpinning indirect links which affect the environment as much as everything else.

Violence and criminality (Targets 16.1, 16.2, and 16.4), access to justice (Target 16.3), corruption and accountability (Targets 16.5 and 16.6), participation and access to information (Targets 16.7, 16.8, and 16.10), and having a legal identity (Target 16.11) are all important background factors which have to be properly addressed. Unless and until they are, the ability of a state to focus on the other SDGs is going to be hampered.

The links between conflicts and environmental degradation was well-established, whether it was the deliberate burning of Kuwaiti oil fields by retreating Iraqi armed forces during the 1991 Gulf War, the pressure put on refugee camps by displaced peoples as a result of the wars in Syria or Ukraine, or the environmental impact of depleted uranium munitions or nuclear weapons. The war in Ukraine, though not specifically caused by resources, has had a significant impact on global grain and oil prices.

In addition to causing environmental degradation, conflicts are caused by environmental degradation. Shortages of water, land, fuel, or food have all caused conflicts and will continue to do so without fundamental societal changes.

Conflicts which have been linked to natural resources are twice as likely to recur within five years of a ceasefire, so the risk is significant.

5.18 SDG 17: Partnerships for the Goals

This is a unique SDG insofar as there is no particular action associated with it. The focus of the goal is more about enhancing levels of international cooperation mobilizing resources, sharing knowledge, promoting the creation and transfer of environmentally sound technologies, and building capacity.

There is tremendous scope for making the existing global financial system more sustainable by integrating the environment dimension, but as with most of the calls for better cooperation contained in the 16 other SDGs, progress on this has been extremely patchy.

The ongoing reverberations from the COVID pandemic and the war in Ukraine on this aspect are going to be interesting, as the majority of the globe is likely to experience severe financial hardship over the short-, medium-, or long-term.

5.19 Assessment of SDGs

The 17 UN SDGs cover a huge range of activities, approaches, and areas of life. In 2022 they are approaching the halfway point of their life, having started in 2016 and mostly ending in 2030. The UN is open that the majority of the goals have not yet been met, and that progress will need to improve dramatically if some of the goals are ever to be met.

Trinity College Dublin (TCD)[10] identified in 2017 five positive things and five criticisms about the SDGs, and the following sections are largely based on TCDs original ideas.

5.19.1 Positives

Aspirational
The targets set by the goals are largely aspirational, in that there is no enforcement body which can take action if the target is not met. Indeed, a large proportion of the targets eschew any specific date – be that a percentage reduction, a financial value, or anything else. Most are expressed in terms of phrases like "substantial reduction," "strengthen," or something similar. This is advantageous because it allows for more ambitious targets to be set. The argument is that is you set an ambitious but unenforced target, people/states are likely to make more progress towards it than if you set a very unambitious but enforceable target.

Collective
The targets are not for individual states alone to meet; they are collective – by state, by continent, and by region. This means, at least in theory, that even though there is no formal enforcement mechanism, there will be mutual pressure from neighbouring/trading states to succeed. The reverse of this is also true, of course, and peer pressure can work negatively as well as positively.

Universal

The targets are universal in nature, as opposed to the MDG goals, which were criticised for being focused on what richer nations could do *for* or *to* poorer nations. This will help foster the sense of a collective responsibility and is a more realistic approach since the effects of failure will be felt universally – though not, of course, to the same level.

Poverty Reduction

There is a strong underpinning commitment to end poverty which builds on the original MDG 1, which undertook to eradicate extreme poverty. Poverty is both a cause and result of climate change, and so it is right that it is central to the SDG focus. Poorer states and individuals are less likely to be able to afford cleaner technologies, while simultaneously being less likely to be resilient to the impacts of not doing do. As we saw in Chapter 3, when we looked at environmental and climate justice, one of the best indicators for longevity and health is how wealthy or not the area was where you were born.

Equality Promotion

There is also a strong commitment to reduce inequality in all its forms. This again addresses issues that occur between states and within states, regions, towns, and communities. As we saw earlier in Section 5.6, excluding women from economies, political decision-making, and other aspects of life means that not only is the majority population left largely unheard, but also, decisions which are better for the environment are left unmade.

5.19.2 Negatives

Lack of Ambition

The targets are not ambitious enough and do not necessarily recognise the immediacy of the threats. This is likely down to the change in predictions by IPCC and others in the decades since the SDGs were negotiated, but the goals have remained as originally cast. A good example of this was Target 15.1, which did not create any new targets and merely called upon states to do the things they were already legally obliged to do under other international instruments.

Embedded Inequalities

There are embedded inequalities in the international system, and the SDGs work within the context of these inequalities rather than seeking to replace or remove them. Richer and more powerful states (the two categories largely overlap) exert a lot more influence than poorer and less-powerful states. The argument is that organisations like the UN, World Bank, and the International Monetary Fund largely favour the *status quo*, and without a fundamental shift in these international bodies, nothing will change significantly.

Bureaucratic Process

The goals are largely top-down and bureaucratic, and there is no sufficient engagement with local needs. Different states have different processes, political systems, and priorities, and a uniform approach to the SDGs means that some states have a lot more work to do than others. Rather than requiring all states, rich or poor, developed or developing, North or South, to achieve an equal percentage rise in, say, the "proportion of informal employment in total employment, by sector and sex" (Goal 8, Target 8.3, Indicator 8.3.1), it might be more effective to encourage states where there is already a high proportion to work with those where there is a low proportion.

Soft Law
The aspirational nature of the targets means that they are not binding, so if they become difficult to achieve, they can be ignored. This is likely to become more and more of an issue in the post-COVID world and as the global economic slow-down starts to become more pronounced. Laws and policy are usually only as good as the enforcement that surrounds them. We have discussed Oliver Wendell Holmes's "bad man" theory in Chapter 1, so you are hopefully familiar with the concept of the person who only obeys rules solely as a result of their fear of punishment.

Lack of Data
The lack of reliable and consistent data means that accurately assessing progress towards the goals is not possible. This is true across the SDGs, and for many of them, the majority of states have never reported any progress. Not only does this make it impossible to track overall progress, but it also makes it impossible to share good practice between similar states. It also means that whatever follows on from the SDGs in 2030 will most likely be based on an inaccurate foundation.

ACTIVITY

As discussed earlier, Trinity College Dublin identified five positive aspects and five negative aspects of the UN SDGs.

Assess whether the positives outweigh the negatives.

What lessons should be learned from these positive and negative aspects when designing any replacement to the SDGs to begin in 2030?

What remains important overall, notwithstanding the patchy and partial progress that has been made to achieve them, is that without the MDGs in 2000 and the SDGs in 2015, the planet could have found itself in an even more parlous state.

In the next chapter, we will use the UK energy policy as a vehicle for looking at how sustainability can be embedded into policy and law.

SUMMARY

- SDGs are part of a continuum that started with the MDGs and will extend beyond 2030.
- Most SDG targets will not be met.
- There is considerable overlap between the different SDGs – most are complementary, but some can be contradictory.
- Significant additional expenditure by developed nations is needed.

SAMPLE ESSAY QUESTION

"The legal obligation to develop sustainably within ecological limits does not require a new ecocentric ethic, but is compatible with the anthropocentric ethic on which the 'people-centred' set of SDGs and targets are premised" (Kim R. E., 2016, "The Nexus between International Law and the Sustainable Development Goals," *Review of European Community and International Environmental Law*, 25(1)).

In light of the preceding quote, assess the extent to which the UN SDGs can ever find a satisfactory balance between the social, economic, and environmental strands of sustainable development, and solve the "profit vs planet," "people vs planet," and "planet vs planet" conflicts which Kim identifies.

1. Outline the three strands of sustainable development.
2. Assess selected SDGs giving a rationale for why they were selected (the number selected will depend on the length of the essay, but three for a 2,000-word essay is sufficient).
3. Analyse the selected SDGs in light of the three strands and three conflicts.
4. Conclude.

Further Reading

Dalin, C., Wada, Y., Kastner, T., & Ouma, M.J., 2017, Groundwater Depletion Embedded in International Food Trade, *Nature*, 543(7647), 700–704

FAO, IFAD, UNICEF, WFP, & WHO, 2022, *The State of Food Security and Nutrition in the World 2022*. Repurposing Food and Agricultural Policies to Make Healthy Diets More Affordable, Rome: FAO, https://doi.org/10.4060/cc0639en

Hallegatte, S., Green, C., Nicholls, R.J., & Corfee-Morlot, J., 2013, Future Flood Losses in Major Coastal Cities, *Nature Climate Change*, 3, 802–806

Hoornweg, D., & Pope, K., 2014, *Socioeconomic Pathways and Regional Distribution of the World's 101 Largest Cities*, Global Cities Institute Working Paper No. 04, https://www.daniels.utoronto.ca/work/research/global-cities-institute

Norgaard, K., & York, R., 2005, Gender Equality and State Environmentalism, *Gender & Society*, 19(4), 506–522

Rigaud, K.K., De Sherbinin, A., Jones, B., Bergmann, J., Clement, V., Ober, K., Schewe, J., Adamo, S.B., McCusker, B., Heuser, S., & Midgley, A., 2018, *Groundswell: Preparing for Internal Climate Migration*, Washington, DC: The World Bank, https://doi.org/10.7916/D8Z33FNS

Salmon, H., 2022, The Effect of Women's Parliamentary Participation on Renewable Energy Policy Outcomes, *European Journal of Policy Research*, https://doi.org/10.1111/1475-6765.12539

Summers, N., & Van Heuvelen, T., 2017, Heterogeneity in the Relationship between Country-Level Affluence and Environmental Concern, *Social Forces*, 96(1), 329–359

UN, 2022b, *The Sustainable Development Goals Report*, https://unstats.un.org/sdgs/report/2022/

Notes

1 Declaration of the United Nations Conference on the Human Environment, UN Doc. A/Conf.48/14/Rev. 1 (1973)
2 UN General Assembly, 2017, *UN General Assembly Resolution 72/222*. Education for Sustainable Development in the Framework of the 2030 Agenda for Sustainable Development
3 UN, 2022, *SDG 5 Gender Equality: Progress and Info 2022*, United Nations, https://sdgs.un.org/goals/goal5
4 UN, 2022, *SDG 6 Clean Water and Sanitation: Progress and Info 2022*, United Nations, https://sdgs.un.org/goals/goal6
5 USAEC, 1954, *Remarks Prepared by Lewis L Strauss, Chairman, US Atomic Energy Commission*, USAEC, 16 September 1954, New York: NY, US AEC, p. 9
6 Summers, N., & Van Heuvelen, T., 2017, Heterogeneity in the Relationship between Country-Level Affluence and Environmental Concern, *Social Forces*, 96(1), 329–359, 353
7 Executive Order 14013 of February 4, 2021 "Rebuilding and Enhancing Programs to Resettle Refugees and Planning for the Impact of Climate Change on Migration"
8 Adapted from: Hallegatte, S., Green, C., Nicholls, R.J., & Corfee-Morlot, J., 2013, Future Flood Losses in Major Coastal Cities, *Nature Climate Change*, 3, 802–806, Table 2, 804; Hoornweg, D., & Pope, K., 2014, *Socioeconomic Pathways and Regional Distribution of the World's 101 Largest Cities*, Global Cities Institute Working Paper No. 04, https://www.daniels.utoronto.ca/work/research/global-cities-institute
9 UN, 2022, *The Sustainable Development Goals Report*, p. 57, https://unstats.un.org/sdgs/report/2022/
10 TCD, 2017, *Achieving Sustainable Development*, www.futurelearn.com/info/courses/achieving-sustainable-development/0/steps/35496

6

Energy Policy

Friday, 21 April 2017, was a watershed moment in UK energy use, as it was the first day that the UK went a whole day without using coal to generate electricity since the 1880s. Predictions are that 2025 will see the first fossil-fuel-free day of electricity generation.

In this chapter we will consider the general area of the UK's energy policy, with a focus on the links to sustainability. It is rather a misnomer to refer to "UK energy policy" as though it was one coherent strategy. It is in fact a series of strategies that have been adopted, amended, and dropped by successive (and often the same) government and is as much at the mercy of political point-scoring and trend-following as any other area of policy (as we saw in Chapter 4). The policy area also bleeds into other areas – integrated transport, housing, communications, education, defence, and healthcare all have significant energy usage, and significant changes in policy will greatly impact them. The following image (Figure 6.1) represents some of the key elements which impact energy policy.

6.1 Influences on UK Energy Policy

6.1.1 The Energy Regulator

The energy regulator for Great Britain is the Office of Gas and Electricity Markets (OFGEM), which sits under the Gas and Electricity Markets Authority (GEMA), which was created by the Utilities Act 2000.[1] The regulators control the price that can be charged for electricity and gas by suppliers, as well as working to ensure fair practice. Whilst the regulator does not directly influence government policy, they have an indirect influence insofar as they identify what they feel to be gaps in existing and proposed policy developments.

6.1.2 Academic Work

Research undertaken by academics links to most of the other influencing factors in the diagram. We have seen already in Chapter 4 how the academic research undertaken in relation to plastic pollution gradually fed into policy discussions, and the same is true of energy-related research. One of the most potentially groundbreaking pieces of energy research being carried out currently is the UK Atomic Energy Authority's Joint European Torus (JET) project in Culham, near Oxford. JET, along

DOI: 10.4324/9781003137214-6

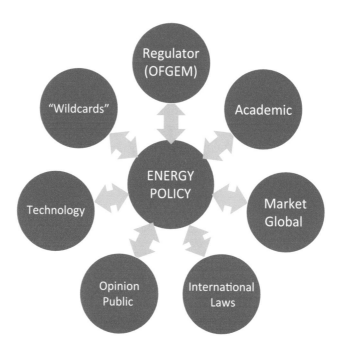

Figure 6.1 Influences on UK energy policy.

with the larger International Thermonuclear Experimental Reactor (ITER) project in France, is looking into the possibilities of generating clean, sustainable, and cheap energy through nuclear fusion. If the projects are successful, the research will have a fundamental impact on energy policies in the UK and globally.

6.1.3 The Global Energy Market

The UK has been both an importer and an exporter of energy, and the global market dictates the price that can be charged for difference types of energy, in the same way it can for any traded commodity. There is a little bit of a curveball in relation to the oil market, however, which is the Organization of Petroleum Exporting Countries (OPEC). OPEC is a 13-state organisation funded in 1960, the members of which control over 40 per cent of the global oil supply. The members of OPEC decide whether to increase or reduce oil production levels to either decrease or increase the unit price.

In 2022, we also saw the vulnerability of many European nations to gas imported from Russia. Though the war in Ukraine was a "wildcard" event (see following text), the issue of "gas security" has been concerning the European Commission for many years.

QUOTATION

"As demonstrated by the EU-wide stress tests in 2014, national policies do not sufficiently take into account the security of supply situation in their neighbouring countries. There are also serious shortcomings in taking into account external risks which includes the lack of access to information on commercial gas supply contracts."

European Commission, 2016, Security of Gas Supply Regulation, http://ec.europe.eu

6.1.4 International Laws and Obligations

The UK's international obligations in terms of energy production and consumption have had a dramatic impact on energy policy – notably through the UN Framework Convention on Climate Change and associated protocols. In 2019, the UK was one of the first major economies to put in place a statutory obligation to reach net zero on all greenhouse gas emissions by 2050. The Climate Change Act 2008 (2050 Target Amendment) Order 2019[2] changed the original target of an 80 per cent reduction contained in Section 1 of the Climate Change Act 2008[3] to 100 per cent. This was described as "legally binding" by the government, but there is no sanction in the Climate Change Act for failure to meet the target, and fundamentally, the constitutional principle of parliamentary sovereignty means that any future Parliament is free to change the law.

Although net zero is not just about energy production, the energy industry contributes around one-fifth of UK emissions, so there are significant energy policy implications for this pledge.

6.1.5 Public Opinion

Whilst not exerting a direct pressure on energy policy, the public does play an indirect role. It was public pressure, bolstered by scientific evidence, that led directly to the government's decision in 2019 to suspend "fracking" (see later text) despite the fact that licenses had already been granted.

....

Definition

Fracking, or *hydraulic fracturing*, is a method of obtaining oil and gas from bedrock. Water and sand or other particles are typically pumped at high pressure into the bedrock to create cracks in the rock. When the water dissipates, the sand (etc.) holds the cracks open so that the fossil fuels can be accessed.

It is praised as a way of releasing otherwise-inaccessible oil and gas which can be used as fuel in place of coal, thus lowering CO_2 emissions.

It is criticised because of the associated risks of earthquakes, groundwater contamination, surface-water pollution, noise pollution, air pollution, and a range of negative health impacts.

....

The public, either individually or as part of a group, also exerts an influence on policy through bringing cases for judicial review. Most of the cases involving energy in the UK are either about the lawfulness or otherwise of a policy decision or relate to trespass and criminal acts by protestors. The *de facto* ban was reversed by the Truss government in October 2022, and the reversal itself was a reversal by the Sunak government in November 2022. This is an excellent example of the speed in which real or imagined public opinion can lead to changes in policy.

6.1.6 Technology

New technology creates the need for new policies to deal with it. This links back to the point which was made in Chapter 1 about early laws being reactive – the Alkali Act 1863[4] being a reaction to the pollution caused by the soda ash industry, for example. From an energy perspective, most of the technology in the early days concerned the efficiency of the fuel source, the generator design, and so on. Today, the energy sector is one of those included under the Environmental Permitting (England and Wales) Regulations 2016[5] (see Chapter 10), and it is also covered by Section 4 of the Electricity Act 1989. It is thus a criminal offence to generate electricity (beyond the *de minimis* 10 megawatt-hour limit) without a licence.

LEGISLATION

(1) A person who –
  (a) generates electricity for the purpose of giving a supply to any premises or enabling a supply to be so given;
  (b) participates in the transmission of electricity for that purpose;
    (bb) distributes electricity for that purpose;
  (c) supplies electricity to any premises,
  (d) participates in the operation of an electricity interconnector; or
  (e) provides a smart meter communication service,

shall be guilty of an offence unless he is authorised to do so by a licence.

S4(1), Electricity Act 1989, as amended

The format of the licence will vary depending upon which aspect of the permission is required, but if a novel technology is going to be used to generate electricity, then it will be subject to the licensing regime.

6.1.7 Wildcards

Historically, the energy policy has been affected enormously by unpredictable events which often take place far away from the UK. Despite the evidence that the accidents had nothing to do with the reactor design, the nuclear accident at Chernobyl in 1986 and Fukushima Daiichi in 2011, for example, painted nuclear power generation in a very unfavourable light, and the UK and many other countries moved away from nuclear as a source of electricity generation as a result. The 2022 war in Ukraine and subsequent cessation of gas importation from Russia have had a significant impact on energy prices in the UK and were a fundamental reason for the Truss government's now-rescinded plan to reintroduce "fracking" despite the scientific evidence of its instability and unsuitability.

It is perhaps surprising to realise that a considerable quantity of the UK's energy is generated through steam power, as it has been for over a century. The first working steam engine was an enormous static machine designed by Thomas Newcomen in the early 1700s and was used to pump water out of coal mines in Staffordshire (1712) and tin mines in Cornwall. The engine was popular, despite its alleged 1 per cent efficiency, meaning, that 99 per cent of the energy used to power the machine was lost. In 1768, James Watt improved the engine by adding a separate condenser and, in partnership with Matthew Boulton, developed an efficient steam engine, powered by coal. The Boulton and Watt engine used cast-iron cylinders bored by John Wilkinson, who adapted technology he had used for making cannons.

In power stations today, the fuel source may be coal, oil, gas, biomass, or nuclear. In almost all cases, the heat from the fuel source is used to turn water into steam. The steam powers the turbines, which create electricity.

The chapter will separate energy policy into different fuel sources, dealing first with the different unsustainable fossil fuels, moving through current renewable energy strategy, and concluding by considering possible future energy sources.

6.2 Coal

As we saw in previous chapters, ascribing the term "policy" to an area of 18th- and 19th-century law is a little flattering. The reality was that there was a series of disconnected, reactive, and piecemeal measures driven by practical concerns about human health, productivity, and new technology. This is exactly what we saw with coal.

Coal was used by the Romans in Britain around 2,000 years ago, but its use seems to have dissipated after the Romans left, not starting again until the 12th century. As we saw in Chapter 1, it was not long after this reintroduction that problems of emissions and smoke started to become problematic.

Coal and wood were the fuels that powered the Industrial Revolution and led to the pollution which has become associated with it. Despite this, it is important to remember that the UK had become heavily reliant on coal as a fuel source well before the 1700s. Coal was one of the nation's staple industries, but it was the extractive element of the industry to which any policy related, rather than the energy it produced.

The current recognition of and fears about the finite levels of coal and other fossil fuels were not widespread issues, although there were some who were more prescient than the majority. The author Jules Verne, though writing fiction in the late 1860s, was clear to point out that coalfields are not inexhaustible and were not likely to last longer than 300 years at what were then the current rates of consumption.[6]

As the 20th century progressed, coal use was less about producing steam to move vehicles and more about electricity generation and domestic fires. It was initially an industry comprising many private firms – an estimated 2,500 in the period between the First and Second World Wars.

The widening recognition that many coal seams were becoming uneconomic to mine, that coal was indeed a finite resource, and that coal miners were often exploited by mine owners led to the passage of the Coal Industry Nationalisation Act 1946[7] and the creation of the National Coal Board (NCB) on 1 January 1947.

LEGISLATION

Assets to be transferred without option.
Unworked coal and mines of coal (and certain associated minerals).

(1) Interests in unworked coal, and in mines of coal, of colliery concerns and of the Coal Commission [subject to some provisions]
(2) Interests of the Coal Commission in minerals other than coal, and interests of colliery concerns and of subsidiaries thereof in unworked minerals other than coal being minerals which can only be economically worked in association with the working of coal or which can only be economically brought to the surface by the use of a mine of coal an interest in which vests in the Board.

Collieries, and colliery coke ovens and manufactured fuel plants.

2 Interests of colliery concerns and of class A subsidiaries thereof in fixed and movable property used for colliery activities, coal carbonisation and coal products distillation activities allied with colliery activities, or manufactured fuel activities.

Schedule 1, Part 1, Coal Industry Nationalisation Act 1946

By 1947, the rationalisation of the coal industry had led to the closure of over 60 per cent of coal mines across Britain – from 2,500 in 1913 to only 1,100 in 1947 – and yet the overall coal production fell by less than 30 per cent, from 290 million tonnes to 200 million tonnes. This fall, it should be noted, predated widespread concerns about climate change, and by the time the industry was renamed as British Coal Corporation by the 1980s, there were only 16 deep mines across the country.

In 1994, under the Coal Industry Act,[8] the administrative and regulatory provisions and ownership of the unworked and closed mines of British Coal were separated out to the Coal Authority, and the assets were privatised and became UK Coal. The company closed in 2015, and in June 2021, the government announced that all use of coal for electricity generation in UK will cease by 2024. It should be noted that this does not apply to coal use in heavy industries like steel production or in domestic settings. However, as discussed in Chapter 4, there is still opportunity for politicians to present this gradual change as being "radical" and portray the UK as "leading the way in consigning coal power to the history books,"[9] despite the fact that Austria, Belgium, Portugal, and Sweden had already stopped using coal for power production by mid-2022.

Despite the possibility that this deadline may slip back to its original 2025 date as a result of the energy crisis sparked by the war in Ukraine, there is no doubt that the use of coal in the electricity generation sector is rapidly going to cease.

6.3 Oil and Gas

The oil and gas industries are significantly younger than the coal industry in the UK but nonetheless date back to the 19th century. Both oil and gas emit less carbon when burned than coal – for oil, the figures are about 72 per cent, and for gas around 55 per cent. This makes both more attractive than coal in terms of their use for fuel and power, as governments are able to meet carbon reduction targets without significant changes to the infrastructure.

The oil industry was the first of the three fossil fuel industries to be nationalised, and this happened through the Petroleum (Production) Act 1934,[10] and as a result, licences from the board of trade were needed to even explore for oil. The Gas Act 1848[11] not only nationalised the gas industry but also created area gas boards and a Gas Council to advise the government.

LEGISLATION

It shall be the duty of every Area Board as from the vesting date

a) To develop and maintain an efficient, co-ordinated and economical system of gas supply for their area and to satisfy, as far as is economical to do so, all reasonable demands for gas in their area

b) To develop and maintain the efficient, co-ordinated and economical production of coke, other than metallurgical coke;

c) To develop and maintain efficient methods of recovering by-products obtained in the process of manufacturing gas

S1(1), Gas Act 1948

Also, in line with the coal industry, political expediency meant that both the oil and gas industries were later privatised. Oil was part privatised in 1976 to raise funds during the balance of payments crisis, and by the mid-1980s, the industry was effectively in private hands. British Gas was privatised at the end of 1986.

The Petroleum Act 1998[12] was passed to consolidate the previous, disparate legislation around petrochemicals that had evolved over the decades. The Act reiterates that the ownership of oil and gas reserves resides with the Crown. The privatisation of oil and gas has not affected this, and private companies now operate in oil and gas fields that are technically owned by the Crown. The Act was passed six years after Article 4(2)(a) of the UN Framework Convention on Climate Change had required the UK, among other nations, to reduce emissions to 1990 levels by 2000. Despite this, there is no mention in the 1998 Act about reducing the UK's reliance of oil and gas for energy production.

ARTICLE

The developed country Parties and other Parties included in Annex I commit themselves specifically as provided for in the following:

(a) Each of these Parties shall adopt national policies and take corresponding measures on the mitigation of climate change, by limiting its anthropogenic emissions of greenhouse gases and protecting and enhancing its greenhouse gas sinks and reservoirs. These policies and measures will demonstrate that developed countries are taking the lead in modifying longer-term trends in anthropogenic emissions consistent with the objective of the Convention, recognizing that the return by the end of the present decade to earlier levels of anthropogenic emissions of carbon dioxide and other greenhouse gases not controlled by the Montreal Protocol would contribute to such modification, and taking into account the differences in these Parties' starting points and approaches, economic structures and resource bases, the need to maintain strong and sustainable economic growth, available technologies and other individual circumstances, as well as the need for equitable and appropriate contributions by each of these Parties to the global effort regarding that objective.

Article 4(2)(a) UN Framework Convention on Climate Change 1992

The Act was amended in 2015 and 2016, and new sections were inserted to cover fracking (hydraulic fracturing), which is a method or extracting gas and sometimes oil from bedrock which was being artificially fractured. This provision places the responsibility for granting a consent largely in the hand of the Secretary of State.

LEGISLATION

The OGA [Oil and Gas Authority, now the North Sea Transition Authority] must not issue a well consent for a well situated in the English onshore area that is required by an onshore licence for England or Wales unless the well consent imposes –

(a) a condition which prohibits associated hydraulic fracturing from taking place in land at a depth of less than 1000 metres; and

(b) a condition which prohibits associated hydraulic fracturing from taking place in land at a depth of 1000 metres or more unless the licensee has the Secretary of State's consent for it to take place (a "hydraulic fracturing consent").

S4(4A)(1), Petroleum Act 1998 (as amended by the Infrastructure Act 2015[13] and the Petroleum (Transfer of Functions) Regulations 2016)[14]

The granting of planning permission by local authorities to companies who wish to engage in fracking, and the policy decision itself, has been the subject of a number of judicial review cases. None of those relating to the granting of permission was successful, but there was a partial success in relation to the challenge to policy framework. The phrase "unconventional hydrocarbons" remains in the 2021 revisions to the National Planning Policy Framework in Annex 2 as part of the definition of "mineral resources of local and national importance," but the clause mentioned in the judicial review has been removed.

JUDGMENT

R (ex parté Stevenson) v Secretary of State for Housing and Communities and Local Government (2019) EWHC 519 (Admin)

This case concerned the consultation which led to the addition of a new Paragraph 209(a) into the National Planning Policy Framework. The new paragraph said:

"209. Minerals planning authorities should:

a) recognise the benefits of on-shore oil and gas development, including unconventional hydrocarbons, for the security of energy supplies and supporting the transition to a low-carbon economy; and put in place policies to facilitate their exploration and extraction."

The claimant argued that the Secretary of State "failed to carry out a lawful consultation exercise" (para 3), and the court found that "that the consultation on the draft revised Framework . . . was so flawed in its design and processes as to be unlawful."

(Per Dove, J at para 62)

As Figure 6.2 demonstrates, the prices of petrol, oil, and gas have fluctuated greatly over the last two decades. This not only has an impact on the profitability of the energy companies but also affects the cost-effectiveness of the renewable

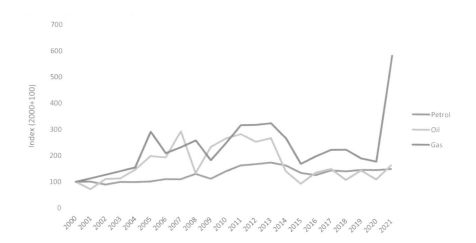

Figure 6.2 Petrol, oil, and gas price, 2000–2022.

Sources: Petrol Price – RAC Foundation; Oil Price (December of each year) – Macrotrends and Department of energy and Climate change; Gas (December of each year) Clifford Talbot.

energy sector. In essence, when oil is expensive, alternatives seem much more economically attractive than when oil is cheap.

Current policy was in flux, even before the advent of the war in Ukraine. In 2021, a revised Oil and Gas Authority strategy came into force, and in March 2022, the Oil and Gas Authority changed its name to the North Sea Transition Authority (NSTA). Whilst the key focus of the NSTA is still oil and gas extraction, the authority also controls the carbon capture and storage (CCS) industry. The use of fracking, which had originally been approved by the government, was suspended in 2011 after being linked to earthquakes near Blackpool. It was reapproved in 2012, banned in 2019 by the High Court in Stephenson (mentioned earlier), re-approved again (in September 2022, under PM Liz Truss), and then disapproved (in October 2022, under PM Rishi Sunak).

CCS is not a single approach or technological fix, but the term refers to the different methods of capturing carbon emissions and processing it so that it can be stored under the seabed inside the rock formations, or within the spaces left by exhausted oil and gas reservoirs. Proponents argue that the technology, which does not currently exist on a large scale, will eventually lead to 50 million tonnes of carbon a year being stored and is a vital part of new zero. Opponents argue that reliance on an end-of-pipe fix for emissions as opposed to serious systemic change in industrial strategy will encourage governments to reduce the pressure on industry to reduce emissions. Overall, it seems that a combination of both approaches is necessary to reach new zero as rapidly as possible.

The oil and gas industry illustrates, perhaps more than any other part of the energy industry, the issues of energy security and fragility of supply. As Figure 6.2 demonstrates, the price of gas almost trebled in 2021. This was as a result of an increase in demand post-pandemic and a shortage of supply. The issues were compounded in 2022 with the war in Ukraine leading to tight restrictions on the levels of gas being pumped from Russia.

6.4 Nuclear Fission

The UK was involved with nuclear science from close to the beginning of the discipline. Nuclear fission is often called "splitting the atom," but the two are significantly different. Ernest Rutherford created the first artificial nuclear reaction in 1917 in Manchester and supervised John Cockcroft and Ernest Walton, who successfully split the nucleus of an atom in Cambridge in 1932. It was, however, a team led by Enrico Fermi and Leo Szílard in the United States who managed to create the first self-sustaining nuclear reactor, a feat they achieved in 1942 in some converted squash courts under Stagg Field at the University of Chicago. The UK joined the fray in 1949 with the Graphite Low Energy Experimental Pile (GLEEP), near Oxford. Producing usable electricity from a nuclear reactor was achieved in 1949, with the EBR-1 reactor in Idaho, and connection to a local grid happened near Moscow in 1954.

British scientists, along with colleagues from Canada, had moved to the United States during the Second World War to work on the Manhattan Project, the project led by Robert Oppenheimer which led to the first nuclear weapons. This linkage between the nuclear reaction required to create energy and that required to create a weapon has been at the heart of public and governmental uneasiness about nuclear power ever since.

The year 1946 was pivotal for nuclear energy. The very first resolution of the United Nations General Assembly was to look at ways of controlling unidentified "problems" caused by the very discovery of atomic energy.

1(1) ESTABLISHMENT OF A COMMISSION TO DEAL WITH THE PROBLEMS RAISED BY THE DISCOVERY OF ATOMIC ENERGY

Resolved by the General Assembly of the United Nations to establish a commission, with the composition and competence set out hereunder, to deal with the problems raised by the discovery of atomic energy and related matters

Resolution 1(1) of the United Nations General Assembly

In the United States, 1946 saw the passage of the McMahon Act (the Atomic Energy Act),[15] which passed the responsibility for atomic energy from the Manhattan Project to a new Atomic Energy Commission. The Act also made sharing any technology relating to atomic energy to a foreign power a potentially capital offence, which provoked consternation among the British scientists who were then unable to return to the UK to continue their work in the field.

In the UK, the Atomic Energy Act 1946[16] put all nuclear research under the control of the government but took it outside the control of the Minister of Fuel and Power, giving instead to the Ministry of Supply.

LEGISLATION

An Act to provide for the development of atomic energy and the control of such development, and for purposes connected therewith.

1 General duty of Minister of Supply.
   It shall be the general duty of the Minister of Supply (in this Act referred to as "the Minister") to promote and control the development of atomic energy.

Introductory Text and S1, Atomic Energy Act 1946

There was an economic driver behind this, and Prime Minister Clement Attlee was keen that even though the uses for, and the economic significance of, atomic energy had not been fully identified, it was a worthy avenue for research. As such, he proposed in the commons debate on the Act in 1946 that universities and commercial firms be encouraged by government funding to pursue atomic research as much as possible.[17] It will be noted that Section 1 of the Atomic Energy Act 1946 gives the Minister of Supply a *duty* rather than a *power* to promote the development of atomic energy.

We can also see a very good example of a form of proactive decision-making within the atomic energy sector, in that the Atomic Energy Authority Act 1954[18] created a body which was tasked with taking over control of the atomic energy industry, which would not exist in any meaningful capacity until the reactor at Calder Hall was switched on two years later.

LEGISLATION

An Act to provide for the setting up of an Atomic Energy Authority for the United Kingdom, to make provision as to their powers, duties, rights and liabilities, to amend, consequentially on the establishment of and otherwise in connection with that Authority, the Atomic Energy Act, 1946, the Radioactive Substances Act, 1948, and certain other enactments, and for purposes connected with the matters aforesaid.

Long Title, Atomic Energy Authority Act 1954

Nuclear power, at its peak in the 1990s, contributed around 25 per cent of the UK's energy. However, accidents at Three Mile Island in the United States in 1973 and Chernobyl in the USSR in 1986, as well as minor leaks from Windscale/Sellafield plant in Cumbria, began to shift public opinion, and thus political willpower, away from nuclear power. The last plant to come on stream was Sizewell B in Suffolk. It was given the go-ahead after a lengthy (pre-Chernobyl) public inquiry which sat from 1982 to 1985 and reported in 1987, and the plant started operations in 1995.

In 2005, the government announced that because nuclear power generates no CO_2 at the point of operation, it was a logical source of sustainable power.

QUOTATION

"The issue back on the agenda with a vengeance is energy policy. . . . [W]e have established a review of the UK's progress against the medium and long-term Energy White Paper goals . . . with the aim of publishing a policy statement on energy [which] will include specifically the issue of whether we facilitate the development of a new generation of nuclear power stations."

Rt Hon Tony Blair, Speech to the CBI Conference, 29 November 2005

Despite the then prime minister's announcement, it was another decade before concrete steps were taken to restart the UK's nuclear programme, and the consultation process was found to have been procedurally unfair.

JUDGMENT

R (ex parté Greenpeace Ltd) v Secretary of State for Trade and Industry (2007) EWHC 311 (Admin)

This case concerns the public consultation which led to the prime minister's 2005 announcement that nuclear energy was "back," and the Energy Challenge Energy Review Report 2006.[19]

The claimants argued the consultation process leading to the decision was procedurally flawed and that therefore the decision was unlawful. The court held that "there was a breach of the claimant's legitimate expectation to fullest public consultation; that the consultation process was procedurally unfair; and that therefore the decision in the Energy Review that nuclear new build 'has a role to play . . .' was unlawful."

(Per Sullivan J, para 120)

In 2010, plans were announced for a number of new nuclear plants, and three of these look likely to be completed. If all three are constructed, they will supply around 18 per cent of the UK's energy and will operate for around 60 years. All will be built adjacent to existing or decommissioned plants, and all three will be financed by a consortium of Électricité de France (EdF) and China General Nuclear Power Group (CGN):

Hinkley Point C (Somerset)	3.2 GW	Construction is underway.
Sizewell C (Sussex)	3.2 GW	Construction to start c. 2024.
Bradwell B (Essex)	2G W	Stage 1 of consultation completed.

As the contribution of coal, oil, and gas falls, that made by nuclear power is set to rise.

Several environmental groups are opposed to nuclear energy. They argue that despite the zero emissions production of electricity, once the plants are complete, mining the uranium is very carbon-intensive, and the risk of accidents makes this an unsuitable part of a future energy mix.

Other environmental groups argue that although there is a risk of accidents, this is less problematic than the certain impacts of climate change and not adopting renewable energy.

Draw up an objective list of the advantages and disadvantages of nuclear energy, and assess whether it should be a part of a future energy mix for the UK.

6.5 Wind

Wind power is nothing new, and windmills have been used for centuries to grind corn or drain farmland, for example. What is relatively new is their use to create electricity. The UK has seen a roughly 20 per cent year-on-year growth in the capacity of wind energy, and the 2019 Conservative Party Manifesto promised 40 gigawatts of offshore wind by 2030, which would require this rate of growth to continue.

As a renewable resource, wind is an ideal contributor to the energy mix, particularly in countries which have predictable and relatively constant flow of wind. There is no technical reason that wind turbines should not operate in regions prone to hurricanes, typhoons, and other extreme weather events, but their effectiveness is compromised by high wind speeds.

There are essentially two different categories of commercial wind farm – onshore and offshore. Onshore has the advantage that it is easier to connect to the existing electricity infrastructure, but the disadvantage is that space required is significant and brings with it considerable planning law implications. Offshore wind farms tend to be larger both in the size of the turbines and the number of turbines, as there are fewer planning considerations to consider. Connection to existing infrastructure is harder, however, adding cost to both the construction and the operational phases.

Whilst there is a lot less controversy around wind power than there is around nuclear power, there are still several concerns that have been raised.

6.5.1 Space

The space needed is a concern. The Hornsea offshore windfarm, off the east coast of England, is the largest in the world. Two phases are completed as of August 2022, and they have a combined generation capacity of 2.5 gigawatts, with two further phases planned which will raise capacity to 6 megawatts. Hornsea I and II (the first two phases) occupy around 1,000 square kilometres. Whitelee Wind Farm in Scotland, the largest onshore wind farm in the UK, used 55 square kilometres of land to generate 0.5 gigawatts. By way of illustration, the Hinkley Point C site (see earlier text), which will have a generating capacity 28 per cent higher than Hornsea I and II, and six times greater than Whitelee, occupies only 1.6 square kilometres.

6.5.2 Noise

Wind farms do not operate in silence. As with almost all machinery, there is noise which is emitted as a result of their operation. Noise pollution, however, is a matter for statutory nuisance rather than environmental law. Noise is also covered as one of the elements which must be addressed by a developer as part of their application for an environmental permit under the Environmental Permitting (England and Wales) Regulations 2016[20] (see Chapter 10).

CASE

R (ex parté Lee) v Secretary of State for Communities and Local Government, Maldon District Council, Npower Renewables (2011) EWHC 807 (Admin)

This case concerned planning permission granted for the construction of a ten-turbine onshore windfarm near Bradwell-on-Sea in Essex. The claimant, who was appearing on behalf of the community group Bradwell and Tillingham Tackling Lost Environment (BATTLE), argued that the planning inspector should not have used noise data from Npower, even though that data was not disputed by the local planning authority. BATTLE did not provide its own noise data.

The court held that the planning inspector was entitled to rely on noise data from studies produced by Npower, who were applying for planning permission.

6.5.3 Birds

The potential impact to birds caused by the construction and operational phases of a wind farm could occur through direct bird strike on the blades or habitat loss through inappropriate constriction location. There seems to be contrary evidence as to the severity of this impact, however, and there remains work to be done in order to come to a conclusive view. Larsen found that birds "are astonishingly good at flying around or over the turbines,"[21] and Nature Scot/Nàdar Alba state that well-sited wind farms "have limited effects on birds."[22] Fox and Pedersen, on the other hand, sound a note of caution and, while recognising the contribution of wind farms to renewable energy, suggest we also need to focus on technologies which do not have a "cost to migratory bird populations."[23]

6.5.4 Fish

Concerns over the relationship between offshore wind farms and the fishing industry have been raised for many years. Problems have been identified with fishing vessel gear snagging on the undersea cables which take power from the wind farm to shore, and this not only endangers the crews of the fishing vessels but also potentially interrupts the flow of electricity.

From an ecological perspective, the construction of wind farms can disturb species of fish and shellfish and may lead some species to relocate to less-favourable grounds. Once they are built, fishing vessels are often excluded (sometimes voluntarily) from wind farm sites (to reduce the risk of accidents). Whilst this means that the areas may become pseudo-havens for some species, the knock-on effect is that fishing is moved to other, less-sustainable areas.

6.5.5 Benefits

On the plus side, unlike nuclear power, the use of wind energy does not produce highly radioactive waste, and the construction of plants is considerably less expensive. Using the examples from earlier in this section, Hornsea I cost £4.2bn, Whitelee cost £500m, and Hinkley Point C will cost around £25bn. They are also quicker to construct – from planning consent to operation took 5 years for

Hornsea I, 3 years for Whitelee, and will likely take 15 years for Hinkley Point C from the granting of a nuclear site licence in 2012 to the estimated start of operations in 2027.

In September 2022, as part of a suite of policy announcements by the new government, it was announced that the *de facto* rather than *de jure* restrictions on new onshore wind farms would be relaxed and treated the same way as other national infrastructure projects.

QUOTATION

6.6 Biomass and Energy from Waste

6.6.1 Biomass

Biomass energy is a catch-all heading which technically includes all energy produced from living or once-living organisms. Technically, this would include coal, oil, and gas, but the term is usually applied to renewable sources of energy, such as wood chips, manure, and household waste (even if some of that was never living organisms).

The argument is partly that biomass is a renewable resource – rather than waiting millions of years for peat to be turned into coal, wood can be planted, grown, felled, burned, and replanted in a reasonably short time period. If the carbon produced by the burning of the wood is absorbed by the replacement tress which have been planted, then the system could work as close to net zero carbon emissions.

Sterman et al.[24] suggest that biofuels will not even have a short-term benefit, as a CO_2 molecule from wood burning has the same impact on the climate as a CO_2 molecule from coal burning. This can be offset if the production of wood is increased dramatically to offset the carbon. Even then, a newly planted sapling does not immediately absorb the same amount of carbon as was released by a mature tree, and thus the carbon debt could take several decades to be repaid.

There are additional complications for biofuel, which are that a significant proportion of it has to be imported from overseas, thus contributing to carbon emissions from shipping, and the fact that in many countries the growth of biofuels has been linked to significant rises in deforestation, and the knock-on impacts of biodiversity. This occurs either because illegal or unscrupulous businesses have identified a growth market and are clear-cutting established, and sometimes protected, areas of forest, or because, at a governmental level, the export of biofuels is a good generator of currency. This is a pattern which was well-established by the growth of palm oil in the 1990s.

In the UK, biomass is used to generate around 7.2 per cent of the UK's energy demand, and solid biomass accounts for about 4.3 per cent of the UK total. These figures include EfW.

Drax Power Station in Yorkshire is the largest power station in the UK. It has converted four of its six turbines to run on biomass rather than coal and will convert the remaining two to operate as part of a combined cycle gas turbine system. Conversion of coal-fired power stations to biomass-fired is attractive for businesses because it is relatively straightforward, and therefore less expensive, since the only significant change is the source of fuel. Drax imports the majority of the wood pellets it needs from the logging industries in the Eastern United States, and this has caused some controversy over the claims that it is a truly "green" way of operating.

6.6.2 Energy from Waste (EfW)

Although, as we saw earlier, energy from waste is often included as part of biomass energy, there are some significant differences that need exploring. The use of municipal waste as fuel to create energy has the advantage that it partially solves two different issues – it diverts waste from landfill, and any energy produced means a reduction in energy required from other sources.

The 1975 Waste Framework Directive[25] introduced the idea of the preferred ways for member states to deal with waste, and this was crystallised into the "waste hierarchy" by the 2008 Waste Framework Directive.[26] Figure 6.3 shows this hierarchy.

Energy recovery is preferable to landfill as a treatment for waste, but the direction of travel is to prevent municipal waste as much as possible and, where this is not possible, to reuse or recycle material before it enters the waste stream. This poses an interesting conundrum for the EfW sector – the better the UK's performance in terms of the waste hierarchy, the less the material available to use for EfW.

The 2021 Waste Management Plan issued by the Department of the Environment, Food, and Rural Affairs calls for more EfW plants to recover heat as well as energy, the idea being that this can be used for heat networks and further reduce the use of other energy sources, particularly gas.

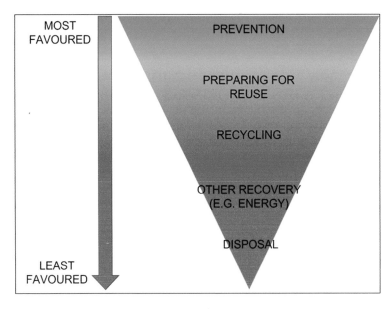

Figure 6.3 Waste hierarchy (Article 4, 2008 WFD).

Source: Directive 2008/98/EC of the European Parliament and of the Council of 19 November 2008 on waste.

QUOTATION

> "To deliver net zero virtually all heat will need to be decarbonised and heat networks will form a vital component of this. Energy from waste has a role to play in supplying this heat, but currently only around a quarter of energy from waste plants operate in combined heat and power mode, despite most being enabled to do so. We want to see this number increase. We are targeting energy from waste incinerators to produce heat for heat networks as this substantially reduces their emissions by making use of the otherwise wasted heat to displace gas boiler heating. This will support a shift from using high carbon gas generation to lower carbon generation in heat networks."
>
> DEFRA, 2021, Waste Management Plan for England, Department of the Environment, Food, and Rural Affairs, London: TSO, p. 12

EfW plants do not generate energy without producing CO_2, however. Some estimates put the total emissions from the EfW sector as 11 million tonnes equivalent of CO_2, while producing 2.5 per cent of the UK's energy. This is significant enough that carbon capture and storage (CCS) plans are being considered (see Section 6.2), but it is insignificant when contrasted to the emissions from gas and coal.

There are currently 54 municipal waste incinerators operating in the UK, and more are planned. Between them in 2021, they used nearly 15 million tonnes of waste, which amounts to around 56 per cent of the UK's residual waste.

ACTIVITY

Energy from waste is a growth industry. Parallel government policies call for an "elimination of all avoidable waste" by 2050 (DEFRA, 2021, Waste Management Plan for England).

Is EfW a sustainable industry, given the commitment to effectively remove its fuel source?

6.7 Hydroelectric and Solar

6.7.1 Hydroelectric

The use of water to drive machinery is not a recent concept. Different forms of waterwheel were regularly being used in Ancient Greece, Rome, China, India, the Norse kingdoms, and the Islamic world 2000 years ago. The use of the same technology to generate electricity dates back to the late 19th century in the North of England, and shortly afterwards at Niagara in the United States. It is one of the many technological advances attributed to the Industrial Revolution.

In addition to the standard model of hydroelectric power production, where a body of water is dammed and the flow directed through turbines to produce energy, there is a second type, known as a "pumped storage" hydroelectricity. These are usually new *consumers* of energy so are not technically about energy production but work on the basis that water is pumped upwards into a holding tank, usually when energy costs are low. When energy costs rise, or in case of a spike in demand, the water is released to run back through the turbines and generate power.

Globally, the generation of hydroelectric power kicked off in the 1950s and 1960s, and it currently generates around 1.5 terrawatts of energy.[27] Most of the UK's

1.8 gigawatts of hydroelectric power generation take place in Scotland and Wales, for reasons of terrain and rainfall, although there are three plants in England. Hydroelectric power generation does not feature at all in the government's 2022 British Energy Security Strategy, despite the contribution made by Welsh plants. In Scotland, too, hydropower does not receive a lot of attention in the Scottish Energy Strategy.

The rationale for this lack of attention in future energy polices appears to be that the hydroelectric capacity of the UK has reached maturity, and there are very few commercially viable opportunities to expand this type of energy production. Hydroelectric will continue to play a role in the generation of renewable energy, and it remains a significant player. Globally, the International Energy Agency calculated that hydropower grew faster than any other renewable energy type in the decade to 2020.

There are issues with expanding hydropower, however. The standard dam-and-turbine model requires significant reservoir of water to function effectively. The only way to achieve this is to flood what was previously a river valley, causing displacement of animal species and any people who lived there, and causing the flooded vegetation to die and rot, emitting methane, a powerful greenhouse gas. The 22-gigawatt Three Gorges Dam on the Yangtze River in China, for example, created a reservoir of almost 40 square kilometres, stretching nearly 600 kilometres (longer than the distance between Dover and Newcastle-upon-Tyne) and resulted in the forced relocation of over 1 million people.

6.7.2 Solar

The first solar cells were produced in the United States in the late 19th century, but these were far too inefficient to become commercially viable. Solar energy is one of the areas which has seen the most dramatic reduction in technology costs in recent years. Solar panels are now around one-tenth of the price they were in 2010, and about one-third more effective.

Installation of solar panels on a domestic buildings is usually considered to be part of "permitted development," so specific planning permission is not required. A commercial "solar farm" – anything with more than 4 or 5 solar panels – will need planning permission, in the same way as onshore windfarms. Solar farms require a significant amount of space – the largest in the UK is in North Wales and needs 1 square kilometre to generate 72 megawatts of energy (this is the same amount of space as Hinkley Point C, but only 2 per cent of the power). The space occupied by a solar farm, however, can simultaneously be used to farm sheep and poultry, which offsets some of the spatial requirements.

CASE

Lark Energy Ltd v Secretary of State for Communities and Local Government (2014) EWHC 2006

This case concerned a proposed expansion to a planned 14-megawatt solar farm. Planning permission had been granted for the original project, but a proposed expansion to 24 megawatts, which had been approved by the planning inspector, was rejected by the Secretary of State on the basis that the benefit was outweighed by the harm caused to the character of the area.

The court held that the Secretary of State had failed in his duty to consider the project in light of the local authority's development plan.

In July 2022, a team of researchers in Japan announced that they had created an efficient solar panel which was "near-invisible." He et al. predict that efficiency levels of 79 per cent can be reached with scaled-up designs,[28] and this raises the likelihood that solar panels will be used as windows in future building construction.

This new design opens up the possibility of a massive expansion in the use of solar power, even in temperate climates such as the UK. At present, the technology is in its infancy, and there are no policy guidelines as to its use. However, given the precedent set by allowing visible solar panels on domestic properties to largely be covered by permitted development, it follows that "near-invisible" panels will not trigger significant planning issues and will not require any additional use of space. This is partly supported by the 2022 British Energy Security Strategy, which outlines several ways of streamlining the planning processes involved with solar installation and making the installation of renewable energy the presumptive norm for all new buildings. This is a significant step, as if all new buildings are designed with integrated elements of renewable energy, the focus can be on retrofitting these technologies to existing buildings.

These are proposals, of course, and as yet have not developed into concrete policy or legislation, but they do indicate the likely direction of travel.

6.8 Future Energy Sources

As the UK moves closer to a net zero or even zero carbon energy sector, the bulk of the power is likely to be generated from technologies which already exist. Energy demand per appliance is likely to fall as efficiency is increased, but overall energy demand may rise as policies such as the end of new petrol and diesel vehicles start to take effect over the next few years.

To counter this, and to make the UK as energy secure as possible, there are several technologies which are being researched. Some of these are currently in operation but are only small-scale.

6.8.1 Nuclear Fusion

Current nuclear technology is based on sustained nuclear fission reactions, which produce large amounts of heat but also produce large quantities of waste material which will remain highly radioactive for centuries. Nuclear fusion, on the other hand, involves creating a reaction by firing particles into each other at high speed, fusing them together. The reaction causes significant heat but does not produce any long-term radioactive waste. The creation of a self-sustaining nuclear fusion reaction similar to that which takes place in the heart of the sun has been described as the "holy grail" of renewable energy, as it will provide large amounts of clean energy.

The downside is that nuclear fusion is technically hard to achieve. There are several research projects looking at fusion. The UK Atomic Energy Authority's Joint European Torus (JET) project in Culham, the International Thermonuclear Experimental Reactor (ITER) project in France, and the Korea Superconducting Tokamak Advanced Research (KSTAR) are significant players. In September 2022, KSTAR announced that they had achieved a nuclear fusion reaction that lasted for 30 seconds – the longest yet recorded.

The UK government published a Green Paper in late 2021 on possible ways of regulating a new nuclear fusion industry. Their response was published in June 2022, and the regulatory framework is included as Clause 110 of the Energy Security Bill, which, at the time of writing, is progressing through the House of Lords.

110   Fusion energy facilities: nuclear site licence not required
(1)   Section 1 of the Nuclear Installations Act 1965 (restriction of certain nuclear installations to licensed sites) is amended as follows.
(2)   After subsection (2) insert –
(2A)   Subsection (1) does not apply to a fusion energy facility.
(2B)   In subsection (2A), "fusion energy facility" means a site that is –
(a)   used for the purpose of installing or operating any plant designed or adapted for the production of electrical energy or heat by fusion, and
(b)   not also used for the purpose of installing or operating a nuclear reactor.

Clause 110, Energy Security Bill

If the bill completes its progress through Parliament and receives royal assent, then the potential future role for nuclear fusion in the UK's energy mix is likely to be significant.

6.8.2 Wave and Geothermal Energy

Both wave energy and geothermal energy are currently being used in the UK, but they are in this section because they have the potential for growth in the future.

Wave energy was first researched in the 1970s and 1980s, and the projects can be separated into two broad categories. The first type are those generators which float on, or below, the surface of the water. The constant swell of the ocean moves the individual components, and energy is generated in the connecting links. The other type are those which are shore-mounted. As waves come in, they push water upwards through a column, and as the waves retreat, the water falls again. In both directions, the movement of the water through the column generates energy.

Almost a decade ago, the UK government identified the potential of wave energy to contribute to the UK energy mix, but to date, less than a third of the potential has been achieved.

KEY FACTS

■   Wave and tidal stream energy has the potential to meet up to 20 per cent of the UK's current electricity demand, representing a 30- to 50-gigawatt (GW) installed capacity.
■   Between 200 and 300 megawatts (MWs) of generation capacity may be able to be deployed by 2020, and at the higher end of the range, up to 27GWs by 2050.

DBEIS, 2013, "Wave and tidal energy: part of the UK's energy mix," Department for Business, Energy & Industrial Strategy, London: TSO

Geothermal energy, too, was considered in the 1970s, as global oil prices spiked. There are three categories of geothermal power, and for each the main benefits are that they are carbon zero once completed and not weather-dependent. The main disadvantage is the cost associated with the initial drilling and construction phase.

Shallow Geothermal. This is mostly accessed through ground-source heat pumps, and these have the advantage that they access the relatively constant heat of the ground at a depth of around 15 metres. they are expensive to install, however, and the Energy Saving Trust's figures for October 2022 show that it would take between 12 and 200 years for the savings to pay off the initial installation cost, depending on what type of system it was replacing.[29]

Aquifer. This type of system relies on the heat stored in groundwater at around 1,500–4,000 metres below ground, where is it considerably hotter. The scale needed for this type of system makes it uneconomic at anything less than a district level, and there is only one operational system in the UK, in Southampton. A second is planned for Stoke-on-Trent, but this is already three years behind schedule.

Deep Geothermal. These systems require similar depth drilling as the aquifer type, around 1,000 metres for heat-only projects and 4,000–5,000 metres for power projects. In 2009, the Department of Energy and Climate Change launched the Deep Geothermal Challenge Fund, which is funding projects in Cornwall, Southampton, Newcastle, and County Durham.

Other than the planning requirements needed to drill deep boreholes and the standard licencing needed to generate electricity, there are no specific licensing requirements for geothermal plants.

Both wave and geothermal have significant potential, but both will require significant funding to unlock that potential.

6.8.3 Space-Based Solar and Airborne Wind Turbines

Both of these technologies are being actively researched, but neither is currently operational in a large-scale way.

Space-Based Solar

The principle behind space-based solar power is that the sun's rays are filtered by the Earth's atmosphere, so even the most efficient solar panels fitted at ground level only generate a fraction of the power which could be generated from a solar panel outside the atmosphere.

In 2021, the Department for Business, Energy, and Industrial Strategy commissioned an independent report into space-based solar, which concluded that with an investment of £16bn over 18 years, space-based solar power could be operational in 2040 and play a significant role in allowing the government to meet its net-zero by 2050 target. The report predicts that a global strip of SBS installations could, on its own, produce enough power to meet global demand 100 times over.

In September 2022, the first demonstration of long-range wireless energy transmission, of the type which would be needed for space-based solar to operate, was successfully demonstrated in Germany, so it is looking increasingly likely that this technology will develop significantly in the next decade. In November 2022, the European Space Agency announced a three-year project called SOLARIS to investigate the feasibility of space-based solar power.

Airborne Wind

Airborne wind turbines (sometimes called flying wind turbines) can work on a similar principle to a kite, or by using a balloon. The generator part of the design can either be ground-based (in which case the energy is based by the flying part rising and falling in the wind) or airborne (in which case the energy is transmitted to the ground via a cable, microwave, or laser).

High-level winds tend to be stronger than those at ground level, and so the idea behind this type of energy generation is that it will take advantage of the higher wind speed. As wind speed doubles, the power potential increases eightfold, and thus the turbines do not need to be as large. Marvel et al.[30] suggest that whereas surface-level turbines could generate 400 terawatts of energy, high-altitude turbines could produce over 1,800 terawatts. There are significant disadvantages to this type of energy, however, most significantly being the associated risks of the turbines occupying the same airspace as aircraft.

Figure 6.4 shows some interesting shifts in market share. Nuclear and petroleum contribute roughly the same in 2021 as they did in 1990. The share taken by natural gas has increased significantly, as has that taken by a combination of bioenergy and waste. Wind, solar, and hydro have increased, but less dramatically. The biggest fall is unsurprisingly in the use of coal, falling from around 35 per cent in 1990 to well under 10 per cent in 2021. As we explored earlier, this share will fall to almost zero in the next few years. What Figure 6.4 does not show is the growth in the size of the energy market overall, which has fallen from 214 million tonnes (of oil equivalent) in 1990 to 170 million tonnes in 2021.

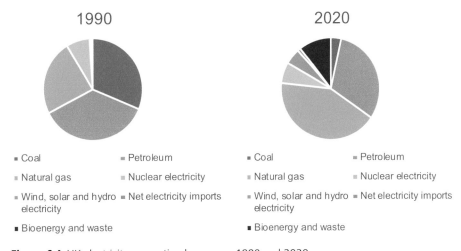

Figure 6.4 UK electricity generation by source, 1990 and 2020.

Source: Digest of UK Energy Statistics (DUKES), 2022.

SUMMARY

- The clear shift in UK energy policy has been from a near-total reliance on fossil fuels to a near-total (and total by 2035) reliance on renewable generation.

- UK's policy on sustainable energy use is triggered by its international obligations under the Paris Agreement, but also by an increasing recognition that reliance on imported energy makes the country vulnerable to external forces.

- Reducing the pressure that can be exerted by the global market may lead to a more stable development of policy.

- However, energy policy announcements in the wake of the war in Ukraine were rushed through with, in the case of fracking, little regard for scientific concerns.

SAMPLE PROBLEM QUESTION

Due to the expansion of Midtown, in the East Midlands, a decision has been reached to construct a 100-megawatt-hour power station on the banks of the river. The site is a brownfield site which was previously used for warehousing and can easily be reconnected to the mainline railway network. Downstream of the site is an area designated as a site of special scientific interest and Ramsar site (see Chapter 7) because of the birds which use it.

Assess the advantages and disadvantages of the following types of power station, and advise the developers which is the favoured option.

- Nuclear fusion
- Energy from waste
- Wind farm
- Hydroelectric
- Solar
- Geothermal

1. Identify any specifics for the site – proximity to railway, close to river, upstream from SSSI, brownfield site – and any limitations these might pose.
2. For each type of power:
   a. Identify current government policy and the impact it might have on the ease of approval.
   b. Identify positive and negative impact on the site-specific issues.
   c. Analyse the level of public support.
3. Conclude, and advise.

Further Reading

Crossley, P., 2019, *Renewable Energy Law: An International Assessment*, Cambridge: CUP

Frazer-Nash Consultancy, 2021, *Space Based Solar Power De-risking the Pathway to Net Zero*, FNC 004456–52265R Issue 1B, London: TSO

Gao, Y., Skutsch, M., Drigo, R., Pacheco, P., & Masrer, O., 2011, Assessing Deforestation from Biofuels: Methodological Challenges, *Applied Geography*, 31(2), 508–518

Hunter, T., Herrera, I., Crossley, P., & Alvarez, G., eds., 2020, *Routledge Handbook of Energy Law*, London: Routledge

Partanen, R., & Korhonen, J.M., 2020, *The Dark Horse: Nuclear Power and Climate Change*, Helsinki: National Library of Finland

Usher, B., 2019, *Renewable Energy: A Primer for the Twenty-First Century*, Columbia: Columbia University Press

Notes

1 2000, c.27
2 SI 2019/1056
3 2008 c.27
4 (26 and 27 Vict. c. 124)
5 SI 2016/1154
6 Verne, J., 1864, *A Journey to the Centre of the Earth*, New York: Scribner & Co
7 1946, c.59
8 1994, c.21
9 Rt Hon Anne-Marie Trevelyan MP, Energy and Climate Change Minister, June 2021
10 1934, c.36
11 1848, c.67
12 1998, c.17
13 2015, c.7
14 SI 2016/898
15 Public Law 585
16 1946 c. 80 (Regnal. 9 and 10 Geo 6)
17 Attlee, C., 1946, Atomic Energy Bill, HC Deb08 October 1946, vol 427, c47
18 1954 c. 32 (2 and 3 Eliz 2)
19 https://assets.publishing.service.gov.uk/government/uploads/system/uploads/attachment_data/file/272376/6887.pdf
20 SI 2016/1154
21 Jesper Kyed Larsen, October 2020, *Birds Are Good at Avoiding Wind Turbines*, Denmark: VattenfallAB
22 Nature Scot/Nàdar Alba, 2020, *Wind Farm Impact on Birds*, www.nature.scot/
23 Fox, A.D., & Petersen, I.K., 2020, Offshore Wind Farms and Their Effects on Birds, *Dansk Ornitologisk Forenings Tidsskrift*, 113(2019), 86–101, 98
24 Sterman, J.D., Siegel, L., & Rooney-Varga, J.N., 2018, Does Replacing Coal with Wood Lower CO2 Emissions? Dynamic Lifecycle Analysis of Wood Bioenergy, *Environmental Research Letters*, 13, 015007
25 Directive 75/442/EEC on waste
26 Directive 2008/98/EC on waste
27 1.5 terawatts is 1,500 gigawatts. To put this figure into perspective, the UK's total household energy consumption in 2018 was 105 terawatts.
28 He, X., Iwamoto, Y., Kaneko, T., & Kato, T., 2022, Fabrication of Near-Invisible Solar Cell with Monolayer WS2, *Scientific Reports*, 12, 11315, https://doi.org/10.1038/s41598-022-15352-x
29 Installation cost of c£30,000. Annual savings v. A-rated Gas Boiler £145. Annual savings v. old electric storage heaters £2500. Source: https://energysavingtrust.org.uk/advice/ground-source-heat-pumps/
30 Marvel, K., Kravitz, B., & Caldeira, K., 2013, Geophysical Limits to Global Wind Power, *Nature Climate Change*, 3, 118–121, 118

7

Wildlife Protection and Wildlife Crime

One of the issues which adds to the complexity of wildlife protection is the fact that there are so many different pressures to balance. The increased value of species which are scarce makes them ideal targets for criminal groups, who regard endangered species as commodities to be traded on the illicit market. The trade follows the same basic supply-and-demand model as any other commodity. The higher the demand, or the lower the supply, then the higher the price. The price charged for the bones of an endangered tiger (*Panthera tigris*), therefore, will be much higher than that charged for the bones of its South American cousin the jaguar (*Panthera onca*), which is not endangered, despite the significant similarities in the chemical makeup of the bones. You will see as you progress through the chapter that almost all the legislative provisions attempt to block the supply side of the trade, by making the buying and selling of particular species a criminal offence. There is much less legislative provision aiming to tackle the demand side of the trade. In essence, this aspect is left to the field of education, and so there is a clear link to Sustainable Development Goal 4 (see Chapter 5).

Although this chapter will focus on animals, it is important to note that this trade involves not just species of animals but also plants. In terms of the animal species, however, it may involve the sale of live examples to collectors or to those seeking exotic pets. It may also involve the sale of animal derivatives – eggs, skins, bones, teeth, or other body parts – either as trophies or for decoration or for their use in traditional medicines. The money raised by organised criminal groups, which is estimated by Interpol to be up to US$20bn a year, makes a significant contribution to their overall income and is linked to the trafficking of people, narcotics, and firearms, as well as corruption and money laundering.

Wildlife crime therefore is a significant issue globally, both from an environmental perspective and a wider criminal one.

Originally, "conservation" was perceived both nationally and internationally as a way of obtaining the optimum sustainable resource yield to secure maximum supply of food and other products. The idea of conserving species for their own value, not simply as resources, is a comparatively recent mainstream one. The importance of biological diversity (biodiversity) and the

DOI: 10.4324/9781003137214-7

conception that wildlife is not an inexhaustible resource seems today like common sense. In some cultures, the view that certain habitats need protection has been entrenched for centuries, even where it was not specifically for wildlife protection reasons. In what is now India, for example, the 7th-century religious encyclopaedia the *Agni Purana* repeatedly encouraged people to worship and protect particular trees as a means of conveying benefits both in this life and the afterlife, and in England, the New Forest in Dorset was created in the 11th century by order of King William I as a private hunting ground. Despite neither of these being done overtly for the protection of nature and wildlife, their effect was to create protected ecosystems.

However, the recognition that wildlife could be hunted without consequences was not something that was present among early European settlers in the United States. In a relatively short time period, the Carolina parakeet (*Conuropsis carolinensis*), great auk (*Pinguinus impennis*), Eastern cougar (*Puma concolor couguar*), and ivory-billed woodpecker (*Campephilus principalis*) were hunted to extinction. This was partly for sporting reasons, partly for the protection of domesticated species, and partly by accident. Even at governmental level, some species were considered to be so prolific that there was no chance of their extinction. The legendary passenger pigeon (*Ectopistes migratorius*), for example, was reported by the Ohio State Legislature to be so numerous that it could be shot at will with no impact on the overall population. Despite the very confident wording of the report, the reality is that indiscriminate shooting of the passenger pigeon led to their extinction in the wild only 43 years after the report was published. The last passenger pigeon, a female named Martha, died in Cincinnati Zoo in 1914.

This chapter will trace the development of national and international legislative provisions which protect wildlife though criminal sanctions and through the creation of protected spaces. Species need spaces, so protecting one while ignoring the other means that efforts will be far less successful. You should remember, though, that there is another legislation which has an indirect wildlife protection role in non-protected areas. Planning law, transport policy, housing policy, farming, energy – in fact, anything which has an impact on human use of space – will have an impact on the space available for wildlife.

AIMS AND OBJECTIVES

After reading this chapter, you should be able to:

■ Identify the main international wildlife and habitat provisions.

■ Identify the linkages between these and UK provisions.

■ Recognise the inherent human/non-human conflicts which relate to land use.

7.1 1940 Western Hemisphere Convention

In 1936, Dr John C. Philips (founder of the American Committee for International Wildlife Protection) arranged for a study of the species of mammal which had either become extinct in the recent past or appeared to be in danger of doing so in the near future. This was the largest study of its kind ever undertaken and proved to be the basis for the approach which would be taken by all future wildlife protection measures. The purpose of the study was both to form a baseline study of what mammals were at imminent risk of extinction and also to identify the factors which had driven those species to that level.

Work on the study (carried out by Allen and Harper) began in mid-1937, almost the same day that William Temple Hornaday, the one-time director of the Bronx Zoo, died. Hornaday was a significant influence on the creation of Allen's study and had warned about the patchy and inadequate legal system decades earlier. He identified that animals were being killed for sport (both legally and illegally) far more quickly than they were breeding, and that a continuation of this would only have one outcome – extinction. The refusal of legislators and society to publicly acknowledge this meant, he argued, as a sign that "we are living in a fool's paradise."[1]

Hornaday's work influenced Allen and Harper's study, and also the negotiations towards the 1940 Convention on Nature Protection and Wildlife Preservation in the Western Hemisphere (sometimes referred to as the Western Hemisphere Convention), which was signed at the Pan American Union (the precursor to the Organisation on America States) in Washington, DC. The Convention was originally signed by only 13 states, with a further five signing in 1941, meaning, that the Convention was only technically binding on a relatively small number of states, with a relatively small range of wildlife. The preamble to the Convention makes is clear that the links had been drawn between human activities and species extinction but also recognised the futility of protecting species without also protecting the habitat which they need to survive.

ARTICLE

Preamble

The Governments of the American Republics, wishing to protect and reserve in their natural habitat representatives of all species and genera of their native flora and fauna, including migratory birds, in sufficient numbers and over areas extensive enough to assure them from becoming extinct through any agency within man's control; and

Wishing to protect and preserve scenery of extraordinary beauty, unusual and striking geologic formations, regions and natural objects of aesthetic, historic or scientific value, and areas characterized by primitive conditions in those cases covered by this Convention; and

Wishing to conclude a convention on the protection of nature and the preservation of flora and fauna to effectuate the foregoing purposes.

Preamble to the 1940 Western Hemisphere Convention

Despite the promises hinted at by the preamble, this was, in practice, a Convention which was more aspirational than enforceable as it lacked any provisions at all for enforcement. Lyster[2] called it a "sleeping convention" and argued that by the 1980s it was of only limited value to most of the signatories. Rogers and Moore are a little kinder to the treaty, although they, too, argue that the levels of activity under it have done little "to belie its dormant reputation."[3]

The criticisms of both Lyster and Rogers and Moore about the lack of enforcement under the Convention is tempered to some extent by their recognition that it is a clear signal of intent and a significant improvement on the vacuum which preceded it and marked a concrete step towards multinational agreements to increase the protection for species, whether vulnerable or not.

7.2 The IUCN and International Species Protection Conventions

National and regional protection measures for specific species have been passed for many years and are summarised briefly in Figure 7.1. St Cuthbert's 7th-century law to protect seabirds off the Farne Islands, the Cruel Treatment of Cattle Act 1822[4] (Martin's Act), or the International Convention for the Regulation of Whaling, for example. The idea of a *global* list of all endangered species of flora and fauna which needed protection was not proposed until 1963, however. The proposal was from the naturalist Peter (later Sir Peter) Scott, and the first attempt to create a list was in the World Wildlife Fund's first report, "The Launching of a New Ark," in 1964. Scott argued that the groundwork for his ideas was done by, *inter* alia, Hornaday, Allen, and Harper, and the link is made clearer when it is understood that IUCN and WWF founding director Harold Coolidge Jr. wrote the forewords both for Allen's 1942 publication and the IUCN's 1969 Red Book.[5] In 1966, the "Red Data Book" was published as a specialist text for the International Union for the Conservation of Nature (IUCN), and this was followed by a version intended for a wider audience in 1969. Out of the same IUCN environment which had spawned the Red Book came a resolution at the IUCN General Assembly in Nairobi in 1963 which called for the creation of a convention to protect endangered species.

In 1972, the UN Conference on the Human Environment (UNCHE) took place in Stockholm, Sweden. This was a pivotal event, as it established the UN Environment Programme (UNEP) and led to the establishment of the World Conservation Strategy (WCS) in 1980, the World Charter for Nature (WCN) in 1982, and the World Conference on Environment and Development (WCED) in 1987. UNCHE also set out two of the fundamental principles of wildlife conservation on an international scale.

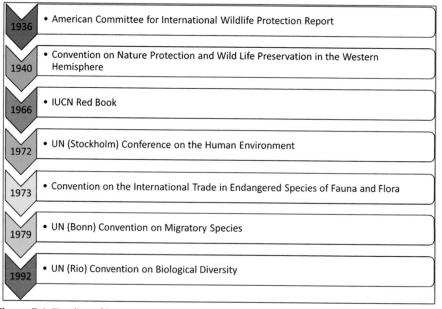

Figure 7.1 Timeline of key species protection measures.

Principle 2

The natural resources of the earth, including the air, water, land, flora and fauna and especially representative samples of natural ecosystems, must be safeguarded for the benefit of present and future generations through careful planning or management, as appropriate.

Principle 4

Man has a special responsibility to safeguard and wisely manage the heritage of wildlife and its habitat, which are now gravely imperilled by a combination of adverse factors. Nature conservation, including wildlife, must therefore receive importance in planning for economic development.

Principle 7

States shall take all possible steps to prevent pollution of the seas by substances that are liable to create hazards to human health, to harm living resources and marine life, to damage amenities or to interfere with other legitimate uses of the sea.

Principles 2, 4, and 7 of the Stockholm Declaration of the United Nations Conference on Human Environment, 1973

The declaration of UNCHE, in line with all declarations of this type, is much more of a declaration of intent, or "soft law," rather than a binding piece of legislation, or "hard law." As such, it is useful as a tool for identifying possible future developments.

7.2.1 Convention on the International Trade in Endangered Species of Wild Fauna and Flora (CITES)

The IUCN's call for an *international* agreement was answered a decade later when the Convention on the International Trade in Endangered Species of Wild Fauna and Flora (CITES) was signed in Washington in May 1973. CITES entered into force in July 1975 after ten ratifications, and since then, membership has grown to 184 parties (2022). The preamble to the Convention recognises both the importance of species protection and habitat protection.

ARTICLE

Recognizing that wild fauna and flora in their many beautiful and varied forms are an irreplaceable part of the natural systems of the earth which must be protected for this and the generations to come;

Conscious of the ever-growing value of wild fauna and flora from aesthetic, scientific, cultural, recreational and economic points of view;

Recognizing that peoples and States are and should be the best protectors of their own wild fauna and flora;

Recognizing, in addition, that international co-operation is essential for the protection of certain species of wild fauna and flora against over-exploitation through international trade.

Preamble, Convention on the International Trade in Endangered Species of Fauna and Flora, 1973.

The Convention identifies the importance of international cooperation in the preamble, and also the link between endangered species and trade. The species which are deemed to need protection are listed in three appendices to the Convention. Appendix I lists the species that are at most risk of extinction, Appendix II lists those which are at some risk, and Appendix III those which are at risk in particular jurisdictions.

ARTICLE

Article II (1)

Appendix I shall include all species threatened with extinction which are or may be affected by trade. Trade in specimens of these species must be subject to particularly strict regulation in order not to endanger further their survival and must only be authorized in exceptional circumstances.

Article II (2)

Appendix II shall include:

(a) all species which although not necessarily now threatened with extinction may become so unless trade in specimens of such species is subject to strict regulation in order to avoid utilization incompatible with their survival; and

(b) other species which must be subject to regulation in order that trade in specimens of certain species referred to in sub-paragraph (a) of this paragraph may be brought under effective control.

Article II (3)

Appendix III shall include all species which any Party identifies as being subject to regulation within its jurisdiction for the purpose of preventing or restricting exploitation, and as needing the co-operation of other Parties in the control of trade.

Article II, Convention on the International Trade in
Endangered Species of Fauna and Flora, 1973

The debate on whether species need to be moved in or out of the different appendices is based in scientific data on species numbers, observed threats, and the trend in numbers. The IUCN Red List, which forms the basis of these decisions, puts all species into one of nine different categories (see Figure 7.2) and also gives a population trend which can be increasing, stable, or decreasing.

The categorisation for many species is in need of updating, and one of the weaknesses of CITES is the data, the collecting of which requires proper funding from the CITES parties.

The "threatened categories" (VU, EN, CR) are all calculated using a set of five criteria (A–E), and if a species meets any of those criteria, then it is put into the respective category. Although the specific levels are of course different for each of the threatened categories, broadly speaking, the categories are:

Category A: Reduction in population size
Category B: Geographic range in the form of either B1 (extent of occurrence) *or* B2 (area of occupancy) *or* both

Not Evaluated (NE)	Data Deficient (DD)	Least Concern (LC)	Near Threatened (NT)	Vulnerable (VU)	Endangered (EN)	Critically Endangered (CR)	Extinct in the Wild (EW)	Extinct (EX)

Figure 7.2 IUCN Red List categories.

Source: IUCN 2022. The IUCN Red List of Threatened Species. Version 2022–1. www.iucnredlist.org

Category C: Population size future estimates of decline
Category D: Current population size (CR <50, EN <250, VU <1,000)
Category E: Probability of extinction in the wild in next 100 years (max) (CR 50 per cent, EN 20 per cent, VU 10 per cent)

Since the ninth meeting of the Conference of the Parties (COP) in Fort Lauderdale in 1994, the approach has been to err on the side of caution (effectively using the precautionary principle) when changing the designation of species. As you can see earlier, much of the data is based on estimates, calculations, and probabilities, and the cautious approach is preferred because of the risks which might result from acting too quickly.

ARTICLE

"When considering proposals to amend Appendix I or II, the Parties shall, by virtue of the precautionary approach and in case of uncertainty either as regards the status of a species or the impact of trade on the conservation of a species, act in the best interest of the conservation of the species concerned and adopt measures that are proportionate to the anticipated risks to the species."

CITES, Annex IV, adopted by Conf. 9.24

The COP meets roughly every two years, and the 19th COP was in Panama City, Panama, in late 2022, and there were 52 proposals put forward to move species across appendices or to change the rules for some species in certain states. These changes are summarised in Table 7.1.

Sadly, over the almost half century of CITES, it is clear that more species are being added or moved from Appendix II to Appendix I than the reverse. This supports other evidence that biodiversity levels are dropping, and species extinction is becoming more commonplace.

CRITIQUING THE LAW

Does the second part of the preamble to CITES (emphasising the "aesthetic, scientific, cultural, recreational and economic" value of wildlife) identify it as an essentially anthropocentric (i.e. human-focused – see Chapter 2) convention?

Is this a good thing or a bad thing for a convention which is intended to protect wild species of fauna and flora?

Table 7.1 CITES COP 19 Proposals for Changes to the Appendices

Downgrade (Appendix I to Appendix II)	8 species, including the white rhinoceros (Ceratotherium simum simum)
Upgrade (Appendix II to Appendix I)	6 species, including the hippopotamus (Hippopotamus amphibius)
Previously not on appendices but add to Appendix II	34 species, including the Chinese water dragon (Physignathus cocincinus)
Previously not on appendices but add to Appendix I	2 species, including pygmy bluetongue lizard (Tiliqua adelaidensis)

CITES, by its very nature, only covers species which fulfil two criteria: they are already endangered or at risk of becoming endangered, and they are traded internationally. The Convention does not require signatory states to do anything at all about species which are commonplace or, indeed, species which are endangered but only traded internally.

7.2.2 Bonn Convention on the Conservation of Migratory Species of Wild Animals

Many species are, by their nature, relatively fixed in their location – they are born, live, and die within a territory which happens to coincide with the territory of a single state. This makes the entire lives of those species governed by whatever national measures are in place.

Other species migrate from the territory of one state to the territory of others. For those species which live aquatic lives, their territory may stray into areas which are outside national controls. What this means in practice is that a species may have protection until it crosses the border into the territory of another state, and from a preservation of biodiversity perspective, this is a clearly suboptimal solution.

There are several examples of bilateral or trilateral conventions which cover species that only have a relatively limited migratory pattern. The 130,000 Porcupine caribou (*Rangifer tarandus granti*) spends the vast part of its life in Canada but also crosses into Alaska annually. The 1988 US–Canadian Agreement on the Conservation of the Porcupine Caribou Herd, as the name suggests, is a bilateral agreement between the United States and Canada which has as its two objectives the conservation of this species and the maintenance of traditional ways of life in the Yukon and Alaska regions. The agreement delegated specific decisions to the Porcupine Caribou Management Board, which has put measures in place to limit hunting and also preserve habitat. In the three decades or so since the agreement was signed, Porcupine caribou numbers have risen by 70 per cent to around 220,000.

Whilst smaller agreements and approaches such as this are useful in some cases, there was no coherent system for creating them. To avoid this patchy approach, the UN Convention on the Conservation of Migratory Species of Wild Animals was signed in Bonn in 1979. The Convention sets out the parameters which the 133 state parties should observe for the creation of individual agreements. Canada, China, Russia, and the United States have not signed the Convention, which means that although they are able to, and do, create agreements involving migratory species, they will not necessarily conform to the typology set out by the Bonn Convention.

ARTICLE

Article II: Fundamental Principles

1. The Parties acknowledge the importance of migratory species being conserved and of Range States agreeing to take action to this end whenever possible and appropriate, paying special attention to migratory species the conservation status of which is unfavourable, and taking individually or in co-operation appropriate and necessary steps to conserve such species and their habitat.

2. The Parties acknowledge the need to take action to avoid any migratory species becoming endangered.

3. In particular, the Parties:

   a) should promote, co-operate in and support research relating to migratory species;

b) shall endeavour to provide immediate protection for migratory species included in Appendix I; and

c) shall endeavour to conclude AGREEMENTS covering the conservation and management of migratory species included in Appendix II.

Article III, UN Convention on the Conservation of Migratory Species of Wild Animals

Appendix I is a list of migratory species that are "endangered" (Article III (1)), and the term is used here in a way which broadly (but not exactly) corresponds with the term in the CITES Convention. Appendix II is a list of migratory species which have an "unfavourable conservation status" (Article IV (1)). *Unfavourable* is not defined in the Convention, but following the pattern established for Appendix I language, the standard is likely to conform to "vulnerable" or "near threatened" or somewhere between the two.

CRITIQUING THE LAW

How useful is an international agreement on how to make international agreements?

7.2.3 Convention on Biological Diversity (CBD)

The CBD, which was signed as part of the raft of documents at the UN Conference on Environment and Development in Rio de Janeiro in 1992, entered into force in 1993. 196 countries have ratified the CBD, with the notable exception of the United States of America, which signed in 1993 and, after a failed attempt to get ratification approved by Congress, has not gone any further towards ratification. Despite the absence of the United States, which is ironic, given that it was the state responsible for the original wildlife protection convention in 1940, the CBD is the most widely ratified treaty of its type ever created.

One reason which may explain the willingness of states to ratify the convention is the fact that its aims are generally expressed as aspirational goals, as opposed to tightly defined objectives. The goals themselves, in an approach which was mirrored by the UN Sustainable Development Goals (see Chapter 5), are expressed in quite broad terms. The provisions are solid enough, but the phrase "each contracting party shall, as far as possible and appropriate . . ." mitigates the impact of Articles 5, 6, 7, 8, 9, 10, 11, and 14, which makes the Convention weaker than it needs to be.

Despite the promise of the CBD, the latest in the series of periodical Global Biodiversity Outlook publications (GBO 5) admits that progress has not been satisfactory, and that most of the Aichi biodiversity targets have not been met.

There have been two protocols to the CBD.

The **Cartagena Protocol** on Biosecurity (2000). This Protocol concerns the risks associated with the use of new organisms created as a result of modern biotechnology industry, and their interaction with existing biodiversity. It also covers the safe storage, use, and transfer of such new organisms.

The **Nagoya Protocol** on Access to Genetic Resources and the Fair and Equitable Sharing of Benefits Arising from Their Utilization (2014). This Protocol is also called the ABS (Access and Benefit Sharing) Treaty and aims at sharing any benefits which arise from the use of genetic resources in a fair and equitable way. The Protocol gives weight to Article 15 of the CBD.

ARTICLE

Further weight was added to the CBD by the Aichi biodiversity targets, which ran from 2011 to 2020. The 20 targets were collated together into five goals, and despite the UN Secretary General's previous assertion that most of the goals were not met, the sad truth is that not one of them was met in full. However, as with the UN SDGs, it remains likely that progress towards the targets was greater than it would have been without them.

ARTICLE

COP 15 of the CBD takes place in December 2022, and the intention is to determine a new set of measures for biodiversity. A first draft of the global biodiversity framework was released in 2021 and included four long-term goals with a deadline of 2050 to enhance the integrity of all ecosystems (Goal A), enhance nature's contributions to people (Goal B), ensure the fair use of genetic resources (Goal C), and close the gap on finance (Goal D). The IUCN added that in order to meet these targets, an additional investment of between 0.7 per cent and 1 per cent of global GDP is needed, amounting to between US\$670bn and US\$960bn a year.

It remains to be seen how the participants at COP 15 will react to the proposals (and, indeed, the level of financing suggested by IUCN), and the hope is that they are stronger and better financed and enforced than the original goals. However, given the engagement with financial provision under the UN Framework Convention on Climate Change, it is perhaps more of a hope than an expectation.

7.3 International Habitat Protection Measures

A lot of the species protection measures also include provisions to protect the relevant habitat of the species concerned, for obvious reasons. This section will briefly address some of the major international measures which are primarily designed to protect habitat rather than any specific species. It will not look at smaller regional conventions, like the 1991 Salzburg Convention concerning the protection of the Alps, which only included as members the eight Alpine states. These are important, but these are too numerous to include.

7.3.1 The Antarctic Treaty (1959)

The Antarctic is named from the ancient Greek *"anti"* (opposite to) and *"arcticos"* (both "northern" and "of the bear"), and the name applies to the continent as well as the region which sits more than 60 degrees south.

The Antarctic holds the vast bulk of the world's ice, and due to rising sea and air temperatures caused by climate change, that ice is melting considerably faster now than it was in the 1990s. This, in turn, contributes to rising sea levels and the problems associated with that. The Antarctic is also the location of the most significant thinning of the ozone layer (see Chapter 9), and this may have had an impact on the rate of warming (and thus melting). On the positive side, the Antarctic is also the only continent never to have had a war.

Although there is one specific Antarctic treaty, there is an additional protocol and two further conventions which form what is called the "Antarctic Treaty Series."

1959 Antarctic Treaty

The 1959 Treaty is relatively short and runs to only 14 articles. The parties agreed that the continent should be used for exclusively peaceful purposes and not be a space for nuclear testing or dumping (Articles I and 5) and that priority should be given to scientific investigation and cooperation (Article II and III).

The states further agreed not to claim any new jurisdiction of the Antarctic (Article IV), and although seven states, including the UK, have made territorial claims historically, they are not widely recognised. This lack of formal recognition itself is in contrast with the wording of Article IV, which asserts that no act under the Treaty is the basis for denying a claim to sovereignty.

The Treaty covers the region of Antarctica (that below 60 degrees south) as opposed to the continent. There are 43 consultative parties to the Treaty (which are entitled to take part in meetings of the Secretariat of the Antarctic Treaty) and 26 non-consultative parties, which can attend the meetings but not participate.

1972 London Convention for the Conservation of Antarctic Seals

This Convention covers the region of Antarctica. The text makes reference to Article IV of the Antarctic Treaty and requires parties to confirm that they will not seek to apply sovereignty to any part of the area covered.

There are currently 17 parties to the Convention, and its purpose is to stop the hunting of seals for fur and meat, and its initial standpoint is a complete ban on the hunting and killing of six species of seal. This is accompanied by a range of caveats as to reasons which could be given by states not to comply with the terms of the Convention.

The rationale for what might seem to be a weakening of the provisions of the Convention is that states are at least bound to observe the processes and procedures embedded within it, and if the ban was absolute, those states which were likely to want to use exceptions would not sign and thus not be bound at all.

1982 Convention on the Conservation of Antarctic Marine Living Resources (CCAMLR)

The Convention was created after concerns about the over-exploitation of the seas around the Antarctic. It is a good example of the tragedy of the unmanaged commons (see Chapter 2), as ironically one side effect of the Antarctic Treaty itself was that none of the waters around the Antarctic were sovereign territory.

ARTICLE

1. This Convention applies to the Antarctic marine living resources of the area south of 60° South latitude and to the Antarctic marine living resources of the area between that latitude and the Antarctic Convergence which form part of the Antarctic marine ecosystem.
2. Antarctic marine living resources means the populations of fin fish, molluscs, crustaceans, and all other species of living organisms, including birds, found south of the Antarctic Convergence.

Article 1, CCAMLR

The region covered by the Convention is not as straightforward as that covered by the 1972 London Convention, as it is part based on the area south of 60 degrees south and part on the limits of the "Antarctic Convergence," a line defined in Article 1 as being at latitudes from 45 degrees to 60 degrees south, depending on the longitude. There are 37 parties to the Convention.

1991 Protocol to the Antarctic Treaty (The Madrid Protocol)

This Protocol adds to the provisions of the Treaty and, *inter* alia, prohibits mineral exploitation (other than for scientific purposes). There are estimated to be 500 billion barrels of oil under the continent, compared to annual global oil consumption of 100 million barrels in 2021–2022. This means that the estimated Antarctic oil reserves would supply global demand for oil for five millennia. There have been suggestions over the last few years that Russian-flagged ships have been actively seeking oil reserves, and this has led to concerns that Russia might flout its obligations under the Treaty and the Protocol and start exploiting the colossal oil reserves.

Overall, the Antarctic Treaty Series provides a comprehensive framework for protection of species, habitat, and resources.

ACTIVITY

Consider the following short examples and assess whether they breach the provisions of any part of the Antarctic Treaty Series.

- The Filipino trawler MV *Manila* drops its nets close to a shoal of fin fish. The nets are dropped just to the north of the 60 degrees south line, but the oceanic currents move them south of the line, which is where the fish are caught.

- A New Zealand–registered ship is involved in hunting crab-eater seals (*Lobodon carcinophagus*) just off the coast of the Antarctic continent.

- A submarine registered in Russia is known to have been seeking oil and gas reserves below the ice shelf, although no exploratory drilling has yet taken place.

7.3.2 The Ramsar Convention (1971)

The Ramsar Convention on Wetlands of International Importance Especially as Waterfowl Habitat has the title of the oldest intergovernmental environmental agreement, by dint of the fact that the Antarctic Treaty has a remit much wider than simply environmental issues.

It is a short Convention, running to only 12 sections, and its purpose was to encourage member states to designate areas of internationally important wetlands ("Ramsar sites") within their own territory, on the basis that a large proportion of waterfowl are migratory.

What has become interesting about the Ramsar Convention is that many of the c150 Ramsar sites in the UK overlap with the 650+ SACs ("special areas of conservation" under the Habitats Directive) and/or the 280 SPAs ("specially protected areas" under the Birds Directive), which are covered in more detail in Section 7.4.1, which follows, despite the designations being under different regimes.

ARTICLE

Article 2

1. Each Contracting Party shall designate suitable wetlands within its territory for inclusion in a List of Wetlands of International Importance, hereinafter referred to as "the List" which is maintained by the bureau established under Article 8. The boundaries of each wetland shall be precisely described and also delimited on a map, and they may incorporate riparian and coastal zones adjacent to the wetlands, and islands or bodies of marine water deeper than six metres at low tide lying within the wetlands, especially where these have importance as waterfowl habitat.
2. Wetlands should be selected for the List on account of their international significance in terms of ecology, botany, zoology, limnology, or hydrology. In the first instance wetlands of international importance to waterfowl at any season should be included.
3. The inclusion of a wetland in the List does not prejudice the exclusive sovereign rights of the Contracting Party in whose territory the wetland is situated.
4. Each Contracting Party shall designate at least one wetland to be included in the List when signing this Convention or when depositing its instrument of ratification or accession, as provided in Article 9.
5. Any Contracting Party shall have the right to add to the List further wetlands situated within its territory, to extend the boundaries of those wetlands already included by it in the List, or, because of its urgent national interests, to delete or restrict the boundaries of wetlands already included by it in the List and shall, at the earliest possible time, inform the organization or government responsible for the continuing bureau duties specified in Article 8 of any such changes.
6. Each Contracting Party shall consider its international responsibilities for the conservation, management, and wise use of migratory stocks of waterfowl, both when designating entries for the List and when exercising its right to change entries in the List relating to wetlands within its territory.

Article 2, Ramsar Convention 1971

The "monitoring bureau" mentioned is the IUCN, and an interesting aspect of this Convention is that states have to designate at least one area of wetland before they can be part of the Convention. This ensures that any state which wishes to benefit from the protective regime established by the Convention must either designate or create an area of wetland.

The designation of Ramsar sites was just one of the three pillars of the Convention, the other two being the promotion of "wise use" of wetlands in each country and better international cooperation to further wise use. *Wise use* is never actually defined in the Convention itself, but this can be seen as a positive element, as it allows for a range of interpretations.

QUOTATION

"[T]he flexibility and conceptual vagueness that characterises wetland 'wise use' and 'ecological character' serves to enable communication with and among contracting parties in situations where consensus is neither desired nor possible. This is understandable given that 170 diversely socio-political national governments are committed to the Convention obligations."

Joshi, D., et al, 2021, "Ramsar Convention and the Wise Use of Wetlands: Rethinking Inclusion," *Ecological Restoration*, 39(1/2), March/June 2021, p. 37
https://muse.jhu.edu/article/793658

There are currently over 170 parties to the Ramsar Convention, and the areas designated as Ramsar sites cover around 2.5 million square kilometres (this is an area approximately twice the size of South Africa). A longitudinal study in 2014 found that bird species were twice as abundant in Ramsar-designated wetland sites as they were in non-protected wetland sites, although the team did concede that this might have been because only the higher-quality sites were designated in the first place.

Paris Protocol (1982)

This short Protocol was adopted by the parties in order to remove the provision in the convention itself that the English-language version was the only authentic version. The rationale for doing so was twofold. Parties acknowledged that the effectiveness of the convention would be improved with wider participation and that this could be facilitated by "authentic language versions."

7.3.3 The Bern Convention on the Conservation of European Wildlife and Natural Habitats (1979)

The Bern Convention was introduced under the auspices of the Council of Europe (CoE) but has extended the potential for membership so that there are now 50 parties to the Convention, drawn mostly from CoE member states, but also including five non-member states (Belarus, Burkina Faso, Morocco, Senegal, and Tunisia). This makes the reach of the Convention far more restricted than the Ramsar Convention, but greater (in terms of parties, rather than space) than the Antarctic Treaty.

The Convention requires parties to take steps to conserve wild flora and fauna, as well as their habitats. There is particular attention given to "endangered and vulnerable" species which are left undefined by the text of the Convention. The classifications, whilst using the same language as the IUCN Red List (mentioned earlier), are not based on that list. The list of endangered and vulnerable *flora* species is based on the IUCN's list but tailored for endemic European species. The list of endangered and vulnerable *fauna* species is based on lists created by the European Committee for the Conservation of Nature and Natural Resources (a CoE advisory committee).

ARTICLE

Article 1

The aims of this Convention are to conserve wild flora and fauna and their natural habitats, especially those species and habitats whose conservation requires the co-operation of several States, and to promote such co-operation. Particular emphasis is given to endangered and vulnerable species, including endangered and vulnerable migratory species.

Article 2

The Contracting Parties shall take requisite measures to maintain the population of wild flora and fauna at, or adapt it to, a level which corresponds in particular to ecological, scientific, and cultural requirements, while taking account of economic and recreational requirements and the needs of sub-species, varieties, or forms at risk locally.

Articles 1 and 2, Bern Convention

One of the interesting differences of this Convention compared to the others we have considered is the language used. Many other international legal instruments are couched in aspirational terms (see, for example, earlier discussions on the CBD). The Bern Convention uses considerably stronger language, and this, combined with a standing committee to rule on potential breaches, makes the provisions more powerful than they would otherwise have been. To paraphrase Shakespeare, though the Convention be but small, it is fierce.

QUOTATION

"Two aspects of the convention are especially noteworthy. The first is that almost every one of its provisions is mandatory, as opposed to being couched in the hortatory language favoured by many conservation treaties. The second is the system of administration it has created to promote and oversee its implementation, which represents a major advance from earlier regional wildlife conventions."

Bowman, M.; Davies, P.; and Redgewell, C., 2010, *Lyster's International Wildlife Law*, 2nd ed. Cambridge, CUP, p. 268

A similarity that the Bern Convention has with many conservation treaties is the inherent contradiction between conservation and development which is at the heart of sustainable development. To offset this, the standing committee set up the "Emerald Network" of protected sites in 1989, which is the main way for parties to demonstrate their correct implementation of the Convention. The Emerald Network is strengthened by the EU's membership of the Bern Convention, as the network of "Natura 2000" sites established under the Habitats Directive[6] (see later text) is counted as contributions from EU member states.

7.4 UK Law

As we saw at the start of the chapter, species need spaces – whether on land or in water, and whether permanent homes or temporary resting places. UK law is still currently based heavily on measures introduced as a result of EU law, and this section will focus partly on the two main residual EU measures, the Birds and Habitats Directives, but will begin by considering the development of laws in the

UK from the 19th century and the obligations which stem from international measures.

7.4.1 UK Law: Fauna, Flora, and Habitat

Prior to the start of the 19th century, the main emphasis in the UK's conservation laws was on the protection of habitats and the species that lived in them for the purposes of hunting. As we saw at the start of the chapter, the New Forest was created by the king in the 12th century as a private hunting area, and penalties for anyone caught poaching were severe.

There followed a period from the 19th to mid-20th century when acts were passed in a reactive and disjointed way, as they were in other areas of environmental law. The Sea Bird Protection Act 1869[7] introduced the idea of a "close season," where seabirds should not be killed.

LEGISLATION

"Any person who shall kill, wound, or attempt to kill or wound, or take any sea bird, or use any boat, gun, net, or other engine or instrument for the purpose of killing, wounding, or taking any sea bird, or shall have in his control or possession any sea bird recently killed, wounded, or taken, between the first day of April and the first day of August in any year, shall, on conviction of any such offence before any justice or justices of the peace in England or Ireland, or before the sheriff or any justice or justices of the peace in Scotland, forfeit and pay for every such sea bird so killed, wounded, or taken, or so in his possession, such sum of money not exceeding one pound as to the said justices or sheriff shall seem meet, together with the costs of the conviction; provided always, that this section shall not apply where the said sea bird is a young bird unable to fly."

S2, Sea Birds Protection Act 1869

The fine of £1 per bird is equivalent to around £95 at 2022 values, which is a relatively low fine by modern standards. Not long afterwards, the Wild Birds Preservation Act 1880[8] widened the offence to all wild birds (rather than just seabirds) and effectively imposed a close season from 1 March to 1 August, when trapping or killing any wild bird would result in a £1 fine for the first bird, and 5 shillings (25p) for any subsequent bird.

Most conservation work at that time was carried out by voluntary organisations – the National Trust was established in 1907, and the RSPB (as the Society for the Protection of Birds) in 1889. There was little official enforcement or monitoring of compliance with the patchy legislation. The Protection of Birds Act 1954,[9] for example, which provided a great deal of the underpinnings to the current WCA, was introduced as a private member's bill on behalf of the RSPB.

Indeed, if we discount areas which were protected for hunting, etc., the current global strategy of identifying specific areas that might need protection, designating them under some sort of scheme, and giving them additional protection was also introduced by voluntary organisations. Cley Marshes, on the North Norfolk coast, was purchased by the Norfolk Naturalist Trust in 1926 as a way of providing for a perpetual breeding ground for birds. Romney Marsh in Kent, which now forms part of the wider Dungeness RSPB Reserve, was bought by the RSPB in 1929. Both of these sites (and others like them) suffered from a fundamental problem, however. Their only protection came from common law, property law, and tort law – there was no specific statutory protection which could be relied upon. The same was true for flora and other fauna too. Common law does not protect wild creatures, but property rights can be used, as animals which are present on land can be protected from interference by anyone who is not the holder of the proprietary interest. This situation was clearly untenable for the effective protection of species.

For flora and fauna, therefore, statutory protection was needed to overcome the limitations of common law. The main piece of legislation in the UK which was introduced to counter these limitations is the Wildlife and Countryside Act 1981, as amended. Those parts of the WCA which relate to bird species will be covered later, in Section 7.4.2, and here we will focus briefly on the statutory protection for other fauna and flora. The introduction of "non-native" species is a provision introduced to protect native species. The grey squirrel (*Sciurus carolinensis*), which was introduced to the UK in the 1870s and deliberately released by the Zoological Society of London in 1921, has caused massive displacement and population collapse of the native red squirrel (*Sciurus vulgaris*), for example.

QUOTATION

"Some dozen years ago the Zoological Society of London obtained a number of individuals from a private collection in Bedfordshire, for the purposes of inducing them to breed at liberty in the gardens at Regent's Park."
Anon, 1921, "Grey Squirrels," *The Times*, Tuesday, 20 Dec 1921, p. 11

LEGISLATION

14 Introduction of new species etc (E+W)

(1) Subject to the provisions of this Part, if any person releases or allows to escape into the wild any animal which –

(a) is of a kind which is not ordinarily resident in and is not a regular visitor to Great Britain in a wild state; or

(b) is included in Part I, IA or IB of Schedule 9, he shall be guilty of an offence.

(2) Subject to the provisions of this Part, if any person plants or otherwise causes to grow in the wild any plant which is included in Part II of Schedule 9, he shall be guilty of an offence.
S14(1) and S14(2), WCA 1981, as amended

For species which are already present (including the red squirrel), Schedule 5 of the WCA lists the 115 species of animals which are protected, including 25 species of butterfly. For these species, it is an offence under Section 9 to intentionally kill, injure, take, disturb, sell, offer for sale, transport for sale, or advertise any live or dead specimen, in whole or in part.

Schedule 8 of the WCA lists 167 species for which picking, uprooting, or destroying, or sale or advertisement of sale, is an offence to intentionally damage, destroy, or obstruct any structure used for shelter or disturbing animal while it occupies a structure.

The original lists for both Schedules were bolstered by additions from the Conservation (Natural Habitats, Etc.) Regulations 1994[10] with "European Protected Species," which are those designated as such by the Habitats Directive (see following).

ACTIVITY

Consider the following examples and assess whether they breach Section 14(1) or 14(2) of the Wildlife and Countryside Act.

- Jeremy owns a number of captive-bred finches, including greenfinches (*Chloris chloris*), elegant euphonia (*Euphonia elegantissima*), and 'I'iwi (*Drepanis coccinea*). One day, he leaves both the hatch of his indoor aviary ajar, and the window open, and ten greenfinches and six 'I'iwi escape into the nearby park.

- Elaine is a keen gardener and wants to offset the cost-of-living crisis by growing her own food. She buys seed for Good King Henry (*Blitum bonus-henricus*), a native version of spinach, and plants them. Unknown to her, some of the seeds are of duck potato (*Sagittaria latifolia*), which spreads beyond her garden boundaries and rapidly colonises the nearby riverbank.

- Richard buys some cowslip (*Primula vulgaris*) plants from the local nursery, and the seeds self-set in the nearby park.

In terms of habitat, the 1940 Western Hemisphere Convention (previous) allowed for and encouraged the creation of national parks, national reserves, natural monuments, and wilderness reserves as soon as possible, and this predates seminar moves in the UK by a few years. The UK provisions were triggered by the publication of two reports in the 1940s, the Huxley Report (1945) and the Ritchie Report (1949).

- ■ Conservation of Nature in England and Wales 1945 (the Wildlife Conservation Special Committee – the Huxley Committee)
- ■ Final Report on Nature Reserves in Scotland 1949 (the Scottish Wildlife Conservation Committee – the Ritchie Committee)

These reports contributed to the National Parks and Access to the Countryside Act 1949[11] (NPACA), which allowed for the creation of national parks, nature reserves, and sites of special scientific interest (SSSI), which remain the cornerstones of habitat protection in the UK nearly 75 years later.

National Parks

The National Parks Commission was set up under Section 1 of the NPACA and was given the responsibility of identifying large areas of the UK which were both attractive and useful for recreation and designating them as national parks. The role of the National Parks Commission is currently undertaken by Natural England.

LEGISLATION

National Parks.

(1) The provisions of this Part of this Act shall have effect for the purpose –
    (a) of conserving and enhancing the natural beauty, wildlife and cultural heritage of the areas specified in the next following subsection; and
    (b) of promoting opportunities for the understanding and enjoyment of the special qualities of those areas by the public.
(2) The said areas are those extensive tracts of country in England as to which it appears to Natural England that by reason of –
    (a) their natural beauty, and

(b) the opportunities they afford for open-air recreation, having regard both to their character and to their position in relation to centres of population, it is especially desirable that the necessary measures shall be taken for the purposes mentioned in the last foregoing subsection.

(3) The said areas, as for the time being designated by order made by Natural England and submitted to and confirmed by the Minister, shall be as known as, and are here-inafter referred to as, National Parks.

S5, NPACA, as amended

Unlike the other designations covered next, national parks were given their own planning authorities by Section 63 of the Environment Act 1995,[12] and it is these rather than the planning authorities of whichever county or borough the park sits in which make decisions.

There are 15 national parks in the UK, and they cover around 22,000 square kilometres, making this the largest classification by area.

1951: Peak District (England); Lake District (England); Snowdonia (Wales); Dartmoor (England)

1952 Pembroke Coast (Wales); North York Moors (England)

1954 Yorkshire Dales (England); Exmoor (England)

1956 Northumberland (England)

1957 Brecon Beacons (Wales)

1989 The Norfolk and Suffolk Broads (England) (technically not a national park but recognised through the Norfolk and Suffolk Broads Act 1988[13] as having the same status as a national park)

2002 Loch Lomond and the Trossachs (Scotland)

2003 Cairngorms (Scotland)

2005 New Forest (England)

2010 South Downs (England)

National Nature Reserves

The idea for nature reserves in the UK was introduced by Section 15 of the NPACA, and the current wording was inserted by the Natural Environment and Rural Communities Act 2006.[14]

LEGISLATION

15 Meaning of "nature reserve."

(1) In this Part, "nature reserve" means –

(a) land managed solely for a conservation purpose, or

(b) land managed not only for a conservation purpose but also for a recreational purpose, if the management of the land for the recreational purpose does not compromise its management for the conservation purpose.

(2) Land is managed for a conservation purpose if it is managed for the purpose of –

(a) providing, under suitable conditions and control, special opportunities for the study of, and research into, matters relating to the fauna and flora of Great Britain and the physical conditions in which they live, and for the study of geological and physiographical features of special interest in the area, or

(b) preserving flora, fauna or geological or physiographical features of special interest in the area, or for both those purposes.

S15, NPACA, as amended by the Natural Environment and Rural Communities Act 2006

The first designated national nature reserve was Bienn Eighe in northwest Scotland, which was designated in 1951. There are currently nearly 400 national nature reserves across the UK, covering around 2,700 square kilometres. The largest is the Cairngorm Mountains in Scotland, which is around 250 square kilometres, and the smallest is *Dan yr Ogof* in Wales, which is only 5,000 square metres.

National nature reserves are usually designated for their broader ecological value rather than for the presence of any specific species. If there are any specific species of habitats in need of additional protection, they will be duly designated under other schemes (e.g. SSSI, discussed next).

Sites of Special Scientific Interest

SSSIs were created under Section 28 of the NPACA and are currently designated under Section 28 of the Wildlife and Countryside Act 1981.

LEGISLATION

28 Sites of special scientific interest (E+W)
  (1) Where Natural England are of the opinion that any area of land is of special interest by reason of any of its flora, fauna, or geological or physiographical features, it shall be the duty of Natural England to notify that fact –
    (a) to the local planning authority (if any) in whose area the land is situated;
    (b) to every owner and occupier of any of that land; and
    (c) to the Secretary of State.
      S28, Wildlife and Countryside Act 1981, as amended by the Natural Environment and Rural Communities Act 2006[15] and the Marine and Coastal Access Act 2009[16]

The body responsible for notification of SSSIs has changed over the years, but the basic rationale of "special interest due to its flora, fauna, geological or physiographical features" has not changed. There are currently over 7,000 SSSIs in the UK, and in total, they cover around 10,000 square kilometres (which is about 7.5 per cent of total UK land area). Some SSSIs are massive (the Wash in Norfolk, for example, is around 620 square kilometres), and some are very small (Sylvan Barn in Gloucestershire is only 4.5 square metres), but the process of identification and notification is the same for all.

■ Natural England (NE) must notify LPA, all owners and occupiers, and SSE when they find (or are referred to) an area which meets the criteria for SSSIs.

■ The notification by NE is provisional, and there is a three-month period during which representations or objections can be made.

■ NE decides, after considering any objections, whether to reject notification, confirm with modifications, or confirm without modifications.

■ If conformation of the decision is not made within nine months of the initial notification, then it lapses.

■ During the notification period, NE specifies what it considers to be "damaging operations." These are actions, rather than inactions, so doing nothing is not covered, even if doing nothing would lead to a loss or deterioration of the things which make the site special.

■ Before carrying out an action which is potentially a "damaging operation," an owner or occupier must notify NE in writing.

- The action can proceed four months after notification (or earlier, if written consent is obtained from NE); the delay period is designed to give NE time to prepare a management plan.
- If there is an emergency (or if planning permission has been granted), the operation can go ahead without notification.

English Nature (the predecessor body to Natural England) started an ambitious programme to assess the condition of all SSSIs in England in March 1997. The baseline study was completed in March 2003, and less than 60 per cent of the SSSIs assessed were deemed to be in "favourable" or "unfavourable (recovering)" condition.

KEY FACTS

Natural England categorises the condition of SSSIs as one of the following:

- **Favourable** – habitats and features are in a healthy state and are being conserved by appropriate management
- **Unfavourable (recovering condition)** – if current management measures are sustained the site will recover over time
- **Unfavourable (no change)** or **unfavourable (declining condition)** – special features are not being conserved or are being lost, so without appropriate management the site will never reach a favourable or recovering condition
- **Part destroyed or destroyed** – there has been fundamental damage, where special features have been permanently lost and favourable condition cannot be achieved
  DEFRA, 2022, "Sites of special scientific interest: managing your land," Department of the Environment, Food, and Rural Affairs, London: TSO

This prompted a significant programme of SSSI protection, and Natural England, which was established in 2006, was given the objective of achieving "favourable" status for all SSSIs. The latest NE report (March 2020) shows that 93 per cent of SSSIs are currently in a "favourable" or "unfavourable recovering" condition, and although this is a significant improvement, it nonetheless falls well below the objectives set.

CRITIQUING THE LAW

In addition to the types of protected sites covered here, there are also areas of outstanding natural beauty, heritage coast, marine protected areas, and others. Most of the land-based designations overlap. Does that mean the system is too complex?
Why do you think marine protection is so far behind terrestrial?

7.4.2 Residual EU Law

Even though the UK has left the EU, at the time of writing, new legislation had not been passed to replace or amend the EU standards on wildlife and habitat protection. Given the commitment of the UK and the EU under their international treaty obligations is very similar, it seems doubtful that there will be much clear water between the two sets of provisions going forward.

Birds Directive[17]

The Directive extends to cover all species of wild birds living on the European territory of member states as well as nests, eggs, and habitats. This means that dependencies and territories outside Europe will not be counted. For most EU member states, this is a relatively straightforward calculation, but the five *"départements et régions d'outre-mer"* (departments or regions overseas – French Guiana, Guadeloupe, Martinique, Mayotte, and Réunion) are regarded as being integral parts of France, and hence the EU.

The Directive identifies in the preamble that there has been a rapid decline in the numbers of some species in the territories of some member states, and that the migratory nature of many species makes protection a transboundary issue. What this means is that harmonisation of protection is the only logical way of preserving species – if a species of bird is protected in Austria but not in Germany, for example, then the protection is not going to be effective.

ARTICLE

Article 2

"Member States shall take the requisite measures to maintain the population of the species referred to in Article 1 at a level which corresponds in particular to ecological, scientific and cultural requirements, while taking account of economic and recreational requirements, or to adapt the population of these species to that level."

Article 6

"1. Without prejudice to paragraphs 2 and 3, Member States shall prohibit, for all the bird species referred to in Article 1, the sale, transport for sale, keeping for sale and the offering for sale of live or dead birds and of any readily recognisable parts or derivatives of such birds.

2. The activities referred to in paragraph 1 shall not be prohibited in respect of the species referred to in Annex III, Part A, provided that the birds have been legally killed or captured or otherwise legally acquired.

3. Member States may, for the species listed in Annex III, Part B, allow within their territory the activities referred to in paragraph 1, making provision for certain restrictions, provided that the birds have been legally killed or captured or otherwise legally acquired."

Article 2, Directive 2009/147/EC on the conservation of wild birds (codified version)

The general protective regime created by the Directive includes the same measures as international conventions (e.g. the 1971 Ramsar Convention, earlier).

Annexe 1 193 species listed (also applies to regularly migrating birds), which have their habitats classified as specially protected areas and then notified to the Commission.

MS must protect wetlands of international importance.

The sale of live or dead birds and any readily recognisable derivatives or parts is prohibited.

Annexe 2 Part 1 lists 25 species that can be hunted anywhere in MS territory, provided it does not "jeopardise conservation efforts" (Art. 7). Part 2 lists a further 58 species that may be hunted only in specifically mentioned states or areas. Hunting must comply with "wise use and ecologically balanced" control of species of birds concerned.

Annexe 3 This is effectively lists two bird species which can be sold, offered for sale, etc., provided they have been legally killed. Part A I lists the seven species of birds to which this applies across the EU (mallard duck, ptarmigan, three species of partridge, pheasant, and common wood pigeon). Part B lists 19 species which individual member states have applied to have included. The species on Annexe 3 tend to be those which are hunted for sport or regarded as vermin or both.

The Directive also bans a range of methods of hunting and killing birds in Article 8 and Annex IV, and this includes things like using explosives or automatic weapons and blinding or mutilating birds to use as bait.

It is possible for member states to derogate from the limitations imposed by the Directive for a range of reasons – for example, to cull birds as a way of controlling the spread of the highly pathogenic avian influenza (HPAI) outbreak in 2021/2022, which was the largest ever recorded.

UK implementation of the Directive is through the Wildlife and Countryside Act 1981[18] (as amended), which was passed to include the 1979 iteration of the Directive. The WCA is a wide-ranging piece of statute and also covers the protection of fauna species other than birds, and habitat.

LEGISLATION

An Act to repeal and re-enact with amendments the Protection of Birds Acts 1954 to 1967 and the Conservation of Wild Creatures and Wild Plants Act 1975; to prohibit certain methods of killing or taking wild animals; to amend the law relating to protection of certain mammals; to restrict the introduction of certain animals and plants; to amend the Endangered Species (Import and Export) Act 1976; to amend the law relating to nature conservation, the countryside and National Parks and to make provision with respect to the Countryside Commission; to amend the law relating to public rights of way; and for connected purposes.

Wildlife and Countryside Act 1981, long title

There are several sections of the WCA which have been given different form in their application to England and Wales on the one hand, and Scotland on the other, by virtue of the Wildlife and Natural Environment (Scotland) Act 2011.[19] For ease, however, this section will focus on the provisions as they apply in England and Wales.

Sections 1–8 focus on the protection of birds and prevention of poaching. The language used is broadly similar to that of Article 6 of the Directive, and there are seven schedules which deal with the protection of birds and their nests:

Schedule ZA1   Birds which re-use their nests: golden eagle, white-tailed eagle, and osprey. The offence is extended to include damage to or taking of the next even when it is not being used.

Schedule A1   Protected nests and nest sites (birds): golden eagle and white-tailed eagle. Offence is extended as per Schedule ZA1, but this only applies in Scotland.

Schedule 1   Birds which are protected by special penalties: 80 species of rarer birds listed. Offence widened to disturbing the birds or their dependent young, and penalty for committing an offence is increased to level 5 on the standard scale – currently £5,000.

Schedule 1A   Birds which are protected from harassment: golden eagle, white-tailed eagle, hen harrier, red kite. The Schedule applies only to Scotland.

Schedule 2	Birds which may be killed or taken: Part I lists 25 species which may be killed or taken outside the close season. Part IA is a sublist of 17 of those species that must not be killed on a Sunday or Christmas Day in Scotland.
Schedule 3	Birds which may be Sold: 19 species can be sold if alive, ringed, and bred in captivity, and the wood pigeon can be sold dead. There are additional provisions for Scotland.
Schedule 4	Birds which must be registered and ringed if kept in captivity: all falcons, hawks (except vultures), and ospreys.

The difficulty in protecting birds, particularly those birds which prey on other birds, is the balance which is given to each species.

JUDGMENT

R (ex parté McMorn) v Natural England (2015) EWHC 3297 (Admin)

This case is interesting because it revolves around the refusal of Natural England to grant a licence to a gamekeeper to kill buzzards. The licence was requested because the predation by the buzzards was making the gamekeeper's pheasant shooting business not economically viable.

Buzzards are protected under the WCA but are not endangered. Natural England was ruled to have acted unlawfully by treating buzzards and other raptors differently to other species given the same level of protection under the WCA.

The case revealed that the "substantial reason for the difference in approach was some hostile public opinion."

(Per Ouseley J. @para 185)

The WCA does go further than the Directive in the restrictions it imposes, and this is down to the fact that in addition to transposing the Directive, the Act was a restatement of the Protection of Birds Acts, which predated the UK's membership on the EU.

Habitats Directive[20]

The Habitats Directive is, as the name suggests, concerned with conserving the natural habitats of wild fauna and flora. The Directive was passed in 1992 as a result of the Bern Convention (discussed earlier), which the EU had ratified in 1982.

Much of the structure comes from the Bern Convention, and thus, EU member states were required by both provisions to identify and designate areas which needed protection. There is a well-defined process for doing this.

Firstly, the site is considered nationally, in terms of both the type of habitat and species present. If the habitat is listed in Appendix I and the species in Appendix II, then the site is a nationally important site and must be designated as such.

The second state is to repeat the exercise, but with an EU focus. This ensures that each member state has to contribute in proportion to the representation within its territory of natural habitat types and the habitats of species potentially threatened by habitat loss listed in annexes.

The completion of the two stages means a site can be designated as a special area of conservation and will form part of the coherent European ecological network of special conservation areas called "Natura 2000," which also satisfied the EU's requirements under the Bern Convention's Emerald Network (see previous text).

SUMMARY

In this chapter we have looked at the development and operation of a range of different measures which have been put into place at different levels to protect or conserve flora, fauna, and habitat. There are many other measures which have not been covered, as this is an extremely complex and evolving area.

- There has been fundamental shift in human attitude over time.
- The threat of extinction was originally not widely considered to be serious.
- Today, the Convention for Biological Diversity has been accepted by almost every nation on Earth.
- Implementation is the weak point.
- Many countries which have ratified international instruments are not complying with them.
- Reasons could be political, social, economic, or ideological, but without proper implementation, we will not achieve a fraction of what is needed.

In the next chapter, we will look at different aspects of animal law – from experimentation to use in films.

SAMPLE ESSAY QUESTION

Given the constantly evolving nature of the UK landscape, how should the decisions be made as to whether it is, for example, the 15th-, 17th-, 19th-, or 21st-century version of a landscape that should be protected/restored?

1. State the law – the National Parks and Access to the Countryside Act 1949 (as amended) is key here, but also consider the Wildlife and Countryside Act 1981, the Natural Environment and Rural Communities Act 2006, and the Marine and Coastal Access Act 2009, among others.
2. Is there any guidance in statute as to which iteration of an area is the one most worth protecting?
3. Select an area – an essay can be made more powerful by the use of specific examples rather than writing in generalisations.
4. Trade the development of that area over time – and assess whether it has become more urbanised, industrialised, or drained, to make farmland, for example.
5. Analyse these states with the provisions of the statute.
6. Conclude.

Further Reading

Allen, G. M., 1942, *Extinct and Vanishing Mammals of the Western Hemisphere with the Marine Species of all the Oceans*, Lancaster, PA: American Committee for International Wild Life Protection Special Report Number 11

Fisher, J., Simon, N., & Vincent, J., 1969, *The Red Book: Wildlife in Danger*, Cambridge: International Union for the Conservation of Nature and Natural Resources

Fitter, R., & Fitter, M., eds., 1984, *The Road to Extinction: Problems of Categorizing the Status of Taxa Threatened with Extinction: A Symposium Held by the Species Survival Commission, Madrid 1984*, Cambridge: International Union for the Conservation of Nature and Natural Resources

Hornaday, W.T., 1913, *Our Vanishing Wild Life: Its Extermination and Preservation*, New York: Charles Scribner's Sons

IUCN, 1966, *Animals and Plants Threatened with Extinction*, Cambridge: International Union for the Conservation of Nature and Natural Resources

Jeffery, M., Firestone, J., & Bubna-Litic, K., 2008, *Biodiversity, Conservation, Law + Livelihoods: Bridging the North-South Divide*, Cambridge: IUCN Academy of Environmental Law Research Studies

Lyster, S., 1985, *International Wildlife Law: An Analysis of International Treaties Concerned with the Conservation of Wildlife*, Cambridge: Grotius Publications

Rogers, K., & Moore, J., 1995, Revitalizing the Convention on Nature Protection and Wild Life Preservation in the Western Hemisphere: Might Awakening a Visionary But "Sleeping" Treaty be the Key to Preserving Biodiversity and Threatened Natural Areas in the Americas? *Harvard International Law Journal*, 36, 465

Scott, P., ed., 1964, *The Launching of a New Ark: The First Report by the World Wildlife Fund*, London: Collins

Notes

1   Hornaday, W.T., 1913, *Our Vanishing Wild Life: Its Extermination and Preservation*, New York: Charles Scribner's Sons, p. ix

2   Lyster, S., 1985, *International Wildlife Law: An Analysis of International Treaties Concerned with the Conservation of Wildlife*, Cambridge: Grotius Publications, p. 242

3   Rogers, K., & Moore, J., 1995, Revitalizing the Convention on Nature Protection and Wild Life Preservation in the Western Hemisphere: Might Awakening a Visionary But "Sleeping" Treaty be the Key to Preserving Biodiversity and Threatened Natural Areas in the Americas? *Harvard International Law Journal*, 36, 465, 475–476

4   3 Geo 4 c.71

5   Scott, P., Burton, J., & Fitter, R., 1987, Red Data Books: The Historical Background, in Fitter, R., & Fitter, M., eds., *The Road to Extinction: Problems of Categorizing the Status of Taxa Threatened with Extinction: A Symposium Held by the Species Survival Commission, Madrid 1984*, Cambridge: International Union for the Conservation of Nature and Natural Resources, p. 3

6   Directive 92/43/EEC on the conservation of natural habitats and of wild fauna and flora, as amended

7   32 and 33 Vict. c17

8   43 and 44 Vict. c.35

9   1945 c.30

10 SI 1994/2716

11 12, 13, and 14 Geo 6, c.97

12 1995 c.25

13 1988 c.4

14 2006 c.16

15 2006 c.16
16 2009 c.23
17 Directive 2009/147/EC on the conservation of wild birds (codified version)
18 1981 c.69
19 2011, asp 6
20 Directive 92/43/EEC on the conservation of natural habitats and of wild fauna and flora, as amended

177

NOTES

8

Animal Law

This chapter focuses on the human interaction with animals. The best way of summing up this relationship is also the title of Herzog's 2010 book on the topic: *Some We Long, Some We Hate, Some We Eat*. Not everyone loves dogs, or hates rats, or eats meat, and the differentiation between animal species will vary depending on where you are in the world.

There is no international law on animal welfare, which may come as a surprise. The closest is likely to be the draft framework for a UN Convention on Animal Health and Protection (UNCAHP), which was launched in 2019, with hopes expressed that it could potentially be adopted by the General Assembly before 2029.

This chapter will use the Animal Welfare Act 2006[1] (as amended) as the vehicle to consider the different aspects of animal law. Where there are elements which are specifically excluded from the AWA (such as animal experimentation, which is the sole preserve of the Animals (Scientific Procedures) Act 1986[2]), these will be dealt with separately.

The traditional approach used in what we can broadly classify as "animal welfare legislation" was to limit or prohibit harm being caused to animals. The AWA takes the innovative and welcomed step of adding to this with a raft of provisions to promote animal welfare.

AIMS AND OBJECTIVES

After reading this chapter, you should be able to:

- Identify and discuss the moral and ethical issues around the use of animals.
- Discuss the different uses of animals and the accompanying legal frameworks.
- Identify the issues surrounding the use of animals in sport.

DOI: 10.4324/9781003137214-8

8.1 Morality, Ethics, Philosophy, and the Origins of the AWA

The Animal Welfare Act (AWA) stems from the philosophical, moral, and ethical majority views of early 21st-century UK:

- Humans are superior to animals.
- There is a hierarchy between animals.
- Harm should be avoided unless necessitated by a larger good. This aligns to a consequentialist or utilitarian view, where if an action can be demonstrated to stop more harm than it creates, then it is "good."
- For the protection of society as a whole, animal cruelty and failure to ensure animal welfare should be regarded as issues for criminal law rather than civil law.

Looking more broadly at our relationship with animals, the ethical standpoint has changed over time. In the Elizabethan times of the 16th century, bullbaiting and bear-baiting, were as popular for ordinary people as going to the theatre. The blood sports involved tying a bull or a bear to a stake driven into the ground, setting dogs onto it, and gambling about how long it would take the staked animal to die, and how many dogs it would kill. To 21st-century minds, this is likely to seem barbaric, but at that time, cockfighting, dogfighting, goose-pulling, rat-fighting, and other forms of animal sports were also popular, with a wide range of the public. Boddice reports that cockfighting "was a truly national sport, played by commoners and kings."[3]

The 18th-century artist William Hogarth's etching *First Stage of Cruelty* (1751) suggests a link between cruelty to animals by children and criminality in adult-hood – the subsequent images in the series show the boy (Tom Nero) who is cruel to a dog slipping further into depravity until he eventually kills a woman, is executed, and then is publicly dissected (in line with the Murder Act 1751[4]).

Hogarth then was of the view that animal cruelty was not something to be ignored, not necessarily because it was inherently wrong, but because it would lead to worse crimes. Although blood sports were a major feature of the 17th and 18th centuries, their support was by no means universal. Primatt was among those who found blood sports to be abhorrent, arguing that "if a man is cruel to his beast . . . he is a wicked man."[5]

Today, the dominant view in the UK is that activities which involve cruelty to, or mistreatment of, animals are morally and ethically wrong. Some have argued that there is a class distinction – dogfighting, goose-pulling, badger-baiting, hare-coursing, and the other blood sports of the working class were all banned long before fox hunting, for example. As we have seen, cockfighting occupied a kind of middle ground, as it was universally popular.

ACTIVITY

The predominant morality of the UK has changed considerably from the times when bullbaiting and cockfighting were considered to be mainstream sports. However, bull-fighting is still popular in Spain, and cockfighting is legal in Puerto Rico, the Dominican Republic, and the Philippines, among others.

To what extent should the UK be able to export its own moral standards and insist that other nations make legislative provisions to ban these types of pastimes?

Is this disparity an area in which the United Nations should become involved?

At the heart of the Animal Welfare Act (and the devolved versions) are the "five freedoms" of animal welfare. These can be traced back to Ruth Harrison's 1964 book *Animal Machines* and the subsequent 1965 report published by the "Technical Committee to Inquire into the Welfare of Animals Kept under Intensive Livestock Husbandry Systems" (the Brambell Committee), which concluded that an animal "should have at least sufficient freedom of movement to be able without difficulty, to turn round, groom itself, get up, lie down and stretch its limbs."[6] This is, it should be noted, a threshold (a minimum acceptable level) rather than a target (the best level of welfare).

In 1964, the EEC (as it was then) passed the first of its animal welfare–related legislation, Directive 64/432/EEC.[7] As we have seen previously, the primary focus on the EEC was economic parity across the member states, and so it is no surprise to see that is the case here. The priority is the intra-community trade in bovines (cattle) and swine (pigs) and to control any animal health issues that might affect this. The primary purpose of this Directive was not to promote animal welfare but to harmonise health laws to allow for smoother import/export without risking zoonotic epidemics (diseases which can transfer from animals to humans). The EU followed a similar pattern with the second Directive on this area,[8] although recognition of the animal cruelty aspect was expressed more strongly.

LEGISLATION

Whereas the national legislation now in force in the field of protection of animals presents disparities of such a nature as to affect directly the functioning of the common market;

Whereas the effect of the costs arising from these requirements are variable from one Member State to another;

Whereas the Community should also take action to avoid in general all forms of cruelty to animals;

Whereas it appears desirable, as a first step, that this action should consist in laying down conditions such as to avoid all unnecessary suffering on the part of animals when being slaughtered;

Whereas in this respect the practice of stunning animals by appropriate recognized techniques should be generalized;

Whereas, however, it is necessary to take account of the particular requirements of certain religious rites,

Preamble to Directive 74/577/EEC

The Council of Europe has also passed animal welfare legislation, starting in the late 1960s and continuing to this day:

- European Convention for the Protection of Animals during International Transport (1968 – revised in 2003). The 1968 version signed and ratified by the UK; the 2003 version not ratified by the UK. The Convention (in both versions) covered aspects of transporting live animals, from their fitness to travel to the standards of the vehicles.

- European Convention for the Protection of Animals Kept for Farming Purposes (1976). Signed and ratified by the UK. Main focus was on avoiding suffering, not promoting welfare, but there are provisions for ensuring appropriate living conditions. The Convention created a standing committee which periodically produces species-specific guides.

- European Convention for the Protection of Animals for Slaughter (1979). Signed but not ratified by the UK. Covers slaughterhouses and the process of slaughtering and is designed to make the process more humane.

- European Convention for the Protection of Vertebrate Animals Used for Experimental and Other Scientific Purposes (1986, amended in 1998). Signed and ratified by the UK. This plus later evolutions of the EC/EU Directives were the foundations for ASPA 1986 (see following text).

- European Convention for the Protection of Pet Animals (1987). Not signed or ratified by the UK. Covers keeping, breeding, and aspects like tail docking of dogs and declawing cats.

By the end of the 1970s, the five freedoms had evolved considerably, and the versions most currently used today are:

- Freedom from hunger and thirst
- Freedom from discomfort
- Freedom from pain, injury, or disease
- Freedom to express normal behaviour
- Freedom from fear and distress

The AWA does not use this specific language, but Section 9 does reflect the general tone of the five freedoms.

LEGISLATION

9 Duty of person responsible for animal to ensure welfare

(1) A person commits an offence if he does not take such steps as are reasonable in all the circumstances to ensure that the needs of an animal for which he is responsible are met to the extent required by good practice.

(2) For the purposes of this Act, an animal's needs shall be taken to include –

(a) its need for a suitable environment,
(b) its need for a suitable diet,
(c) its need to be able to exhibit normal behaviour patterns,
(d) any need it has to be housed with, or apart from, other animals, and
(e) its need to be protected from pain, suffering, injury, and disease.

S9, AWA 2006

We can say that the AWA does not adopt any overtly philosophical stance, but that it does take a largely consequentialist approach to ethics:

- Excluding any deliberate harm to animals if it is approved under A(SP)A.
- Allowing for tail docking only if medically appropriate (S6).
- Allowing destruction of animals if deemed to be in their best interests.
- Allowing destruction of animals involved in fighting if it is in the best interests of society.

However, thinking back to Chief Seattle/Seathl, Murray Bookchin, and James Lovelock (see Chapter 1), it appears that the AWA unsurprisingly adheres to the dominant Western philosophical tradition that humans are superior to animals. It also makes several value judgments about which types of animals are "superior" (and therefore more worthy of protection):

- Humans vs non-human animals (S1)
- Vertebrates vs invertebrates (S1)
- Domesticated animals vs wild animals (S2)

It could also be argued that some of these distinctions have their basis in pragmatism and economics rather than anything more complex.

Humans. As we have seen in previous chapters, the dominant view in UK environmental legislation has consistently been anthropocentric in nature, and the distinction between human and non-human animals is thus inevitable.

Vertebrates. The rationale for not extending the protections of the AWA to invertebrates was due to the belief that only vertebrates were sentient (able to perceive of feel things), and therefore invertebrates could not suffer. There is provision made in Section 1(3)(b) for the definition of animal to be extended, and with the establishment of the Animal Sentience Committee under Section 1 of the Animal Welfare (Sentience) Act 2022[9] and the 2021 recognition that "crabs, octopus and lobsters" will be recognised as sentient in government decision-making, this may change.

Wild animals. Non-domesticated and wild animals are not subject to the same levels of control as domestic animals – there is no "ownership" as such. In fact, for those species not specifically identified by legislation (see Chapter 7), the control of wild animals depends on where they are. If they are on or over land, then they are subject to standard proprietary rights. If they are in or over water, then the same rules apply, unless the water is outside territorial limits.

Domesticated animals include both those domesticated as pets and those domesticated as farm animals, which brings in the economic argument. The meat farming industry taken as a whole in the UK is an economic colossus, generating £14bn in 2021 across beef, pig, sheep, and chicken, with the dairy side of the trade being around £20bn. Mariam Stamp Dawkins makes the strong point that many improvements in farm animal welfare standards will require additional cost, and as a result, "the case will have to be particularly clear and watertight, because every excuse will be found to turn it down."[10]

For the most part, the higher the standards of animal welfare, the more expensive they are to comply with. If, for example, the amount of space deemed appropriate for a chicken is doubled, then the number of chickens that can be kept in a defined area is halved. The price charged for chicken and eggs will have to increase to offset the loss to the farmer.

Under a legal positivist view, of the sort promoted by Jeremy Bentham, among many others, the only rights that matter are legal rights, which are enshrined in law. If something is not set out in statute, it doesn't count. Legally (and thus "enforceably"), animals have the rights that we (as humans) give them. Over time, those rights have changed, as societal pressure forces change in the law. Changes in the law affect what the majority see as "acceptable" or "unacceptable," and thus the cycle begins again.

ACTIVITY

Assess whether animal welfare standards are predominantly a legal, ethical, or moral issue.

There have also been several instances (from Plato onwards) of animals being tried for various offences. Sometimes it has been specific animals which had killed a person – pigs and cows have both been executed for this. On other occasions, it was insects which were devouring crops, or even rats.

QUOTATION

This case took place in Autun, southern France, in the 1520s. Crops were being eaten, and culprits were assumed to be rats. The citizens issued a citation to the rats to appear before *le tribunal ecclesisatique d'Autun*, on the charge that they had eaten or destroyed the barley crop of local farmers.

Local lawyer Barthélemy de Chassenée defended the rats, who had failed to appear on the first day of the trial. He pointed that in order for the summons to be valid, each one of his clients had to be served individually.

The judge agreed that this was a valid point, and a summons was duly posted in the churches of all neighbouring towns.

The rats failed to appear on the second day and were found to be in contempt of court. De Chassenée argued that the unpaved and unlit road from his clients' several residences to the Autun Courthouse, especially in 1508, was fraught with deadly peril: cats, dogs, and hostile people, none of which were neutral in the case.

Simply, it was unsafe for his clients to attend the Autun courtroom.

A change of venue was pointless since his clients would suffer the same peril anywhere in France. The rats were acquitted.

Slabbert, M., 2004, "Prosecuting Animals in Medieval Europe: Possible Explanations," *Fundamina: A Journal of Legal History*, 2004(10), 159–179 (p. 163)

Since animal welfare is such an emotive issue, it is inevitable that the legislation have an ethical background which is relatively easy to trace. We have moved beyond sending animals to trial for some action or inaction, but as a society, we still cling to our ideas about hierarchies of animals. Nowhere is this more clearly displayed than in the area of animal experimentation.

8.2 Animal Experimentation

Ethical concerns about animal experimentation have changed over the years. Experimenting on animals, whether for sheer scientific curiosity or in order to find cures or treatment for medical and health conditions (in animals or humans), is a well-established practice, from Aristotle onwards. Almost as longstanding have been the voices of objectors, those who believe the suffering of animals can skew the results of the experimentation. The language used is equally polarised – those in favour talk of "scientific procedures," and those opposed talk of "vivisection."

Notable proponents and practitioners of animal experimentation:

Robert Boyle (17th-century Anglo-Irish scientist, philosopher, and theologian). Boyle did not carry out vivisection himself but believed it was very useful.

Antoine Lavoisier (18th-century French chemist). Lavoisier carried out experiments on the breathing of humans and animals to develop his work on naming oxygen and hydrogen.

Louis Pasteur (19th-century French chemist and microbiologist). Pasteur, who invented the process of pasteurisation, experimented extensively on animals in developing vaccines for anthrax, cholera, and rabies.

Emil von Behring (20th-century Prussian physiologist). Von Behring worked with fellow Prussian Paul Ehrlich to develop a vaccine for diphtheria by injecting it into horses.

Frederick Banting (20th-century Canadian physician) and John Macleod (20th-century Scottish biochemist). Banting and Macleod discovered insulin by making dogs diabetic.

Jonas Salk (20th-century American virologist). Developed a polio vaccine through a programme of testing on rhesus macaques (*Macaca mulatta*).

QUOTATION

"We have also parks and enclosures of all sorts of beasts and birds which we use not only for view or rareness, but likewise for dissections and trials; that thereby we may take light what may be wrought upon the body of man. . . .

We try also all poisons and other medicines upon them, as well of chirurgery, as physic. By art likewise, we make them greater or taller than their kind is; and contrariwise dwarf them, and stay their growth: we make them more fruitful and bearing than their kind is; and contrariwise barren and not generative.

Also we make them differ in colour, shape, activity, many ways. We find means to make commixtures and copulations of different kinds; which have produced many new kinds, and them not barren, as the general opinion is. We make a number of kinds of serpents, worms, flies, fishes, of putrefaction; whereof some are advanced (in effect) to be perfect creatures, like beasts or birds; and have sexes, and do propagate. Neither do we this by chance, but we know beforehand, of what matter and commixture what kind of those creatures will arise."

Bacon, F., 1627 (1884), *The New Atlantis*, London: George Bell & Sons (p. 18)

Sir Francis Bacon was writing in an unfinished novel of a possible future where not only do we have zoos and wildlife parks for education and entertainment but where we also carry out genetic experiments on, and crossbreeding of, animals to achieve a set of goals.[11]

If we were to take a consequentialist approach, all these medical and scientific advances have saved countless human lives, albeit at the cost of many more animal lives. However, society has largely moved on since the 18th and 19th centuries, and in the UK, animal experimentation is governed by the Animals (Scientific Procedures) Act 1986 (ASPA) which, as we saw earlier, was significantly influenced by the Council of Europe Convention for the Protection of Vertebrate Animals Used for Experimental and Other Scientific Purposes (also 1986) and various EU Directives. It was, however, preceded by the Cruelty to Animals Act 1876,[12] which prohibited "painful" experiments on animals.

> 2. A person shall not perform on any living animal and experiment calculated to give pain, except subject to the restrictions imposed by this Act. Any person performing or taking part in performing any experiment calculated to give pain, in contravention of this Act, shall be guilty of an offence under this Act, and shall, if it be the first offence, be liable to a penalty not exceeding fifty pounds, and if it be the second or any subsequent offence, be liable, at the discretion of the court by which he is tried, to a penalty not exceeding one hundred pounds, or to imprisonment for a period not exceeding three months.
>
> S2, Cruelty to Animals Act 1876

Section 3 of the Act did allow for experiments by licenced persons which inflicted pain, but which were performed under anaesthetic and were intended to advance physiological knowledge, save (human) life, or alleviate (human) suffering. The fines for contravening the Act would equate to £4,400 and £8,800 at 2022 values.

There may be more experiments on animals than you would think, although since the introduction of A(SP)A, they are referred to as "scientific procedures" rather than "experiments." In 2021, the UK carried out 3.1 million scientific procedures on live animals, which is a rise from 2020, but continues the gradual downward trend that started in 2015. This drop may be a genuine reflection of fewer procedures being carried out, but it is also possible it is due to the change in classification in 2014 whereby the number of completed procedures was counted as opposed to the number of procedures *started*.

The hierarchy mentioned earlier in terms of animals is starkly illustrated by Section 5(6) of the Act, although there is no rationale stated for this disparity.

LEGISLATION

> (6) The Secretary of State shall not grant a project licence authorising the use of cats, dogs, primates [apes and monkeys] or equidae [horses, donkeys, asses] unless he is satisfied that animals of no other species are suitable for the purposes of the programme to be specified in the licence or that it is not practicable to obtain animals of any other species that are suitable for those purposes.
>
> S5(6), Animals (Scientific Procedures) Act 1986

The outcome of the procedures from an animal health perspective is divided into five categories. Four of these originated in Schedule 8 of the Directive 2010/63/EU[13] (the Animal Directive), and this remains the case post-Brexit. The fifth category is "sub-threshold," which simply means it is more minor than the "mild" classification.

LEGISLATION

> Non-recovery:
>
>> Procedures which are performed entirely under general anaesthesia from which the animal shall not recover consciousness shall be classified as "non-recovery."

Mild:

> Procedures on animals as a result of which the animals are likely to experience short-term mild pain, suffering or distress, as well as procedures with no significant impairment of the well-being or general condition of the animals shall be classified as "mild."

Moderate:

> Procedures on animals as a result of which the animals are likely to experience short-term moderate pain, suffering or distress, or long-lasting mild pain, suffering or distress as well as procedures that are likely to cause moderate impairment of the well-being or general condition of the animals shall be classified as "moderate."

Severe:

> Procedures on animals as a result of which the animals are likely to experience severe pain, suffering or distress, or long-lasting moderate pain, suffering or distress as well as procedures, that are likely to cause severe impairment of the well-being or general condition of the animals shall be classified as "severe."
>
> Annex VIII, Part 1, Directive 2010/63/EU, on the protection of animals used for scientific purposes

There are very strict licensing conditions for animal experimentation, both to protect the welfare of the animals involved and also to protect those carrying out the testing, as there have been several high-profile cases involving anti-vivisection protest groups.

The rest of this section will focus on the two main types of animal testing – generic modification and medical research – but will also look briefly at the testing of cosmetics and non-medical products on animals, which is still permitted in many countries.

Note

Huntingdon Life Sciences was a company carrying out animal research under licence in the UK. It is now part of the Envigo Group.

The company, its employees, and its suppliers were subjected to a long-term protest by "Stop Huntingdon Animal Cruelty" (Shac). Injunctions were imposed on Shac by the High Court on several occasions in relation to their harassment of different companies linked to HLS.

Several members of SHAC were jailed for conspiracy to blackmail in 2009 and harassment in 2010.

8.2.1 Genetic Engineering and Cloning

Genetic modification was not originally covered by the Act, and the provisions were inserted by the Animals (Scientific Procedures) Act 1986 Amendment Regulations 2012.[14]

LEGISLATION

(3B) The breeding of an animal is a regulated procedure if –
   (a) the animal is bred from an animal whose genes have mutated or been modified or from a descendant of an animal whose genes have mutated or been modified;
   (b) the animal is to be allowed to live until after it has attained the stage of its development when it is a protected animal; and
   (c) after the animal has attained that stage the animal may experience pain, suffering, distress or lasting harm of a level mentioned in subsection (1) by reason of the mutation or modification referred to in paragraph (a).

S2(3B), Animals (Scientific Procedures) Act 1986

Of the 3.1 million procedures carried out in 2021, 1.3 million were for the creation or breeding of genetically altered (GA) animals, which is a marked drop from previous years.

KEY FACTS

Results of GA creation and breeding (2021)

Sub-threshold procedures	73%
Mild	23%
Moderate	2%
Nonrecovery	0.1%

Home Office, 2022, Annual Statistics of Scientific
Procedures on Living Animals Great Britain 2021, London: TSO, p. 29

This shows that most GA procedures were not fatal to the animals involved but still means that around 13,000 animals died. Much of the GA work being carried out is related to the breeding of existing lines (1.2 million) rather than the creation of new lines (0.1 million). Although some of the processes might appear similar, the government is very clear that cloning is not the same as genetic modification, and that animals produced through this type of cloning should be regarded and treated in the same was as other animals. Partly, they admit that this is a practical issue, as it would be impossible to distinguish the cloned animal(s) from their "parent." There is currently a ban on cloning humans (Human Reproductive Cloning Act 2001),[15] but there are no such restrictions on animal cloning.

Definition

3. Cloning methods being used in farmed animals [somatic cell nuclear transfer] do NOT involve genetic modification: the intention with cloning is to reproduce an existing animal, rather than to create one with novel DNA that has not existed before.

DEFRA/FAnGR, 2016, statement on cloning of farm animals,
Department of the Environment, Food, and Rural Affairs and
Farm Animal Genetic Resources Committee, London: TSO p. 2

8.2.2 Medical Research

Of the 3.1 million procedures carried out in 2021, 1.7 million were for procedures which were not linked to GA animals. More than half of these procedures were on mice (54 per cent), and fish, birds, and rats accounted for a combined 40 per cent. The majority of experiments were carried out for reasons of research into neurology (the nervous system), immunology (the immune system), or oncology (cancer).

LEGISLATION

2 Regulated procedures.

(1) Subject to the provision of this section, "a regulated procedure" for the purposes of this Act means any procedure applied to a protected animal for a qualifying purpose which may have the effect of causing the animal a level of pain, suffering, distress or lasting harm equivalent to, or higher than, that caused by the introduction of a needle in accordance with good veterinary practice.

(1A) A procedure is applied to an animal for "a qualifying purpose" if –

(a) it is applied for an experimental or other scientific purpose (whether or not the outcome of the procedure is known); or

(b) it is applied for an educational purpose.

S2, Animals (Scientific Procedures) Act 1986

In terms of severity, the majority of these experiments were classed as mild (50 per cent), and the proportion of sub-threshold experiments has risen from 10 per cent in 2018 to 20 per cent in 2021. Around 4 per cent of experiments are classed as non-recovery, which equates to around 60,000 animal fatalities.

It is a requirement set by the Medicines and Healthcare Products Regulatory Agency that all human medicines be tested on animals before they are tested on humans. There is increasing pressure on this stance to be changed and for the increased use of "in-vitro" or laboratory-based experiments instead, as they do not require live animal subjects. The efficacy of in vitro testing varies depending on the product being tested, although the "three Rs" do require the government to keep in mind the ideas of replacement, reduction, and refinement in granting licences and otherwise operating under the Act. This means that future use of in vitro testing is likely to increase as the science behind it develops further.

LEGISLATION

2A Principles of replacement, reduction, and refinement

(1) The Secretary of State must exercise his or her functions under this Act with a view to ensuring compliance with the principles of replacement, reduction, and refinement.

(2) For the purposes of this Act –

(a) the principle of replacement is the principle that, wherever possible, a scientifically satisfactory method or testing strategy not entailing the use of protected animals must be used instead of a regulated procedure;

(b) the principle of reduction is the principle that whenever a programme of work involving the use of protected animals is carried out the number of protected animals used must be reduced to a minimum without compromising the objectives of the programme;

(c) the principle of refinement is the principle that the breeding, accommodation and care of protected animals and the methods used in regulated procedures applied to such animals must be refined so as to eliminate or reduce to the minimum any possible pain, suffering, distress or lasting harm to those animals.]

S2A, Animals (Scientific Procedures) Act 1986

8.2.3 Tobacco, Cosmetics, and Domestic Products

These types of tests are not covered under ASPA, but all are de facto banned in the UK. ASPA dos not specifically mention tobacco or cosmetics, but a Home Office guidance note[16] on the operation of ASPA makes it clear that licences will not be granted for any work involving the following:

- Testing cosmetics.
- Developing or testing alcohol or tobacco products (however, we may consider the use of alcohol or tobacco as research tools for investigating disease or novel treatments).
- Developing or testing offensive weapons (but we may consider licences for developing and testing ways of protecting or treating servicemen and service-women, or the population as a whole).
- Using great apes (chimpanzees, pygmy chimpanzees, gorillas, and orangutans).
- Using stray animals of a domestic species.

The testing of domestic products (e.g. cleaning products) on animals was introduced in the UK in 2015, again by a policy announcement about granting of licences.

QUOTATION

From 1 November 2015, the testing of finished Household Products under the Animals (Scientific Procedures) Act 1986 will be subject to a policy ban. The use of animals to test finished Household Products is therefore prohibited from this date.

In addition to the ban on finished Household Products, the testing on animals of ingredients primarily intended or expected to be used in Household Products will be prohibited unless:

- The proposed testing has a regulatory requirement, for example under REACH (Registration, Evaluation, Authorisation and restriction of Chemicals); and
- No other method or testing strategy for obtaining the results sought, not entailing the use of a live animal, is recognised under the legislation of the European Union.

Home Office, 2015, Advice Note 01/2015 Animals (Scientific Procedures) Act 1986 Policy on Testing Household Products, London: TSO, p. 4

Animal testing of cosmetic products was banned across the EU by Regulation 1223/2009.[17]

ARTICLE

1. Without prejudice to the general obligations deriving from Article 3, the following shall be prohibited:
   (a) the placing on the market of cosmetic products where the final formulation, in order to meet the requirements of this Regulation, has been the subject of animal testing using a method other than an alternative method after such alternative method has been validated and adopted at Community level with due regard to the development of validation within the OECD;

(b) the placing on the market of cosmetic products containing ingredients or combinations of ingredients which, in order to meet the requirements of this Regulation, have been the subject of animal testing using a method other than an alternative method after such alternative method has been validated and adopted at Community level with due regard to the development of validation within the OECD;

(c) the performance within the Community of animal testing of finished cosmetic products in order to meet the requirements of this Regulation;

(d) the performance within the Community of animal testing of ingredients or combinations of ingredients in order to meet the requirements of this Regulation, after the date on which such tests are required to be replaced by one or more validated alternative methods listed in Commission Regulation (EC) No 440/2008 of 30 May 2008 laying down test methods pursuant to Regulation (EC) No 1907/2006 of the European Parliament and of the Council on the Registration, Evaluation, Authorisation and Restriction of Chemicals (REACH) (15) or in Annex VIII to this Regulation.

Article 18, Regulation 1223/2009

The mention at the end of Article 18 of the REACH Directive is interesting, because there is currently a debate about a decision in 2020 by the European Chemicals Agency. The Agency ruled that in order to comply with the terms of the REACH Directive, a German company *must* test two products on animals, even though those products were only for use in cosmetics. The case *Symrise v ECHA Case* T-656/20 is currently being appealed before the Court of Justice. Given the inclusion of REACH as one of the Home Office's exceptions for animal testing of domestic product ingredients (mentioned earlier), the outcome of this case could have a dramatic impact on animal testing of products sold in the UK.

What we can see is that there have been arguments for and against the validity of testing substances on animals for many centuries. There has been a growing recognition that this is no longer appropriate in many instances (cosmetics and domestic products, for example), and the alternatives to animal testing for medical products are increasing in effectiveness, so this is a fluid and dynamic area of regulation.

ACTIVITY

Consider whether any of the following examples of animal experimentation could be justified either legally or morally.

- XYZ Ltd is an English company which wants to develop a cure for a particularly nasty virus which has the potential to become a pandemic. Their proposal is to infect 50 rhesus macaque (*Macaca mulatta*) with the virus and test different antiviral drugs. They expect most of the procedures to be non-recoverable, but an antiviral drug has the potential to save many human lives.

- Medizinischer Betrug GmbH is a German company which thinks that by splicing together the genetic material from a frog and a chicken, it can create a new form of chicken which is immune to H5N1 avian flu. This will improve chicken welfare and increase profitability for farmers.

- Dà Jiémáo is a Chinese company. They produce raw materials which are used both on the food production and cosmetics industries. They have experimented on the Chinese slug (*Meghimatium bilineatum*) to produce a substance which makes lipstick glossier and food glaze more long-lasting.

8.3 Farming

The RSPCA estimates that over 1 billion animals and many millions of fish are reared every year in the UK. This makes the potential impact of the farming sector on animal welfare enormous. The Humane Slaughter Association produces estimates for the numbers slaughtered for human consumption, but these estimates do not include those slaughtered overseas and imported as meat products.

KEY FACTS

Annual slaughter for human consumption:

Cattle (beef)	2,600,000
Pig (pork, ham)	10,000,000
Sheep (lamb, hogget, mutton)	14,500,000
Fish	80,000,000
Birds	950,000,000

Humane Slaughter Association, 2022,
"How many animals are slaughtered in the UK?" www.hsa.org.uk/

8.3.1 Legal Standards

Section 4 of the AWA makes it an offence to cause *unnecessary* suffering (as opposed to *any* suffering) of a protected animal and goes on to outline what is taken into account in deciding what is and is not unnecessary.

LEGISLATION

(3) The considerations to which it is relevant to have regard when determining for the purposes of this section whether suffering is unnecessary include –
  (a) whether the suffering could reasonably have been avoided or reduced;
  (b) whether the conduct which caused the suffering was in compliance with any relevant enactment or any relevant provisions of a licence or code of practice issued under an enactment;
  (c) whether the conduct which caused the suffering was for a legitimate purpose, such as –
    (i) the purpose of benefiting the animal, or
    (ii) the purpose of protecting a person, property or another animal;
  (d) whether the suffering was proportionate to the purpose of the conduct concerned;
  (e) whether the conduct concerned was in all the circumstances that of a reasonably competent and humane person.

S4(3), Animal Welfare Act 2006

Specific elements linked to farming are covered by different statutory provisions. Those relating to the use of agricultural machinery, the sale of food, and the intricacies of farming tenancies will not be covered here, but the Department of the Environment, Food, and Rural Affairs has guidance documents relating to all areas of farming. Other than the running of the farm, the two key areas of livestock farming which impact on animal welfare are the transportation and killing of the animals.

Transport

Animals will need to be transported live from one farm to another or when they are bought and sold. The provisions for this derive from Council Regulation (EC) No. 1/2005[18] and cover the general promotion of animal welfare before, during, and after the journey.

ARTICLE

3 General conditions for the transport of animals

No person shall transport animals or cause animals to be transported in a way likely to cause injury or undue suffering to them.

In addition, the following conditions shall be complied with:

(a) all necessary arrangements have been made in advance to minimise the length of the journey and meet animals' needs during the journey;

(b) the animals are fit for the journey;

(c) the means of transport are designed, constructed, maintained and operated so as to avoid injury and suffering and ensure the safety of the animals;

(d) the loading and unloading facilities are adequately designed, constructed, maintained and operated so as to avoid injury and suffering and ensure the safety of the animals;

(e) the personnel handling animals are trained or competent as appropriate for this purpose and carry out their tasks without using violence or any method likely to cause unnecessary fear, injury or suffering;

(f) the transport is carried out without delay to the place of destination and the welfare conditions of the animals are regularly checked and appropriately maintained;

(g) sufficient floor area and height is provided for the animals, appropriate to their size and the intended journey;

(h) water, feed and rest are offered to the animals at suitable intervals and are appropriate in quality and quantity to their species and size.

Article 3, Council Regulation 1/2005

In addition, for invertebrates which are not covered by the AWA, transportation is covered by the Welfare of Animals (Transport) (England) Order 2006[19] and equivalent legislation on the devolved nations.

One of the most contentious issues in relation to the transportation of live animals is when that transport involves their export onto the European continent. The practice is currently legal, provided the provisions of the Animal Welfare Act are complied with and the journey is the shortest route available.

JUDGMENT

R (ex parté MAS Group Holdings Ltd) v Secretary of State for the Environment, Food and Rural Affairs (2019) EWHC 158 (Admin)

This case was brought as a challenge to the Secretary of State's policy on not authorising livestock export licences unless the route taken was the shortest available.

The court held that the policy decision was valid and complied with EU Regulation 1/2005.

(Per Morris J @para 180)

The Animal Welfare (Kept Animals) Bill is currently progressing through the parliamentary process and is expected to receive royal assent in early 2023. The Bill will impose a ban on the export of livestock (i.e. live animals) from Great Britain, contravention of which could lead to up to 51 weeks' imprisonment.

CLAUSE

40 Prohibition of export of livestock for slaughter etc.

(1) A person may not export relevant livestock from Great Britain for slaughter.

(2) A person who contravenes subsection (1) commits an offence.

(3) A person "exports" relevant livestock from Great Britain if –

(a) the person sends, or attempts to send, relevant livestock from a place in Great Britain to anywhere outside the British Islands,

(b) the person transports, or attempts to transport, relevant livestock from or through Great Britain to anywhere outside the British Islands, or

(c) the person organises, or attempts to organise, the transport of relevant livestock from or through Great Britain to anywhere outside the British Islands

(4) A person exports relevant livestock "for slaughter" if the person exporting the relevant livestock knows, or could reasonably be expected to know, that the relevant livestock is being exported –

(a) for the purposes of being slaughtered, or

(b) for the purposes of being fattened for slaughter.

S40(1)–(4), Animal Welfare (Kept Animals) Bill 2022

Abattoirs

The Welfare of Animals at the Time of Killing (England) Regulations 2015[20] sets out the licence requirements for operating a slaughterhouse or abattoir, which are issued by the Food Standards Agency.

LEGISLATION

12. Subject to regulations 14 and 23(2), no person may carry out an operation specified in regulation 13 except under and to the extent authorised by a licence registered with the competent authority.

13. The operations referred to in regulation 12 are any of the following operations carried out other than in a slaughterhouse –

(a) an operation specified in any of sub-paragraphs (b) to (f) of Article 7(2) carried out for the purposes specified in Article 10 (private domestic consumption) by a person other than the owner of the animal;

(b) an operation specified in any of sub-paragraphs (b) to (f) of Article 7(2) carried out for the purposes specified in Article 11 (direct supply of small quantities of poultry, rabbits and hares);

SS12 and 13(a)–(b), Welfare of Animals at the Time of Killing (England) Regulations 2015

Article 7(2) referred to in the Regulations is Article 7(2) of Regulation (EC) No. 1099/2009,[21] which set out the requirements involved in killing animals whilst causing the minimum amount of stress.

ARTICLE

1. Killing and related operations shall only be carried out by persons with the appropriate level of competence to do so without causing the animals any avoidable pain, distress or suffering.
2. Business operators shall ensure that the following slaughter operations are only carried out by persons holding a certificate of competence for such operations, as provided for in Article 21, demonstrating their ability to carry them out in accordance with the rules laid down in this Regulation:

   (a) the handling and care of animals before they are restrained;
   (b) the restraint of animals for the purpose of stunning or killing;
   (c) the stunning of animals;
   (d) the assessment of effective stunning;
   (e) the shackling or hoisting of live animals;
   (f) the bleeding of live animals;
   (g) the slaughtering in accordance with Article 4(4)

   Regulations 7(1) and (2), Regulation (EC) No 1099/2009
   on the protection of animals at the time of killing

8.3.2 Voluntary Standards

In addition to the statutory provisions, there are a series of voluntary standards which can be applied to livestock farming. In no case are they mandatory standards, but they all have their own criteria, which may or may not be backed up by statute.

Red Tractor

The Red Tractor is the logo of a standard set by Assured Food Standard, a not-for-profit limited company set up under the National Farmers Union of England and Wales (NFU) and which covers livestock and arable farming. It is not legally binding, but as with fair trade and other certification schemes, if a product wishes to display the logo, it must meet the criteria and pay a royalty fee.

QUOTATION

"Together we work to ensure that all livestock are healthy with the right living space, food and water. All our farmer members share our priorities to strive for the very best in animal health and wellbeing."

Assured Food Standard, 2022, "About Red Tractor,"
https://redtractor.org.uk/about-red-tractor/

There have been several controversies involving Red Tractor–certified farms, and when they have been uncovered, the farms have been dropped from the certification scheme.

Organic

The set of requirements for organic production originated in Council Regulation (EC) No. 834/2007,[22] and UK legislation still links back to these criteria.

Article 4 Overall principles

Organic production shall be based on the following principles:

(a) the appropriate design and management of biological processes based on ecological systems using natural resources which are internal to the system by methods that:

(i) use living organisms and mechanical production methods;

(ii) practice land-related crop cultivation and livestock production or practice aquaculture which complies with the principle of sustainable exploitation of fisheries;

(iii) exclude the use of GMOs and products produced from or by GMOs with the exception of veterinary medicinal products;

(iv) are based on risk assessment, and the use of precautionary and preventive measures, when appropriate;

(b) the restriction of the use of external inputs. Where external inputs are required or the appropriate management practices and methods referred to in paragraph (a) do not exist, these shall be limited to:

(i) inputs from organic production;

(ii) natural or naturally derived substances;

(iii) low solubility mineral fertilisers;

(c) the strict limitation of the use of chemically synthesised inputs to exceptional cases these being:

(i) where the appropriate management practices do not exist; and

(ii) the external inputs referred to in paragraph (b) are not available on the market; or

(iii) where the use of external inputs referred to in paragraph (b) contributes to unacceptable environmental impacts;

(d) the adaptation, where necessary, and within the framework of this Regulation, of the rules of organic production taking account of sanitary status, regional differences in climate and local conditions, stages of development and specific husbandry practices.

Article 4, Council Regulation (EC) No. 834/2007

The organic label can be awarded by one of six approved control bodies in the UK, and to qualify for the label, the awarding body must be content that the produce meets the criteria outlined earlier:

■ Organic Farmers and Growers CIC

■ Organic Food Federation

■ Soil Association Certification Ltd

■ Biodynamic Association Certification

■ Quality Welsh Food Certification Ltd

■ OF&G (Scotland) Ltd

The argument is that by giving animals an environment which is as natural as possible, the stress levels of the animal are reduced, which in turn leads to a reduced need for antibiotics. The Association also publishes specific guidance on standards for different types of livestock.

Ethical Dairy

In 2016, a farm in Dumfries and Galloway in Scotland started to develop "ethical dairy" as a concept, where calves are kept with their mothers for 5–6 months, as opposed to the standard practice of removing the calf at birth. This approach, also called "calf at foot," is not without its critics but is being trialled at around 400 farms across Europe and seems to be generating benefits for both animal welfare and production.

QUOTATION

Compared to an average dairy farm, already the Ethical Dairy has:

- Cut greenhouse gas emissions by more than half
- Reduced energy use by more than half
- Cut antibiotic use by 90%
- Cut agro-chemical use by 90%
- Doubled the productive life of cows
- Increased our farm biodiversity five-fold
- Increased the net amount of food in our food system by 80%
- Exceeded the highest standards of animal welfare

Ethical Dairy, 2022, "About the Ethical Dairy," www.theethicaldairy.co.uk/about-ethical-dairy

What we can see in relation to livestock and dairy farming is that the legislative framework provides a backstop of the minimum standards of animal welfare permissible in the sector. Individual farms are of course free to adopt higher voluntary standards which give more regard to animal welfare standards, and many have done so. The advantages can be healthier and more productive animals, as well as a reduction in need for chemical and antibiotic use. The downside is the additional cost, not all of which can be passed on to the consumer.

CRITIQUING THE LAW

If an organisation is able to demonstrate that "higher" ethical standards can be commercially viable and also have other benefits (e.g. reduced chemical use and GHG emissions), should that standard become the new baseline for the industry?

8.4 Pets

Companion animals and pets are covered by the AWA, provided they meet the criteria for animals set out in the Act. In addition, the Dangerous Wild Animals Act 1976[23] requires a licence to keep a range of dangerous wild animals in captivity. The local authority issues the licences if it is convinced that it is not contrary to the public interest or safety to do so and that the applicant is an appropriate person to keep such an animal. Prior to the Act, it was possible to buy and keep wild animals without any licencing – for example, the case of Christian the Lion bought in Harrods in 1969.

The Animal Welfare (Kept Animals) Bill 2022 includes provisions for restricting the keeping of primates as pets to those who have a license, which would be renewable every six years.

CLAUSE

2 Primate licences

(1) A primate licence authorises its holder to keep, during the period for which the licence has effect, such number of primates of such species at such premises as the licence may specify.

(2) A primate licence has effect for a period of six years from the date on which it comes into force, subject to the following provisions of this Chapter.

S2, Animal Welfare (Kept Animals) Bill 2022

Owned pets are regarded as property so are protected by normal property rights as well as the avoidance of suffering/promotion of welfare provisions of the AWA.

Guide dogs, assistance dogs, and pets as therapy (PAT) animals don't have any specific protection (the AWA is broad), but they are exempt from rules about going into shops, etc., under the Equalities Act 2010.

Under Section 14 of the AWA, the Department of Environment Food and Rural Affairs (and the Welsh equivalent) has the power to issue and revise codes of practice in relation to any aspect of the Act. They are not legally enforceable in their own right but provide guidance on how to comply with the legal provisions of the Act.

JUDGMENT

R (ex parté Electronic Collar Manufacturers Association and Petsafe Ltd v the Secretary of State for the Environment, Food and Rural Affairs (2021) EWCA Civ 666

This case was an attempted judicial review brought by the manufacturers of remote-controlled handheld electronic collars which were used for training cats and dogs (these are also called "shock collars"). The Secretary of State announced in 2018 that shock collars would be banned under Section 12 of AWA.

The basis for the review was that the evidence of the welfare effects of these devices was unchanged, but previously Secretaries of State had deemed that the same evidence did not warrant a ban.

The court held that it was

> very difficult to see how it can be irrational for a decision maker to change his mind about whether a ban is appropriate, or that he should be required to give reasons, let alone "cogent reasons" for changing his mind, even if the underlying evidence is the same.

(Per Laing LJ @para 101)

What is interesting about this case is not just that the judicial review failed and the enaction of a ban was adjudged to be within the powers of the Secretary of State, but that four years later, no ban has actually been introduced in England or Scotland. In Wales, the Animal Welfare (Electronic Collars) (Wales) Regulations 2010[24] does not ban the manufacture, sale, possession, or ownership of shock collars but does ban their use.

··

  2 Prohibition on use of electronic collars

    (1) It is prohibited for a person to –

        (a) attach an electronic collar to a cat or a dog;

        (b) cause an electronic collar to be attached to a cat or a dog; or

        (c) be responsible for a cat or a dog to which an electronic collar is attached.

S2, Animal Welfare (Electronic Collars) (Wales) Regulations 2010

CRITIQUING THE LAW

If the welfare of pets is of paramount importance, should the breeding and selling of breeds of animal which are inherently unhealthy be banned under Section 9(2)(e) of the Animal Welfare Act 2006 on the basis that the animals need to be protected from pain, suffering, injury, and disease?

8.5 Sport and Entertainment

Animals have been used in sports and other types of entertainment for thousands of years. Horse racing, chariot racing, bearbaiting, and other activities where animals were pitted against humans for entertainment (e.g. *venatio*, where exotic species were hunted in the amphitheatre, forum, or stadium, often as a warm-up to gladiatorial contests) or punishment (e.g. *damnatio ad bestias*, where a convicted prisoner was killed by wild animals like lions or bears) were common in Ancient Rome and Greece. Camel wrestling in the Middle East and South Asia, cricket fighting in China, horse racing in Central Asia, horse fighting in South-East Asia, and cockfighting across the world all date back at least 1,000 years. Most of these sports were partly about providing entertainment but were also about opportunities for gambling on the outcome.

In the UK today, blood sports are banned, and although organised dogfights do occur, all animal fights are banned by the AWA, which takes a strong stance on the issue.

LEGISLATION

··

  8 Fighting etc.

    (1) A person commits an offence if he –

        (a) causes an animal fight to take place, or attempts to do so;

        (b) knowingly receives money for admission to an animal fight;

        (c) knowingly publicises a proposed animal fight;

        (d) provides information about an animal fight to another with the intention of enabling or encouraging attendance at the fight;

        (e) makes or accepts a bet on the outcome of an animal fight or on the likelihood of anything occurring or not occurring in the course of an animal fight;

        (f) takes part in an animal fight;

        (g) has in his possession anything designed or adapted for use in connection with an animal fight with the intention of its being so used;

(h) keeps or trains an animal for use for in connection with an animal fight;

(i) keeps any premises for use for an animal fight.

(2) A person commits an offence if, without lawful authority or reasonable excuse, he is present at an animal fight.

(3) A person commits an offence if, without lawful authority or reasonable excuse, he –

(a) knowingly supplies a video recording of an animal fight,

(b) knowingly publishes a video recording of an animal fight,

(c) knowingly shows a video recording of an animal fight to another, or

(d) possesses a video recording of an animal fight, knowing it to be such a recording, with the intention of supplying it.

SS8(1)–(3), Animal Welfare Act 2006

Punishments under this section also include the seizure of any animal which may be involved in the commission of a Section 8(1) or 8(2) offence, in addition to a fine, imprisonment, deprivation of the animal involved, or disqualification from owning any other animal, either temporarily or permanently.

Not all sport or entertainment involving animals is designed to cause them harm, however, and the remainder if this section will look briefly at racing, zoos, circuses, and hunting and fishing.

The welfare of animals involved in horse racing and greyhound racing and those kept in zoos and circuses is covered by the general provisions of the AWA discussed earlier. For each, however, there are additional provisions which apply.

8.5.1 Racing Animals – Horses

Horse racing has been a leisure pursuit across the world for many centuries, although "modern" professional horse racing in the UK started in the 18th century. The welfare of horses (and riders) comes under the auspices of the British Horseracing Authority (BHA), which came into being after the merger in 2007 of the Horseracing Regulatory Authority (which regulated animal welfare, discipline, and integrity in the sport and was a transitional body that took over the role from the Jockey Club in 2006) and the British Horseracing Board (which had more of a promotional and commercial role and took that over from the Jockey Club in 1993).

The BHA has the power to bring proceedings against jockeys, breeders, trainers, and others involved in the sport for ill-treatment of horses. Any judgment of the BHA disciplinary panel is separate from any enforcement action taken under the AWA.

8.5.2 Racing Animals – Dogs

Hare coursing, which uses greyhounds, has been a popular sport since at least the time of the ancient Greek historian Arrian of Nicomedia (1st century) and has been banned in Britain since the early 21st century (see earlier text). Coursing relies on "sight hounds" like greyhounds – dogs which hunt and chase prey by sight, rather than smell. Modern oval track greyhound racing was introduced in the 1920s in the United States and crossed the Atlantic shortly afterwards. The Greyhound Board of Great Britain (GBGB) is the sport's regulatory authority in Britain.

In addition to the AWA provisions, the Welfare of Racing Greyhounds Regulations 2010[25] covers the sport and makes a series of provisions which focus on the issuing of licences to those who would want to run a greyhound racing track. In a 2016 report, the House of Commons Environment, Food, and Rural Affairs

Committee[26] concluded that GBGB was doing a good job of regulation but called for more transparency in data, especially around injuries, euthanasia, and rehoming.

8.5.3 Zoos

The operation of a zoo in the UK is covered partly by the standard provisions of the AWA, but also by the Zoo Licensing Act 1981.[27]

LEGISLATION

1 Licensing of zoos by local authorities.

(1) Subject to this section it is unlawful to operate a zoo to which this Act applies except under the authority of a licence issued under this Act by the local authority for the area within which the whole or the major part of the zoo is situated.

(2) In this Act "zoo" means an establishment where wild animals (as defined by section 21) are kept for exhibition to the public otherwise than for purposes of a circus (as so defined) and otherwise than in a pet shop (as so defined)

(2A) This Act applies to any zoo to which members of the public have access, with or without charge for admission, on seven days or more in any period of twelve consecutive months.

SS1(1)–(2A), Zoo Licensing Act 1981

If someone has a small collection of animals (under 120), or they are mostly the same species (i.e. a deer park), or their premises are not open to the public, then they may not need a licence. Organisations holding a zoo licence are required to undergo regular inspections by vets and by the local authority (which is responsible for licensing), and these inspections will cover the welfare of the animals, suitability of their accommodation, training of the staff, and other relevant issues.

8.5.4 Circuses

The use of animals in circuses was widespread at one point and is one of the areas of law where the devolved nations on the UK have the power to pass their own legislation. Globally, around 50 countries have national bans or restrictions on the use of wild or all animals in circuses, and in addition, several states in the USA have also enacted bans or restrictions. In recent years, three acts across the UK have banned the use of wild animals in circuses.

England

The Wild Animals in Circuses Act 2019[28] bans the use of wild animals (those not normally domesticated in the UK) from travelling circuses in England.

LEGISLATION

1 Prohibition on use of wild animals in travelling circuses in England

(1) A circus operator may not use a wild animal in a travelling circus in England.

(2) For the purposes of this section, a circus operator uses a wild animal in a travelling circus if the animal performs or is exhibited as part of the circus.

SS1(1) and 1(2), Wild Animals in Circuses Act 2019

There is a loophole whereby a static circus could still display or use wild animals in their activities, but this is not an issue in reality as there are no static circuses in England which currently use wild animals. There are circuses which use horses, and as these are not subject to the provisions of the Act, they can continue to do so.

Scotland

The Wild Animals in Travelling Circuses (Scotland) Act 2018[29] bans the use of wild animals (those not normally domesticated in the UK) from travelling circuses in Scotland.

LEGISLATION

1 Wild animals in travelling circuses: offence

(1) A person who is a circus operator commits an offence if the person uses, or causes or permits another person to use, a wild animal in a travelling circus.

(2) An offence under this section is committed in relation to a travelling circus only if the wild animal is transported, whether regularly or irregularly, from one place to another where it is used in the travelling circus, but –

(a) the animal need not be in the course of being transported for the offence to be committed,

(b) it is immaterial to the commission of the offence whether or not the transportation of the animal is with, or is part of, the travelling circus.

(3) For the purpose of this section, a wild animal is used if the animal –

(a) performs, or

(b) is displayed or exhibited.

(4) A person who commits an offence under this section is liable on summary conviction to a fine not exceeding level 5 on the standard scale.

S1, Wild Animals in Travelling Circuses (Scotland) Act 2018

As with the English version which followed it, the Scottish Act technically allows the use of wild animals in static (non-travelling) circuses and the continued use of domesticated animals, such as horses.

Wales

Perhaps unsurprisingly, the Wild Animals and Circuses (Wales) Act 2020[30] follows the pattern established by the equivalent Acts in England and Scotland, with the same caveats.

Northern Ireland

There has been no ban enacted in Northern Ireland, but given the ban across the rest of the United Kingdom and a similar ban put in place in the Republic of Ireland (the Circuses (Prohibition on Use of Wild Animals) Regulations 2017[31]), the opportunities for animals to be used in circuses in Northern Ireland are extremely low.

8.5.5 Hunting and Fishing

We have covered a lot of the restrictions on hunting and trapping birds and certain species of mammals covered by the Wildlife and Countryside Act 1981 in Chapter 7, so those provisions will not be revisited here.

Hunting

The Protection of Wild Mammals (Scotland) Act 2002[32] and the Hunting Act 2004[33] ban the hunting of several species of mammals with dogs across Great Britain. There is no such restriction on Northern Ireland, and the Northern Ireland Assembly voted against a ban in December 2021. The Acts both make exceptions for "flushing out" game using dogs and using dogs to retrieve lawfully killed game birds.

LEGISLATION

1 Offences

(1) A person who deliberately hunts a wild mammal with a dog commits an offence.

(2) It is an offence for an owner or occupier of land knowingly to permit another person to enter or use it to commit an offence under subsection (1).

(3) It is an offence for an owner of, or person having responsibility for, a dog knowingly to permit another person to use it to commit an offence under subsection (1).

S1, Protection of Wild Mammals (Scotland) Act 2002

LEGISLATION

1 Hunting wild mammals with dogs

A person commits an offence if he hunts a wild mammal with a dog, unless his hunting is exempt.

2 Exempt hunting

(1) Hunting is exempt if it is within a class specified in Schedule 1.

(2) The Secretary of State may by order amend Schedule 1 so as to vary a class of exempt hunting.

3 Hunting: assistance

(1) A person commits an offence if he knowingly permits land which belongs to him to be entered or used in the course of the commission of an offence under section 1.

(2) A person commits an offence if he knowingly permits a dog which belongs to him to be used in the course of the commission of an offence under section 1.

SS1–3, Hunting Act 2004

The Schedule I exemptions mentioned in Section 2(1) of the Act are quite extensive and include the use of dogs to prevent damage that the wild animal might cause to a range of interests, or to flush out game birds so that they can be shot.

Hare coursing (pursuit of hares by "sight hounds," for example, species like greyhounds which hunt by sight, not by scent) is also banned across Great Britain, and the Police, Crime Sentencing, and Courts Act 2022[34] has subsequently created additional offences for those who are trespassing in order to engage in hare coursing.

LEGISLATION

(1) A person commits an offence if they trespass on land with the intention of –

(a) using a dog to search for or to pursue a hare,

(b) facilitating or encouraging the use of a dog to search for or to pursue a hare, or

(c) enabling another person to observe the use of a dog to search for or to pursue a hare.

S63, Police, Crime Sentencing, and Courts Act 2022

Fishing

There was significant debate during the preparations for the AWA to make sure that freshwater fishing was deliberately excluded from animal welfare rules, amid concerns that if it were to be included, practices such as the use of barbed hooks would be criminalised.

Freshwater fishing is usually divided into coarse fishing and fly fishing. Coarse fishing is purely a recreational activity. It gets its name because fish are regarded as being too "coarse" (i.e. rough, or unpalatable) to be desirable as food so are caught and returned to the water. Fly fishing is named after the use of a "fly" which is cast in the water to attract game fish. In the UK, fish caught this way are almost exclusively salmonids (salmon, trout, and char). Both types of fishing require a rod licence to be obtained from the local authority, and there are lots of site-specific and local rules, which we will not explore here.

It is also possible to fish in the sea from shore. This does not require a licence, but salmon and trout caught in this manner may only be kept by a person who possesses a valid freshwater fishing licence.

To a much greater extent than freshwater fishing, commercial sea fishing must pay due regard to the limits of territorial waters (see Chapter 2). From the late 1950s to early 1970s, for example, we saw the "Cod Wars," a series of confrontations between the UK and Iceland over a disagreement over control of North Atlantic fishing rights. This escalated into ramming incidents and fears over global security issues, as Iceland threatened to withdraw from NATO if it did not get the result it wanted. At the same time, cod stocks off the coast of Newfoundland in Canada fell by over 80 per cent as a result of overfishing, making the remaining cod more valuable.

In 1967, there were two consolidation acts which were passed in order to simplify the legal regime around commercial fishing. The Sea Fisheries (Shellfish) Act 1967[35] and Sea Fish (Conservation) Act 1967[36] continue to be the basis of legislation on commercial sea fishing, although there is a raft of secondary legislation concerning catch limits for different species. Enforcement is carried out by one of the ten Inshore Fisheries and Conservation Authorities, which were set up along with the Marine Management Organisation (MMO) by the Marine and Coastal Access Act 2009.[37] The Fisheries Act 2020[38] created the "fisheries objectives," which is a series of eight linked objectives which are placed on the "fisheries policy authorities" (which are effectively the relevant Secretaries of State in England and the devolved nations).

LEGISLATION

1 Fisheries objectives

   (1) The fisheries objectives are –

      (a) the sustainability objective,

      (b) the precautionary objective,

      (c) the ecosystem objective,

      (d) the scientific evidence objective,

      (e) the bycatch objective,

      (f) the equal access objective,

      (g) the national benefit objective, and

      (h) the climate change objective.

S1(1), Fisheries Act 2020

The Fisheries Policy Authorities (FPAs) must prepare a Joint Fisheries Statement (JFS) (s2(1)), which sets out how they are going to approach the objectives. Following a consultation process, the JFS was published on 23 November 2022, and the JFS will be reviewed at least every six years. The JFS sets out a shared ambition for the FPAs (following text) and identifies three main areas of focus for delivery of this ambition.

KEY FACTS

Our ambition is to deliver world class, sustainable management of our sea fisheries and aquaculture across the UK, and to play our part in supporting delivery of this globally. . . . We aim to deliver this ambition through three main areas:

■ Protecting and, where necessary, recovering our fish stocks.
■ Reducing the adverse effects of fishing on the marine and coastal environment.
■ Supporting a modern, resilient and environmentally responsible fishing industry.

Joint Fisheries Statement, November 2022, p. 13

SUMMARY

■ The Animal Welfare Act 2006 is the keystone of modern animal welfare laws in the UK, but there are many other legislative provisions which relate to different aspects of human interaction with animals.

■ In addition, there is a wide range of regulatory bodies which issue licences, monitor, inspect, and prosecute different aspects of human–animal interaction.

■ Development of this relationship between people and animals over the last few millennia has been more dramatic in some areas than in others.

■ Religion and belief have played a role here, too, whether it is the belief that some species of animal should not be eaten by humans at all (e.g. Hinduism and cows) or on particular days (e.g. Catholicism and meat on a Friday), or the belief that animals must be killed in a specific manner before they are eaten (e.g. halal or kosher), or the belief that no animals should be eaten by humans (e.g. Jainism).

■ To end the chapter by paraphrasing Herzog, some we love, some we hate, some we kill, some we inject, some we race, some we fear, some we fight, some we eat, and some we protect.

The next chapter will consider the legal frameworks around pollution of the air and the wider issues of climate change.

SAMPLE PROBLEM QUESTION

Police officers and RSPCA officers visited a farm near Camtonside (in Midshire, England) after getting a tip-off that there were a number of alpacas kept on the property in very poor conditions. On arrival at the farm, animals were found to be sick, injured, diseased, and malnourished, and carcasses and bones were left around the site.

After a full investigation, the RSPCA concluded the following:

- The alpaca had been kept in unsuitable, dirty, and crowded accommodation, with a significant lack of nourishment and care.
- Failure to engage a vet meant that animals suffered and died without proper attention and unrelieved by humane euthanasia, and those that were dying were left with the living.
- The animals were left to suffer without any recourse to positive input of any kind, such as food, management, treatment, alleviation of overcrowding, or prudent care from a competent and caring owner.

The farm is run by Bob, and the other worker involved in the alpaca side of the farm business is Harvey (a new employee, who has only been employed for one month). Bob claimed he did not have sufficient funds to keep the animals in better conditions.

Advise Bob and Harvey on whether they are in contravention of the provisions of the Animal Welfare Act 2006 and what sanctions may be imposed upon them.

> 1. Identify the specific elements of the AWA which might apply (specifically Section 4 (unnecessary suffering) and Section 9 (duty to ensure welfare)).
> 2. Assess whether the behaviours were due to acts or omissions and whether they were deliberate or due to negligence.
> 3. Assess the difference between Section 4 and Section 9 – one is to avoid cruelty; one is to promote welfare.
> 4. Identify appropriate/likely sanctions (Sections 33–42).
> 5. Conclude.

Further Reading

Harrison, R., 1964, *Animal Machines: The New Factory Farming Industry*, London: Vincent Stewart Publishing

Herzog, H., 2010, *Some We Love, Some We Hate, Some We Eat: Why It's so Hard to Think Straight about Animals*, London: HarperCollins

Primatt, H., 1776, *A Dissertation on the Duty of Mercy and the Sin of Cruelty to Brute Animals*, London: R. Hett

Robertson, I.A., 2015, *Animals, Welfare and the Law: Fundamental Principles for Critical Assessment*, London: Routledge

Stamp Dawkins, M., 2012, *Why Animals Matter: Animal Consciousness, Animal Welfare, and Human Well-Being*, Oxford: OUP

Steier, G., 2023, *Farm Animal Welfare Law: International Perspectives on Sustainable Agriculture and Wildlife Regulation*, Boca Raton: CRC Press

Sweeney, N., 2017, *A Practical Approach to Animal Welfare Law*, 2nd ed., Great Easton: 5m Publishing

Tyson, E., 2020, *Licensing Laws and Animal Welfare: The Legal Protection of Wild Animals*, London: Palgrave Macmillan

Notes

1 2006 c.45
2 1986 c.14
3 Boddice, R., *Beastly Pleasures: Blood Sports in England, c1776–1876*, York: University of York, p. 125
4 25 Geo 2 c 37
5 Primatt, H., 1776, *A Dissertation on the Duty of Mercy and the Sin of Cruelty to Brute Animals*, London: R. Hett, p. 87
6 Technical Committee to Inquire into the Welfare of Animals Kept under Intensive Livestock Husbandry Systems, para 37
7 DIR 64/432/EEC on animal health problems affecting intra-Community trade in bovine animals and swine
8 DIR 74/577/EEC on stunning animals before slaughter
9 2022, c.22
10 Stamp Dawkins, M., 2012, *Why Animals Matter: Animal Consciousness, Animal Welfare, and Human Well-Being*, Oxford: OUP, p. 4
11 This is echoed in HG Wells' 1896 novel "The Island of Dr Moreau" which charts the catastrophic consequences of this type of approach
12 39 and 40 Vict. c. 77
13 Directive 2010/63/EU on the protection of animals used for scientific purposes
14 S.I. 2012/3039
15 2001, c.23
16 Home Office, 2014, *Guidance on the Operation of the Animals (Scientific Procedures) Act 1986*, London: TSO, p. 50
17 Regulation 1223/2009 on cosmetic products
18 Council Regulation (EC) No 1/2005 on the protection of animals during transport and related operations and amending Directives 64/432/EEC and 93/119/EC and Regulation (EC) No 1255/97
19 SI 2006/3260
20 SI 2015/1782
21 Regulation (EC) No 1099/2009 on the protection of animals at the time of killing
22 Council Regulation (EC) No 834/2007 on organic production and labelling of organic products with regard to organic production, labelling and control
23 1976 c.38
24 SI 2010/943 (W.97)
25 SI 2010/543
26 EFRA, 2016, *Greyhound Welfare, HC 478: House of Commons Environment, Food and Rural Affairs Committee*, 2nd Report of 2015–16, London: TSO, p. 25
27 1981 c.37. The Act does not apply to Northern Ireland
28 2019 c.4
29 2018 asp.3
30 2020 asc2
31 SI No. 482/2017
32 2002 asp6
33 2004 c.37
34 2022 c.32
35 1967 c.83
36 1967 c.84
37 2009 c.23
38 2020 c.22

9

Climate Change and Air Pollution

By its very nature, air pollution is the most mobile form of pollution. It can have local, regional, or global impact, depending upon the nature of the pollutant. Since climate change is being driven by substances introduced into the air by human activity, it is also within the remit of the chapter.

In terms of focus, this chapter looks at three separate but linked effects of air pollution and allows you to explore the difficulties inherent in dealing with each of them. The three are:

- Acid rain
- Ozone layer depletion
- Climate change

There is a mixture of UK legislation addressing the different aspects of atmospheric pollution prevention. Some of these predate International and European initiatives, and some were introduced as a direct response to them. Broadly, they fall into two categories: that dealing with pollution prevention from large industrial premises and that dealing with smaller premises and vehicles. For each of the three elements of air pollution, we will look at international law, EU law (to the extent it has not been amended post-Brexit), and UK laws. The implications for industrial polluters will act as a theme running through all of them and will thus be the initial focus of the chapter.

AIMS AND OBJECTIVES

After reading this chapter, you should be able to:

- Understand the theory and application of the best appropriate technique standard.
- Explain the international legislative approaches to tackling acid rain, ozone layer depletion, and climate change.
- Identify the UK approach to smoke and statutory nuisance.

DOI: 10.4324/9781003137214-9

9.1 Industrial Pollution Control

Industrial pollution control has a long history in the UK, going back at least as far as the Alkali Act 1863.[1] There is a direct lineage between the role of the alkali inspector in 1863 and the chief inspector in 1874 to the inclusion of other airborne industrial pollutants under the Alkali &c Works Order 1958[2] through to the creation of the Industrial Air Pollution Inspectorate in 1983 and the merger with the Radiochemical Inspectorate, the Hazardous Waste Inspectorate, and Water Inspectorate to create Her Majesty's Inspectorate of Pollution (HMIP) in 1987. The process culminated with the merger of HMIP and the National Rivers Authority to create the Environment Agency in 1996. This process of repeated mergers has subsequently been rationalised again so that at the current time, there are four main environmental regulatory bodies across the UK:

The Environment Agency (England). Formed in 1996 by Section 1 of the Environment Act 1995,[3] which merged the responsibilities of HMIP, the National Rivers Authority, some of the responsibilities of the waste regulation authorities and waste disposal authorities, and the role of the chief inspector under the Radioactive Substances Act 1993.[4]

The Scottish Environmental Protection Agency/*Buidheann Dìon Àrainneachd na h-Alba* (Scotland). Formed in 1986 by Section 20 of the Environment Act 1995, which merged the roles of the Rover Purification Boards and waste, pollution, and radioactive substances inspectors.

Natural Resources Wales/*Cyfoeth Naturiol Cymru* (Wales). Formed in 2013 by the Natural Resources Body for Wales (Establishment) Order 2012,[5] which merged the Environment Agency Wales, Countryside Council for Wales, and the Forestry Commission Wales.

The Northern Ireland Environment Agency (Northern Ireland). Formed in 2016 after the dissolution of the Environment and Heritage Service.

In the 1970s, the now-disbanded Royal Commission on Environmental Pollution recognised that in order for industrial pollution to be controlled effectively, an integrated approach would need to be taken.

QUOTATION

"The reduction of emissions to the atmosphere can lead to an increase in wastes to be disposed of on land or discharged into water. If the optimum environmental solutions are to be found, the controlling authorities must be able to look comprehensively to all forms of pollution arising from industrial processes where different control problems exist."

RCEP, 1976, Air Pollution Control: An Integrated Approach,
Fifth Report (Cmnd 6371), London: HMSO

The RCEP was predicting that if a separate approach were to be taken, then an unscrupulous corporate polluter would look for the lowest cost-alternative method for disposing of industrial waste – what some have referred apocryphally to as the "CATNIP" approach (cheapest alternative technique not involving prosecution). With an integrated approach, the idea of, for example, liquefying a previously gaseous emission and releasing it into the water rather than the air would no longer be viable. The RCEP also recommended that a single regulatory body would be needed to oversee this integrated approach.

The legislative framework covering industrial pollution control has also undergone a range of changes since the 1860s, and the current provisions in England and Wales stem from the Pollution Prevention and Control Act 1999[6] and the Environmental Permitting (England and Wales) Regulations 2016[7] (as amended). The water- and groundwater-related elements of the Permitting Regulations will be covered in Chapter 10. The Permitting Regulations apply to "regulated facilities" and cover a wide range of activities which require permission to operate.

LEGISLATION

(1) In these Regulations, "regulated facility" means any of the following –

    (a) an installation,
    (b) mobile plant,
    (c) a waste operation,
    (d) a mining waste operation,
    (e) a radioactive substances activity,
    (f) a water discharge activity,
    (g) a groundwater activity.
    (h) a small waste incineration plant;
    (i) a solvent emission activity;
    (j) a flood risk activity.
    (k) a medium combustion plant;
    (l) a specified generator

(2) But the following are not regulated facilities –

    (a) an exempt facility,
    (b) an excluded waste operation,
    (c) the disposal or recovery of household waste from a domestic property within the curtilage of that property by a person other than an establishment or undertaking.
    (d) an excluded flood risk activity

(3) In these Regulations, a reference to a class of regulated facility is a reference to a class in paragraph (1).

(4) A regulated facility of any of the following classes may be carried on as part of the operation of a regulated facility of another class –

    (a) waste operation;
    (b) mining waste operation;
    (c) water discharge activity;
    (d) groundwater activity.
    (e) a small waste incineration plant;
    (f) a solvent emission activity;
    (g) a flood risk activity.
    (h) a medium combustion plant;
    (i) a specified generator

Reg 8, Environmental Permitting (England and Wales) Regulations 2016

In terms of air pollution, the Permitting Regulations include this within the wide definition of "emission."

"Emission" means –

(a) in relation to a Part A installation, the direct or indirect release of substances, vibrations, heat or noise from individual or diffuse sources in the installation into the air, water or land,

(b) in relation to a Part B installation, the direct release of substances or heat from individual or diffuse sources in the installation into the air,

(c) in relation to Part A mobile plant, the direct or indirect release of substances, vibrations, heat or noise from the mobile plant into the air, water or land,

(d) in relation to Part B mobile plant, the direct release of substances or heat from the mobile plant into the air,

(e) in relation to a waste operation, the direct or indirect release of substances, vibrations, heat or noise from individual or diffuse sources related to the operation into the air, water or land,

(f) in relation to a mining waste operation, the direct or indirect release of substances, vibrations, heat or noise from individual or diffuse sources related to the operation into the air, water or land, and

(g) in relation to a radioactive substances activity, the direct or indirect release of radioactive material or radioactive waste;

(h) in relation to a small waste incineration plant, the direct or indirect release of substances from individual or diffuse sources in the regulated facility into the air or water;

(i) in relation to a medium combustion plant, the release of substances from the plant into the air;

(j) in relation to a specified generator, the release of substances from the plant into the air;

Reg 2, Environmental Permitting (England and Wales) Regulations 2016

Operating a regulated facility without a permit is an offence, as is releasing emissions in contravention of the details of a permit. The Sentencing Council released a set of guidelines in 2014 for environmental offences, and these apply both to individuals and to corporate bodies. For corporations, the guidelines divide corporate bodies into five categories by scale of turnover:

Very Large Organisations. Undefined, but must "very greatly exceed" the limit for large organisations.

Large Organisations. £50m or higher.

Medium Organisations. £10m–£50m

Small Organisations. £2m–£10m

Micro Organisations. Under £2m.

The guidelines also separate offences by their scale (category 1–4) and by the *mens rea* element which can be attributed to the corporation (low culpability, negligent, reckless, deliberate) and include a "starting point" for a fine as well as an upper and lower range of potential fines, depending on the severity and culpability. Figure 9.1 illustrates the range of fines available just for a "large" organisation.

This gives the courts a very flexible approach to fining a corporation, with the maximum fine listed in the guidance being £3m (large corporation, category 4 offence, deliberate action) and the minimum fine listed being just £100 (micro corporation, category 1 offence, low/no culpability).

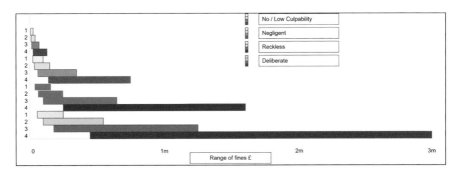

Figure 9.1 Range of fines recommended for a large corporation.

Source: Sentencing Council, www.sentencingcouncil.org.uk/sentencing-and-the-council/about-sentencing-guidelines/about-published-guidelines/environment/.

9.1.1 Best Appropriate Technique (BAT)

As we have seen, the integrated pollution prevention and control regime is predicated on the requirements of the Directive 2010/75/EU,[8] which built on Directive 2008/1/EC[9] and Directive 96/61/EC.[10] The original Directive was transposed into UK law by virtue of the Pollution Prevention and Control Act 1999,[11] and it is this Act which is the "enabling" Act under which the Environmental Permitting Regulations sit.

The definition of "environmental pollution" in the Act is very extensive:

LEGISLATION
....

(2) In this Act –

"activities" means activities of any nature, whether –

(a) industrial or commercial or other activities, or

(b) carried on particular premises or otherwise,

and includes (with or without other activities) the depositing, keeping or disposal of any substance;

"environmental pollution" means pollution of the air, water or land which may give rise to any harm; and for the purposes of this definition (but without prejudice to its generality) –

(a) "pollution" includes pollution caused by noise, heat or vibrations or any other kind of release of energy, and

(b) "air" includes air within buildings and air within other natural or man-made structures above or below ground.

(3) In the definition of "environmental pollution" in subsection (2), "harm" means –

(a) harm to the health of human beings or other living organisms;

(b) harm to the quality of the environment, including –

(i) harm to the quality of the environment taken as a whole,

(ii) harm to the quality of the air, water or land, and

(iii) other impairment of, or interference with, the ecological systems of which any living organisms form part;

(c) offence to the senses of human beings;

(d) damage to property; or

(e) impairment of, or interference with, amenities or other legitimate uses of the environment (expressions used in this paragraph having the same meaning as in Directive 2010/75/EU).

S1(2) and (3), Pollution Prevention and Control Act 1999

The definition is extended in relation to potential air pollution by the Environmental Permitting (England and Wales) Regulations 2016.

LEGISLATION

Schedule 1 of the EP regulations continues the three levels of permit which had been introduced under the Pollution Prevention and Control (England and Wales) Regulations 2000,[12] namely, Part A(1), Part A(2), and Part B. the category into which a permit falls is calculated by the scale of the operation.

Part A(1) Larger operations from installations and mobile plant which are regulated by the environment agency.

Part A(2) Smaller operations from installations and mobile plant which are regulated by the relevant local authority, although the local authorities will be in consultation with the relevant environment agency (see earlier text).

All Part A operations will be regulated "for the purpose of achieving a high level of protection of the environment taken as a whole by, in particular, preventing or, where that is not practicable, reducing emissions into the air, water and land" (EP Regulations, Reg 3).

Part B activities are also regulated by the local authority, and Regulation 6 sets a threshold for Part B activities where they cannot release any of the substances listed in Subsection 3, or a release at a level "so trivial that it is incapable of causing pollution or its capacity to cause pollution is insignificant."

LEGISLATION

There is a general, overarching provision that all regulated activities must comply with "BAT" (best available techniques), which are defined in Article 2(12) of Directive 2008/1/EC.[13]

Definition

Article 3 Definitions . . .

(10) "best available techniques" means the most effective and advanced stage in the development of activities and their methods of operation which indicates the practical suitability of particular techniques for providing the basis for emission limit values and other permit conditions designed to prevent and, where that is not practicable, to reduce emissions and the impact on the environment as a whole:

(a) "techniques" includes both the technology used and the way in which the installation is designed, built, maintained, operated and decommissioned;

(b) "available techniques" means those developed on a scale which allows implementation in the relevant industrial sector, under economically and technically viable conditions, taking into consideration the costs and advantages, whether or not the techniques are used or produced inside the Member State in question, as long as they are reasonably accessible to the operator;

(c) "best" means most effective in achieving a high general level of protection of the environment as a whole;

(11) "BAT reference document" means a document, resulting from the exchange of information organised pursuant to Article 13, drawn up for defined activities and describing, in particular, applied techniques, present emissions and consumption levels, techniques considered for the determination of best available techniques as well as BAT conclusions and any emerging techniques, giving special consideration to the criteria listed in Annex III;

(12) "BAT conclusions" means a document containing the parts of a BAT reference document laying down the conclusions on best available techniques, their description, information to assess their applicability, the emission levels associated with the best available techniques, associated monitoring, associated consumption levels and, where appropriate, relevant site remediation measures;

Article 2(10)–(12), Directive 2010/75/EU of the European Parliament
and of the Council on Industrial Emissions (Integrated Pollution
Prevention and Control)

BAT is not a static standard and is a good illustration of the symbiotic relationship between law and science in this area. Annex III, specifically Part 12, allows for the standard to be incrementally tightened as scientific standards are improved.

ARTICLE

Annex III Criteria for determining best available techniques

1. the use of low-waste technology;
2. the use of less hazardous substances;
3. the furthering of recovery and recycling of substances generated and used in the process and of waste, where appropriate;
4. comparable processes, facilities or methods of operation which have been tried with success on an industrial scale;
5. technological advances and changes in scientific knowledge and understanding;
6. the nature, effects and volume of the emissions concerned;
7. the commissioning dates for new or existing installations;
8. the length of time needed to introduce the best available technique;

9. the consumption and nature of raw materials (including water) used in the process and energy efficiency;
10. the need to prevent or reduce to a minimum the overall impact of the emissions on the environment and the risks to it;
11. the need to prevent accidents and to minimise the consequences for the environment;
12. information published by public international organisations.

Annex III, Directive 2010/75/EU of the European Parliament and of the Council on Industrial Emissions (Integrated Pollution Prevention and Control)

Annex II of the Directive sets out an indicative list (NB, not an exhaustive list) of the main polluting substances which need to be taken into account if they are relevant.

ARTICLE

Air

1. Sulphur dioxide and other sulphur compounds.
2. Oxides of nitrogen and other nitrogen compounds.
3. Carbon monoxide.
4. Volatile organic compounds.
5. Metals and their compounds.
6. Dust including fine particulate matter.
7. Asbestos (suspended particulates, fibres).
8. Chlorine and its compounds.
9. Fluorine and its compounds.
10. Arsenic and its compounds.
11. Cyanides.
12. Substances and preparations which have been proved to possess carcinogenic or mutagenic properties or properties which may affect reproduction via the air.
13. Polychlorinated dibenzodioxins and polychlorinated dibenzofurans.

Annex II, Directive 2010/75/EU of the European Parliament and of the Council on Industrial Emissions (Integrated Pollution Prevention and Control)

Article 13 encourages the exchange of information between member states in relation to BAT in order to promote harmonisation of standards across the EU. These BAT Reference Documents (or BREF Documents), which are prepared by a combination of industry and NGOs, were included in the old regimes but are made stronger in the 2010 Directive, where Articles 14 and 15 set out that the BREF documents should be the reference point used by member states.

ACTIVITY

Now that the UK has left the EU and has the ability to deviate from the provisions of Annex III, Directive 2010/75/EU, how should the criteria for establishing BAT be changed?

9.2 Acid Rain

Standard rainwater in the UK is usually mildly acidic, with a pH of between 5 and 5.5, so the term "acid rain" is a little bit of a misnomer. Nonetheless, "acid" rain is caused when certain pollutants (generally oxides of nitrogen and sulphur dioxide) rise in the air and are incorporated into the standard weather patterns. The pollutants then mix with naturally occurring water vapour and eventually fall as rain, with a pH of around 4.2–4.5. The pH ("potential of hydrogen") scale which is used to measure acidity and alkalinity runs from 0 (highly acidic, for example, battery acid) to 14 (highly alkaline, for example, liquid drain cleaner), with distilled water having a pH of 7 (neutral). The scale is logarithmic in nature, which means that each change in digit means a tenfold increase or decrease in acidity. Acid rain, with pH of 4.5, is therefore ten times more acidic than "standard" rain, with a pH of 5.5.

The elevated acidity caused by pollutants can cause significant problems for the environment onto which the rain falls. The majority of plant and animal species have an optimum pH range of between 5 and 8, so the more acidic the rain, the greater the impact it will have.

It is possible for the pollutants which cause acid rain to be emitted by natural processes, and there is little that can be done to control these. Over the last century, there have been increasing levels of emissions from anthropogenic (human-made) sources, such as vehicle exhaust pipes, industrial chimneys, and so on. The 1970s and 1980s saw episodes of "forest death" across Europe, where acid rain decimated areas of forest and the biodiversity which relied upon them. The majority of forests in what was then Czechoslovakia (now the Czech Republic and Slovakia), as well as major parts of forests in Germany, Poland, and the former Soviet Union, were damaged by acid rain (Rose, 1988).

In addition to the death of forests, several Scandinavian countries also reported that fish stocks had fallen dramatically.

QUOTATION

"In southern Norway regional damage is now documented in an area of 33,000 km2, 13,000 km2 of which are devoid of fish. Several major southern salmon rivers are now barren. In Sweden more than 2500 lakes are documented to be affected. This corresponds to 3%–4% of the total lake area. An additional 6,000 lakes are assumed to be affected by acidification."

Muniz, I. P., 1984, The Effects of Acidification on Scandinavian Freshwater Fish Fauna, Philosophical Transactions of the Royal Society of London. Series B, *Biological Sciences*, Vol. 305, No. 1124, Ecological Effects of Deposited Sulphur and Nitrogen Compounds (May 1, 1984), pp. 517–528

Conceptually, the solutions to acid rain are among the simplest of all types of air pollution to create. Reducing emissions of sulphur dioxide, oxides of nitrogen, volatile organic compounds (VOCs), and so on will reduce the level at which acid rain is created, and since the cause-and-effect is not contentious, the impacts of acid rain can be solved.

Unfortunately, the implementation of such measure has proved to be more complex, although there are provisions to do so at international, regional, and local levels.

9.2.1 Long-Range Transboundary Air Pollution Convention

The Long-Range Transboundary Air Pollution Convention (LRTAP), which was briefly mentioned in Chapter 1, was a significant first step in the process of internationally agreed targets for the reduction of airborne pollutants.

LRTAP was created under the umbrella of the United Nations Economic Commission for Europe (UNECE), which itself sits under the UN Economic and Social Council. UNECE has 56 member states. These are mostly in Europe but also include Canada and the United States, several countries in Central Asia, and Israel. The Convention has 51 parties (all the UNECE member states, except Andorra, Israel, Tajikistan, Turkmenistan, and Uzbekistan). The Convention was agreed and signed in Geneva in 1979 and entered into force in 1983.

The basic principle is that states should limit and then reduce their levels of air pollution, especially that with a transboundary impact.

ARTICLE

Article 2: FUNDAMENTAL PRINCIPLES

The Contracting Parties, taking due account of the facts and problems involved, are determined to protect man and his environment against air pollution and shall endeavour to limit and, as far as possible, gradually reduce and prevent air pollution including long-range transboundary air pollution.

Article 2, LRTAP

The idea of transboundary liability for pollution is not particularly new and was established four decades earlier in the Trail Smelter Arbitration (*USA v Canada*, 3 RIAA 1907 (1941)), which was discussed briefly in Chapter 1. The LRTAP sets out what it means by *air pollution*, and you can see that these include a range of anthropocentric (human health, living resources, material property, and amenities) and ecocentric (ecosystems) approaches.

ARTICLE

Article 1

(a) "Air Pollution" means the introduction by man, directly or indirectly, of substances or energy into the air resulting in deleterious effects of such a nature as to endanger human health, harm living resources and ecosystems and material property and impair or interfere with amenities and other legitimate uses of the environment;

(b) "Long-range transboundary air pollution" means air pollution whose physical origin is situated wholly or in part within the area under the national jurisdiction of one State and which has adverse effects in the area under the jurisdiction of another State at such a distance that it is not generally possible to distinguish the contribution of individual emission sources or groups of sources

Article 1, LRTAP

What LRTAP does is create a framework whereby parties can share information and develop their existing policies on reducing air pollution (Art. 4), cooperate in research and development (Art. 7), and generally work together to combat air pollution. The thinking behind the Convention is that if national pollution levels are reduced, levels of transnational air pollution will be reduced, and their impact will abate.

Since the Convention itself is more of a framework, the details are contained in the protocols to the Convention. There have been eight protocols thus far:

■ 1984 (Geneva) Protocol on Long-Term Financing of the Cooperative Programme for Monitoring and Evaluation of the Long-Range Transmission of Air Pollutants in Europe (EMEP). This Protocol set up the EMEP, which collects data, monitors, and models dispersion on SO_2, NOx, VOC, and other pollutants.

- 1985 (Helsinki) Protocol on the Reduction of Sulphur Emissions or Their Transboundary Fluxes by at Least 30 Per Cent. This protocol required parties to put in place policies and strategies for reducing sulphur emissions by 30 per cent from 1980 levels by 1993 at the latest. These targets were generally not met.

- 1988 (Sofia) Protocol Concerning the Control of Nitrogen Oxides or Their Transboundary Fluxes. This protocol replicated the Helsinki Protocol provisions on sulphur and applied them to NOx, as scientific data had revealed the importance of NOx reductions is reducing acid rain. Unlike Helsinki, there is no specific reduction target contained in the Protocol.

- 1991 (Geneva) Protocol Concerning the Control of Emissions of Volatile Organic Compounds or Their Transboundary Fluxes. This protocol called for a 30 per cent reduction on VOC emissions (based on a target year of "between 1984 and 1990" to be achieved by 1999).

- 1994 (Oslo) Protocol on Further Reduction of Sulphur Emissions. This protocol effectively replaces and builds on the 1985 Helsinki Protocol. It acknowledges in the preamble that the provisions of the UN FCCC will be expected to lead to reductions in sulphur emissions. Annex II set specific targets for each party to achieve by 2000, 2005, and 2010.

- 1998 (Aarhus) Protocol on Heavy Metals (amended 2012). The aim was to cut heavy metal emissions (cadmium (Cd), lead (Pb), and mercury (Hg)) from industrial sources, combustion (including road transport), and waste incineration.

- 1998 (Aarhus) Protocol on Persistent Organic Pollutants (POPs) (amended 2009). This set the goal of eventual elimination of POPs – substances which do not break down rapidly in the natural environment and cause health issues when injected. Things like pesticides and industrial chemicals come within this category. Interestingly, the pesticide DDT (dichlorodiphenyltrichloroethane) was listed in Annex I as a substance which should be eliminated as soon as a viable replacement could be found. The use of DDT was also the trigger for Rachael Carson's 1962 book *Silent Spring*, which is regarded as one of the triggers for the environmental movement.

- 1999 (Gothenburg) Protocol to Abate Acidification, Eutrophication, and Ground-Level Ozone (amended 2012). This protocol builds on previous provisions to set emissions ceilings for SO_2, NOx, VOCs, and ammonia (NH_3) and required both annual reporting and annual future forecasting of emissions by parties.

9.2.2 EU

In addition to the wider UNECE measures, the European Union has, in its different incarnations, passed legislation which will have the effect of lowering air pollution.

The first of these was Directive 70/220/EEC,[14] which, although it links very strongly to air pollution from positive ignition engines (i.e. petrol, as opposed to diesel, which are "compression ignition" engines), is more about maintaining the "level playing field" of the EEC. It was triggered by two differing sets of regulations on exhaust emissions issued at a national level in Germany in 1968 and France in 1969 and fears over the impact this could have on trade.

The Directive creates a new EEC level approval system, and member states are forbidden from denying approval if a vehicle meets criteria set out in the Directive.

ARTICLE

No Member State may refuse to grant EEC type approval or national type approval of a vehicle on grounds relating to air pollution by gases from positive-ignition engines of motor vehicles

- from 1 October 1970, where that vehicle satisfies both the requirements contained in Annex I, with the exception of those in items 3.2.1.1 and 3.2.2.1, and the requirements contained in Annexes II, IV, V and VI;
- from 1 October 1971, where that vehicle satisfies, in addition, the requirements contained in items 3.2.1.1 and 3.2.2.1 of Annex I and in Annex III

Article 2, Directive 70/220/EEC

Whilst the 1970 Directive did have an impact on exhaust emissions (most member states were not setting national levels at that time), the first Directive to specifically address air pollution was Directive 80/779/EEC.[15] This Directive set "limit values" and "guide values" for sulphur and suspended particulates (grit, smoke, dust, and other particulate matter). Put simply, "limit values" must not be exceeded, and "guide values" must be attempted.

ARTICLE

Whereas, in order to protect human health in particular, it is necessary to set for these two pollutants limit values which must not be exceeded in the territory of the Member States during specified periods; whereas these values should be based on the findings reached in the framework of the WHO, particularly with regard to the dose/effect relationships established for sulphur dioxide and suspended particulates taken together; . . .

Whereas guide values should also be set to serve as long-term precautions for health and the environment and as reference points for the establishment of specific schemes within zones determined by the Member States

Preamble, Directive 80/779/EEC

This Directive has been amended several times, and the current version is the Ambient Air Directive,[16] which has pulled together a range of different directives into one place:

- Council Directive 96/62/EC of 27 September 1996 on ambient air quality assessment and management
- Council Directive 1999/30/EC of 22 April 1999 relating to limit values for sulphur dioxide, nitrogen dioxide, and oxides of nitrogen, particulate matter, and lead in ambient air
- Directive 2000/69/EC of the European Parliament and of the Council of 16 November 2000 relating to limit values for benzene and carbon monoxide in ambient air
- Directive 2002/3/EC of the European Parliament and of the Council of 12 February 2002 relating to ozone[17] in ambient air

- Directive 2004/107/EC of the European Parliament and of the Council of 15 December 2004 relating to arsenic, cadmium, mercury, nickel, and polycyclic aromatic hydrocarbons in ambient air

Benzene (Dir 2000/69/EC) is a solvent, part of what gives petrol its smell, and is carcinogenic (cancer-causing). Polycyclic aromatic hydrocarbons (PAH, Dir 2004/107/EC) are a wider range of POPs (see earlier) formed of two or more benzene rings.

The 2008 Directive also includes provision aimed at $PM_{2.5}$, which is fine particulate matter (grit, dust, etc.) with a diameter of less than 2.5 microns (μm). By comparison, a human hair is around 70 microns, so 28 times thicker. $PM_{2.5}$ is so small it is easily inhaled and then adheres to the lining of the lungs, leading to potentially serious health implications. The Directive takes a pragmatic perspective on levels of $PM_{2.5}$.

ARTICLE

Fine particulate matter ($PM_{2.5}$) is responsible for significant negative impacts on human health. Further, there is as yet no identifiable threshold below which PM2.5 would not pose a risk.

Recital 11, Directive 2008/50/EC

Despite this acknowledgement that there is essentially no safe level of PM 2.5, Annexe XIV sets a series of targets to be met by 2010, 2015, and 2020, peaking at a concentration of 20μg/m3.

CRITIQUING THE LAW

Given the understanding that no levels of PM 2.5 are safe, is the EU doing enough by setting targets of more than 0? Should the UK mandate a lower level?

UK provisions on air quality are given effect by the Air Quality Regulations 2010[18] as amended. The Regulations require the Secretary of State to divide up the UK into "zones and agglomerations" (Reg 4(2)) and, once that is done, to assess the air quality in each zone/agglomeration once every five years. Table 9.1 illustrates the specific provisions that link to each type of pollutant. The standards are currently those set by the 2008 Directive, although this may change in the future as either that Directive or domestic law are amended.

Schedule 2 sets the limit values, Schedule 3 sets the target values, and Schedule 5 sets the alert thresholds for SO_2, NO_2, and ozone. If the alert values are exceeded,

Table 9.1 Statutory Provision for What Needs to Be Assessed

What Must Be Assessed	Statutory Provision
SO2, NO2, NOx, particulate matter,[19] lead, benzene, CO	Reg. 5(1)
Ozone	Reg. 8(1)
Arsenic, cadmium, nickel, mercury, benzo(a)pyrene, and other polycyclic aromatic hydrocarbons	Reg. 10(1)

the Secretary of State is under an obligation to inform the public "by means of radio, television, newspapers or the internet" (Reg. 21).

LEGISLATION

Sulphur dioxide

Averaging period	Limit value
One hour	350 µg/m3 not to be exceeded more than 24 times a calendar year
One day	125 µg/m3 not to be exceeded more than 3 times a calendar year

Nitrogen dioxide

One hour	200 µg/m3 not to be exceeded more than 18 times a calendar year
Calendar year	40 µg/m3

Benzene

Calendar year	5 µg/m3

Lead

Calendar year	0.5 µg/m3

PM_{10}

One day	50 µg/m3, not to be exceeded more than 35 times a calendar year
Calendar year	40 µg/m3

$PM_{2.5}$

Calendar year	20 µg/m3 (by 1st January 2020)

Carbon monoxide

Maximum 8hr daily mean 10 mg/m3

Schedule 2, Air Quality Regulations 2010

The extensive regulations at different levels have led to the reduction in some of the pollutants linked to acid rain, and in Europe and North America particularly, the situation has notably improved since the 1970s. This is not the case globally, however, and in areas with less-robust pollution controls, such as parts of SE Asia, the problem persists.

9.3 Ozone Layer Depletion

Ozone (O_3) occurs at different levels. Low-level, or tropospheric, ozone, which occurs close to ground level, is, as we saw in the previous section, a constituent part of smog and contributes to ill-health (particularly respiratory health) to such an extent that the Secretary of State must issue a warning if the levels get too high. It is also the third most potent greenhouse gas, after CO_2 and methane (CH_4). It is caused by the chemical reaction of sunlight on hydrocarbons from exhaust emissions.

High-level, or stratospheric, ozone acts as a screen for up to 99 per cent of the ultraviolet rays contained in sunlight. The "ozone layer" is not uniformly distributed and tends to be thicker around the equator.

From the early 1970s onwards, scientists have been investigating the potential of certain manmade substances or activities to damage ozone. The impacts of nitrogen oxides, hydrogen oxides, chlorine oxides, and supersonic air travel were all the subject of reports from 1970 to 1974, and in 1976, the National Academies of Sciences Engineering and Medicine in the United States published a report which identified the impact of halocarbons on stratospheric ozone. The impact of the report was a ban by the US Environmental Protection Agency in March 1978 on the use of CFCs as propellants in aerosols.

In 1985, scientists announced that there was a significant thinning of the ozone layer over Antarctica, and this was an annual occurrence. The fear of the international community was that this thinning would lead to a lower level of protection from ultraviolet light and, since the link between ultraviolet light and cancer had been recognised in the late 1950s, an increase in cancer.

The substances understood to cause the most significant damage to the ozone layer were those like chlorofluorocarbons (CFCs), hydrochlorofluorocarbons (HCFCs), and bromotrifluoromethane (halon), which are very stable compounds used in a range of processes, from aerosols to cooling systems. Because of their stability, these substances rise into the lower stratosphere, where they are broken down and their chlorine or bromine molecules are released. These, in turn, break down ozone into free oxygen, which does not share she same ultraviolet-absorption qualities.

9.3.1 Vienna Convention

The Vienna Convention on the Ozone Layer was created by the United Nations and signed in 1985. Thinking back to the political decision-making cycle outlined in Chapter 4, which outlined the potential for time delay in decision-making, the Convention was signed relatively quickly after the issues with a thinning ozone layer were identified. This gives some indication to the level of importance which was attached to the ozone layer thinning. The Convention currently has 198 signatories, the most recent being the state of Palestine in 2019.

ARTICLE

Aware of the potentially harmful impact on human health and the environment through modification of the ozone layer . . .

Aware that measures to protect the ozone layer from modifications due to human activities require international co-operation and action, and should be based on relevant scientific and technical considerations . . .

Determined to protect human health and the environment against adverse effects resulting from modifications of the ozone layer.

Preamble (excerpts), the Vienna Convention for the Protection of the Ozone Layer 1985

The convention requires signatories to undertake research on substances that were thought likely to pose a risk to the ozone layer, and to cooperate, collaborate, and share data as much as possible.

ARTICLE

Article 2: General Obligations

1. The Parties shall take appropriate measures in accordance with the provisions of this Convention and of those protocols in force to which they are party to protect human health and the environment against adverse effects resulting or likely to result from human activities which modify or are likely to modify the ozone layer.

Article 2 (1), the Vienna Convention for the Protection of the Ozone Layer 1985

The language makes it clear that this convention is adopting the *precautionary principle* to provisions, as there are threats of serious or irreversible damage both to human health and the environment, and the Convention is not using the lack of full scientific certainty as a reason to postpone measures.

Annex I of the Convention lists "chemical substances of natural and anthropogenic origin [which] are thought to have the potential to modify the chemical and physical properties of the ozone layer," and these are separated into five groups:

Carbon Substances. CO, CO_2, CH_4 (methane), and "non-methane hydrocarbon species" (e.g. acetone, benzene, ethanol).

Nitrogen Substances. N_2O (nitrous oxide), NO_x.

Chlorine Substances. Fully halogenated alkanes, partially halogenated alkanes (these substances include CFCs and HCFCs).

Bromine Substances. Fully halogenated alkanes (e.g. halon).

Hydrogen Substances. This includes water vapour.

This is interesting and demonstrates the importance of the Convention's focus on research, as CFCs and HCFCs, which were later identified as significant players in ozone layer depletion, are only mentioned in Annex I as one of the substances that need monitoring.

The Montréal Protocol (to the Convention on Substances That Deplete the Ozone Layer) was signed in 1988 and has subsequently been "adjusted and amended" eight times by the 2nd, 4th, 7th, 9th, 11th, 19th, 28th, and 30th Meetings of the Parties.

It is the Protocol which contains the specific targets for the reduction of "ozone-depleting substances" (ODS), although it does not use that phrase. There are five annexes which contain the details of the "controlled substances," where it allocated them an "ozone-depleting potential" of between 0 (the lowest potential) and 1.0 (the highest potential) and a "100-year Global Warming Potential."

Definition

The Global Warming Potential (GWP) was developed to allow comparisons of the global warming impacts of different gases. Specifically, it is a measure of how much energy the emissions of 1 tonne of a gas will absorb over a given period of time, relative to the emissions of 1 tonne of carbon dioxide (CO2). The larger the GWP, the more that a given gas warms the Earth compared to CO2 over that time period.

US EPA, 2022, Understanding Global Warming Potentials, epa.gov

The Protocol also sets target dates for the cessation of production of the controlled substances.

1996: Carbon tetrachloride (Article 2D(2))
Chlorofluorocarbons (CFC) (Article 2A(4))
Chloroform (Article 2E(3))
Hydrobromofluorocarbons (HBFC) (Art 2G)
Non-methane hydrocarbons (Article 2C(3))
2002: Bromochloromethane (Article 2I(3))
2010: Bromotrifluoromethane (halon) (Article 2B(4))
2015: Methyl bromide (Article 2H(5*ter*))
2020: Hydrochlorofluorocabons (HCFC) (Article 2F(6))

With the legal production and use of ODS being almost entirely stopped, two phenomena have been identified. Firstly, the levels of thinning in the ozone layer over Antarctica have reduced. Most of the ODS are quite stable, so it will take decades, if not centuries, before the ozone layer is returned to its pre-anthropocentric levels, but this is a positive outcome.

A negative consequence has been identified by INTERPOL, which is the illegal smuggling of ODS. Operation DEMETER VII, a joint operation between the UN Office of Drugs and Crime and INTERPOL in October 2021, involving over 100 law enforcement agencies, seized nearly 7 metric tonnes of ODS and nearly 500 items (e.g. refrigerators) which contained ODS.

9.3.2 EU

The Vienna Convention was approved by the EEC in October 1988, although action on some of the substances contained in the Convention had already been taken. Council Decision 80/372/EEC,[20] for example, required MS to take all appropriate measures both to ensure no growth in production capacity of CFC-11 and CFC-12 (Article 1(1)) and also to reduce use of CFC-11 and CFC-12 in aerosol cans by 30 per cent of 1976 levels by the end of 1981 (Article (1)(2)).

Current EU regulation is centred on Regulation 1005/2009,[21] which imposed bans on some ODS in advance of what was required under the Vienna Convention. Annexes I and II of the Regulations lists "controlled substances" (which are copied across from the annexes of the amended Montréal Protocol) and bans production (Article 4), placing on the market and use (Article 5), and "[p]lacing on the market of products and equipment containing or relying on controlled substances" (Article 6), other than in very limited cases which meet the exemption criteria in Part III.

As an EU Regulation, this was directly applicable in the UK, and the Ozone-Depleting Substances and Fluorinated Greenhouse Gases (Amendment, etc.) (EU Exit) Regulations 2019[22] ensures that the provisions remain in place post-Brexit.

ACTIVITY

The causal links between anthropogenic emissions and both acid rain and ozone layer depletion were relatively easy to establish, and international agreement was relatively rapid. As a result, both have shown significant signs of improvement.

To what extent is it important that we adopt a precautionary approach (see Chapter 1) to transboundary pollution of this type?

Assess the advantages and disadvantages of such an approach.

9.4 Climate Change

Climate change (often referred to as "global warming" or the "(enhanced) greenhouse effect") is a significant topic, which will only be addressed at an outline level here. One part of the Intergovernmental Panel on Climate Change Sixth Report, for example, runs to over 3,000 pages, so it would not be feasible to cover the topic in significant depth in this chapter.

It is important to set out early on that the "greenhouse effect," which is the trapping of warmth from the sun by the Earth's atmosphere, is what makes life on Earth possible. Without the warmth caused by this effect, the Earth would likely have a similar temperature to Mars, which averages about –80°C. The basic concern about climate change is that human activity is contributing to a warming atmosphere, and that this anthropocentric warming will lead to unfavourable conditions for human life, including:

- Reduced crop yields. Even if temperature is warmer, nights will be just as long, flowers will be out of synch with pollinators, etc.
- Increased flooding. A rise in sea level of 1 metre will flood one-fifth of Bangladesh, and recent estimates are that if all the ice on Antarctica melts, sea level will rise by 40 metres.
- Species death for those species which lack the ability to migrate or adapt.
- Desertification.
- Increased likelihood and severity of forest fires.

Almost a quarter of a century ago, Pier Vellinga and Willem van Verseveld from the Vrije Universiteit Amsterdam were predicting that human-induced climate change was likely to lead to an increase in extreme weather events. They concluded "with reasonable but no absolute confidence"[23] that emissions of greenhouse gases (including CO_2) were affecting global weather patterns, as well as the frequency and severity of "extreme weather events," such as hurricanes and cyclones.

Whilst it is impossible to directly attribute any one weather occurrence to climate change, 2021 saw records being broken for heat (48.8°C in Sicily is the hottest temperature ever recorded in Europe), rainfall (for the first time at Summit Point in Greenland), wind speed (149 miles per hour winds in Louisiana during Hurricane Ida), the worst flooding in decades in Nigeria and Niger, and drought (Nevada's Lake Mead falling to its lowest level ever recorded).

There are several greenhouse gases (GHG) which are known to contribute to climate change. The three main ones are:

Carbon Dioxide (CO_2). The burning of any organic material will release CO_2, and most notably, this includes oil, natural gas, and coal, the three main fossil fuels. It also includes wood, so the increase in forest fires will see a further release of CO_2. Carbon has always been released from natural sources, but the level of emissions has increased dramatically since the mid-1800s. Natural carbon sequestration (the absorption of carbon by growing plants) used to balance out the emissions, but now there is less material to absorb the greater quantities of gas.

Methane (CH_4). Any organic material which rots produces methane, as does the normal gastrointestinal process of many animals, including humans. Ironically, as discussed in Chapter 6, the flooding of the Three Gorges Valley in China to create a massive hydroelectric dam has led to increased methane emissions. As the climate warms, much of the methane which was trapped in the permafrost of the Northern Hemisphere (e.g. Canada, Greenland, Siberia) is now being released.

Ozone (O_3). See discussion in Section 9.3 earlier.

Conceptually, reducing emissions on the three main GHG is as straightforward as dealing with acid rain and ozone layer depletion. Replacing fossil fuels with renewable energy sources and increasing carbon sequestration are both avenues which are available. The difficulty arises where there is any uncertainty about predictions which can be seized upon by politicians. In Chapter 8, we encountered Mariam Stamp Dawkins's argument that any moves to improve animal welfare would have to be backed up by unshakeable science, as policymakers would do everything to avoid incurring additional costs. The same is true of climate change, where the precise impacts are (a) difficult to predict, (b) will not happen for some time, and (c) for most policymakers, will be felt far away. Little wonder that Bell et al. say that "addressing the problem of climate change has proved to be a much greater challenge than achieving consensus on the problem of ozone depletion."[24]

The difficulty with persuading all parties that these measures are needed is that the issues associated with climate change are generally going to take some time to manifest, and there is still a level of uncertainty about quite how catastrophic they will be. UN Secretary General António Guterres, for example, has been criticised for being overly despondent in his choice of words. In an interview in *The Guardian* newspaper in late 2022, he called present policies "catastrophic" and said that unless the developed and developing world could find a way of working together to solve the crisis, humanity was "doomed."[25]

There is a thriving industry in "carbon offsetting" whereby individuals and companies can join schemes to remove carbon to the equivalent level of that individual or company's calculated emissions. For example, if a company emits 100 tonnes of carbon annually, they can engage in a scheme to plant a sufficient number of trees to absorb 100 tonnes of carbon from the atmosphere. The Environment Agency carried out a review of offsetting schemes in 2021 and ranked them as high/mild/low performing in a number of categories. Of the 13 schemes they assessed, none was high performing across all areas, seven were "low performing" in terms of their speed of impact, and six were "low performing" in terms of the scientific confidence of their impact. Replating woodland was the best performer, but it was slow to have an impact.

9.4.1 UNFCCC

The UN Framework Convention on Climate Change (FCCC) was agreed by over 150 countries as part of the UN Conference on Environment and Development in Rio de Janeiro in 1992. It is, as the name suggests, a framework convention so did not contain a great deal of specific content. It is instead a broad document which sets out the general direction in which countries should travel over the subsequent years. There is an inherent recognition in the FCCC of issues around environmental and climate injustice (see Chapter 3).

ARTICLE

Acknowledging that change in the Earth's climate and its adverse effects are a common concern of humankind,

Concerned that human activities have been substantially increasing the atmospheric concentrations of greenhouse gases, that these increases enhance the natural greenhouse effect, and that this will result on average in an additional warming of the Earth's surface and atmosphere and may adversely affect natural ecosystems and humankind,

Noting that the largest share of historical and current global emissions of greenhouse gases has originated in developed countries, that per capita emissions in developing countries are still relatively low and that the share of global emissions originating in developing countries will grow to meet their social and development needs,

Preamble, UN FCCC 1992

The Kyoto Protocol (1997) contained a lot of the detail which had been missing from the FCCC itself. The Protocol takes as a standard "base year" (the year against which reductions in emissions will be judged as 1990, although states are free to select their own base year). The amount by which states need to reduce their emissions, and the range of mechanisms which states may choose to utilise in achieving this, is set out in Annex B.

ARTICLE

Article 2

1. Each Party included in Annex I, in achieving its quantified emission limitation and reduction commitments under Article 3, in order to promote sustainable development, shall:

(a) Implement and/or further elaborate policies and measures in accordance with its national circumstances, such as:
   (i) Enhancement of energy efficiency in relevant sectors of the national economy;
   (ii) Protection and enhancement of sinks and reservoirs of greenhouse gases not controlled by the Montreal Protocol, taking into account its commitments under relevant international environmental agreements; promotion of sustainable forest management practices, afforestation and reforestation;
   (iii) Promotion of sustainable forms of agriculture in light of climate change considerations;
   (iv) Research on, and promotion, development and increased use of, new and renewable forms of energy, of carbon dioxide sequestration technologies and of advanced and innovative environmentally sound technologies;
   (v) Progressive reduction or phasing out of market imperfections, fiscal incentives, tax and duty exemptions and subsidies in all greenhouse gas emitting sectors that run counter to the objective of the Convention and application of market instruments;
   (vi) Encouragement of appropriate reforms in relevant sectors aimed at promoting policies and measures which limit or reduce emissions of greenhouse gases not controlled by the Montreal Protocol;
   (vii) Measures to limit and/or reduce emissions of greenhouse gases not controlled by the Montreal Protocol in the transport sector;
   (viii) Limitation and/or reduction of methane emissions through recovery and use in waste management, as well as in the production, transport and distribution of energy;

Article 2(1)(a), Kyoto Protocol 1997

The Paris Agreement, adopted at COP 21, entered into force on 5 October 2016 and put in place legally binding targets and gave parties until 2020 to submit their plans for climate action. These plans, also called "nationally determined contributions," or NDCs, needed to set out how the state was going to meet their emissions targets and also build resilience. Despite significant levels of scepticism, all 193 parties to the Agreement issued a first NDC, more or less by the deadline, and close to 80 per cent have subsequently issued a new or updated NDC.

The 27th Conference of the Parties (COP 27) in Sharm-el-Sheikh, Egypt, in November 2022 is the latest in the series of meetings which are intended both to set targets, address the failure to meet previous targets, and agree on future approaches.

9.4.2 EU

EU is signatory to UN Framework Convention on Climate Change and the Kyoto Protocol and bound by the terms of both to reduce overall emissions by 8 per cent by

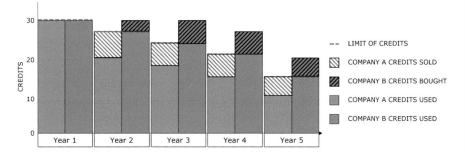

Figure 9.2 Example "cap and trade" system.

2012. In February 2010, the new Directorate-General for Climate Action (DG CLIMA) was formed and reports that the EU overall is on track with emission reductions.

DG CLIMA controls the EU Emissions Trading System (EU ETS), which was implemented in 2005 under the auspices of the Kyoto Protocol via Directive 2003/87/EC.[26] The EU ETS is a "cap and trade" system – it works by capping the total quantity of emissions permitted and then allowing a trade to develop.

The theory is that with a fixed number of credits, which reduces in every round, those companies which reduce their emissions will have "spare" credits that they can sell to the companies that are less efficient at emissions reduction. As the total number of credits reduces, the price rises, and there is more impetus on the less-efficient companies to pay to improve their efficiency, rather than pay for additional credits. Figure 9.2 shows the relationship between two companies who are the only players in a fictitious ETS. In year 1, the total number of available credits is 60 (30 per company), and this total is reduced to 30 (15 per company) in year 5. Company A is very efficient at reducing emissions so has "spare" credits to trade from year 2 onwards. Company B is less efficient and so must purchase the spare credits from Company A. The system is successful overall, as the total emissions has fallen by year 5 in line with targets. In reality, of course, any ETS system is far more complex than this, and the chargeable price of spare credits will rise and fall depending on the quantity available, and the demand.

Only certain industries currently cover the EU ETS. Broadly speaking, the categories are:

- Energy activities
- Production and processing of ferrous metals
- Mineral industries
- "Others," which cover pulp and paper production

Directive 2008/101[27] (amending Directive 2003/87/EC so as to include aviation activities in the scheme for greenhouse gas emission allowance trading) added "all flights which arrive at or depart from an aerodrome situated in the territory of a Member State to which the Treaty applies shall be included" in the EU ETS from 1 January 2012.

CASE

Arcelor SA v European Parliament (T-16/04) (2010) Env LR D7
This case concerned a challenge to the legality of the ETS on the basis that it breached the community objective of freedom of establishment.
The court rejected the argument and found that the ETS was legitimate.

ACTIVITY

Consider whether the following examples are valid examples of schemes for offsetting carbon emissions:

■ Greenwash Ltd offers to plant pine trees on land it plans to buy in Canada and promises that the trees will immediately offset the emissions of any company which subscribes to their scheme.

■ Bob owns a Christmas tree farm in the North of England. He offers companies the chance to "adopt" some of his trees, which have already been planted, as a way of offsetting their emissions. He does not restrict the adoption of any individual tree to just one company.

■ Wildmere Marsh Restoration Trust is offering companies the chance to part-fund their ambitious plans to restore Wildmere Marsh, a salt marsh of the east coast. The Trust claims that the completed restoration will increase the carbon sequestration potential of the marsh and thus allow offsetting.

9.5 Statutory Nuisance and Air Pollution

Emissions that cause a nuisance under Part 3 of the Environmental Protection Act 1990[28] are actionable as statutory nuisances, and their abatement is the responsibility of the local authority. This section will focus on those statutory nuisances that are airborne.

LEGISLATION

79 Statutory nuisances and inspections therefor.

(1) Subject to subsections (1A) to (6A) below, the following matters constitute "statutory nuisances" for the purposes of this Part, that is to say –

(a) any premises in such a state as to be prejudicial to health or a nuisance;

(b) smoke emitted from premises so as to be prejudicial to health or a nuisance;

(c) fumes or gases emitted from premises so as to be prejudicial to health or a nuisance;

(d) any dust, steam, smell or other effluvia arising on industrial, trade or business premises and being prejudicial to health or a nuisance;

(e) any accumulation or deposit which is prejudicial to health or a nuisance;

(f) any animal kept in such a place or manner as to be prejudicial to health or a nuisance;

(fa) any insects emanating from relevant industrial, trade or business premises and being prejudicial to health or a nuisance;

(fb) artificial light emitted from premises so as to be prejudicial to health or a nuisance;

(g) noise emitted from premises so as to be prejudicial to health or a nuisance;

(ga) noise that is prejudicial to health or a nuisance and is emitted from or caused by a vehicle, machinery or equipment in a street or in Scotland, road

(h) any other matter declared by any enactment to be a statutory nuisance

and it shall be the duty of every local authority to cause its area to be inspected from time to time to detect any statutory nuisances which ought to be dealt with under section 80 below or sections 80 and 80A below and, where a complaint of a statutory nuisance is made to it by a person living within its area, to take such steps as are reasonably practicable to investigate the complaint.

S79(1), Environmental Protection Act 1990

Local authorities have the power to enter any land with whatever personnel and equipment they consider necessary and can carry out tests, make measurements, and may take any samples and articles.

Once a statutory nuisance has been detected, the local authority is under a duty to serve a notice requiring the abatement of the nuisance on the person causing the nuisance or, if they cannot be found, the owner or occupier of the site. The local authority has a residual power to carry out the works. It is a criminal offence for a person not to comply with an abatement notice.

It is a defence for some instances of statutory nuisance if the polluter can demonstrate that they used the best practicable means (BPM) to "prevent, or to counteract the nuisance" (S80(7)).

LEGISLATION

(9) In this Part "best practicable means" is to be interpreted by reference to the following provisions –
  (a) "practicable" means reasonably practicable having regard among other things to local conditions and circumstances, to the current state of technical knowledge and to the financial implications;
  (b) the means to be employed include the design, installation, maintenance and manner and periods of operation of plant and machinery, and the design, construction and maintenance of buildings and structures;
  (c) the test is to apply only so far as compatible with any duty imposed by law;
  (d) the test is to apply only so far as compatible with safety and safe working conditions, and with the exigencies of any emergency or unforeseeable circumstances;
and, in circumstances where a code of practice under section 71 of the Control of Pollution Act 1974 (noise minimisation) is applicable, regard shall also be had to guidance given in it.

S79(9), Environmental Protection Act 1990

These matters are only statutory nuisances if they are prejudicial to health or a nuisance. It is not necessary to show that something is <u>both</u> prejudicial to health *and* a nuisance.

JUDGMENT

Betts v Penge Urban District Council (1942) 2 KB 154
This case concerns a landlord and tenant dispute and focused on the words repeatedly used in the Public Health Act 1936,[29] "prejudicial to health or a nuisance," and the court held that the two elements needed to be read disjunctively, and that if something has been deemed to constitute a nuisance, it did not need also be prejudicial to health.
(Per Caldecote CJ @159)

Definition

"Prejudicial to health" means injurious, or likely to cause injury, to health.
S79(7), Environmental Protection Act 1990

National Coal Board v Neath BC (1976) 2 All ER 478
This case held that *nuisance*, as used in the Public Health Act 1936, took on the same meaning as *public nuisance* or *private nuisance* at common law.

In other words, an act which either physically damages property or interferes with the enjoyment of, or interests in land, or an act or omission which materially affects the reasonable comfort and convenience of life of a class of the public.

9.6 Smoke

As we have seen in earlier chapters, the historical background to air pollution in the UK began with medieval legislation relating to smoke emissions, but in modern times, its starting point was the Alkali Act 1863, followed by 60 years of Public Health Acts (1875 to 1936), which contained provisions concerning smoke emissions. Domestic and industrial smoke emissions began to be comprehensively controlled by the provisions of the Clean Air Act 1956,[30] which were triggered by the "Great Smog" of 1952, which led to thousands of excess deaths. The 1956 Act was amended by the Clean Air Act 1968,[31] and the current provisions now sit in the Clean Air Act 1993.[32]

Subsequently, the introduction, in turn, of the Integrated Pollution Control (IPC), Integrated Pollution Prevention and Control (IPPC), and Environmental Permitting Systems meant that anything licensed under those systems was removed from the ambit of the Clean Air Act.

This leaves the Clean Air Act as the governing legislation covering domestic and smaller industrial activities which fall below the threshold required for the permitting regime.

LEGISLATION

1 Prohibition of dark smoke from chimneys.

  (1) Dark smoke shall not be emitted from a chimney of any building, and if, on any day, dark smoke is so emitted, the occupier of the building shall be guilty of an offence.

  (2) Dark smoke shall not be emitted from a chimney (not being a chimney of a building) which serves the furnace of any fixed boiler or industrial plant, and if, on any day, dark smoke is so emitted, the person having possession of the boiler or plant shall be guilty of an offence. . . .

2 Prohibition of dark smoke from industrial or trade premises.

  (1) Dark smoke shall not be emitted from any industrial or trade premises and if, on any day, dark smoke is so emitted the occupier of the premises and any person who causes or permits the emission shall be guilty of an offence.

SS1(1) and (2) and S2(1), Clean Air Act 1993

In addition, local authorities are given the power under Part III of the Act to create "smoke control areas" (SCA), and if they believe that local authorities have not sufficiently tackled smoke emissions in the area, then the Secretary of State also has the power to impose an SCA over the local authority area. In a smoke control area, it is an offence to emit any smoke.

The main offence under the Clean Air Act, however, relates to "dark smoke," which is defined in the Act with reference to the Ringelmann chart.

LEGISLATION

3 Meaning of "dark smoke."

(1) In this Act "dark smoke" means smoke which, if compared in the appropriate manner with a chart of the type known on 5th July 1956 (the date of the passing of the Clean Air Act 1956) as the Ringelmann Chart, would appear to be as dark as or darker than shade 2 on the chart.

(2) For the avoidance of doubt it is hereby declared that in proceedings –

(a) for an offence under section 1 or 2 (prohibition of emissions of dark smoke); the court may be satisfied that smoke is or is not dark smoke as defined in subsection (1) notwithstanding that there has been no actual comparison of the smoke with a chart of the type mentioned in that subsection.

(3) Without prejudice to the generality of subsections (1) and (2), if the Secretary of State by regulations prescribes any method of ascertaining whether smoke is dark smoke as defined in subsection (1), proof in any such proceedings as are mentioned in subsection (2) –

(a) that that method was properly applied, and
(b) that the smoke was thereby ascertained to be or not to be dark smoke as so defined, shall be accepted as sufficient.

S3, Clear Air Act 1993

The Ringelmann chart referred to in the Act dates back to the 1880s, and the version contained in British Standard 2742 (2009) is a five-shade scale on white cards, ranging from 0 per cent black (level 0) to 100 per cent black (level 5). Anything darker than shade 2 is deemed to be dark smoke. Figure 9.3 gives a graphical impression of the different shades of smoke used in the chart.

CRITIQUING THE LAW

Is it useful to have a smoke categorisation system based on visual inspection rather than chemical or other content?

Once dark smoke has been identified, then the occupier of the premises from where the smoke is being emitted must be notified. If the premises and operation are not exempt from the Act (e.g. they are licensed under the Permitting Regulations), then the occupier may be able to use one of the listed defences.

0	1	2	3	4	5

Ringelmann Chart (Illustrative)

Figure 9.3 The Ringelmann chart.
Source: Author created, based on the 1888 Ringelman chart.

1 Prohibition of dark smoke from chimneys. . . .

(4) In any proceedings for an offence under this section, it shall be a defence to prove –

(a) that the alleged emission was solely due to the lighting up of a furnace which was cold and that all practicable steps had been taken to prevent or minimise the emission of dark smoke;

(b) that the alleged emission was solely due to some failure of a furnace, or of apparatus used in connection with a furnace, and that –

(i) the failure could not reasonably have been foreseen, or, if foreseen, could not reasonably have been provided against; and

(ii) the alleged emission could not reasonably have been prevented by action taken after the failure occurred; or

(c) that the alleged emission was solely due to the use of unsuitable fuel and that –

(i) suitable fuel was unobtainable and the least unsuitable fuel which was available was used; and

(ii) all practicable steps had been taken to prevent or minimise the emission of dark smoke as the result of the use of that fuel;

or that the alleged emission was due to the combination of two or more of the causes specified in paragraphs (a) to (c) and that the other conditions specified in those paragraphs are satisfied in relation to those causes respectively. . . .

2 Prohibition of dark smoke from industrial or trade premises. . . .

(4) In proceedings for an offence under this section, it shall be a defence to prove –

(a) that the alleged emission was inadvertent; and

(b) that all practicable steps had been taken to prevent or minimise the emission of dark smoke.

SS1(4) and S2(4), Clean Air Act 1993

Since the 1993 Act is a consolidation act, the exemptions are carried over from regulations which followed the Clean Air Act 1968.

LEGISLATION

1. Timber and any other waste matter (other than natural or synthetic rubber or flock or feathers) which results from the demolition of a building or clearance of a site in connection with any building operation or work of engineering construction (within the meaning of section 176 of the Factories Act 1961).[33]

2. Explosive (within the meaning of the Explosives Act 1875[34]) which has become waste; and matter which has been contaminated by such explosive.

3. Matter which is burnt in connection with –

(a) research into the cause or control of fire or

(b) training in fire fighting.

4. Tar, pitch, asphalte and other matter which is burnt in connection with the preparation and laying of any surface, or which is burnt off any surface in connection with resurfacing, together with any fuel used for any such purpose.

5. Carcases of animals or poultry which –

   (a) have died, or are reasonably believed to have died, because of disease;

   (b) have been slaughtered because of disease; or

   (c) have been required to be slaughtered pursuant to the Diseases of Animals Act 1950.[35]

6. Containers which are contaminated by any pesticide or by any toxic substance used for veterinary or agricultural purposes; and in this paragraph container includes any sack, box, package or receptacle of any kind.

Schedule 1, Clean Air (Emission of Dark Smoke) (Exemption) Regulations 1969[36]

SUMMARY

■ Air pollution is extremely mobile, and efforts to tackle the problem work more effectively when three parameters are met:

1. There is overwhelming agreement as to the cause–effect relationships of human activity and pollution.

2. There is international legislation which is ratified by the vast majority of nations.

3. The legislation creates specific targets to be met.

■ Acid rain has been tackled quite well in Europe, as LRTAP has satisfied all three of these parameters. In SE Asia, however, where the parameters have not been met, acid rain still poses a significant problem.

■ Ozone layer depletion has not been "solved" per se but is very much on the right track towards being solved, and again, the three parameters have been met.

■ Climate change, on the other hand, is causing many more problems. There are still global leaders who deny that there is a link between anthropocentric pollution and climate change and will argue that the changing climate is part of a natural cycle of warming and cooling.

■ Efforts to tackle climate change are at the mercy of national politics – when a country elects a climate change sceptic, that country is more likely to renege on its previous promises to reduce emissions, in favour of short-term national benefits.

SAMPLE ESSAY QUESTION

The impending climate crisis or "*climate apocalypse*" has the potential to cause incalculable and irreversible levels of harm to life on Earth. Assess, using examples, the extent to which current global legislative and political measures are likely to result in (a) avoiding or (b) offsetting these impacts.

> 1. Identify what is meant by climate crisis and climate apocalypse. Consider sources like the IPCC and whether they regard these issues as still being avoidable.
> 2. Find examples of global measures (for example, the UN Framework Convention on Climate Change).

3. Assess whether the measures announced at the most recent COP have been met by action or rhetoric.
4. How likely is the planet to miss the 1.5°C target outlined by IPCC?
5. Identify and assess efforts which have been made to "live with" or offset the effects of climate change.
6. Conclude.

Further Reading

Bodansky, D., Brunnée, J., & Rajamani, L., 2017, *International Climate Change Law*, Oxford: OUP

Dessler, A.E., 2021, *Introduction to Modern Climate Change*, Cambridge: CUP

Mayer, B., 2018, *The International Law on Climate Change*, Cambridge: CUP

Rose, C., 1988, The Forest is Dying, *New Internationalist*, 5 June 1988, Issue 184

Thunberg, G., 2022, *The Climate Book*, London: Allen Lane

Underdal, A., & Hanf, K., 2020, *International Environmental Agreements and Domestic Politics: The Case of Acid Rain (Routledge Revivals)*, London: Routledge

Vellinga, P., & van Verseveld, W.J., 2000, *Climate Change and Extreme Weather Events*, Gland: WWF

Yoshida, O., 2020, *The International Legal Regime for the Protection of the Stratospheric Ozone Layer*, 2nd ed., Leiden: Brill-Nijhof

Notes

1   26 and 27 Vict c 124
2   SI 1958/497
3   1995 c.25
4   1993 c.12
5   SI 2012/1903 (W. 230)
6   1999 c.24
7   SI 2016/1154. The "Permitting Regulations"
8   Directive 2010/75/EU of the European Parliament and of the Council on industrial emissions (integrated pollution prevention and control)
9   Directive 2008/1/EC of the European Parliament and of the Council of 15 January 2008 concerning integrated pollution prevention and control
10 Council Directive 96/61/EC of 24 September 1996 concerning integrated pollution prevention and control
11 1999 c.24
12 SI 2000/1973
13 Directive 2008/1/EC of the European Parliament and of the Council of 15 January 2008 concerning integrated pollution prevention and control
14 Council Directive 70/220/EEC of 20 March 1970 on the approximation of the laws of the member states relating to measures to be taken against air pollution by gases from positive-ignition engines of motor vehicles
15 Council Directive 80/779/EEC of 15 July 1980 on air quality limit values and guide values for sulphur dioxide and suspended particulates
16 Directive 2008/50/EC of the European Parliament and of the Council of 21 May 2008 on ambient air quality and cleaner air for Europe

17 The ozone referred to here is tropospheric (low-level) ozone, which is a health hazard and constituent part of smog. See section 9.3 below

18 SI 2010/1001

19 In this provision, *particulate matter* is PM_{10}, so that with a diameter of 10 microns or under

20 Council Decision 80/372/EEC concerning chlorofluorocarbons in the atmosphere

21 Regulation (EC) 1005/2009 of the European Parliament and of the Council of 16 September 2009 on substances that deplete the ozone layer

22 SI 2019/583

23 Vellinga, P., & van Verseveld, W.J., 2000, *Climate Change and Extreme Weather Events*, Gland: WWF, p. 1

24 Bell, S., McGillivray, D., Pederson, O., Lees, E., & Stokes, E., 2017, *Environmental Law*, 9th ed., Oxford: OUP, p. 542

25 Harvey, F., 2022, UN Chief Warns 'We Will Be Doomed' without Historic Climate Pact, *The Guardian*, 4 November 2022

26 Directive 2003/87/EC of the European Parliament and of the Council of 13 October 2003 establishing a scheme for greenhouse gas emission allowance trading within the community and amending Council Directive 96/61/EC

27 Directive 2008/101/EC of the European Parliament and of the Council of 19 November 2008 amending Directive 2003/87/EC so as to include aviation activities in the scheme for greenhouse gas emission allowance trading within the community

28 1990 c.43

29 Public Health Act 1936 c.49. the phrase "prejudicial to health or a nuisance" occurs 11 times in the Act

30 1956 c.52

31 1968 c.62

32 1993 c.11

33 1961 9 and 10 Eliz 2 c. 34

34 1875 38 and 39 Vict c.17

35 1950 c.36

36 SI 1969/1263

10

Water and Marine Pollution

Seven-tenths of the surface of the Earth is covered by water, and between 55 per cent and 60 per cent of the human body is made up of water. Contaminated drinking water is responsible for hundreds of thousands of human deaths every year, and anthropocentric pollution of the oceans contributes to millions of annual animal deaths. Changing weather patterns caused by climate change mean that rainfall levels are increasing in some areas, leading to floods, and decreasing in others, leading to drought. Many predict that as alternatives to fossil fuels are developed, the next global conflict will be centred on access to healthy and drinkable water.

Water is essential to life, and in this chapter, we will look at both fresh water and seawater and the controls which exist in relation to each. The chapter will start by looking at the international measures which have been put into place in relation to maritime pollution before looking more closely at domestic freshwater and groundwater pollution controls.

AIMS AND OBJECTIVES

After reading this chapter, you should be able to:

■ Identify the key legislative provisions relating to maritime pollution control.

■ Describe the UK approach to water pollution control.

■ Understand the importance of, and application of laws to, groundwater protection.

10.1 Marine Pollution

Prevention of pollution of the seas lends itself more to international rather than domestic action. As such, the UK is a signatory to and has ratified many international conventions and agreements, such as:

DOI: 10.4324/9781003137214-10

1954 International Convention for the Prevention of Pollution of the Sea by Oil (OILPOL 1954)

This was a convention created by the Inter-Governmental Maritime Consultative Organization (IMCO), which was a United Nations agency set up in 1948. The Convention banned what was then the common practice of rinsing out oil tankers and cargo ships with seawater and letting the oily waste go into the sea, but the ban only applied to "special areas" which were environmentally sensitive. The Convention was replaced by MARPOL (see following text) in 1973, and the IMCO became the International Maritime Organisation (IMO) in 1982. OILPOL 1954 was important as it marked the start of an ongoing process of developing international legislative measures to protect the oceans from pollution.

The 1956 United Nations Conference on the Law of the Sea (sometimes known as "UNCLOS I") led to four thematically linked treaties being agreed in Geneva in 1958.

1958 Convention on the High Seas

This Convention defined what was meant by the "high seas" and enshrined access to the high seas to all states, whether or not they had a coastline.

ARTICLE

Article 1

The term "high seas" means all parts of the sea that are not included in the territorial sea or in the internal waters of a State.

Article 2

The high seas being open to all nations, no State may validly purport to subject any part of them to its sovereignty. Freedom of the high seas is exercised under the conditions laid down by these articles and by the other rules of international law. It comprises, inter alia, both for coastal and non-coastal States: (1) Freedom of navigation; (2) Freedom of fishing; (3) (4) Freedom to lay submarine cables and pipelines; Freedom to fly over the high seas. These freedoms, and others which are recognized by the general principles of international law, shall be exercised by all States with reasonable regard to the interests of other States in their exercise of the freedom of the high seas.

Articles 1 and 2, 1958 Convention on the High Seas

1958 Convention on the Continental Shelf

This Convention clarified the definition of the continental shelf and the rights of states over the areas of continental shelf that were attached to their coastline.

1958 Convention on the Territorial Sea and Contiguous Zone

This convention created the right of innocent passage by vessels from one state through the territorial waters of another. It also established the limits of territorial waters.

1958 Convention on Fishing and Conservation of Living Resources of the High Seas

This Convention acknowledged the rights of all nations to fish on the high seas despite their being outside any national control (see Chapter 2 on the "global (unmanaged) commons") and calls for all states to adopt measures to conserve resources. However, Article 2 makes very clear that the purpose of these resources is primarily to benefit humans.

ARTICLE

As employed in this Convention, the expression "conservation of the living resources of the high seas" means the aggregate of the measures rendering possible the optimum sustainable yield from those resources so as to secure a maximum supply of food and other marine products. Conservation programmes should be formulated with a view to securing in the first place a supply of food for human consumption.

Article 2, 1958 Convention on Fishing and Conservation of
Living Resources of the High Seas

Taken together, these four conventions established a new system of rights and obligations for all states with regard to the sea and things living in it. Despite the fact that these rights were mostly expressed in the sense of exploiting marine resources and the obligations in terms of protecting marine resources for future exploitation, the Conventions did provide the foundations on which the newer, more environmentally focused provisions could be built. All the conventions were effectively replaced by the UN Convention on the Law of the Sea (also, somewhat confusingly, called UNCLOS) in 1982 (which follows).

1969 International Convention Relating to Intervention on the High Seas in Cases of Oil Pollution Casualties ("INTERVENTION 1969")

This is an IMCO/IMO Convention which was agreed in the wake of the Torrey Canyon oil spill in Cornwall in 1967.

Note

The Liberian-registered, BP-chartered, and US-owned SS Torrey Canyon was built in the United States in 1959 and was an oil tanker with a capacity of 120,000 tonnes. The ship ran aground off the Cornish coast en route to Milford Haven docks in Wales in March 1967.

The ship started to break up and leak its cargo of oil. The Royal Navy and Royal Air Force embarked on a campaign to destroy the ship using bombs, rockets, and over 1,000 tonnes of napalm to set the oil alight.

The ship eventually sank and was, at that time, the largest oil tanker ever to do so. The total oil spill was around 30 million gallons, and the environmental impact was exacerbated by the incorrect use of detergents to try to break up the spill.

The rationale for the Convention was to legitimise the use of this type of militaristic action against a ship registered in a different state if the purpose was to minimise pollution and environmental damage from a stricken vessel.

ARTICLE

Parties to the present Convention may take such measures on the high seas as may be necessary to prevent, mitigate or eliminate grave and imminent danger to their coastline or related interests from pollution or threat of pollution of the sea by oil, following a maritime casualty or acts related to such a casualty, which may reasonably be expected to result in major harmful consequences.

Article 1, INTERVENTION 1969

In 1973, the Convention was added to by a protocol which added other hazardous substances to the scope of the Convention.

1969 International Convention on Civil Liability for Oil Pollution Damage (CLC 1969)

This is a second IMCO/IMO Convention passed in the aftermath of the Torrey Canyon oil spill and requires commercial (non-military) vessels carrying over 2,000 tonnes of oil to have sufficient insurance to cover the cost of any damage caused by the spillage of that oil. There have been three protocols to the Convention, in 1976, 1984, and 1996, and these were amended in 2000, and all these concerned limits to liability and the alignment to "special drawing rights" (SDRs), which are used by the International Monetary Fund.

1971 International Convention on the Establishment of an International Fund for Compensation for Oil Pollution Damage (FUND 1971)

This IMCO/IMO Convention also addressed the issue of compensation for oil spills and, as the name indicates, created a fund which would be paid into by the shipping industry. The fund would be used both to mitigate the impact on individual ship owners of individual spills and to bolster the level of compensation paid to victims. There were two protocols in 1976 and 1984, but the 1992 Protocol effectively replaced everything which came before it and established a new fund, the "1992 International Oil Pollution Compensation (IOPC) Fund" (also called the "1992 Fund").

1972 Convention for the Prevention of Marine Pollution by Dumping from Ships and Aircraft

Also called the Oslo Convention, this was a regional measure, the terms of which applied only to parts of the North Atlantic and Arctic Oceans and the Baltic and Mediterranean Seas. The Convention banned parties from dumping into the sea any Appendix I substances (substances including organohalogens, organosilicon, and "persistent plastics") and any "significant" levels of Appendix II substances (toxic and persistent chemicals, for example). The Oslo Convention was replaced by the OSPAR Convention (which follows) in 1992.

1972 Convention on the Prevention of Marine Pollution by Dumping of Wastes and Other Matter

This Convention is also known as the London Convention. This is another IMCO/IMO Convention and is the first global anti-dumping convention.

ARTICLE

> Contracting Parties shall individually and collectively promote the effective control of all sources of pollution of the marine environment and pledge themselves especially to take all practicable steps to prevent the pollution of the sea by the dumping of waste and other matter that is liable to create hazards to human health, to harm living resources and marine life, to damage amenities or to interfere with other legitimate uses of the sea.
>
> Article 1, London Convention 1972

There are caveats with the Convention, and it very clearly defines "dumping" as being the deliberate disposal of substances at sea and makes exceptions for anything which is not deliberate.

1973 International Convention for the Prevention of Pollution from Ships (MARPOL 1973)

Another IMCO/IMO Convention, MARPOL 1973 closed the loophole left by the London Convention and specifically included incidental, operational, and accidental pollution. The Convention was agreed in November 1973, and a protocol was adopted in 1978 following several oil tanker accidents in the preceding two years:

- *Olympic Bravery* (English Channel, January 1976)
- *Urquiola* (Spain, May 1976)
- *NEPCO 140* (New York, June 1976)
- MV *Argo Merchant* (Massachusetts, December 1976)
- *Borag* (Taiwan, March 1977)
- MV *Hawaiian Patriot* (Pacific Ocean, February 1977)
- *Venpet* and *Venoil* (South Africa, December 1977)

MARPOL has six annexes which have come into force between 1983 and 2005.

ANNEX I	Regulations for the Prevention of Pollution by Oil, 1983. Amended several times to add the requirement for a double hull on all new oil tankers (1992, as a result of the *Exxon Valdez* oil spill in Alaska in 1989) and retrofitted to all existing oil tankers (2001 and 2003).
ANNEX II	Regulations for the Control of Pollution by Noxious Liquid Substances in Bulk, 1983. Regulated a large number of substances and requires that their residues can only be discharged in officially regulated facilities.
ANNEX III	Prevention of Pollution by Harmful Substances Carried by Sea in Packaged Form, 1992. This Annex required proper and clear labelling and documentation in relation to harmful substances.
ANNEX IV	Prevention of Pollution by Sewage from Ships, 2003. Prohibits the discharge into the sea of sewage from ships, although there are three exceptions. Firstly, if the discharge is in an "approved sewage treatment plant." Secondly, if the sewage is disinfected or *comminuted* (broken up into tiny pieces) and discharged more than three miles from shore. Thirdly, if the sewage is not disinfected or comminuted but is discharged more than 12 miles from shore.
ANNEX V	Prevention of Pollution by Garbage from Ships, 1988. Amongst other provisions relating to different types of garbage, this Annex imposes a complete ban on plastic waste being disposed of into the sea. Annex V is described by the IMO as a "living document," and the latest revisions were in 2017.
ANNEX VI	Prevention of Air Pollution from Ships, 2005. As we saw in Chapter 3, shipping is recognised as being responsible for almost 3 per cent of anthropogenic carbon emissions, and so this Annex aims to reduce levels of emissions from ships.

1974 Convention for the Prevention of Marine Pollution from Land-Based Sources

This was also called the Paris Convention and was introduced following the UN Conference on the Human Environment, which was held in Stockholm in 1973. It is usually "paired" with the Oslo Convention (mentioned earlier) from two years earlier, as the terms apply to the same marine areas, and the "land-based" sources in the Paris Convention complement the "vessels and aircraft" of the Oslo Convention. As with the Oslo Convention, the Paris Convention was subsumed by the OSPAR Convention (see following text) in 1992.

ARTICLE

> The Contracting Parties pledge themselves to take all possible steps to prevent pollution of the sea, by which is meant the introduction by man, directly or indirectly, of substances or energy into the marine environment (including estuaries) resulting in such deleterious effects as hazard to human health, harm to living resources and to marine eco-systems, damage to amenities or interference with other legitimate uses of the sea.
>
> Article 1(1), Paris Convention 1974

Note

UNCLOS I, UNCLOS II, and UNCLOS III refer to the UN *Conferences* on the Law of the Sea held respectively in Geneva in 1956 and 1960, and in New York in 1972.

UNCLOS is the acronym for the UN *Convention* on the Law of the Sea, which emerged out of UNCLOS III.

1982 UN Convention on the Law of the Sea (UNCLOS)

UNCLOS restated many of the definitions from the four 1958 Conventions. We have explored the revised definitions of "territorial sea," "contiguous zones," "exclusive economic zones," and "extended continental shelf" in Chapter 2, as part of the discussions about the global commons. UNCLOS is also covered briefly in Chapter 5 on the UN SDGs, as SDG 14 (life under water) is aligned to the UNCLOS standards.

From an environmental perspective, Part XII of UNCLOS establishes a 46-article obligation on states to "protect and preserve" the marine environment (Article 192), and states must keep this in mind when pursuing their right to exploit their natural resources (Article 193).

Whilst UNCLOS has been generally praised for its role in reducing marine pollution, there have been criticisms that it has not gone far enough to overcome systemic failures. Over-fishing and the decline of marine biodiversity have not halted since UNCLOS, and indeed, in some areas, the rate of decline has increased.

1983 Agreement for Co-Operation in Dealing with the Pollution of the North Sea by Oil

This is also called the Bonn Convention and was another regional convention which was signed by the North Sea states and the EU. It applies to specified areas of the North Sea, defined in Article 2. The Agreement requires the parties to actively assess the relevant areas of the North Sea and, where they find pollution, to take action, either alone or in conjunction with other parties.

1990 Oil Pollution Preparedness, Response, and Cooperation Convention (OPRC 1990)

It may seem surprising to know that prior to OPRC, and despite decades of legislation tying to reduce the frequency and severity of oil pollution, there was no mandatory requirement until OPRC for ships to have an on-board oil pollution emergency plan. The Convention also calls for training for oil pollution incidents and stockpiling of equipment to deal with oil pollution.

1992 Convention for the Protection of the Marine Environment of the North-East Atlantic (OSPAR)

OSPAR gets its acronym because at its heart it is a reinvention of the **OS**lo and **PAR**is Conventions (mentioned earlier), although it also bears in mind the provisions of UNCLOS.

ARTICLE

> The Contracting Parties shall, in accordance with the provisions of the Convention, take all possible steps to prevent and eliminate pollution and shall take the necessary measures to protect the maritime area against the adverse effects of human activities so as to safeguard human health and to conserve marine ecosystems and, when practicable, restore marine areas which have been adversely affected.
>
> Article 1(a) OSPAR, 1992

The language is similar to that used by the Paris Convention but includes an additional requirement for restoration. This makes OSPAR aligned to post-Rio ideas about the importance of restoration.

1996 International Convention on Liability and Compensation for Damage in Connection with the Carriage of Hazardous and Noxious Substances by Sea (HNS Convention)

This IMO Convention was restated by a 2010 version but is not yet in force, as it lacks the requisite number of state ratifications. The Convention has a complex formula in place in Article 46 for its conditions of coming into force. Twelve states must ratify, four of which must have at least 2 million units of gross tonnage (Art 46(1)(a)), and they must contribute at least 40 million tonnes to the "general account" (part of the HNS Fund). At the end of 2022, only six states have ratified (Canada, Denmark, Estonia, Norway, South Africa, and Turkey/ Türkiye).

Article 7 will provide the key "polluter pays" heart of the Convention, and there will be a fund set up similar to the "1992 Fund" discussed earlier. The exceptions signposted in paragraphs 2 and 3 are acts of war, hostility, or other deliberate sabotage.

ARTICLE

> 1 Except as provided in paragraphs 2 and 3, the owner at the time of an incident shall be liable for damage caused by any hazardous and noxious substances in connection with their carriage by sea on board the ship, provided that if an incident consists of a series of occurrences having the same origin the liability shall attach to the owner at the time of the first of such occurrences.
>
> Article 7(1), HNS Convention

ACTIVITY

Is the existing international and regional framework of marine protection sufficient to enable states to meet their targets under SDG 14 (life below water)?

What we can see from the preceding passages is that there has been a significant development in the protection of the marine environment since the middle of the last century. From a position where it was commonplace for ships to dump every conceivable pollutant into the marine environment, we have moved to a much more restrictive situation, with regulations on deliberate dumping, accidental spillage, and more incidental and operational emissions.

10.2 Fresh Water

Fresh water (sometimes called "sweet water" in older texts) is that which is found in lakes, reservoirs, streams, wells, and rivers up to the point where the river becomes an estuary and meets the sea, when the water is described as "brackish" – neither entirely fresh nor entirely salty.

Definition

Purified water:	Sometimes (inaccurately) called distilled water, this is water which has been treated by one of a range of processes to remove all impurities. It is suitable for human consumption and also used commercially.
Drinking water:	Fresh water which has been sufficiently treated to render is safe for human consumption. It is not necessarily as treated as purified water.
Fresh water:	Frozen or liquid water which contains a minimum of dissolved salts. It is not necessarily free from other pollutants and can be suitable for human consumption if treated.
Ground water:	Water which is below the surface of the ground; it may be in soil or rock formations, or underground streams.
Grey water:	Sometimes called "sullage," this is domestic wastewater which has been discharged in showers, sinks, or washing machines, for example. It is suitable for use in central heating systems, crop irrigation, or flushing toilets.
Brackish water:	Water which is less salty than sea water, but more salty than fresh water. It can occur naturally in estuaries or can be produced through activities such as prawn farming.
Seawater:	Water which is found in the world's seas, oceans, and some lakes. It is typically about 3 per cent salt, although there are "hypersaline" bodies of water such as the Dead Sea (34 per cent salt) and Salt Lake in the United States (c. 20 per cent salt).

Land-based mammals, including humans, require suitable water to drink, so there is a strong focus on the quality of water used for livestock and human consumption. Most land-based plants and crops also require fresh or grey water, and so in areas where there is low rainfall, or little water flow, artificial irrigation of fresh or grey water is used to nourish crops. Over-irrigation can have a catastrophic impact on aquifers and underground water levels. This is illustrated well by the situation in the "Texas Panhandle" area of the United States, where water is being pumped from the Ogallala Aquifer faster than it is being replenished. This caused severe water stress to humans, livestock, and crops. This is not likely to be a threat just in Texas – several reservoirs in Northeast Spain are at record low levels. The Sau Reservoir in Catalonia was built in the early 1960s to supply water to

Barcelona, the population of which has grown from around 2.5 million at the time the reservoir was built to around 5.7 million today. A combination of this increased demand and a lack of sustained rainfall means that the reservoir is at under 10 per cent of capacity. It has been forecast that globally 80 per cent of people will be exposed to high threats to water security by 2050.[1]

There is a very long history of legislation in the UK that serves to prevent the pollution of rivers and other inland waters. The various Acts that have been promulgated since Victorian times were consolidated into the Water Resources Act 1991,[2] and this has now been added to by the Environmental Permitting (England and Wales) Regulations 2016[3] (as amended).

10.2.1 History of UK Water Pollution Control

This section will focus on water pollution control as it relates to environmental damage, rather than human health, as the latter was covered in some depth in Chapter 1. Some of the earliest legislation is very much about nature as a resource (primarily fishing) and rivers as an aid to navigation, so an anthropocentric perspective.

Clause 33 of the Magna Carta in 1215, for example, demanded that all fish-weirs should be removed from the river Thames and the river Medway and across the country. Fish-weirs (also known as *kiddles*) are placed across rivers to trap salmon as they swim upstream to spawn. The purpose of the removal of fish-weirs was to improve salmon fishing, but the knock-on effects were a growth in salmon numbers and general river health.

Salmon were also protected by the Salmon Fisheries Act 1861,[4] which forbade the placing of anything which would trap salmon (Section 11) and also made provisions to reduce water pollution that affected the productivity of salmon fishing.

General provisions for rivers started with the Rivers Pollution Prevention Act 1876,[5] which introduced the offences of "causing or knowingly permitting" and "impeding the proper flow" of a river, which have been themes in water pollution legislation ever since.

LEGISLATION

Every person who puts or causes to be put or to fall or knowingly permits to be put or to fall or to be carried into any stream, so as either singly or in combination with other similar acts of the same or any other person to interfere with its due flow, or to pollute its waters, the solid refuse of any manufactory, manufacturing process or quarry, or any rubbish or cinders, or any other waste or any putrid solid matter, shall be deemed to have committed an offence against this Act.

In proving interference with the due flow of any stream, or in proving the pollution of any stream, evidence may be given of repeated acts which together cause such interference or pollution, although each act taken by itself may not be sufficient for that purpose.

S2, Rivers Pollution Prevention Act 1876

The defence under the Act was that the accused had used the "best practicable and available means" to prevent or minimise pollution (Section 3). The Act was repealed 75 years later by the Rivers (Prevention of Pollution) Act 1951,[6] which tidied up the offence and expressly extended its application to local authorities and other bodies corporate.

1) Subject to this Act, a person commits an offence punishable under this section –

   (a) if he causes or knowingly permits to enter a stream any poisonous, noxious or polluting matter; or

   (b) if he causes or knowingly permits to enter a stream any matter so as to tend either directly or in combination with similar acts (whether his own or another's) to impede the proper flow of the water of the stream in a manner leading or likely to lead to a substantial aggravation of pollution due to other causes or of its consequences;

and for the purposes of paragraph (a) of this subsection a local authority shall be deemed to cause or knowingly permit to enter a stream any poisonous, noxious or polluting matter, which passes into the stream from any sewer or sewage disposal works vested in them, in any case where either the local authority were bound to receive the matter into the sewer or sewage disposal works, or they consented to do so unconditionally, or they consented to do so subject to conditions and those conditions were observed.

S2(1), Rivers (Prevention of Pollution) Act 1951

The Act also introduced a discharge consent system for discharge of pollutants (Section 7), and this system, the mechanics of which have been amended several times, forms the basis of the consent system which is used today.

The Act was repealed by the Control of Pollution Act 1974, which pulled together much of the legislation relating to pollution on land, in the air, in water, as well as addressing noise pollution.

The current legislation is the Water Pollution Act 1991,[7] as amended (primarily by the Environmental Permitting (England and Wales) Regulations 2016 (The Permitting Regulations)). The overall operation of the Permitting Regulations in terms of granting licences and so on was discussed in Chapter 9, so this chapter will concentrate on the water and groundwater offences and the case law which relates to them.

10.2.2 Achieving and Maintaining Water Quality

An understanding of the sources of water and groundwater pollution is essential if the regulator stands a hope of controlling pollution and improving water quality. Generally speaking, water pollution comes from three main sources:

■ A specific outlet, such as a discharge pipe. This is sometimes called "point source pollution."

■ Run-off from industrial plants or agricultural land. This can happen either through surface water or by percolation and is referred to as "diffuse pollution."

■ Accidental spillage.

The Royal Commission on Environmental Pollution (RCEP) classified water pollutants into three groups:

Sewage effluent	Sewage tends to be high in nitrogen and phosphorous, and the algae and phytoplankton which bloom have a high biological oxygen demand (BOD), and this reduces the oxygen levels in the water, causing problems for flora and fauna.
Heavy metals	Heavy metals (arsenic, cadmium, chromium, nickel, and zinc, for example), along with organochlorines (solvents and

insecticides like DDT, for example), may have three negative impacts. Some are toxic to humans and animal life (e.g. arsenic). Some are persistent, so they do not break down into harmless or less-harmful compounds (e.g. DDT). Some are bio-accumulative, so while a small dose may not be toxic, organisms do not excrete them, and over time, they accumulate and become toxic (e.g. mercury).

Other pollutants   This is a catch-all category of pollutants which may be problematic. It includes industrial discharges, chemicals, oil, and solid waste.

As with other types of pollution, the UK government classifies water pollution incidents into four categories:

Category 1   Major. Causing serious, persistent, and/or extensive impact. This may include impacts such as:
Significant fish death
Required closure of potable (drinking) water, or industrial or agricultural abstraction
Major effect on amenity (e.g. cessation of water sports)

Category 2   Significant. This may include impacts such as:
Some fish death
Some impact on amenity
Disturbance to a protected area (see Chapter 8)

Category 3   Minor or minimal impact.

Category 4   Negligible impact.

Unsurprisingly, most of the reporting relates to category 1 or category 2 events. In relation to the nine water and sewerage companies operating in England (so excluding all other industrial pollution incidents and any incidents in the devolved nations), the Environment Agency reported in 2022 that the number was increasing.

QUOTATION

"The sector's performance on pollution was shocking, much worse than previous years. Serious pollution incidents increased to 62, the highest total since 2013. There were 8 of the most serious (category 1) incidents, compared with 3 in 2020 and most companies, 7 of the 9, were responsible for an increase in serious incidents compared to 2020."

Emma Howard Boyd, Chair of the Environment Agency,
in Environment Agency, 2021, Research and analysis:
Water and sewerage companies in England: environmental
performance report 2021, www.gov.uk

In order to achieve and maintain water quality, it is first important to assess the current state of a body of water in order that the future improvement and deterioration of them can be monitored. It is then necessary to create standards and objectives to ensure those standards are attained. Finally, there needs to be an enforcement system to ensure that the objectives are met and that the standards achieved are maintained. The stages towards this are:

- Classification
- Setting standards and objectives
- Control of water pollution

Classification

Water quality objectives are not universal, and different standards are required for different bodies of water. The Water Resources Act 1991 specifies that the criteria set for water quality will relate to one of more of the following.

LEGISLATION

(a) general requirements as to the purposes for which the waters to which the classification is applied are to be suitable;

(b) specific requirements as to the substances that are to be present in or absent from the water and as to the concentrations of substances which are or are required to be present in the water;

(c) specific requirements as to other characteristics of those waters;

S82(2), Water Resources Act 1991

The purposes for which water is to be used will include such varied things as swimming (the Bathing Waters Regulations 2013[8]), drinking water (Water Environment (Water Framework Directive) (England and Wales) Regulations 2017[9] – the "WFD Regulations"), habitats (the Conservation of Habitats and Species Regulations 2017[10]), shellfish (the Shellfish Water Protected Areas (England and Wales) Directions 2016[11]), and so on. There will be separate provisions which govern each of those (and other) categories.

We have seen earlier how the RCEP classified water pollutants and water pollution incidents. The way we currently classify water in the UK springs from Directive 2000/60/EC[12] (the Water Framework Directive, or WFD).

ARTICLE

General definition for rivers, lakes, transitional waters, and coastal waters

High   There are no, or only very minor, anthropogenic alterations to the values of the physico-chemical and hydromorphological quality elements for the surface water body type from those normally associated with that type under undisturbed conditions.

The values of the biological quality elements for the surface water body reflect those normally associated with that type under undisturbed conditions, and show no, or only very minor, evidence of distortion.

These are the type-specific conditions and communities.

Good   The values of the biological quality elements for the surface water body type show low levels of distortion resulting from human activity but deviate only slightly from those normally associated with the surface water body type under undisturbed conditions.

Moderate   The values of the biological quality elements for the surface water body type deviate moderately from those normally associated with the surface water body type under undisturbed conditions. The values show moderate signs of distortion resulting from human activity and are significantly more disturbed than under conditions of good status.

Annex V, Water Framework Directive 2000

The WFD does include "poor" and "bad" classifications, but only in the sense that this is how they classify any water that falls below "moderate." Echoing the point made earlier by the Chair of the Environment Agency, the JNCC reported in 2021 that only around one-third of surface water across the whole of the UK was classified as "good" or "high" in 2020, a figure broadly unchanged for the previous decade. It is likely that given the recent publicity around the discharge of sewerage into rivers in the UK, this figure may now be even lower.

In addition to classifying water by its intended use, it is possible to classify it by its contents: specific requirements as to the substances that are to be present or absent in the water and the concentrations of the substances that are to be found in the water. From 1989 to 2013, a series of Surface Water (Dangerous Substances) (Classification) Regulations[13] were passed, which classified substances in line with 1976 Dangerous Substances Directive[14] (as amended). The Water Framework Directive replaced the Dangerous Substances Directive, and the enabling legislation in England and Wales are the 217 WFD Regulations mentioned earlier. In terms of classification, however, the 2017 Regulations use the classifications from Directive 2008/105[15] as amended (the EQS Directive).

There are other characteristics that can be used to classify bodies of water, for example, whether they meet the requirements of the government's 25-year environment plan, which will be given legal effect in due course.

Setting Standards and Objectives

Once the baseline study into a body of water has been set, then there are different standards that can be adopted to make sure that the objectives can be met.

The first of these is "emission standards." These are sometimes called ES, or end-of-pipe standards. This type of standard is adopted where there are permits granted to specific people, and the discharge through a pipe can be monitored.

The advantage of using emission standards is that if a permit-holder breaches the terms of permit (by discharging too much, or at the wrong time, or at the wrong concentration), then prosecution can follow.

The disadvantages of using emission standards are twofold. Firstly, they do not take into account the underlying quality of the body of water into which the discharges are being made. For example, ten permit-holders may be discharging into the same body of water, and none of them may breach the terms of their permit. Taken together and in combination, however, their discharges may lead to the quality of the receiving body of water being downgraded. Secondly, emissions standards cannot, by definition, take account of diffuse pollution from agricultural run-off or industrial run-off.

The second main type of approach is the "environmental quality standard," or EQS. The standard in relation to chemicals that may be discharged into any particular water is set according to the quality of the water receiving the discharge, the receiving water having been classified according to its content. If the water quality deteriorates due to the emissions, then it may be required that emissions cease, or the consent be modified, and may lead to the prosecution of the person making the discharge and/or the downgrading of the water into which the discharge is made.

The advantage of using EQS is that the standard of the receiving body of water can be monitored regularly and will take account of all entry points of pollutants – point source pollution and diffuse pollution. This will help the regulator to better manage the pollution load of the water and take the requisite action.

The disadvantages of this approach are threefold. Firstly, since levels of emissions are set so that the specific receiving water will remain within a certain classification, the standard is based upon a projection of how much a specific water can take of a certain chemical and remain in the classification. The danger is that the emission may not be exceeded but the water is downgraded because the projection was wrong. Secondly, it will not be known whether the projection is correct until the water is found to be failing to meet the standard set for its initial classification, by which time remediation will have become much harder. The third disadvantage is more procedural and is that by just using EQS, a particular polluter may be the root cause of the downgrading of the receiving body of water but cannot be identified (and thus cannot be prosecuted).

The Water Framework Directive adopted both standards in relation to different types of pollution, and that standard has also been adopted by the UK.

Monitoring and Enforcement

Closely linked to issues of standards and objectives is monitoring and enforcement. The Permitting Regulations require that an environmental permit be granted for "water discharge activities."

LEGISLATION

(1) A "water discharge activity" means any of the following –

(a) the discharge or entry to inland freshwaters, coastal waters or relevant territorial waters of any –

    (i) poisonous, noxious or polluting matter,

    (ii) waste matter, or

    (iii) trade effluent or sewage effluent;

(b) the discharge from land through a pipe into the sea outside the seaward limits of relevant territorial waters of any trade effluent or sewage effluent;

(c) the removal from any part of the bottom, channel or bed of any inland freshwaters of a deposit accumulated by reason of any dam, weir or sluice holding back the waters, by causing it to be carried away in suspension in the waters, unless the activity is carried on in the exercise of a power conferred by or under any enactment relating to land drainage, flood prevention or navigation;

(d) the cutting or uprooting of a substantial amount of vegetation in any inland freshwaters or so near to any such waters that it falls into them and failure to take reasonable steps to remove the vegetation from these waters;

(e) an activity in respect of which a notice under paragraph 4 or 5 has been served and has taken effect.

(2) A discharge or an activity that might lead to a discharge is not a "water discharge activity" –

(a) if the discharge is made, or authorised to be made, by or under any prescribed statutory provision; or

(b) if the discharge is of trade effluent or sewage effluent from a vessel.

(3) In determining whether a discharge or an activity is a water discharge activity, no account must be taken of any radioactivity possessed by any substance or article or by any part of any premises.

Paragraph 3, Schedule 21, Permitting Regulations 2016

The definitions of "sewage effluent" and "trade effluent" are carried over from the Water Resources Act 1991.

LEGISLATION

Water discharge activities are broadly the same as the offences under previous legislation, so the case law which has evolved is largely still relevant. It is an offence to operate a regulated facility without a permit, and also to "cause or knowingly permit" a water discharge activity.

LEGISLATION

(1) A person must not, except under and to the extent authorised by an environmental permit –
   (a) operate a regulated facility; or
   (b) cause or knowingly permit a water discharge activity or groundwater activity.

Reg 12(1), Permitting Regulations 2016

If a permit is sought, then the regulator can either:

■ Approve unconditionally
■ Approve with conditions
■ Reject

Conditions may be imposed relating to:

■ The nature, origin, composition, temperature, volume, and rate of discharge
■ The periods during which the discharges can be made
■ Required steps to minimise pollution
■ Metering, sampling, and recording

In line with the polluter pays principle (see Chapter 1), charges are made for the consents, and an annual subsistence fee is also charged. The potential weakness in the system is that it only applies to discharges from specific sources consent and cannot be granted for diffuse pollution – for example, agricultural and industrial run-off.

ACTIVITY

You have been tasked by the Environment Agency with creating a system for regulating diffuse pollution from agricultural and industrial land in an attempt to improve the overall quality of inland freshwater in England.

What steps do you consider would be necessary to do this?

(1)   It is an offence for a person to –

   (a)   contravene regulation 12(1), or
   (b)   knowingly cause or knowingly permit the contravention of regulation 12(1)(a).

(2)   It is an offence for a person to fail to comply with or to contravene an environmental permit condition.

(2A) But it is not an offence for a person to fail to comply with the environmental permit conditions in Part 3 of Schedule 9 (waste operations: management and technical competence conditions).

(3)   It is an offence for a person to fail to comply with the requirements of an enforcement notice or of a prohibition notice, suspension notice, landfill closure notice, mining waste facility closure notice, flood risk activity emergency works notice or flood risk activity remediation notice.

(4)   It is an offence for a person –

   (a)   to fail to comply with a notice under regulation 61(1) requiring the provision of information, without reasonable excuse;
   (b)   to make a statement which the person knows to be false or misleading in a material particular, or recklessly to make a statement which is false or misleading in a material particular, where the statement is made –

      (i)   in purported compliance with a requirement to provide information imposed by or under a provision of these Regulations,
      (ii)   for the purpose of obtaining the grant of an environmental permit to any person, or the variation, transfer in whole or in part, or surrender in whole or in part of an environmental permit, or
      (iii) for the purpose of obtaining, renewing, or amending the registration of an exempt facility;

   (c)   intentionally to make a false entry in a record required to be kept under an environmental permit condition;
   (d)   with intent to deceive –

      (i)   to forge or use a document issued or authorised to be issued or required for any purpose under an environmental permit condition, or
      (ii)   to make or have in the person's possession a document so closely resembling such a document as to be likely to deceive.

(5)   It is an offence for an establishment or undertaking to –

   (a)   fail to comply with paragraph 17(3) or (4) of Schedule 2, or
   (b)   intentionally make a false entry in a record required to be kept under that paragraph.

(6)   If an offence committed by a person under this regulation is due to the act or default of some other person, that other person is also guilty of the offence and liable to be proceeded against and punished accordingly, whether or not proceedings for the offence are taken against the first-mentioned person.

Reg 38, Permitting Regulations 2016

The sanctions for committing offences under Regulation 38 are set out in Regulation 39.

(1) Subject to paragraph (2), a person guilty of an offence under regulation 38(1), (2) or (3) is liable –

   (a) on summary conviction to a fine or imprisonment for a term not exceeding 12 months, or to both;

   (b) on conviction on indictment to a fine or imprisonment for a term not exceeding 5 years, or to both.

(2) A person guilty of offence under regulation 38(1), (2) or (3) in respect of a flood risk activity is liable –

   (a) on summary conviction to a fine or imprisonment for a term not exceeding 12 months, or to both;

   (b) on conviction on indictment to a fine or imprisonment for a term not exceeding 2 years, or both.

(3) In relation to an offence committed before 2nd May 2022, paragraphs (1)(a) and (2)(a) have effect as if for "12 months" there were substituted "6 months".

(4) A person guilty of an offence under regulation 38(4) is liable –

   (a) on summary conviction to a fine;

   (b) on conviction on indictment to a fine or imprisonment for a term not exceeding 2 years, or to both.

(5) An establishment or undertaking guilty of an offence under regulation 38(5) is liable on summary conviction to a fine not exceeding level 2 on the standard scale.

Reg 39, Permitting Regulations 2016

As with most other offences, the statute is a starting point for definitional issues, and a body of case law has evolved which adds interpretation to the statutory provisions.

10.2.3 Case Law

Some of the earlier cases added weight to factual issues which needed clarification.

CASE

Macleod v Buchanan **(1940) 2 All ER 179**

This case is not linked to water pollution but involves a breach of Section 35 of the Road Traffic Act 1930,[16] which made it an offence to "cause or permit" someone to use a car without insurance.

The House of Lords held that "cause" and "permit" were to be read disjunctively, effectively creating two separate offences.

NRA v Egger UK Ltd **(1992) Env LR 130**

This was a Crown Court case which concerned the entry into water of chipboard waste from a wood processing company. The court held that "polluting matter" was matter (including inert matter) which had the *potential* to cause harm and contrasted it with matter which had *actually* caused harm.

JUDGMENT

R v Dovermoss (1995) Env. LR 258

This case concerns a company which caused slurry (a mixture of cow manure and water used as fertiliser) to be spread on two fields. A blocked stream caused water to run across the field, taking the slurry into an area from which drinking water was extracted.

Three interesting things emerged from the case:

1. The court held that a watercourse continued to be a watercourse even when it had overflowed, arguing that: "In our judgment, water that overflows from a river, stream or ditch does not cease to be water of the watercourse" (per Stuart-Smith LJ @ 263).
2. The court held that a watercourse continued to be a watercourse even when it was dried up, saying, "This is obviously good sense because watercourses such as these do not cease to be watercourses simply because they are dry at any particular time. Ditches are often dry for a great part of the year. They do not cease to be watercourses" (per Stuart-Smith LJ @264).
3. The court rejected the argument that some harm must be caused.

> "Pollute", "pollutant" and "pollution" are ordinary English words. The relevant definition of "pollute" in the Oxford English Dictionary is: "to make physically impure, foul or filthy; to dirty, stain, taint, befoul." It is quite clear that it is intended to have a different meaning from "poisonous or noxious matter," since these words appear in the section. "Noxious" means harmful.
>
> (Per Stuart-Smith LJ @255)

On the facts of the case, Dovermoss were acquitted, but the interpretation by the court nonetheless created a useful precedent.

JUDGMENT

National Rivers Authority v Biffa Waste Services Ltd (1996) Env. LR 227

This case involved the waste management company Biffa, which drove caterpillar-tracked vehicles along a riverbed, causing the river to become discoloured by mud and silt.

The court held that Biffa had not committed an offence because they had not caused anything to enter the river that was not there already.

> It seems to me that the justices were right to find that Biffa Waste Services had not committed this offence because they had not caused anything to enter the watercourse which was not there already. They had stirred it up but they had not introduced any matter.
>
> (Per Staughton LJ @231)

As an obiter statement, Rougier J added a note of caution:

> It should not, however, be assumed that such a decision gives to a contractor or plant operator carte blanche to disturb as much as he wishes of that which lies beneath any watercourse and to any depth. What is properly to be described as the bed of a river will vary according to the nature of the river and its subsoil. In certain circumstances it might turn out to be a very narrow stratum indeed.
>
> (Rougier J @231)

Despite the fact that the words "causing" and "knowingly permitting" have been used in legislation since at least the Rivers Pollution Prevention Act 1876, the terms themselves have been finessed much more recently.

JUDGMENT

Alphacell Ltd v Woodward (1972) AC 824; (1972) 2 WLR 1320

This case concerned polluted water being emitted from the premises of a paper manufacturer as the result of drainage pump strainers not stopping brambles and leaves from blocking the impeller.

Alphacell were charged and convicted with causing polluting matter to enter a river, contrary to Section 2(1) of the Rivers (Prevention of Pollution) Act 1951, and argued in their defence that "causing" should include some element of mens rea.

The House of Lords held that there was "no valid reason for reading the word 'intentionally,' 'knowingly' or 'negligently' into section 2 (1) (a) and a number of cogent reasons for not doing so" (per Salmon LJ @848).

Furthermore, Section (91)

> evidently contemplates two things – causing, which must involve some active operation or chain of operations involving as the result the pollution of the stream; knowingly permitting, which involves a failure to prevent the pollution, which failure, however, must be accompanied by knowledge. I see no reason either for reading back the word 'knowingly' into the first limb, or for reading the first limb as, by deliberate contrast, hitting something which is unaccompanied by knowledge. The first limb involves causing and this is what has to be interpreted.
>
> (Per Wilberforce LJ @834)

Subsequent cases led to different interpretations of whether "causing" needed to be a positive action or whether a failure to act could also suffice. This was settled by the Court of Appeal following a reference to the Attorney-General.

CASE

Attorney General's Reference (No.1 of 1994) (1995) 1 WLR 599

This case was a referral on three points of law from the Attorney-General to the Court of Appeal, under the powers in Section 36 of the Criminal Justice Act 1972.[17]

1. Could the offence of "causing" be committed by more than one person?
2. If a sewage company accepted waste which was then disposed of into a stream by a faulty pumping system, it was enough to be a "chain of operations" – and enough to be a positive act that was sufficient to amount to "causing."
3. Would failure to maintain a pumping system (negligently, or in breach of a statutory duty) be a positive act that was sufficient to amount to "causing"?

The court held that:

1. "Obviously, if there is a joint enterprise the answer is 'Yes.' But the question relates to different and separate acts by more than one person. On behalf of the Attorney-General it was argued that the answer is still 'Yes'" (per Taylor CJ @613).
2. "In our judgment, where a sewerage company sets up and owns a plant or system (such as the system in the present case) to carry out its statutory duties, then, if sewage passing through that system pollutes controlled waters, the company has participated in an 'active operation or chain of operations involving as the result the pollution of the stream'" (per Taylor CJ @614).
3. "In our view, where a party has undertaken the day-to-day running and maintenance of a sewerage system, such as the system in the present case, if it fails properly to maintain the system and runs it in an unmaintained state, that would be sufficient to entitle the jury to find that party guilty of 'causing' pollution to controlled waters resulting from lack of maintenance" (per Taylor CJ @615).

The courts have subsequently taken quite a hard line on the things that will constitute "causing."

JUDGMENT

CPC (UK) Ltd v National Rivers Authority (1995) Env. LR 131

This case involved a leak of an alkaline cleaning fluid akin to caustic soda through a faulty pipe onto a roof and then into a river. The defendants argued that the leak was caused by the faulty installation of the pipe by sub-contractors of the building's previous owner.

The court held that

> [t]he fact that the appellants were unaware of the existence of the defect and could not be criticised for failing to discover it, meant that the defect was latent rather than patent, so far as they were concerned, but this was not relevant in law, because the statute does not require either fault or knowledge to be provided against them.
>
> (Per Evans LJ @137–8)

On that basis, CPC's appeal against conviction was rejected.

The CPC case suggests that failure to carry out an effective maintenance process – which would have uncovered the latent defect in the pipe – is a sufficiently positive act to satisfy the text in *Alphacell v Woodward*. There are also two contrasting cases which involve *novus actus interveniens* or the intervening actions of a third party.

JUDGMENT

Impress (Worcester) Ltd v Rees (1971) 2 All ER 357

Empress Car Co (Abertillery) Ltd v National Rivers Authority (1999) 2 AC 22

In both of these cases, an unknown third party was opening an unlocked tap or valve of a fuel or diesel tank and causing polluting matter to enter a river.

In the case of *Impress*, the court held that the stranger's act was "so powerful an intervening cause" that it rendered any behaviour by Impress to be merely "part of the surrounding circumstances." Impress were thus acquitted.

In the case of *Empress*, the House of Lords held that:

> The prosecution need not prove that the defendant did something which was the immediate cause of the pollution: maintaining tanks, lagoons or sewage systems full of noxious liquid is doing something, even if the immediate cause of the pollution was lack of maintenance, a natural event or the act of a third party.
>
> (Per Hoffman LJ @35)

Empress were thus found to have caused the pollution to enter the river.

The key element that distinguished *Empress* appeared to be that because the tap was easily accessible from outside the property, the company should have ensured that it was kept locked.

Whist there are many cases in which the courts have addressed the meaning of "causing" pollution, there are relatively few which address the second leg of the offence, "knowingly permitting." Several of those cases do not relate to water pollution, but the precedent still holds.

CASE

Ashcroft v Cambro Waste Products (1981) 1 WLR 1349

This case concerns a conviction under Section 3(1)(a) of the Control of Waste Act 1974,[18] which makes it an offence *inter* alia to "knowingly permit controlled waste to be deposited on any land."

The court considered the question of whether it is "necessary for the prosecution to prove that the defendant had knowingly permitted the alleged breach of the conditions as well as having knowingly permitted the deposit of controlled waste" (per Boreham J @1357).

As Boreham J concluded: "My answer to that question is 'No'" (@1357).

The *Ashcroft* case concerns the level of knowledge of the details of an act in a scenario where the potential defendant has some control. It concludes that it is sufficient to know that the act is taking place, and that detailed knowledge of the legality of the action was not required. A different situation arose in *Schulmans*, where the relevant act was not one which the company had permitted, or about which it was aware until the spillage.

JUDGMENT

Schulmans Incorporated Ltd v National Rivers Authority (1993) Env. LR D1

In this case, there was a spillage of fuel oil from premises adjacent to land owned by Schulmans. The oil passed across their land and entered the river.

Schulmans were charged and convicted of "knowingly permitting" the oil to cross their land and enter the water (contrary to Section 107(1) of the Water Act 1989[19]) and of "knowingly permitting" liquid to enter water, making the water poisonous to fish (contrary to Section 4(1) of the Salmon and Freshwater Fisheries Act 1975[20]).

They appealed, and the High Court found that:

> In my judgment the essential reason, even if there were no other, why neither conviction can be upheld, is that there was no finding and, as far as we can tell, no evidence that the Appellants could have prevented the escape of fuel oil into the brook sooner than they did, or that there was an escape during any period when they could have prevented but failed to prevent it.
>
> (per Leggatt LJ)

The following two cases build on the approach set out in *Ashcroft*, and both involve broadly similar circumstances.

CASE

Shanks & McEwan (Teesside) Ltd v Environment Agency (1999) QB 333

In this case, the Shanks & McEwan were convicted under Section 33(1)(a) of the Environmental Protection Act 1990,[21] which made it an offence *inter* alia to "knowingly permit controlled waste to be deposited."

The court held that "section 33(1)(a) makes clear that . . . a defendant must know that controlled waste is to be deposited in or on any land. Once he knows this, the strict obligation imported by the rest of section 33(1)(a) comes into play" (per Mance J @ 345).

JUDGMENT

Walker and Sons (Hauliers) Ltd v Environment Agency (2014) EWCA Crim 100

This case concerns the offence of "knowingly permitting the operation of a regulated facility without a permit" contrary to the Environmental Permitting (England and Wales) Regulations 2007[22] Regulation 38.

The appellant had used a contractor to demolish some buildings, and the contractor used the site to burn waste and as an illegal waste station.

The appellant knew of some of the activities taking place on the site (the waste burning) and argued that they did not know that these were taking place without a permit, and therefore they could not be "knowingly permitting" the offence.

The Court of Appeal continued the line of reasoning from *Ashcroft v Cambro Waste Products* (1981) 1 WLR 1349 and *Shanks & McEwan (Teesside) Ltd v Environment Agency* (1999) QB 333 (earlier).

> The words "knowingly" and "permit" relate to knowledge of the facts and not as to the existence and scope of the permission or conditions of a licence. The prosecution does not have to show that a defendant knew that the matters of which it was aware were not permitted.
>
> (Per Simon J @para 29)

What becomes clear through the evolution of these cases is twofold.

- Firstly, if you know that someone is doing something and don't stop them from doing it, it does not matter whether you were aware that the thing they were doing required a permit.

- Secondly, if you discover that an act is taking place, then if you can demonstrate that there was nothing further you could have done to prevent it, you are likely to be acquitted.

ACTIVITY

How beneficial would it be to make water pollution an absolute liability offence and remove both the distinction between "causing" and "knowingly permitting" and the issuing of licences to pollute?

10.3 Groundwater

The provisions we have covered earlier relate to fresh water which flows above ground. In addition, there is a considerable amount of water which is under the ground, in what is called a "saturation zone" (also called the *phreatic* zone). This is the area below the water table and is the source of springs, wells, and streams.

LEGISLATION

3. (1) Subject to sub-paragraphs (2) and (3), "groundwater activity" means any of the following –

(a) the discharge of a pollutant that results in the direct input of that pollutant to groundwater;

(b) the discharge of a pollutant in circumstances that might lead to an indirect input of that pollutant to groundwater;

(c) any other discharge that might lead to the direct or indirect input of a pollutant to groundwater;

(d) an activity in respect of which a notice under paragraph 10 has been served and has taken effect;

(e) an activity that might lead to a discharge mentioned in paragraph (a), (b) or (c), where that activity is carried on as part of the operation of a regulated facility of another class.

(2) A discharge or an activity that might lead to a discharge is not a "groundwater activity" if the discharge is –

(a) made, or authorised to be made, by or under any prescribed statutory provision; or

(b) of trade effluent or sewage effluent from a vessel.

Regulation 3(1) and (2), Schedule 22, Permitting Regulations 2016

The requirement for a permit is set out in Regulation 12 (earlier), and the offence is still "causing or knowingly permitting," and so the preceding case law will apply equally to groundwater pollution. The pathway between a pollutant being released and entering the groundwater is rarely as straightforward as that for water pollution. A good example of this is the *Cambridge Water* case.

CASE EXAMPLE

Cambridge Water Co Ltd v Eastern Counties Leather Plc (1994) 2 AC 264

This case, which is often included within lists of cases about foreseeability, concerns a company (Eastern Counties Leather) which, over many years, spilled a range of industrial chemicals onto their land. The precise dates of the spillages were unknown, but they were known to have occurred prior to 1976 (when a ban on the particular chemical spilled came into force).

Over the succeeding 15 years, the chemicals leached (soaked) into the ground and gradually moved towards a borehole owned by Cambridge Water 1.3 miles away. The pollutants then percolated into the water, contaminating it.

The case hinged on whether the damage was foreseeable (it wasn't).

However, considering the post-*Alphacell* case law earlier, it is clear to see that this would now be classed as a groundwater activity.

10.3.1 Defences

Defences to the provisions of the Permitting Regulations (whether they relate to water discharge activities or groundwater activities) are covered by Regulation 40 of the Environmental Permitting (England and Wales) Regulations 2016.[23]

LEGISLATION

(1) It is a defence for a person charged with an offence under regulation 38(1), (2) or (3) to prove that the acts alleged to constitute the contravention were done in an emergency in order to avoid danger to human health in a case where –

(a) the person took all such steps as were reasonably practicable in the circumstances for minimising pollution; and

     (b) particulars of the acts were furnished to the regulator as soon as reasonably practicable after they were done.

(2) A person who knowingly permits a water discharge activity or groundwater activity where the discharge is water from an abandoned mine or an abandoned part of a mine is not guilty of an offence under regulation 38(1) unless –

     (a) the person is the owner or former operator of the mine or that part of it; and

     (b) the mine or the part of the mine was abandoned after 31st December 1999.

(3) In paragraph (2), "abandoned", in relation to a mine, and "mine" have the meaning given in section 91A of the 1991 Act.

Regulation 40, Permitting Regulations 2016

The emergency defence in Regulation 40(1) replaces that from the Water Resources Act 1991, Section 89(1), which was very similar in wording. "Danger to life or health" was replaced with "danger to human health," but the "all such steps as were reasonably practicable in the circumstances" is the same.

JUDGMENT

Express Ltd (t/a Express Dairies Distribution) v Environment Agency (2003) EWHC 448 (Admin)

This case relates to a vehicle crash leading to the entry of milk into controlled waters contrary to Section 85 of the Water Resources Act. Express Ltd were convicted and appealed on the basis that the spillage had happened because their driver had to pull onto the motorway hard shoulder after a tyre blow-out so as to avoid "damage to life or health."

The factual chain of causation between the tyre blow-out and the milk spillage was unbroken.

> In my judgment, therefore, one is entitled to focus upon the chain of causation and ask whether the act which actually caused the entry was done in an emergency in order to save life or health. In this case, at least on the assumed facts, it clearly was.
>
> (per Hale LJ @588)

CRITIQUING THE LAW

Is there enough emphasis placed on concerns about the environment rather than human health?

SUMMARY

- Water is essential for life, and there are global inconsistencies in access to healthy drinking water.
- In the UK, legislative protection of water, whether it is intended for human consumption, industrial or agricultural use, or as an ecosystem, has improved dramatically in recent years.
- 2022 has seen a number of high-profile cases involving water companies who have released sewage into river and the sea.
- The Secretary of State for the Environment has suggested that the maximum fines for such activity will be raised to £250m. It remains to be seen what amendments to the legislative provisions will be made.

■ Internationally and nationally, efforts to prevent the pollution of water have been strengthened, partly as a result of increased public and state awareness, and partly as a result of improved scientific understanding.

SAMPLE ESSAY QUESTION

Consider the following seven examples. Which do you think amounts to a water- or groundwater-polluting activity?

Albert stores silage (fermented grass used as animal fodder over winter) in a tank which he had constructed on his land, using industry standard processes. After exceptional and unusual rainfall, the tank overflows and the silage enters the river, harming wildlife.

Brian stores silage in a tank which he built himself, on his land, using his own plans, using materials he found on his farm. One morning, he arrives at the site to discover that vandals have broken part of the tank so that the silage has entered the river, harming wildlife.

Claudia is a licensed carrier of hazardous waste and has all the requisite licensing. Her lorry carrying liquid ammonium sulphate for the fertiliser industry is involved in a road traffic accident on the M5, and as a result, diesel fuel leaks out into the neighbouring field.

Diane is a licensed carrier of hazardous waste and has all the requisite licensing. Her lorry carrying acryloyl chloride for the chemical industry is involved in a road traffic accident on the M5 motorway, and as a result, a quantity of acryloyl chloride leaks out onto the carriageway.

Ernie restores classic cars at his garage. Over the years, Ernie has poured wastewater containing oil and chemicals down the drain on his site. No damage to wildlife has ever been directly attributable to his actions.

Francesca restores classic cars at her garage. Over the years, oil and chemicals have leached through the soil and into the groundwater. No damage to wildlife has ever been directly attributable to her actions.

Giovanni lives in a house on the east coast of England. Rather than take his old cooking oil to the local recycling centre, he stores it in plastic bottles which are washed into the sea as the coast erodes.

1. Identify the offences under the Environment Permitting Regulations.
2. Apply the regulations to each character in the question.
   a. Consider the nature of their acts (deliberate, negligent).
   b. Consider the relevance of damage being caused to wildlife.
   c. Consider foreseeability.
3. Consider defences and applicable case law – which may be sources from previous legislation.
4. Conclude.

Further Reading

Boisson de Chazournes, L., 2021, *Fresh Water in International Law*, Oxford: OUP

Clark, R.B., Frid, C., & Attrill, M., 2001, *Marine Pollution*, 5th ed., Oxford: OUP

Dahak, D., 2022, *Water and the Law: Resources, Legal System and Conflicts*, eBook, Seattle, WA: Kindle

JNCC, 2021, *UK Biodiversity Indicators B7 – Surface Water Status*, https://jncc.gov.uk/our-work/ukbi-b7-surface-water-status/

Vörösmarty, C.J., et al., 2010, Global Threats to Human Water Security and River Biodiversity, *Nature*, 467, 555–561

Weiss, J.N., 2014, *Marine Pollution: What Everyone Needs to Know*, Oxford: OUP

Notes

1 Vörösmarty, C.J., et al., 2010, Global Threats to Human Water Security and River Biodiversity, *Nature*, 467, 555–561
2 1991 c.57
3 SI 2016/1154
4 24 and 25 Vict. c.109
5 39 and 40 Vict. c.75
6 14 and 15 Geo. 6. c.64
7 1991 c.57
8 SI 2013/1675
9 SI 2017/407
10 SI 2017/1012
11 SI 2016/138
12 Directive 2000/60/EC of the European Parliament and of the Council of 23 October 2000 establishing a framework for Community action in the field of water policy
13 There were 4 of these in 1989, 1992, 1997, and 1998
14 Council Directive 76/464/EEC of 4 May 1976 on pollution caused by certain dangerous substances discharged into the aquatic environment of the Community
15 Directive 2008/105/EC of the European Parliament and of the Council of 16 December 2008 on environmental quality standards in the field of water policy
16 20 and 21 Geo 5. c.43
17 1972 C.71
18 1974 c.40
19 1989 c.15
20 1975 c.51
21 1990 c.43
22 SI 2007/3538
23 SI 2016/1154

11

Conclusion

Over the course of this book, you have read about, and thought about, an enormous range of issues that relate to environmental law. Some of you have read this book in a "pick and mix" fashion, dipping into different chapters as your interest dictates. Others may have read it more systematically, though probably not in one sitting. The book was designed to focus primarily on UK environmental law and to give the reader a broad range of topics while simultaneously trying not to make the book unmanageably weighty. The further/additional reading sections at the end of each chapter are indicative, and once you start a "deep dive" into a particular area, you will find new authors to propel you on your journey.

We started out looking at where the law came from and considered the difficulties with actually defining what the environment might be. As you will have realised going through the later chapters, very little of the statute or case law hinges on the exact definition of the term; nonetheless, accuracy of terminology is crucial to a law student. Even the definitions which appear at first glance to be all-encompassing, such as Brundtland's "where we all live," turn out to be overly restrictive. The environment extends, after all, to the areas of the planet where we do not live – the oceans, the air, and the global commons.

We have also seen how legal frameworks have emerged and evolved over the centuries, and how society has evolved alongside – or perhaps how the laws have evolved alongside – societal changes. The book has tried to give you as broad a perspective as possible, and wherever it was feasible to do so, examples and writers from a broad spectrum have been included. Some of these will perhaps be less familiar to you than others, and I would encourage you to read as widely as possible.

The UK has moved an enormous way in the last two centuries. In 1822, we had a largely rural society where most people had a real connection to nature and the environment. Neither of the two longest-reigning monarchs (Queen Victoria and Queen Elizabeth II) had acceded to the throne, the Industrial Revolution had yet to take off, and most people did not travel a great distance from home except in times of war. In environmental terms, the average human life expectancy was about 30 years, and contributory factors were things like a lack of sewage, poor medicines, and lack of hygiene. It was this public health

DOI: 10.4324/9781003137214-11

crisis which galvanised much of the early environmental laws, which focused on reducing the risk of catching cholera to improving working and living conditions in urban areas.

In Chapter 2, we took what Coyle and Morrow suggested might be thought of as a "strange" path and looked at philosophy and ethics. Within the myriad of positions and arguments put forward by different environmental philosophies from all sides of the political spectrum, you may have found one to which you are closely aligned. You may not have done that, and what may have become clear is that there is a constant evolution of these positions. Broadly speaking, and this of course overlooks all the nuanced differences, there are a lot of similarities. All recognise that there is a sense of urgency needed, and that humans have caused unprecedented harm to the planet. The philosophical standpoints then split into those which regard capitalism and/or technology as the cause of the world's problems, and those which regard them as the best solution. Even then, there are the "nuclear greens" – environmentalists who overcome their antipathy to nuclear energy and take the pragmatic view that a massive increase in nuclear energy is the only pragmatic way of solving the climate crisis in the time we have available.

We have also seen moves to grant rights to nature, a move which would have been unthinkable to many in the 1820s but which is gaining increasing traction today. Rights and justice also featured heavily in Chapter 3, along with the increasing recognition that the industrialisation process in the developed world has caused, is causing, and will continue to cause problems in the developing world. This imbalance and injustice are reflected at a *macro* level (country by country), a *meso* level (region by region), and also a *micro* level (within one country, or even town). We also explored the links between environmental and climate justice and current human rights provisions in different regions, and this demonstrated that the provision is not uniform. Some areas have progressed further towards recognising that a healthy environment is a human right than others. By contrast, we also considered whether this approach was too overtly anthropocentric, which linked back nicely to the coverage of rights for nature.

Having spent a fair amount of time looking at the more theoretical and philosophical aspects of environmental law, we moved on in Chapter 4 to consider the more practical and procedural elements of how environmental laws come into being. The links between politics and environmental law are very clear to see on a day-to-day basis. You will no doubt have seen that a change in a country's leader can have a dramatic impact on that country's environmental policies and laws. Presidents Trump of the United States and Bolsonaro of Brazil, for example, had very particular views about the reality of climate change, and the policy decisions of their two countries reflected this. Presidents Biden and da Silva, who replaced them, have very different views, and the policies of both countries will likely be very different in the future. We also looked in Chapter 4 at the importance of access to environmental information, and the role played by public engagement with policymaking – whether that is through mainstream actions or protest and civil disobedience.

Chapter 5 looked at the 17 UN Sustainable Development Goals (SDGs) and the roles that they gave to play in shaping environmental law. We saw that although almost none of the many targets set within the SDGs is likely to be met by the 2030 deadline, they nonetheless have been vital in getting state-level engagement with the key issues that face humanity. One of the most visible aspects of sustainability is the use of fossil fuels for energy production, and this was part of the focus of Chapter 6. In the chapter, we considered the development of legislation and policy around the current main sources of energy in the UK and considered how things were likely to develop in the future. This is an area brought into sharp focus in 2022 and 2023 by the ongoing energy crisis, partly triggered by the war in Ukraine. So-called "energy security" (the ability of a country to produce most, if not all, of its own energy) has risen rapidly up the political agenda as a result of the war.

In Chapter 7, our attention turned to crimes involving wildlife and the different provisions which have been put into place to protect wildlife species and the habitats in which they live – after all, species need spaces. We looked at both the international, regional, and UK provisions and spent some time looking at sites of special scientific interest (SSSIs) and other designations which are used for various purposes. Chapter 8 saw our focus shift directly to animals. Recent studies have shown that almost two-thirds of the mammals on the planet today are farmed livestock, whereas only 4 per cent are wild mammals. This makes the laws (primarily in the UK, the Animal Welfare Act 2006) governing our relationship with domesticated animals crucial. Human interest with animals is not just for farming purposes but also for medical experimentation and research and for entertainment. This was a good opportunity to reconsider the societal pressures we discussed in Chapter 4 and explore how laws have changed to give effect to the types of entertainment which were societally acceptable.

In Chapter 9, our attention turned to pollution of the air by human activities. We outlined the provisions of industrial pollution control – for the simple reason that industrial polluters contribute far more to overall pollution levels than individuals. We then looked at three different types of air pollution and explored the international, regional, and UK-based provisions which have been put into place to control them. Politics is important in this section, too, and we saw that where there was broad scientific consensus on the cause–effect relationship between human activities and pollution (e.g. for ozone layer depletion), it was relatively easy to secure the necessary political willpower to act. By contrast, for climate change, even though there is broad scientific consensus, some political leaders continue to regard the issue as largely a naturally occurring phenomenon and refuse to act.

The final chapter looks at water pollution, both fresh water and groundwater, that occur on land, and marine pollution. This chapter links back to issues of the global commons discussed at the start of the book, as the high seas are beyond the control of any particular state, and yet we have passed a series of legislative measures going back 70 years to try to overcome this. In terms of fresh water, again, the importance of industrial pollution was noted. Microplastics, which were mentioned several times in the book, have been found in pretty much every area of water on Earth, and the link between our actions and these consequences cannot be understated.

11.1 The Future

Any attempt to predict the future in more than general terms is doomed to inaccuracy – just look back at any movies from the 1970s or 1980s that are set in 2022! Nonetheless, there are some trends which seem likely to emerge in the next 20 or 30 years, and we will consider them in turn. The linking issue is that laws are still generally reactive rather than proactive. There are good reasons for this – lack of parliamentary time, for example – but it does mean that truly novel techniques may not have a regulatory framework for approval, which will slow down their commercial introduction.

11.1.1 Outer Space

NASA announced in November 2022 that their Artemis Programme was going to make it possible for humans to return to the moon by 2030.

QUOTATION

> "With Artemis missions, NASA will land the first woman and first person of color on the Moon, using innovative technologies to explore more of the lunar surface than ever before. We will collaborate with commercial and international partners and establish the first long-term presence on the Moon. Then, we will use what we learn on and around the Moon to take the next giant leap: sending the first astronauts to Mars."
>
> NASA, 2022, *Artemis*, US National Aeronautics and Space Administration, www.nasa.gov

Artemis is going to be a collaborative programme between government and industry, and if it is successful in its stated aim to get humans to the moon and then Mars, new legal guidelines will be needed. As we saw in Chapter 2, we already have the two UN Conventions which cover how we get to space and what we do once we are there. The 1967 UN Treaty on Principles Governing the Activities of States in the Exploration and Use of Outer Space, Including the Moon and other Celestial Bodies, requires that no state make any claim of territoriality to space, the moon, or any other body. It would seem to be risky not to bolster these provisions and include commercial actors, not least because Artemis will involve the private sector, but also because SpaceX has a greater presence in space than most sovereign nations.

11.1.2 New Forms of Energy

As we saw in Chapter 9, there are several proposals for new ways of generating power. Some (space-based solar power) are effectively using existing technology (solar panels) in a new and as-yet-untested way, and they are by far the most likely to come to fruition in the next ten years or so. Others (nuclear fusion) have been on the card for decades, and although we are inching closer to making them commercially viable, it will perhaps take some decades before nuclear fusion reactors are installed globally.

There are already processes being investigated which use such processes such as extracting the bioluminescent enzymes from jellyfish to make biological fuel cells, using the trace electrical charge of falling raindrops, or harnessing the kinetic energy from a dance floor to generate power.

In the next ten years, there will very likely be new ideas being investigated that have not even been dreamed of today, so perhaps it is necessary to create a global legislative framework not only for licencing these new technologies but also to allow for the type of government and private sector collaboration used in Artemis.

11.1.3 Life on a Changing Planet

With the close of COP 27 in November 2022, it was increasingly apparent that the target of allowing the planet to warm by no more than 1.5 degrees from pre-industrial levels was going to be missed. The failure by global politicians to come to agreements over funding, and their preference for moving decisions to the future, is going to have significant consequences.

To help us cope with the changes that are going to take place over the next 20 or 30 years – increasingly extreme weather, rising sea levels, increasing stress of fresh water, and so on – planning needs to take place to ensure the lowest possible negative impacts. Some governments have started to do this. As we saw in Chapter 5, President Biden's 2021 Executive Order 14013 has already generated a report on the likely impact of climate-induced migration. This, of course, will link back to the issues of environmental injustice and climate injustices covered in Chapter 3, as the worst-affected people will not be from the countries with the highest historic emissions levels. Identifying the scale of the issue is useful, but it is essential to put in place provisions for supporting those who are forced to flee their homes, and perhaps even for those states which cease to exist.

11.1.4 New Foodstuffs

In November 2022, the US Food and Drug Administration (FDA) granted approval to an American company which takes cells from chicken and uses them to produce laboratory-cultivated meat. This was not the first company to do this but was the first (of what will presumably, over time, be many) company to get FDA approval. It looks likely that this type of foodstuff will become increasingly commonplace in the next decade, and as it does so, the price will inevitably fall.

There has been considerable debate over several issues linked to commercial meat farming which may be alleviated by this new approach:

- The amount of land required. This has led some countries (e.g. Brazil) to clear areas of the Amazon to repurpose it as livestock farming land. This then reduces the size of the Amazon and has knock-on effects on biodiversity and carbon sequestration.

- The water requirements of livestock farming. There is a significant difference depending on location and species of animal, but calorie-wise, beef farming requires 10–20 times as much water as cereals and grain.

- The emissions from the livestock industry. Almost two-thirds of greenhouse gas emissions caused by the creation of human foodstuffs is caused by farming of livestock for meat.

QUOTATION

"Global GHG emissions from the production of food were found to be 17,318 TgCO2eq/yr,[1] of which 57% corresponds to the production of animal-based food (including livestock feed), 29% to plant-based foods and 14% to other utilizations."

Xu, X.; Sharma, P.; Shu, S.; Lin, T-S; Caiis, P.; Tubiello, F. N.; Smith, P.; Campbell, N.; and Jain, A. K., 2021, "Global greenhouse gas emissions from animal-based foods are twice those of plant-based foods," *Nature Food*, Vol 2, 724–732

Naturally, lab-grown meat will not appeal to all consumers, and there are many other alternate protein sources which are being developed, from algae to insects. The European Union passed the Novel Food Regulation in 1997,[2] in which "novel food" is defined as that which was not consumed by humans to a significant degree in the EU prior to 1997. This means that both the United States and the EU have proactively introduced regulations through which new foods need to be approved before they can be released onto the market. In the UK, the Food Standards Agency is still working to the requirements set under Regulation 258/97 and is assisted in its decision-making by the Advisory Committee on Novel Foods and Processes (ACNFP).

These predictions may or may not be accurate, and there are likely to be other changes that have not yet been predicted. These four areas do seem to be the most likely to come to fruition in the short- to medium-term, however.

What this book has sought to do is allow you to develop your understanding of several key environmental issues and the relevant legal frameworks and standards which cover them. Some areas are richer in case law than others, and some you will have found more interesting than others. Overall, however, I hope that this book has allowed you to explore ideas about environmental law and has piqued your interest and enthusiasm not only to find out more but also to become part of the change that humanity needs.

Notes

1 TgCO2eq = teragrammes of carbon dioxide equivalent. 1 teragramme is 1,012 grammes, or 1 million tonnes
2 Council Regulation (EC) No 258/97 concerning novel foods and novel food ingredients

Bibliography

Adams, C.F., 1851, *The Works of John Adams*, Vol. V, Boston, MA: Charles C Little & James Brown

ADB et al., 2022, *Poverty and Climate Change: Reducing the Vulnerability of the Poor Through Adaptation* (Joint publication of African Development Bank; Asian Development Bank; UK Department for International Development; EU Directorate-General for Development; German Federal Ministry for Economic Cooperation and Development; Netherlands Ministry of Foreign Affairs Development Cooperation; Organization for Economic Cooperation and Development; United Nations Development Programme; United Nations Environment Programme and The World Bank), www.oecd.org/env/cc/2502872.pdf

Allaby, M., 2003, *Dangerous Weather: Fog, Smog and Poisoned Rain*, New York: Facts on File Inc

Allen, G.M., 1942, *Extinct and Vanishing Mammals of the Western Hemisphere with the Marine Species of all the Oceans*, Lancaster PA: American Committee for International Wild Life Protection Special Report Number 11

Anon, 1921, Grey Squirrels, *The Times*, Tuesday 20 December 1921, p. 11

Assured Food Standard, 2022, *About Red Tractor*, https://redtractor.org.uk/about-red-tractor/

Ayeb-Karlsson, S., 2020, No Power without Knowledge: A Discursive Subjectivities Approach to Investigate Climate-Induced (Im)mobility and Wellbeing, *Social Sciences*, 9(6), 103

Bacon, F., 1597/1996, *Meditationes Sacrae and Human Philosophy*, Whitefish, MT: Kessinger Publishing Company

Bacon, F., 1627 (1884), *The New Atlantis*, London: George Bell & Sons

Banfield, E.C., 1961, *Political Influence: A New Theory of Urban Politics*, New York, NY: The Free Press of Glencoe/Crowell-Collier Publishing Co

Banzhaf, S., Ma, L., & Timmins, C., 2019, Environmental Justice: The Economics of Race, Place, and Pollution. *Journal of Economic Perspectives*, 33(1), 185–208, 190

Bell, S., McGillivray, D., Pederson, O., Lees, E., & Stokes, E., 2017, *Environmental Law*, 9th ed., Oxford: OUP

Boddice, R., 2005, *Beastly Pleasures: Blood Sports in England, c1776–1876*, York: University of York

Bookchin, M., 1982, *The Ecology of Freedom: The Emergence and Dissolution of Hierarchy*, Palo Alto, CA: Cheshire Books

Bourdieu, P., 1991, *Language & Symbolic Power*, Cambridge, MA: Harvard University Press

Bowman, M., Davies, P., & Redgewell, C., 2010, *Lyster's International Wildlife Law*, 2nd ed. Cambridge, CUP

Bullard, R., 2019, *About Environmental Justice*, https://drrobertbullard.com/

Bunyard, P., & Morgan-Grenville, F., 1987, *The Green Alternative Guide to Good Living*, London: Methuen

Burke, E., 1790 (1909), *Reflections on the Revolution in France*, Vol. XXIV, Part 3, Harvard Classics, New York: P.F. Collier & Son

Carson, R., 1962, *Silent Spring*, New York: Houghton Mifflin

Coffee, J., 1981, No Soul to Damn. No Body to Kick: An Unscandalized Inquiry into the Problem of Corporate Punishment, *Michigan Law Review*, 79, 386

Coyle, S., & Morrow, K., 2004, *The Philosophical Foundations of Environmental Law: Property, Rights and Nature*, Portland, OR: Hart Publishing

Dalin, C., et al., 2017, Groundwater Depletion Embedded in International Food Trade, *Nature*, 543(7647), 700–704

Dawkins, R., 1999, *The Extended Phenotype: The Long Reach of the Gene*, Oxford: OUP

DBEIS, 2013, *Wave and Tidal Energy: Part of the UK's Energy Mix*, Department for Business, Energy & Industrial Strategy, London: TSO

DEFRA, 2018, *A Green Future: Our 25 Year Plan to Improve the Environment*, Department of the Environment, Food and Rural Affairs, London: TSO

DEFRA, 2021, *Waste Management Plan for England*, Department of the Environment Food and Rural Affairs, London: TSO

DEFRA, 2022, *Sites of Special Scientific Interest: Managing Your Land*, Department of the Environment, Food and Rural Affairs, London: TSO

DEFRA/FAnGR, 2016, *Statement on Cloning of Farm Animals*, Department of the Environment, Food and Rural Affairs & Farm Animal Genetic Resources Committee, London

d'Eaubonne, F, 1974, *La Féminisme ou la Mort*, Paris: P. Horay

Dhammika, S., 2015, *Nature and Environment in Early Buddhism*, Kandy, Sri Lanka: Buddhist Publication Society

Dobson, A., 1995, *Green Political Thought*, London: Taylor & Francis

Dunn, M., 2020, Evaluating the Impact of the Documentary Blue Planet II on Viewers' Plastic Consumption Behaviors, *Conservation Science and Practice*, 2(10)

EFRA, 2016, *Greyhound Welfare, HC 478: House of Commons Environment, Food and Rural Affairs Committee*, 2nd Report of 2015–16, London: TSO

Ethical Dairy, 2022, *About the Ethical Dairy*, www.theethicaldairy.co.uk/about-ethical-dairy

European Commission, 2016, *Security of Gas Supply Regulation*, http://ec.europe.eu

Fitter, R., & Fitter, M., eds., 1984, *The Road to Extinction: Problems of Categorizing the Status of Taxa Threatened with Extinction: A Symposium Held by the Species Survival Commission, Madrid 1984*, Cambridge: International Union for the Conservation of Nature and Natural Resources

Fitzgerald, P.J., 1966, *Salmond on Jurisprudence*, 12th ed., London: Sweet & Maxwell

Fox, A.D., & Petersen, I.K., 2020, Offshore Wind Farms and Their Effects on Birds, *Dansk Ornitologisk Forenings Tidsskrift*, 113(2019), 86–101

Fox, W., 1986, *Approaching Deep Ecology: A Response to Richard Sylvan's Critique of Deep Ecology*, Occasional Paper, University of Tasmania. Board of Environmental Studies, 20

Frazer-Nash Consultancy, 2021, *Space Based Solar Power De-risking the Pathway to Net Zero*, FNC 004456–52265R Issue 1B, London: TSO

Gadjil, G., 2008, *Ramachandra Guha: The Trouble with Radical Environmentalists*, Pune: Infochange India

Gao, Y., Skutsch, M., Drigo, R., Pacheco, P., & Masrer, O., 2011, Assessing Deforestation from Biofuels: Methodological Challenges, *Applied Geography*, 31(2), 508–518

Hallegatte, S., Green, C., Nicholls, R.J., & Corfee-Morlot, J., 2013, Future Flood Losses in Major Coastal Cities, *Nature Climate* Change, 3, 802–806

Hardin, G., The Tragedy of the Commons, *Science*, 162(3859), 1243–1248

Harrison, R., 1964, *Animal Machines: The New Factory Farming Industry*, London: Vincent Stewart Publishing

Harvey, F., 2022, UN Chief Warns 'We Will Be Doomed' Without Historic Climate Pact, *The Guardian*, 4 November 2022

He, X., Iwamoto, Y., Kaneko, T., & Kato, T., 2022, Fabrication of Near-Invisible Solar Cell with Monolayer WS2, *Scientific Reports*, 12, 11315, https://doi.org/10.1038/s41598-022-15352-x

Herzog, H., 2010, *Some We Love, Some We Hate, Some We Eat: Why It's So Hard to Think Straight about Animals*, London: HarperCollins

HM Treasury, 2022, *Growth Plan 2022 CP743*, London: TSO

Holmes, O.W., 1897, The Path of the Law, *Harvard Law Review*, 10, 457

Home Office, 2014, *Guidance on the Operation of the Animals (Scientific Procedures) Act 1986*, London: TSO

Home Office, 2015, *Advice Note 01/2015 Animals (Scientific Procedures) Act 1986 Policy on Testing Household Products*, London: TSO

Home Office, 2022, *Annual Statistics of Scientific Procedures on Living Animals Great Britain 2021*, London: TSO

Hoornweg, D., & Pope, K., 2014, *Socioeconomic Pathways and Regional Distribution of the World's 101 Largest Cities*, Global Cities Institute Working Paper No. 04, https://www.daniels.utoronto.ca/work/research/global-cities-institute

Hornaday, W.T., 1913, *Our Vanishing Wild Life: Its Extermination and Preservation*, New York: Charles Scribner's Sons

Hughes, D., Jewell, T., Lowther, J., Parpworth, N., & de Prez, P., 2002, *Environmental Law*, 4th ed., Oxford: OUP

Humane Slaughter Association, 2022, *How Many Animals Are Slaughtered in the UK?* www.hsa.org.uk/

ILO, 2019, *Child Labour in Mining and Global Supply Chains*, Geneva: International Labour Organisation

IMF, 2021, *Debt Relief Under the Heavily Indebted Poor Countries (HIPC) Initiative*, International Monetary Fund, www.imf.org

IUCN, 1963, *Eighth General Assembly: Proceedings*, Geneva: International Union for the Conservation of Nature and Natural Resources

Jesper Kyed Larsen, October 2020, *Birds Are Good at Avoiding Wind Turbines*, Denmark: VattenfallAB

Joshi, D., Gallant, B., Hakhu, A., De Silva, S., McDougal, C., Dubois, M., & Arulingam, I., 2021, Ramsar Convention and the Wise Use of Wetlands: Rethinking Inclusion, *Ecological Restoration*, 39(1&2), 37, https://muse.jhu.edu/article/793658

Kim, R.E., 2016, The Nexus between International Law and the Sustainable Development Goals, *Review of European Community and International Environmental Law*, 25(1)

King, M.L., 1968, The Other America, Speech given at Grosse Pointe High School, *Grosse Point*, Michigan, 14 March 1968

La Follette, C., & Maser, C., eds., 2019, *Sustainability and the Rights of Nature in Practise*, Boca Raton, FL: CRC Press

Leopold, A., 1949, *A Sand County Almanac and Sketches Here and There*, Oxford: OUP

Lovelock, J.E., 1979, *Gaia: A New Look at Life on Earth*, Oxford: OUP

Lyster, S., 1985, *International Wildlife Law: An Analysis of International Treaties Concerned with the Conservation of Wildlife*, Cambridge: Grotius Publications

Macrory, R., 2020, *Irresolute Clay: Shaping the Foundations of Modern Environmental Law*, London: Bloomsbury

Manes, C., 1990, *Green Rage: Radical Environmentalism and the Unmaking of Civilization*, Boston, MA: Little, Brown and Co

Marvel, K., Kravitz, B., & Caldeira, K., 2013, Geophysical Limits to Global Wind Power, *Nature Climate Change*, 3, 118–121

Meadows, D.H., Meadows, D.L., Randers, J., & Behrens, W., 1972, *The Limits to Growth: A Report for the Club of Rome's Project on the Predicament of Mankind*, Falls Church, VA: Potomac Associates

Mill, J.S., 1869, *On Liberty*, London: J.W. Parker & Sons

Mingay, G.E., ed., 1977, *The Agricultural Revolution: Changes in Agriculture 1650–1880*, London: Adam & Charles Black

Moore, P., 2005, The Environmental Movement: Greens Have Lost Their Way, *Miami Herald*, 28 January 2005

Muniz, I.P., 1984, The Effects of Acidification on Scandinavian Freshwater Fish Fauna, Philosophical Transactions of the Royal Society of London. Series B, *Biological Sciences*, 305(1124), Ecological Effects of Deposited Sulphur and Nitrogen Compounds (May 1, 1984), 517–528

Næss, A., 1973, The Shallow and the Deep: Long-Range Ecology Movements: A Summary, *Inquiry*, 16, 95–100

NASA, 2022, *Artemis*, US National Aeronautics and Space Administration, www.nasa.gov

Nature Scot/Nàdar Alba, 2020, *Wind Farm Impact on Birds*, www.nature.scot/

Norgaard, K., & York, R., 2005, Gender Equality and State Environmentalism, *Gender & Society*, 19(4), 506–522

Nowotny, H., 1980, The Role of the Experts in Developing Public Policy: The Australian Debate on Nuclear Power, *Science, Technology & Human Values*, 5(2) 14

Organization for Economic Cooperation and Development, 1972, *Recommendation of the Council on Guiding Principles Concerning International Economic Aspects of Environmental Policies*, Paris: OECD

Poynder, J., 1844, *Literary Extracts from English and Other Works; Collected During Half a Century: Together with Some Original Matter*, London: John Hatchard & Son

Primatt, H., 1776, *A Dissertation on the Duty of Mercy and the Sin of Cruelty to Brute Animals*, London: R. Hett

Rawls, J., 1999, *A Theory of Justice*, revised ed., Cambridge, MA: Belnap Press/Harvard University Press

RCEP, 1976, *Air Pollution Control: An Integrated Approach*, Fifth Report (Cmnd 6371), London: HMSO

Rogers, K., & Moore, J., 1995, Revitalizing the Convention on Nature Protection and Wild Life Preservation in the Western Hemisphere: Might Awakening a Visionary But "Sleeping" Treaty be the Key to Preserving Biodiversity and Threatened Natural Areas in the Americas? *Harvard International Law Journal*, 36, 465

Rose, C., 1988, The Forest is Dying, *New Internationalist*, 5 June 1988, Issue 184

Ruse, M., 2013, *The Gaia Hypothesis: Science on a Pagan Planet*, Chicago, IL: University of Chicago Press

Schumacher, E.F., 1973, *Small is Beautiful: A Study of Economics as if People Mattered*, London: Blond & Briggs

Scott, P., ed., 1964, *Launching a New Ark, First Report of the President and Trustees of the World Wildlife Fund, 1961–1964*, London: Collins

Simon, J., 1890, *English Sanitary Institutions: Reviewed in Their Course of Development, and in Some of Their Political and Social Relations*, London: Cassell & Company Ltd

Slabbert, M., 2004, Prosecuting Animals in Medieval Europe: Possible Explanations, *Fundamina: A Journal of Legal History*, 2004(10), 159–179

Smith, H.A., 1887, Early Reminiscences: Number Ten: Scraps from a Diary – Chief Seattle – A Gentleman by Instinct – His Native Eloquence, Etc., *Seattle Sunday Star*, 28 October

Stamp Dawkins, M., 2012, *Why Animals Matter: Animal Consciousness, Animal Welfare, and Human Well-Being*, Oxford: OUP

Sterman, J.D., Siegel, L., & Rooney-Varga, J.N., 2018, Does Replacing Coal with Wood Lower CO2 Emissions? Dynamic Lifecycle Analysis of Wood Bioenergy, *Environmental Research Letters*, 13, 015007

Summers, N., & Van Heuvelen, T., 2017, Heterogeneity in the Relationship between Country-Level Affluence and Environmental Concern, *Social Forces*, 96(1), 329–359

Sunstein, C.R., 2005, *Laws of Fear: Beyond the Precautionary Principle*, Cambridge: CUP

Taylor, P.W., 2011, *Respect for Nature: A Theory of Environmental Ethics*, 25th Anniversary ed., Princeton, NJ: Princeton University Press

TCD, 2017, *Achieving Sustainable Development*, www.futurelearn.com/info/courses/achieving-sustainable-development/0/steps/35496

Thompson, R.C., Olsen, Y., Mitchell, R.P., Davis, A., Rowland, S.J., John, A.W.G. McGonigle, D., & Russell, A., 2004, Lost at Sea: Where Is All the Plastic? *Science*, 304(5672), 838

Thoreau, H.D., 1849, *On the Duty of Civil Disobedience*, Boston, MA: Ticknor & Fields

Turner, C., & Foster, S., 2019, *Unlocking Constitutional and Administrative Law*, 4th ed., London: Routledge

UN, 2022a, *Goal 11: Make Cities Inclusive, Safe, Resilient, and Sustainable*, United Nations, www.un.org/sustainabledevelopment/cities/

UN, 2022b, *The Sustainable Development Goals Report*, https://unstats.un.org/sdgs/report/2022/

UN, 2022c, *All about the NDCs*, www.un.org/en/climatechange/all-about-ndcs

Underwood, E.A. 1947, The History of Cholera in Great Britain, *Proceedings of the Royal Society of Medicine*, XLI, 165–173

UNECE, 2014, *Protecting Your Environment: The Power Is in Your Hands: A Quick Guide to the Arhus Convention*, United Nations Economic Commission for Europe, Geneva

UN Environment Programme, 2016, *Global Gender and Environment Outlook*, Vienna: UNEP

UNEP/WTO, 2005, *Making Tourism More Sustainable*, United Nations Environmental Programme/World Tourism Organisation, https://wedocs.unep.org/20.500.11822/8741

UN General Assembly, 1992, *A/CONF.151/26 (Vol. I) Report of the United Nations Conference on Environment and Development*, Annex I: Rio Declaration on Environment and Development

UN General Assembly, 2017, *UN General Assembly Resolution 72/222. Education for Sustainable Development in the Framework of the 2030 Agenda for Sustainable Development*

UNSC, 2002, *Final Report of the Panel of Experts on the Illegal Exploitation of Natural Resources and Other Forms of Wealth of the Democratic Republic of the Congo S/2002/1146*, Geneva: UN Security Council

US EPA, 2022, *Understanding Global Warming Potentials*, epa.gov

Vellinga, P., & van Verseveld, W.J., 2000, *Climate Change and Extreme Weather Events*, Gland: WWF

Verne, J., 1864, *A Journey to the Centre of the Earth*, New York: Scribner & Co

von Carlowitz, H.C., 1713, *Die Sylvicultura Oeconomica, Oder haußwirthliche Nachricht und Naturmäßige Anweisung zur wilden Baum-Zucht* (On Economic Forestry, or Domestic Message and Natural Instruction for Wild Tree-Cultivation), Leipzig: Verlegts Johann Friedrich Braun

von Schomberg, R., 2012, The Precautionary Principle: Its Use Within Hard and Soft Law, *European Journal of Risk Regulation*, 3(2), 147–156

Vörösmarty, C.J., et al., 2010, Global Threats to Human Water Security and River Biodiversity, *Nature*, 467, 555–561

WCED, 1987, *Report of the World Commission on Environment and Development: Our Common Future*, Vienna: United Nations Department of Economic and Social Affairs, UN General Assembly, A/42/427

White, K., 2018, Connection to Mother Earth Compels Indigenous Women to Protect It, *Truthout*, 8 October 2018, https://truthout.org/articles/connection-to-mother-earth-compels-indigenous-women-to-protect-it/

White, R., 2008, *Crimes Against Nature: Environmental Criminology and Ecological Justice*, London: Routledge

WMO, 2021, *Weather-Related Disasters Increase Over Past 50 Years, Causing More Damage But Fewer Deaths*, World Meteorological Organization, https://public.wmo.int/en

Xu, X., Sharma, P., Shu, S., Lin, T.-S., Caiis, P., Tubiello, F.N., Smith, P., Campbell, N., & Jain, A.K., 2021, Global Greenhouse Gas Emissions from Animal-Based Foods Are Twice Those of Plant-Based Foods, *Nature Food*, 2, 724–732

Index

Wales
    circuses 202
water
    UN SDGs 109–110, 118–119
water pollution *see also* marine pollution
    achieving and maintaining water quality 248–255
    case law 255–260
    fresh water 246–260
    groundwater 260–263
    history of UK water pollution control 247–248
water quality 248–255
wave energy 145–146
well-being
    UN SDGs 106–107

Western Hemisphere Convention (1940) 152–153
Whanganui River 46–47
wildcards 130–131
wildlife protection/wildlife crime 151–152
    international habitat protection measures 160–165
    IUCN and international species protection
        conventions 154–160
    UK law 165–175
    Western Hemisphere Convention (1940) 152–153
wind 138–140, 146–148
work
    UN SDGs 111–112

zoos 201